Paris and the Nineteer

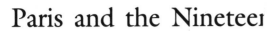

For Kate and Zoë

Paris and the Nineteenth Century

Christopher Prendergast

BLACKWELL
Oxford UK & Cambridge USA

The right of Christopher Prendergast to be identified as author of this work has been
asserted in accordance with the Copyright, Designs and Patents Act 1988

First published 1992
First published in paperback 1995
Reprinted 1996

Blackwell Publishers Inc.
238 Main Street
Cambridge, Massachusetts 02142, USA

Blackwell Publishers Ltd
108 Cowley Road
Oxford OX4 1JF
UK

Library of Congress Cataloging-in-Publication Data
Prendergast, Christopher.
Paris and the nineteenth century / Christopher Prendergast.
p.   cm. – (Writing the city)
Includes bibliographical references and index.
ISBN 0-631-15788-3 (Hbk.) — 0-631-19694-3 (Pbk.)
1. French literature – 19th century – History and criticism.   2. Paris (France) –
Civilization – 19th century.   3. Arts, Modern – 19th century – France – Paris.   4. City
and town life in literature.   5. Paris (France) in literature.   6. Arts, French – France –
Paris.   I. Title.   II. Series.
PQ283.P75   1992
840.9'3244361'09034 – dc20   91-31805
                                                                   CIP

British Library Cataloguing in Publication Data
A CIP catalogue record for this book is available from the British Library.

Typeset in 10 on 12 pt Galliard by Graphicraft Typesetters Ltd, Hong Kong
Printed in Great Britain by Athenæum Press Ltd, Gateshead, Tyne & Wear

This book is printed on acid-free paper

Contents

List of Illustrations

Series Preface

A city's representational life is quite different from its historic, economic, demographic, cartographic, political, ceremonial, cultural life, though of course it may draw on and indirectly reflect or transcribe elements from any or all of these dimensions of the city's existence. And just as it is, in an important sense, true that the city cannot be seen until it has been painted (or depicted), so is it the case that the city cannot be 'read' until it has been 'written'. It is with a consideration of some aspects of the ways in which some of the great cities of the World have been written that this series will concern itself. This does not mean a sort of 'the city in literature' or 'the city and literature' approach. Indeed, the notion is arguably fatuous. The city and literature are coeval, certainly in the West. Homer's Greeks are bent on Troy; Hamlet has come from Wittenberg to Elsinore; Don Quixote rides out of the province of La Mancha; Dante is inseparable from Florence. The novel, indeed, is demonstrably a function, a production of the city. And there is little point in setting out to study, or document, the city as 'background' or 'setting'. The results might well make an interesting supplement to the Blue Guides, but would remain a species of tourist literature. What does seem to be worth studying is some of the ways in which the city has been textualized – alluded to, or 'explored' and inventoried, as, say, Dickens does London, Balzac Paris. But also how it has been constructed in and by various writings – how it has been used as a topos, a topic, a trope. How, for instance, Venice was 'Ruskinized' (to use Henry James's term), and how that 'Ruskinized' Venice then provided a crucial space and place for Proust's imagination, is not simply a matter of academic or biographical interest. It can show us something vital about how great minds appropriate the man-made environment – make it over a second time lexically, turning it into a unique discursive space in which values and meanings can be created, celebrated, contested, transformed. These meanings and values – this discursive appropriation/creation of the city – are vital to all city-dwellers, for, in a very real and important sense, we inhabit the city as it has been written and rewritten as well as the city as it has been built and rebuilt. Obviously to a certain extent a study of the history and culture of cities can quickly come to be a history and study of practically everything of importance – certainly in the Europe of the past few hundred years, as the work of Fernand Braudel and (say) Lewis Mumford sufficiently shows. This series will aim to concentrate more narrowly on how the city has been summoned up, depicted, deployed, dramatized – perhaps rediscovered, reinvented, metamorphosed or transfigured in selected writings. It is to be expected that there will be an inevitable tendency to concentrate on the city as written in the nineteenth and twentieth centuries, this being the period when the city became both mysterious and ubiquitous, unknowable and inescapable, housing the past and determining – or destroying – the future. Increasingly, meaning no longer comes from the church, the court or the manor, but is produced – and reproduced – in the city. How writers have responded to this situation will be one of the areas of interest in the proposed studies.

Tony Tanner

Acknowledgements

Parts of chapters 1 and 2 appeared as an essay in *City Images*, ed. Mary Ann Caws, Gordon and Breach, New York, 1991. On matters both major and minor, I have benefited from the help given me by friends, colleagues and students (in many cases, the categories are happily blurred). In particular I would like to thank the following: Jonathan Arac, Alexander Baumann, Isabella Bertoletti, Victor Brombert, Peter Brooks, Norman Bryson, Richard Burton, Mary Ann Caws, Ross Chambers, Sue Chapman, Tim Clark, David Coler, Peter Collier, Alain Corbin, Kinga Eminowicz-Galicia, Marie Frapin, Hal Foster, Catherine Gallagher, Barbara Goff, Marcel Gutwirth, Leslie Hill, Diana Knight, Carole Kulikowski, Robert Lethbridge, Jean-Michel Massing, George McClintock, Marek Mosakowski, Ian Noble, Linda Nochlin, Elaine O'Brien, Paddy O'Donovan, Jeanine Plottel, Charles Rearick, Michael Riffaterre, Richard Sieburth, Carina Yervasi. Special thanks are due to Alexander Baumann for his truly heroic labours with both typescript and proofs; his sharp eye and indefatigable energy have ensured a far better final text than would otherwise have been the case.

I must also mention two major debts of a collective nature. The first is to the students in my seminar at the Graduate School of the City University of New York; their participation helped me both shape and sharpen the book's final arguments. The second is to my colleagues in the editorial collective of the journal *Social Text*; although we did not discuss the subject matter of this book as such, their example helped me make the most of the extraordinarily fertile circumstance of finding myself writing about nineteenth-century Paris in late twentieth-century New York.

Research in Paris was made possible by grants from the University of Cambridge, the British Academy, the Leverhulme Trust and the Research Foundation of the City University of New York. I am grateful to all four for their support. I should like to thank Claire Barbillon and Nicole Savy of the Musée d'Orsay, who not only placed the museum's resources at my disposal but also invited me to try out some of my ideas in a publication for the museum's series, *Parcours*. I wish also to thank the staff at the Bibliothèque historique de la Ville de Paris for their unfailingly helpful and friendly support.

Christopher Prendergast
New York City

Ne plus aimer Paris, marque de décadence. Ne pouvoir s'en passer, marque de bêtise.

Flaubert, *Carnets*

1

Introduction: Parisian Identities

I

Let us imagine a scene of reading in that novel *par excellence* of imagined (and imaginative) readings, Flaubert's *Madame Bovary*. The year is 1835; the Bovarys have moved from Tostes to Yonville and Balzac's *Le Père Goriot* has just come out in *La Revue de Paris*. In our imaginary scene Emma has procured a copy (perhaps through the good offices of Monsieur Homais) and, on a grey and empty afternoon, is entirely absorbed by its ramifying plot. This is not at all an implausible imagining, since earlier in Tostes Emma is to be found reading Balzac, indeed so enthusiastically that she even brings his novels to the dining table: 'elle lut Balzac et George Sand, y cherchant des assouvissements imaginaires pour ses convoitises. A table même, elle apportait son livre, et elle tournait les feuillets pendant que Charles mangeait en lui parlant.'[1] Balzac, moreover, has contributed to the state of awe-struck wonder in which, from the perspective of provincial Normandy, she has constructed a version of Paris. Paris, for Emma, is 'Paris', a magical proper name ('Comment était ce Paris? Quel nom démesuré . . .'[2]), around which fantasy and desire fluctuate in direct proportion to her feeling of local entrapment.

Already nourished by her previous reading of Balzac, Emma's sense of the 'enormity' of the proper name 'Paris' would doubtless be much enhanced by immersion in the strange adventures of *Le Père Goriot*. In particular, given the way its plot is geared to mystery, reversal and revelation, the novel's most vivid effect on Emma's notions of the metropolitan *là-bas* would probably come with the episode in which the master criminal, Vautrin, is unmasked by the police inspector. Yet, at this climactic moment of the story, where some deep and dark revelation of the nature of the city might be expected, on the subject of Paris Balzac's policeman in fact proves

1

disappointingly tautologous: 'Paris est Paris, voyez-vous' is about the best he can muster, adding portentously, 'Ce mot explique ma vie.'[3] It is, of course, significant that the remark is made by a policeman in a work that is in some ways an embryonic version of what will become the detective novel. The latter is not only a distinctively urban form; it also proposes a specific form of knowledge of the urban itself, predicated on the belief that an increasingly complex and intractable urban reality can be successfully monitored and mastered. Yet, although presented as an exemplary figure of knowledge, an expert in tracking and taming the Parisian labyrinth, Balzac's policeman in fact here combines both power and impotence; at once full and empty, his tautology connotes knowledge, but contains no information and 'explains' nothing.

The logical form of much writing about Paris, and great cities generally, is like this: for those who truly understand the city, 'Paris' ('London', 'New York', etc.) is what goes without saying, according to whatever set of stereotypes is tacitly in play. What, then, does the city represent, and how to represent the city, to see it as form and 'identity' (in the double sense of giving identity to the city and finding identity, individual or collective, in the city)?[4] These, in connection with Paris in the nineteenth century, are some of the questions of this book. But to pose them thus risks resurrecting Balzac's fantasy of omnipotence and control, assuming privileged access to what lies 'behind' tautology and stereotype, to what, in the 'Avant-propos' to the *Comédie humaine*, Balzac calls the 'sens caché' of the modern world.[5] The issue of the identity of the city, and of identities within it, constituted a veritable nineteenth-century obsession. In the later part of the century, Maxime du Camp wrote that never before had the city been so minutely described, monitored, surveyed, classified, generally 'cleaned up' taxonomically as well as practically: 'Il [Paris] est enregistré, catalogué, numéroté, surveillé, éclairé, nettoyé, dirigé, soigné, administré, arrêté, jugé, emprisonné, enterré.'[6] The endless reports and proliferating nomenclatures of the urban bureaucracies (from the police to sanitary inspectors), not to mention the cataloguing descriptions and ordering plots of the novelists, suggest a massive enterprise of mapping the city as a means, both practical and symbolic, of keeping tabs on 'identities'. The city is there to be 'read', often in the form of reading essences, fixed identities, into contingent particulars (of place, speech, dress, etc.). The tautology of Balzac's policeman does not therefore mean that there is no knowledge, but only that it is so immediately and fully to hand that it scarcely needs to be articulated; to the properly positioned subject (whether policeman or novelist), it is as immediately and unproblematically available as it is to the Balzac who, in his early essay, *Histoire et physiologie des boulevards de Paris*, claimed of the Paris boulevards and the instant legibility of their population: 'Autant d'hommes, autant d'habits différents, et autant d'habits, autant de caractères.'[7]

'Identity', then, cannot be at all assumed as a given category or reference point. Much of my argument, on the contrary, will deal with the sheer difficulty of making sense of the modern city and one's place in it, the terms in which the city exceeds both identification and identity, and the price often paid by various artists in their efforts to make the city conform to an intelligible design. We might therefore wish to take the opposite view, that the city lies beyond intelligibility, that, like Newman's city, it is that for which we 'have no map'.[8] But this too is problematical: the view that the city is unmappable, defies understanding, also is, or becomes, a stereotype. In connection with Paris, it has already entered into the stock of city-clichés or *parisianismes*[9] by the 1860s, if not earlier (in a text of 1860 Alfred Delvau, for example, can speak with complete ease, even affectionately, of 'ce sphinx qu'on appelle Paris'[10]); and the proposition that the city is too complex to be understood or known will be increasingly naturalized from the later nineteenth century onwards. Accordingly – and for reasons to be more fully elaborated later – I try to keep constantly active in the argument the claim that there is also a price to be paid for saying that the city has *no* identity, in the now familiar move that breaks a difficult yet essential tension by dissolving ideological notions of fixity and homogeneity into equally ideological or ideologizable notions of free-flowing heterogeneity.

An alternative approach to these issues – and the approach I have sought in many ways to adopt – is that of multiplying critical perspectives within a multiplicity of given perspectives, a juxtaposition, and often a clash, of representations. One image for this way of investigating images is Henry James's figure for the relation between fiction and the world: since I am dealing with a field of representations, taken from an archive so large as to be potentially unmanageable (mainly in literature but also, though to a much lesser extent, in painting), it seemed initially appropriate to proceed by way of a more or less improvised eclecticism – that is, in the spirit of an analogy between the highly diverse nineteenth-century imaginings of Paris and James's house of fiction with its many windows (the possibilities, as well as the limits, of the motif of the 'window' I shall consider at greater length in the next chapter).[11] James's pluralistic metaphor moreover suggests both a model and a further metaphor, whereby one moves about the house and its variegated views in the form of a series of urban walks. This is the model based on that characteristic denizen of the literature of nineteenth-century Paris, the *flâneur*, and the corresponding notion of the city as a special kind of visual field, peculiarly open to the mobile gaze and unforeseen encounter.

I have in large measure organized the book, thematically and topically, around the notion of Paris as a 'space', where space is understood as both physical and social space (roughly in the sense of Kracauer's 'topography of social space'[12]), and hence also space as affected by time, space produced, arranged and altered by history. The itinerary I have followed – more or less

3

randomly carved out – takes in the following *topoi*: the view from the café, the panoramic vista, the underground city (the catacombs and the sewers), the market, the boulevard, the barricade, the park and the canal. I have generally ignored the world of interior and private space, what Balzac describes under the heading of *Scènes de la vie privée* (although the privatizing of domestic space is, of course, one of the constitutive categories of social perceptions of the nineteenth-century city[13]). This approach explains in part the potential relevance of the model of the free-wheeling *flâneur*, as a figure providing a kind of mobile 'window on the world' (to use the Impressionists' terms) through which the diversity of the city, especially the public city, is encountered. Yet here much caution is necessary. For the methodological attractions of the eclectic and the aleatory perspectives can also serve to mask important difficulties of interpretation embedded in the material under consideration itself. The convenience of construing the latter on the analogy of a variegated stroll through the multiform city landscape is simply too convenient, and moreover may well end by uncritically recapitulating a major ideological pattern of the nineteenth-century urban imagination: the idea of the city as a 'free field' of stimulus and adventure for the relaxed and skilful connoisseur.[14]

As a centrally active theme in nineteenth-century literature and painting, the category of *flânerie* is problematical as well as enabling, especially in the complex moves and tensions of Baudelaire's writings. I shall want, in subsequent chapters, to consider in some detail certain versions of the theme of *flânerie*. For the moment, let us simply remind ourselves of the definition supplied by James himself (in *Roderick Hudson*), namely that 'the prime requisite of an expert *flâneur*' is 'the simple, sensuous, confident relish of pleasure'.[15] That, of course, is the view of the comfortably furnished, travelling gentleman, a view amply confirmed and provided for in a welter of nineteenth-century guidebooks and journalistic writing, themselves often constructed in the form of a chapter-by-chapter itinerary through the city. Deconstructing this incarnation of the nineteenth-century *flâneur* is quite straightforward but also essential: as both middle class and male, he is appropriately seen and placed in contrast with two other figures also 'circulating' in the city, and whose condition he commonly ignores or frequently exploits: the vagabond and the prostitute.[16] Working from an analogy with the *flâneur* moving through the 'variety' of the city ('variety', in its more settled and unexamined forms, is not the same as 'heterogeneity'), we quickly end up with the city as pure spectacle, with what Alfred Kazin has identified – precisely in connection with Henry James on the subject of New York – as the logical terminus of literary *flânerie*, the construction of the city as aesthetic object ('The city becomes an esthetic object when you become totally fascinated by the energy and the multifariousness of the surface'[17]).

It will, of course, be abundantly clear how much these preliminary observations on approach and method owe to the work of Walter Benjamin;
indeed the imprint of Benjamin's work can be seen, whether strongly or
faintly, virtually everywhere in the following pages. The Paris I am concerned
with is to a very large extent the Paris that Benjamin called the 'capital of
the nineteenth century', both in his study of Baudelaire and in the
monumental Arcades Project (the *Passagen-Werk*, now available in French
translation under the title *Paris, capitale du XIXe siècle*[18]). By 'capital of
the nineteenth century', Benjamin meant that in the developing urban forms
of life exemplified by Paris we see some of the distinctive features of
'modernity' in general and its complex, unsettling effects on both society
and the psyche. Benjamin's strategy was that of the micrology, the close-
up focus on specific urban phenomena, crucially the nineteenth-century
arcades, but with a view to uncovering a more general social and cultural
logic. The arcade is posed as the site and perfect emblem of the emergence
of the culture of the 'commodity', a culture of movement and dislocation
in which the eye and the mind are increasingly solicited, and threatened, by
an uprecedented range of stimuli masquerading as the utopia of the New.
It is the world described by Balzac in the image of a ceaseless 'turning',
what Lucien de Rubempré, newly arrived in the capital, experiences as 'la
rapidité du tournoiement parisien',[19] a mobile swirling landscape dominated
by chance encounter, fast transaction, frenetic circulation of money, goods
and bodies.

Speed, as Benjamin and others remind us, is one of the fundamental
conditions of the new commodity culture and will return again and again
in the developing lexicon of 'modernity'. Marx talks of the 'agitation' of
modern life, famously elaborating that idea as the experience whereby 'all
that is solid melts into air'.[20] Nietzsche speaks of the 'haste and hurry now
universal . . . the increasing velocity of life', of the 'hurried and over-excited
worldliness' of the modern age.[21] The great sociologist of urban experience,
Georg Simmel, refers to the 'impatient tempo of modern life',[22] its corresponding phenomenon of 'over-excited and exhausted nerves',[23] and gen-
eralizes this to a fundamental psychic condition of life in the city, formulated as 'the dissolution of fixed contents in the fluid element of the soul'.[24]
In their fully generalized forms, some of these accounts will become
problematically implicated in the phenomenon they describe, notably perhaps Simmel's emphasis on the city as the place of the jangled and jaded
sensation-seeker. The recurring preoccupation with speed and velocity,
however, registers a major fact of the modern experience of the city, one
that had profound effects on everyday life, undermining more settled
notions of 'tradition' and 'community', or, as Benjamin's German puts it,
removing from the immediacy of *Erlebnis* the sanctioning framework of
Erfahrung.[25]

It will also implicate the fate of art, both practically through its growing incorporation into the market, and formally in the development of an art more and more committed to the registration of sudden *aperçu*, fluid sensation, mobile point of view and fugitive impression (precisely, in another key, the theme of the 'fugitive', and the attempt to encircle, capture and fix it). Simmel put the point well when, in speaking of Rodin, he claimed that modern 'art not merely mirrors a world in motion, its very mirror has itself become more labile.'[26] And although, in these metaphors of 'mirroring', one must resist the reductive schemes of causal explanation associated with a naive base/superstructure account of culture and society, there can be little doubt as to the validity of Benjamin's argument that the sense of the city as an increasingly uncertain and unpredictable perceptual field is linked to the emergence of an art geared to an entirely new set of rhythms, an art based on the principles of surprise and 'shock', disruption and displacement of any assumption of a coherent 'centre' to experience – whether in the 'snap-shot' technique of later nineteenth-century verse poetry, the jerky, nervous registers of the prose poem, or the fluctuating and disintegrative rhythms of the later forms of the novel. The supreme spokesman in the nineteenth century for the relation between the city and the new art was, of course, Baudelaire, notably in his emphasis on *modernité*, both social and artistic, as based on the exploration and cultivation of 'le transitoire, le fugitif, le contingent',[27] and, more specifically, on the mutual relations of daily life and artistic method around the experience of *speed* (as, for instance, in Baudelaire's comments on the significance of Constantin Guys's method of rapid composition in his sketches of city life).[28]

Benjamin's description of Paris as 'capital of the nineteenth century' was not, however, just shorthand for indicating the city's crucial place in the emerging social and cultural forms of modernity. It is also a kind of summarizing quotation that stands for a whole body of reference within nineteenth-century discourse itself. If, for us, the phrase 'capital of the nineteenth century' has become something of a Benjaminian cliché, we should not forget that it was already such in the nineteenth-century archive Benjamin so tirelessly excavated. Describing Paris in this way had become something of a commonplace from the late eighteenth century onwards. Paris, in these accounts, was variously capital of the century, Europe, nations, the earth and the universe. In his poem, 'Paris', Vigny presented the city not only as 'le pivot de la France', but as 'l'axe du monde'.[29] Balzac, in his early essay 'Paris en 1831', spoke of Paris as 'la capitale du monde' and as 'sans égal dans l'univers'.[30] Even Victor Considérant, in a context of bitter attack, called it 'la capitale des capitales'.[31] And so it went on. Later in the century, Edmond Texier managed to get most of the relevant clichés into a single paragraph, when in his *Tableau de Paris* he described Paris as 'l'œil de l'intelligence, le cerveau du monde, l'abrégé de l'univers, le commentaire de l'homme, l'humanité faite ville'.[32] Texier also collaborated on another book in which one of the more expansive of these clichés appeared in its very title, *Paris, capitale du monde*. This came out in 1867, in time for the Exposition Universelle of that year. So too did the *Paris-Guide*, a collection of essays by diverse hands, including a long preface by Victor Hugo (subsequently published under the title of *Paris*).[33] Hugo, of course, has complex statements to make about contemporary Paris (notably in *Les Misérables*). In the prefatory text written for *Paris-Guide*, however, he echoes the standard idioms in posing Paris as not only the centre of civilization but the motor force of the world-historical future: 'Paris est sur toute la terre le lieu où l'on entend le mieux frissonner l'immense voilure du progrès.'[34]

This is Hugo seeking to gather into an image of urban modernity and futurity all the prestigious connotations associated with the ancient linking of the ideas of *civitas, civilitas* and *humanitas* – the city as the place of civilized man (rarely woman) and the centre of the self-governing republic.[35] But, in the context of the values and objectives represented by the Exposition Universelle, the attempted adaptation of these ancient notions to modern Paris rings hollow. The republican ideal is indeed active in Hugo's text (the city as the focus of a unifying political culture consisting of free and equal citizens). This theme is central to post-revolutionary republican conceptions of the political significance of the city (it should be remembered that the Revolution brought the seat of government back from Versailles to Paris, and it is perhaps significant that in the chapter devoted to its high symbolic moment – the storming of the Bastille – Michelet will begin his account with a dramatic and rhetorical opposition between Paris and Versailles[36]). 1867, however, is the period of the Second Empire. Hugo writes *Paris* from both a position of exile and a feeling of intense personal hatred for Napoleon III, and clearly much of what he writes – in particular the association of Paris with revolution, democracy and the legacy of 1789 – was designed as a provocation to the imperial regime. Yet what strikes us in retrospect in reading his preface is the ease with which Hugo's republican enthusiasms mesh with an official imperial ideology glorifying Paris as a vanguard of technological progress and capitalist expansion. Whatever else divides them, republican and imperial images of modern Paris have a common ideological investment (reflected in the recurrence of identical themes in the World Exhibitions of both the Second Empire and the Third Republic): the assumption of the city as more or less identifiably coherent, as having, precisely, an *identity* binding its members in a shared sense of purpose and a common sense of belonging. Hugo will denounce the miseries of nineteenth-century urban living, but will rarely lose the sense of Paris as a culturally integrated and historically purposive creation; indeed the thrust of his argument in *Paris* is to extend the official image of the Exposition Universelle – as signifying the 'concord of nations' – into a prophetic vision of a future European nation-state of which Paris, as its capital, would be the crowning glory.[37]

Hugo's hymn of praise to Paris as the capital of the future is not, however, merely a matter of historical curiosity. If I introduce Hugo's *Paris* at this stage, and the countervailing and demystifying force of Benjamin (and Baudelaire), it is because in a great deal of recent writing on nineteenth-century Paris the lessons of the latter have been forgotten, displaced by something resembling the tone and approach of Hugo (minus the republican rhetoric). Paris, and especially the Paris of Baron Haussmann and Napoleon III, has been up for rehabilitation. Symptomatic of this new revisionist politics of urban historiography is Donald Olsen's widely praised book, *The City as a Work of Art*. The price paid, in terms of subject matter, is exorbitant. Olsen explicitly excludes from his purview what he calls urban history as 'social pathology'.[38] The terms of the excluded are themselves interesting – they recapitulate a stock nineteenth-century figure, in the reduction of man-made forms of urban misery to the medicalized vocabulary of illness and disease ('Qui a interrogé les entrailles de la grande ville, sondé les plaies de son corps comme le médecin,' exclaim rhetorically the editors of the early nineteenth-century *Nouveau Tableau de Paris*[39]). But, more important, no sooner is the reduction effected than it is despatched to the waste-paper basket of history. Reduced and then removed, what might otherwise obstruct the 'vista' of the aestheticist historian is conveniently forgotten so as to allow the field to be exclusively occupied by a cultural and ideological fiction: the city as a work of art. Not surprisingly, Paris, on this view, becomes, along with imperial London and Vienna, 'a privilege to inhabit', and 'the embodiment of nineteenth-century urban civilization, a realized ideal'.[40] But *whose* privilege, an ideal realized for whom? Clearly so for the property speculator, the genteel resident and the well-to-do tourist (whose perspective, quite literally at the level of quoted sources, is consistently adopted by Olsen); but scarcely so for the ragpicker, the beggar and the slum dweller (in a chapter on working-class housing Olsen omits to tell us that, as fast as Haussmann demolished the slums, they sprang up elsewhere, in the eastern *quartiers* and beyond the *barrières*).

The omission is instructive, since it is an intellectual precondition of the idea of the city as pleasure garden and work of art that it be seen as a 'collectively created complex',[41] the product of a common will and the expression of a high degree of homogeneity in the social and political culture. This, ideologically speaking, is pure Haussmann: the vision of the modern city as unified, centred and fully legible, opened up as a safe and regulated space of leisure and pleasure to all its citizens. An exemplary case in point (which I shall consider in some detail in a later chapter) is furnished by one of Haussmann's major transformations of urban space: the creation or extension of public parks. Only an absurdly partisan account of

Haussmannization could deny the considerable improvement in public amenity represented by the provision of new parks and open spaces (by 1870 there were roughly 4500 acres of municipal parkland as against a mere 47 acres twenty years previously [42]). Yet there is clearly a difference between recognizing a real practical achievement and endorsing the wider ideological claims made on its behalf. In this respect, we may note how Olsen, in discussing the question of the municipal park, quotes with evident approval the astonishing remark of a contemporary observer: 'Paris has been developing into Arcadia.'[43] We shall see, in later chapters, what happens to the attempted importation of pastoral imagery in representations of the city, its ironic cancellation in the novels of Balzac and Zola, the poetry of Baudelaire and Laforgue, the paintings of Manet and Seurat. Certainly, the notion that the park functioned as a space for the bucolic fraternizing of all Parisians, suspending the frictions and divisions of social hierarchy and class conflict, could be dismissed as simply absurd, were it not that it is also symptomatic of the terms and tone of the revisionist approach in general. It gives one very good reason why Olsen's apparent endorsement of the imagery of rustic Arcadia is appropriately met and challenged by the implications of Benjamin's study of the urban arcades.

In attacking the revisionist view, it is, of course, easy to fall victim to a certain kind of disingenuousness: as a lover of Paris – as was Benjamin himself – and hence wholly complicit in that peculiarly 'amorous' idiom which saturates the literature of Parisian *flânerie*, I have reason to be grateful for certain features of Haussmannization (although it was one of the standard themes of the period that Haussmann had destroyed the city of *flânerie*). More important, it is to disfigure history itself, in terms of both intentions and outcomes, to see Haussmannization *solely* as an exercise in counter-revolutionary strategy (city planning as basically an exercise in crowd control) or as the provision of *carte blanche* for the predatory moves of speculative capital. Haussmann's 'achievements' were real, but so too was the gap between practical reform and official ideology. The reforms may have contributed to the blurring of the signs of difference and division, especially in certain public spaces, but they did not obliterate the actual differences themselves. The city certainly became more 'beautiful', in terms of spanking new boulevards, refurbished façades and monumental vistas, but at the cost of hiding much from public view. Physically, the city came to seem more coherent, but socially it remained disturbingly opaque and unpredictable. There was simply too much in 'circulation', and circulating too fast, for a sense of stable identity to remain in place for very long.

'Circulation', according to Didier Gille, is at the very heart of the modern conception of the city.[44] Control the network of circulation, said the earlier reformers, ensure the orderly flow of traffic, waste and bodies, and the rational city will emerge. Above all, regulate the circuits at the margin of society, and the centre will hold. Already during the Restoration and the July Monarchy, Parent-Duchâtelet, that indefatigable collector of statistics and zealous promotor of reform, argued in his reports that a key to the construction of the rational city was control of the sewers and the prostitutes. Creating safe and efficient systems of discharge and evacuation seemed the basis for guaranteeing that the city would be properly ordered and 'policed'. Haussmann's thinking was not so very different. Although – significantly – he did nothing in respect of prostitution (at a time of spectacular increase in the trade), he did embark, with the aid of his engineer, Belgrand, on a programme for renovating the Paris sewerage system. The experiment was in fact limited in scope, and did not deal with the problem of evacuating human bodily waste. One supplementary purpose that it did come to fulfil, however, was that of rapid communication: the use of the sewers to transport the pneumatic tubes in which letters could be moved about the city with great speed.[45]

In its small way, this odd off-shoot of sanitary reform resumes the unfolding paradox of the modern city throughout the nineteenth century: the faster the city becomes, the more its circuits of communication accelerate, the *less* controllable it in fact becomes. Balzac again already hints at this, in his luridly melodramatic way, with the plot of *Splendeurs et misères des courtisanes* – precisely a narrative in which the attempts to manage the flux of male desire around the body of a prostitute are in part undone by a series of wildly circulating letters and messages, a circuit of communication that no one can fully master. We have come, largely through a simplified reading of the works of Foucault, to see the history of the nineteenth-century city as a story of imposed surveillance and attempted mastery, as the progressive emergence of the classified and regimented city under the aegis of an irresistibly powerful 'carceral' ideology. Certainly the endless statistical investigations and the various programmes of reform, especially those devoted to the marginal or marginalizing spaces of the new urban order (the prisons, the hospitals, the slums, the brothels, the cesspits and the sewers), suggest that this was indeed a powerful impulse. Haussmann's way with both Paris overground and Paris underground would seem the exemplary illustration of that enterprise. Haussmann's objective was to produce a coherent and stratified identity for modern Paris (it is no accident that Hausmann provided Paris with its first accurate survey map), a clearly readable system of boundaries and demarcations with everything in its proper place, essentially a city without surprise.

Yet arguably he in fact presided over its opposite: the city as a place of increasing illegibility, in which 'surprise' seemed to be the order of the day, and in which 'identity', psychic and social, would come to be perceived as uncertain and problematical. Vigny, as early as 1844 (in 'La Maison du Berger') will attack the project of the rationalized city (specifically its mechanized forms of transport) as the city of 'calcul silencieux et froid', as exactly a city without surprise, beyond the play of chance ('Plus de hasard').[46] This came to be one of the major themes of complaint about the Paris of the Second Empire and the Third Republic: alongside 'rectiligne' and 'géométrique' (referring to the new layout of the streets and boulevards), the favourite adjective was 'monotone';[47] Verlaine wrote, playing comically with internal rhyme around the theme of boring 'sameness', of 'le long ennui de vos haussmanneries'.[48] Yet, paradoxically, the clearer, cleaner and more uniform the city came to appear physically, the more opaque and mysterious it came to seem socially, as governed by a contingent and chaotic play of forces, transactions and interests, to which one could not attach a correspondingly clear description. Baudelaire, in 'Le Cygne', described the *making* of Haussmann's Paris as a 'bric-à-brac confus'.[49] He was, of course, referring primarily to the physical realities of demolition and rebuilding. But the notion of the city as 'bric-à-brac' remained even after the building was completed, and indeed did so often in relation to the city's architecture itself;[50] planned and rationalized, the city paradoxically no longer seemed to possess coherent form.

II

This sense of the difficulty of 'reading' (and writing) Paris, of holding it in stable focus, is one of the main themes of this book. For problems of readability and interpretation are not only questions for the understanding of Haussmann's Paris (although arguably they are experienced there in particularly acute form). They are also, in varying degrees of severity, problems in the history of the city throughout the whole of the nineteenth century.[51] In the 1830s Balzac mobilizes the routine comparison of Paris with the sea and the ocean, but in order to focus his sense of its 'unfathomability': 'Paris est un océan. Jetez-y la sonde, vous n'en connaîtrez jamais la profondeur.'[52] Towards the end of the century, Barrès, from the perspective of an anxious political right, will describe Paris as a kind of swirling dustbowl ('une nombreuse poussière d'individus . . . sans lien social, sans règle de vie, sans but'[53]), a site of atomistic fragmentation and dispersal on such a scale as to defy intelligibility itself: 'Paris n'est pas un univers saisissable pour nous; c'est un désordre.'[54] Together, the responses of Balzac and Barrès can be said to frame the city as the problem of how to make sense of it.

Indeed this is a theme which, as Marshall Berman has argued, we can take back at least as far as Rousseau's Paris.[55] In *Emile* Paris is compared to the scattering and dispersing energies of the whirlwind ('un tourbillon social').[56] In *La Nouvelle Héloïse* Saint-Preux comes to the city (the hero's arrival in Paris will furnish the narrative matrix of much of the great tradition of the nineteenth-century novel). Its psychic impact is immediate and dramatic: caught in the rhythms of a vertiginous circulation, Saint-Preux experiences the movements of the city as a self-disorientating and self-undoing force that threatens the foundations of identity itself:

> Cependant je commence à sentir l'ivresse où cette vie agitée et tumultueuse plonge ceux qui la mènent, et je tombe dans un étourdissement semblable à celui d'un homme aux yeux duquel on fait passer rapidement une multitude d'objets. Aucun de ceux qui me frappent n'attache mon cœur, mais tous ensemble en troublent et suspendent les affections, au point d'en oublier quelques instans *ce que je suis et à qui je suis.*[57] (my italics)

Rousseau, of course, brings special preoccupations to his view of the city: his belief that it is only beyond the walls of the city, in solitary communion with nature, that 'identity' is properly achieved. In the *Rêveries d'un promeneur solitaire* (notably in Book 5) Rousseau sketches, on 'associationist' principles, a model of psychic equilibrium, whereby a happily integrated subjectivity is built from the unimpeded and harmonious flow into the self of the sights and sounds of the natural world. In thus severing the self from the city, the *Rêveries* effectively found a genre, a literature based on sustained contestation of, and flight from, the urban, and whose major practitioners in nineteenth-century France will include Chateaubriand, Senancour, Lamartine, Vigny, Fourier, George Sand, Nerval and Fromentin. Chateaubriand's North American forests, Senancour's mountains, Lamartine's lakes and landscapes, Vigny's 'Maison du Berger', Fourier's rural phalanstery, Sand's *romans champêtres*, Nerval's country festivals, Fromentin's idyllic farm are so many literary manifestations of a resolute turning away from the city, its blandishments and corruptions.

But if the flight from the city to the countryside in the name of an authentic subjectivity is one side of Rousseau's enormously influential presence in the nineteenth-century rejection of the urban, there is also another, more public side. The existential problem of 'belonging' in and to the city described by Saint-Preux was also a political problem, a politics of belonging. Much of the argument of *Du contrat social* turns on the claim that in the modern city (unlike the smaller ancient city-state) there is no social and material base for the reinvention of the ideals of the polis. The difficulty of being a citizen in the modern world is essentially that there are no cities (with the possible exception of the beloved Geneva) in which to exercise the virtues of citizenship. The problem of 'representing' the city as a coherent and intelligible space thus becomes associated with the problem of representation *in* the city. This, moreover, is not just a matter for Rousseau and his peculiarly radical theory of the inalienability of 'sovereignty'. Even that most urban and urbane of the *philosophes*, Turgot, found it impossible to make sense of the doctrine of political representation in terms that would accommodate the inhabitants of the city, including its wealthiest and most powerful members.

In his *Mémoire sur les municipalités* of 1774, Turgot argued the classic Enlightenment connection between representation and property. Property here meant *landed* property, 'real' property, what Turgot describes in virtually ontological terms as 'la place qu'ils occupent indéliblement sur le sol'.[58] Those without land (which in this context means more than owning a house) are not entitled to full citizenship in the state, not primarily because they are poor, but because, without land, they are without fixed attachment, belong nowhere ('ils n'appartiennent à aucun lieu'[59]). Political identity thus rests not just on what belongs to you, but on where and to what you belong. And this is why Turgot refuses the franchise not only to the propertyless peasant in the countryside, but also to the vast majority of the wealthy in the city. The dominant form of urban wealth is mobile wealth, and 'les richesses mobilières sont fugitives comme les talents.'[60] It does not fix, root: in ceaseless circulation, it is not a 'natural' extension of self, an index of belonging, an 'indelible' trace of grounded being, what is 'proper' to one in the sense of a 'property' that is constitutive of identity and difference; rather – to speak in semiological terms – it is less an index than a sign, and, like all signs, shadowed by the arbitrariness and instability that accompany a system of 'representation' without secure foundations.[61]

Turgot's proposals came to nothing, and in the course of the nineteenth century the concepts of citizenship and political representation will assume quite different forms.[62] The kind of thinking and feeling that lies behind those proposals nevertheless will travel through the nineteenth century in a variety of guises. The effects of mercantilism and capitalism, as systems for making wealth more 'mobile', will make the city a site of permanent anxiety as well as a source of magnetic attraction. If, on the one hand, the city is seen as a centre of *humanitas*, the heart of civilization and culture, there is, on the other hand, a continuing sensitivity to those other ancient notions – the sense of *cultura* as originating in land, agriculture, cultivation, and the implication of *pagus* (from the Greek verb 'to fix'), namely the countryside as a place of fixed boundaries and settled community.

The relative, indeed radical, absence of settled forms of 'community' in the city was, of course, a standard nineteenth-century theme. Paris was regularly described as a city of 'nomads'. But, whereas today the 'nomadic' has become something of a postmodernist shibboleth, the nineteenth-century politics of that analogy were essentially a politics of fear and loathing. Lecouturier, for instance, was giving vent to a sense of alarm and outrage when he wrote in 1848: 'Il n'y a pas de société parisienne, il n'y a pas de

Parisiens. Paris n'est qu'un campement de nomades.'[63] Then there was Haussmann's famous speech deploring the 'rootlessness' of modern Paris and its invasion by 'cette tourbe de nomades'[64] that made up the migrant army of casual labour drawn into the city by his own building programme. 'Nomads', in this context, meant an inferior class of working or unemployed person, and more generally that floating and drifting population which made up much of the urban *bas-fonds* (vagabonds, beggars, criminals); and it was not that long before the class reference came also to acquire a racial overlay, in a generalized dislike of the 'immigrant' and fear of 'contagion'. Dreyfus is not far away, along with Barrès's call for an integrated 'national' culture based on the values of the 'soil'.

Another way of articulating these preoccupations and concerns, alongside the very general contrast of city and country, might be in terms of two conflicting ideas of the city itself: the idea of the city as 'capital' and as 'metropolis'. We can usefully draw here on the distinctions proposed by Anne Querrien (in 'The Metropolis and the Capital'): a capital is a political and cultural 'centre', with the power and authority to dominate and protect a wider 'territory', to keep in place a 'social hierarchy' and to 'subjugate a population . . . to a common heritage'. A metropolis, on the other hand, 'is not a centre and has no centre', it 'has no identity to preserve', it 'begins with the slightest desire to exchange', is 'made up of networks', it 'puts an incongruous mix of beings into circulation' and is 'the place where migrants find their socially predetermined destination'.[65] While we must bear in mind that French 'métropole' has a distinct semantic history which does not itself precisely coincide with this opposition, something of the latter seems to have been at work in the social imagination of the city, particularly in the later nineteenth century. Although the two ideas of the city overlapped, coexisted, waxed and waned according to the pressure of events, it seems that the view of Paris as 'metropolis', as impersonal space of 'circulation' and 'exchange', came more and more to challenge, in ways generally felt to be menacing, the older notion of the city as 'capital'. With that change went corresponding changes at the level of perceived civic and existential relations to the city, broadly those summed up in Auguste Cochin's account of the process whereby 'il y a encore dans Paris des habitants, il n'y a plus de citoyens'[66] (and paradoxically nowhere was this feeling perhaps greater than in the period which saw the restoration of the Republic after 1871).

This, for instance, is part of the context for understanding Barrès. Barrès's fear is essentially a fear of the 'metropolis', all mixture, movement and decentredness. In so far as Barrès wanted a city at all, what he wanted was a 'capital', in the sense of that right-wing adaptation of the notion of a 'centre' radiating out into the nation at large and as such the focus of a collective national identity. 'Le véritable fonds du Français', wrote Barrès in one of the many disquieting sentences of *Les Déracinés*, 'est une nature commune, un produit social et historique, possédé en participation par chacun de nous.' Paris, in *Les Déracinés*, is accordingly desired as 'un lieu national' but, without the 'lien social naturel'[67] which the link with the country (with 'roots') supplies, it becomes an unstructured, deracinated and meaningless cosmopolitan mix 'faite de toutes les races et de tous les pays'.[68] The example of Barrès thus helps us to see that the idea of modern Paris as beyond the powers of coherent and intelligible representation is itself ambiguous. It certainly speaks of real difficulties of perception brought about by real social changes. But it is not thereby itself innocently free of ideological determination. On the contrary, and as we shall have ample occasion to see, very specific sorts of interest and commitment often underlay the diagnosis of modern Paris as unreadable and uncontrollable, although the picture here is complex and involves many different, and often diverging, points of view.

On the one hand, there was that brand of nostalgia for a lost *vieux Paris* which was for the most part little more than a reactionary demand for a return to the more secure and hierarchical taxonomies of the past (the city as 'readable' by virtue of everyone being in, and perceivable as being in, their 'proper' place). Or there was the more openly political version of an intelligibly ordered city of the kind that we get in Barrès's fantasy of recovering an absent centre of control through a return of the spirit of Napoleon I. On the other hand, the sense of the city as acquiring increasingly 'blurred' contours often came to be identified, and even celebrated, in ways that effectively masked what was, at least under appropriate conditions of analysis, eminently 'readable' in the city, as its actual systems of control. 'Blur', of course, is a term that evokes Impressionism, and, as Tim Clark has recently shown, much of the version of 'modernity' we get in Impressionist painting served to promote this view of the city: in its recurring preference for the 'high' view, or its emphasis on urban life as festivity and fashion, or its tendency to reduce distinctions and divisions to the illegible, we have so many perspectives in which the famous Impressionist 'blur' arguably – at least in some cases – serves a whole social way of seeing, or rather a refusal to see significant forms of difference, division and conflict; in Clark's words, if the work of the Impressionists caught an important truth in registering the disappearance from the surfaces of everyday life in the city of a fully coherent sense of '*form*', then this is not the same as saying – although it was precisely this that was often implied in the naturalizing reduction of one to the other – that the city 'lacks *order*'.[69] This in turn generates a further paradox: if the city appears to resist intelligible representation and 'workable forms of visualisation',[70] it may be that appearances are to some extent deceptive; that what truly controls the city (for example, increasingly powerful, mobile capital) seeks to remain hidden, unlocatable, at once fluid and disoriginated. It is one of the myths of the modern city that it 'belongs' to no one in particular, that everything in it is permanently up for grabs to everyone. No belief could have been more convenient to those with an interest in disguising the fact that they actually owned most of it.

III

This oscillation between the notions of Paris as readable or unreadable, as being this side or the other side of representability, raises many of the complex substantive issues in the material with which I shall be concerned in the following chapters. One reason for raising them here, in the introductory chapter, is that they also engage the methodological problems in writing about the material which I mentioned at the beginning. While, in terms of the given genres of scholarly writing, I would like to see this book as a contribution to social and cultural history, it is not, however, offered as a contribution to history in the ordinary sense of describing what was the case, so to speak, on the historical ground. It is not about the referent 'Paris', but about certain symbolic representations, various manifestations of the discursive category 'Paris'.[71] I shall not labour the now notorious distinction between 'discourse' and 'referent' (along with its immensely controversial implications for the category of 'history' itself), since I have assumed that the reader interested in the subject of this book will not be particularly interested in prolonged immersion in theoretical matters (readers entirely *un*interested in such matters are invited to jump to the next chapter). In an important sense, the distinction is in any case artificial, in so far as the symbolic is also part of what was the case; it too belongs to the history in the direct and active sense of helping to produce it. This is essentially what I mean in describing my undertaking as a form of social and cultural history – not simply the social history of art and literature, nor literature and art as 'sources' for social history, but an enterprise concerned with a universe of signs, symbols and representations which themselves participate in the processes whereby a historical reality is produced, maintained, questioned, altered.

On the other hand, if the discourse/referent distinction helps to define the specific area of the book's concerns, it is also something of an embarrassment with regard to several of its ambitions. I shall want to argue, for example, that some representations (largely ideological constructs motivated by or implicated in particular interests) miss, mask or distort the 'reality' of nineteenth-century Paris, and that the significance of several of the accounts I shall be considering lies in the way they function as so many resistances to the terms of an ideologically given or dominant image of the city. Take, for instance, the recurring figure in the literature of the period of the 'industrious' worker, or, more accurately, the description of the worker as finding fulfilment, or at least satisfaction, in the virtues of indus-triousness. But the meaning and value of that description alter from one context to the next, and in order to be understood require grasping what the philosophers sometimes call the relevant 'horizon of concerns' on which the description is situated. These naturally vary in a divided society, and one of the discursive meanings I would want to attach to the metaphor of Paris as a 'space' is that of a space occupied by rival interpretations, often con-flicting and competing with each other for a position of dominance within the field in question.

The image of the industrious worker is a case in point. The meaning of that image is strictly context-bound.[72] Its appearance in, say, the working-class press of the 1830s and 1840s (for example, the newspaper, *L'Atelier*) calls on the values of an older, immensely self-conscious artisanal culture in order to resist the common reduction, in other descriptions, of working-class life and mentality to the imagery of passive fecklessness and brute animality.[73] Conversely, the ideal of the industrious worker reproduced in the 'bourgeois' texts of the period (the *physiologie*, the reformist reports, the hugely influential novels of Eugène Sue, notably *Les Mystères de Paris*) reflects a quite different set of interests: the importance of fashioning a disciplined labour force which is seen to be threatened by those forms of working-class leisure and sociability deemed to lead not only to slackness in the workplace, but ultimately to riotous behaviour, both drunken and insurrectionary, in society at large.[74] These sorts of considerations do not, of course, guarantee direct passage to a 'referent'. There is no comfortable point transcendent to the clash of representations from which they might be adjudicated, and it may be that decisions of this kind simply reflect one's own preferences and allegiances on the battlefield of representations. Yet, when the author of the *Physiologie de l'industrie française* complacently urges upon his readers the view that a worker removed from the din of industrial production in the city to a gentler auditory environment would suffer from acute sensory deprivation, there seems no plausible reason whatsoever to believe that this could possibly have been, or ever be, the case.[75] The brutal assault on the ear by the deafening roar of the industrial workshop of which Michelet speaks in *Le Peuple*[76] or to which Goujet takes Gervaise in Zola's *L'Assommoir*, seems to be much closer to the mark.

The example of industrial noise does, however, raise a further problem, that peculiarly difficult, if not impossible, order of the referent which the phenomenologists describe as the *vécu* (not so much what was the case in the external factual sense, as what was experienced by the consciousness and the body of individual human beings). The statistics of disease and the mortality tables, though indispensable, do not get us very far with that; indeed there is a sense in which 'that' is so ultimately beyond the scope of the historian's inquiry that there is perhaps no point in worrying about it at all. Yet the ideal of a phenomenological history of the nineteenth-century city remains a seductive one, in particular the project of gaining some purchase on the vicissitudes of the urban sensorium, what it felt like to inhabit the city at the level of sight, smell, touch, sound and taste, the city from the point of view of a history of bodily sensations or what Simmel called the changes wrought by urban life in 'the sensory foundations of psychic life'.[77] We want to get inside the skin of the past, not just as metaphor, but as epidermal sensibility, focus of that rich and complex sensorial history which Alain Corbin has recently defended as a vital, if neglected, dimension of social history.[78] In his remarkable book, *The City in History*, Lewis Mumford, writing about the modern industrial city (what he calls the 'paleotechnic town'), invites us to recover it in precisely these terms: 'Approach more closely the paleotechnic town: examine it with eye, ear, nose, touch.'[79] Mumford's unique combination of prodigious learning, moral passion and imaginative sympathy takes us some way towards a realization of that imperative (a paragraph on the lack of sunlight in the urban slum dwelling tells us more about the actual texture of experience than a string of statistics).

I have, to some extent, tried to follow Mumford's injunction in the following pages, and in particular to ensure that the exploration of Paris as a lived 'space' extends beyond its natural domination by the model of sight to include other orders of sensory apprehension. It would, nevertheless, be naïve to assume that we can simply reach back to some primary, unmediated level of urban physical experience. The construction and reconstruction of what we call 'experience' here is subject to many kinds of mediation. Getting inside the 'skin' of the urban past raises in acute form the problems familiar to hermeneutic theory. In the first place, whatever the relations of continuity linking the experience of the nineteenth-century city to that of the late twentieth-century city, there are gaps over which it is difficult for even the most highly attuned empathetic imagination to leap – the disjunction between what we, as modern urban creatures, have grown used to and what was experienced as quite novel, fresh and shocking in the developing nineteenth-century urban environment. Raymond Williams, commenting on the physical and social disconnectedness of the city crowd, reminds us that 'we forget what a novel experience that must have been to people used to customary small settlements.'[80] It is, however, more than a matter of forgetting and remembering; it is also a question of possible incommensurables in transacting between different frames of reference and understanding. The project of grasping the sensory world of the nineteenth-century city from the perspective of our own may be blocked by virtue of different and non-measurable forms of sensitivity and tolerance.

For example, is the late twentieth-century city smellier or noisier than, say, the mid-nineteenth-century city? It is probably noisier (as a result of developments in mass urban transport), and probably not smellier (owing to the extraordinary, and often anthropologically exotic investment in what Corbin has described as the strategy of progressive urban 'deodorization'[81]). But, even if quantitative measurement of a comparative sort were possible, this would not of itself yield a true phenomenology of the *vécu*. Corbin's work on the sense of smell and the olfactory environment tells us, for example, that Paris in the middle of the nineteenth century was almost certainly no smellier than Paris in the middle of the eighteenth century; that what had changed were not the 'facts', but forms of social perception and levels of human tolerance. Perhaps our urban world is in fact noisier than that of the nineteenth century, but this does not tell us much about relative responses to different auditory environments. Simmel wrote that 'interpersonal relations in big cities are distinguished by a marked preponderance of the activity of the eye over the the activity of the ear'. Simmel is here referring to the fact that, as we move about the city, we scarcely talk to each other. It is a point about the quality of communication. But it could also be a point about bodily and psychic reaction to physical stimulus: the noisier the city becomes, the more we switch off as a necessary mechanism of self-defence, the less we actually hear (or think we hear). Perhaps the nineteenth-century city-dweller had less to cope with by way of noise, but, if that is so, how he or she coped (or failed to cope) we can only guess.

A second reason why the enterprise of re-creating the *vécu* may remain beyond our reach is that our only access to it is via representations, mainly written ones, and that the written record, especially in those highly wrought texts we call 'literary', poses special problems of interpretation. Again, I do not propose to linger in the uninviting, and treacherous, theoretical waters into which the hermeneutics of textual mediation of the past lead us. It is not clear that in them one can swim very far, or indeed do anything other than drown in hermeneutical despair. But the difficulty can be briefly illustrated by way of a particular theme in the nineteenth-century literary corpus, what we might call the gastronomic topos. Paris, the city of lovers, is also the city of gourmets, and the pleasures of the table are everywhere found in its literature. From Balzac to Huysmans, the restaurant is a scene of considerable narrative and descriptive attention in the nineteenth-century novel (in Balzac's *Le Cousin Pons* and Huysmans's *A Vau-l'eau*, it becomes, respectively, an object of powerful libidinal attachment and a source of serious libidinal depression). In the genre of the *physiologie*, it becomes the occasion of a veritable sociology; Frédéric Soulié's 'Restaurants et gargotes', in the collectively produced volume, *La Grande Ville, Nouveau Tableau de Paris*, argues that the life of the restaurant furnishes a key to a complete social taxonomy of the contemporary city.[83]

But, apart from anything else, the Parisian restaurant would seem to be not only the gastronome's but also the phenomenologist's paradise. Where else, in public space, is the body, its appetites and sensations, so clearly visible as before this feast for the eyes, the nose and the mouth? We think of Balzac's orgies of food that are also orgies of words, in particular a proliferating banquet of nomination, those dizzying sequences of culinary nouns and adjectives that describe the menus at the ubiquitous Rocher de Cancale. Clearly, these places were 'real' (even when packaged in fictional disguises), as were the sights, smells and tastes they afforded (at least to those who could afford *them*). But it is also clear that the gastronomic topos is not just a matter of neutral description. It is also a constitutive element, a discourse, specifically the discourse of pleasure. Pleasure is very far from being a 'repressed' category in nineteenth-century representations of the city. On the contrary, the capacity of the city to supply all manner of pleasures is often at the heart of its perceived *raison d'être* (Delvau's little book, *Les Plaisirs de Paris*, rang a further change on the theme of the 'capital' in defining Paris as the 'capitale du plaisir', as 'la ville du plasir et des plaisirs par excellence'[84]). The gastronomic theme is at once a privileged form of, and a metonymy for, this inexhaustible capacity. Its *locus classicus* is Brillat-Savarin's *Physiologie du goût*, that celebration of the arts of cuisine, which so impressed Balzac and which impresses upon us the notion that the acme of (male) human happiness is to be found in intelligent conversation with a beautiful woman at the table of a sophisticated Parisian restaurant – a formula which, as Roland Barthes once pointed out, combines, in actuality or in promise, the three basic forms of the pleasures of orality.[85] Taste, indeed – not just in the sense of educated sensitivity to the arts, but also in the sense of physical sensitivity to the pleasures of the body – furnishes a whole generative vocabulary for the nineteenth-century conception of Paris. In a great deal of the relevant literature, Paris is not simply a treasure-house of gustatory delights; the gustatory itself comes to act as a metaphor for the experience of Paris: Paris is above all there to be 'tasted' (as in Balzac's definition of the elite corps of connoisseurs of the city: 'il est un petit nombre d'amateurs . . . qui dégustent leur Paris'[86]).

There are, of course, also counter-moves, an ironic staging of the discourse of pleasure, which challenges and devalues the prestige of the gastronomic model. Flaubert's set meal in *L'Education sentimentale* is also a rhetorical set-piece, whose vocabulary and syntax act to arrest the neo-Rabelaisian flow and gusto of Balzac's gargantuan repasts, freezing the elaborate meal arranged by de Cisy, for example, into dead spectacle. Huysmans's *A Vau-l'eau* takes us into the reduced world of M. Folantin, the hero of a narrative that consists almost entirely of a forlorn journey away from the nauseous 'odeur des potages' infesting his apartment block through the equally re-pellent odiferous ambiance of the cheaper Parisian restaurants. Vallès's famished pauper in *Les Réfractaires* falls into delirium before the smells issuing from a restaurant. Zola, in *Le Ventre de Paris*, will take us back to base, the food market of Les Halles, that belly which supplies the bellies of Paris, abundant yet disgusting, always close in the Zolaesque *imaginaire* to the excretory functions, to the stench of rotting substance. But my main point here is that, however varied the forms of the *vécu* involved with the theme of food, its significance as a theme is highly overdetermined. It gathers up not only a phenomenology of sensory experience, but also a sociology, a social distribution of bodily sensation, an economics of access to resource, and an ideology of urban representations. It is an illusion to think that we can separate the first (as a primary 'referent') from all the others, to imagine that we can peel off the multiple layers of the complex cultural palimpsest to arrive at a simple core of founding bodily experience ('la sensation pure'[87]).

IV

Since I am primarily concerned with literary texts, it is as well to conclude with some introductory remarks on the material I have chosen and the way I propose to treat it, not just because of the sheer embarrassment of riches the subject presents, but also because these questions are intimately connected to the more substantive questions of the book. In many respects, there is inevitably here a risk of being caught up oneself in one of the more suspect practical and ideological forms of nineteenth-century urban 'style', the form known doctrinally as 'eclecticism', and widely interpreted as a symptom of the radical incoherence of the modern city (what, in *La Curée*, Zola called 'ce bâtard opulent de tous les styles'[88]). For example, my use of painting and, very briefly, photography, is for the most part resolutely opportunistic and, in its general lines of approach, hugely derivative of certain branches of recent art history. Indeed the main reason I have included painting is because, in my own view, it is in recent art history that the debate about representations of the city, and specifically Paris, has been at its most challenging and informative. Nevertheless, since I am myself no art historian, I have – apart from one moderately sustained excursus on the Impressionist way with the theme of the urban park – kept painting secondary to the literary sources.

In respect of the latter, I have preferred on the whole to take exemplary ('canonical') texts, and the writers who figure most prominently in the argument are virtually self-selecting: Balzac, Hugo, Michelet, Flaubert, Baudelaire, Zola, Huysmans, Barrès, Laforgue, Vallès. (Conversely, some of my omissions – in particular Stendhal and Maupassant – will, of course, seem quite arbitrary). It will perhaps come as even less of a surprise to learn that the writers who recur most frequently or are discussed in the greatest detail are Balzac, Hugo, Flaubert, Baudelaire and Zola, and that certain texts receive particularly close attention (notably, those quintessentially urban works, *La Fille aux yeux d'or*, *Les Misérables*, *L'Education sentimentale*, *Les*

Fleurs du Mal, Le Spleen de Paris, La Curée and *Le Ventre de Paris*). Beyond
the procession of canonical figures, however, I also sketch in, where appropriate, supporting contexts from some of the minor writers and genres of
the period – the *tableau*, the *physiologie*, the popular novel, guidebooks,
journalism. The point, in this latter connection, is not, of course, to try to
exhaust an archive, but to suggest some of the terms on which certain
standardized discourses of 'Paris' were constructed in the nineteenth century (largely picturesque, touristic and sanitized). These provide contexts
for assessing the far more complex account of Paris and modern urban life
in the work of the great writers of the period.

The potential charge of resurrecting and redeploying the terms of
nineteenth-century eclecticism bears less, however, on my choice of material
than on my method of treatment. As will be seen, the analytic focus varies
considerably, from the wide-angle view to the close-up. For the most part,
however, I have also followed Benjamin's example in adapting the strategy
of micrological analysis he brings to material and social phenomena to my
reading of literary texts: often the analysis proceeds by way of prolonged
attention to a small piece of text (a single poem, an extract from a novel),
especially in the opening chapters. There are many reasons for this (some
merely to do with my own analytical preferences), but the most important
has to do with my desire to resist one particular inherited model for talking
about 'relations' between literature and society: namely, the mechanical
model of 'background', according to which the text passively receives or
reflects information from a social and historical hinterland from which it is
otherwise disconnected. If the more dynamic and dialectical notion of social
and cultural history as a collection of interacting 'signifying practices' is still
insufficiently developed to be anything other than controversial, it nevertheless seems to me to be far more fruitful than the approach which effectively
reduces literature to the status of mere illustration.

One way of putting this is to say that the 'history' is not 'behind' the
text, but *in* the text, in its sinews, textures, syntax, vocabulary, as process
of articulation; and if that shift of preposition begs many questions, it
at least moves us away from the positivist reduction of literary history to
simple 'source' material towards a more active engagement with language
and literature as themselves 'active' forms. The corresponding technique of
reading is that of close textual analysis, or what , in another context, Jean-
Pierre Richard calls 'microlecture'; in the title of one of his more recent
books, *Pages/paysages*,[89] it is a way of reading that collapses *pages* into
pa(ysa)ges. On the other hand, the 'landscapes' of the pages I shall be
examining rarely display the orderly imaginary topography to which the
presuppositions of Richard's approach commit him (indeed in certain places
my argument will be explicitly concerned with the problems of constructing
the city as 'landscape'); and, by the same token, neither does the method

of close reading I employ in any way endorse the paradoxical presupposition of presuppositionless reading often proposed and legitimized by the tradition of 'practical criticism'.

The major theoretical reason why this shift of focus from 'behind' to 'in' has become so important in literary study has to do with our more generally enhanced awareness of the role of language in the social construction of reality. Or, to put this another way, one form of the 'referent' that literature can make peculiarly its own – though again in necessarily mediate fashion – is language (as well as being itself an element in the construction of that referent). This is, of course, now something of a commonplace. But the point to be stressed here is that it has particular force in connection with the history of cities. One question with which several of the texts I shall be considering concern themselves is the fate of text – meaning by this not so much the text of the city as the text *in* the city or, more generally, the circulation of its languages, discourses, idioms. The city 'lives by remembering', remarked Emerson,[90] and, one might add, in large measure by the storage of memories in writing and speech. Memory here means, at least in part, knowledge (the use of written records and specialized discourses to ensure a certain accumulation of cognitive wealth); and knowledge, both of and in the city, means power, the struggle to control both scripture and speech in order to gain domination over the storehouse of information, the transmission of messages, the economy of the city's signs and symbols.

This characteristically generates two clashing models of the discursive life of the city. On the one hand, there is the drive towards extreme centralization, the imposition of a normative language or what Mumford calls the 'monologue of power',[91] seeking either to obliterate or to subordinate the diversity of social speech and the production of counter-discourses. He who masters the languages of the city rules the city. But, then, in the words from Sophocles' *Antigone*, 'A city that is of one man only is no city.' The monologue of power spells the death of the city, as does its opposite, withdrawal from the circuit of communication (dramatized in Baudelaire's astonishing poem, 'Rêve parisien', where a fantasy of artistic mastery of the city culminates in the creation of a terrifying, death-like wordless space, from which not only the strident noise of the city but all dialogue with the other has been excluded). The alternative model embraces the principle of dialogue ('The dialogue is one of the ultimate expressions of life in the city'[92]), the notion of the city as a pluralistic and democratic space of diverse voices, either as civilized intercourse or, in the more conflictual form of the *agon*, as the competition of ideas, the cut and thrust of debate, the rhetorical arts of persuasion.[93]

Several of the texts I shall be concerned with contain statements about, commentaries on and enactments of the place and fate of language in nineteenth-century Paris. Both the centralist and democratic models are

23

relevant here. Balzac's linguistic thinking, for example, is on a par with his ideological commitment to the absolutist state: a stable lexical order goes with a stable political order; you do not take liberties with the lexicon, above all with the word 'liberty' itself.[94] Hugo's views, on the other hand, though fraught with hesitation and equivocation, are more ecumenically liberal, and carry, at least in principle, a commitment to giving literary *droit de cité* to all the languages of the city, and crucially to the demotic.[95] Yet the dominant mode in which nineteenth-century literature both refers to and deploys these two models – that of democratic dialogue and autocratic monologue – is essentially one of critique, often in the form of a corrosive irony working to hold up both as etiolated and vacuous fictions. There are, broadly, two main contexts for this, one political, the other cultural (though the distinction is to some extent arbitrary).

The cultural context concerns the commercialization of language, the abasement of the language of 'democratic' debate and 'free' exchange to commodity status, ideas and words for sale.[96] This development can perhaps be adequately measured by the cultural distance separating two literary versions of that word-spinning milieu of Parisian life, the arcades and galleries of the Palais-Royal: Diderot's *Le Neveu de Rameau* and Balzac's *Illusions perdues*. In the former, the currency of exchange is still the high-minded intellectual coinage of what Cochin will later describe as the Enlightenment 'philosophical society'[97] (although the high-minded discursive values represented by Diderot's *moi* are seriously compromised by the irreverent materialism of *lui*). But by the time we enter the world of Balzac's Palais-Royal we are almost entirely in the hands of the venal word-merchants, those whores of discourse (the analogy between the man of letters and the prostitute is Balzac's) for whom the word 'speculation' has nothing whatsoever to do with the life of the mind and the imagination. Its exemplary figure (along with the publisher and the bookseller) is the journalist. 'The commercialisation of the Press', remarks Kracauer (in the study of Offenbach and Second Empire Paris he wrote at the same time Benjamin was working on his Baudelaire book), 'meant its withdrawal from the battle of rival opinions.'[98] Commercial journalism is the hollow mockery of a culture of democratic exchange and argument, a fake agonistics fuelled only by ambition and greed, a 'circulation' of ideas and opinions geared to the obsession with circulation figures. Balzac gives the first, and seminal, diagnosis of this in *Illusions perdues*, and it will remain an abiding preoccupation, and source of anxiety, through the nineteenth century up to Maupassant's *Bel-Ami*, Vallès's *L'Insurgé* and Barrès's *Les Déracinés*.

The political context in which the literature of nineteenth-century Paris engages with the question of language is particularly rich, perhaps because the project of imposing or encouraging a uniform 'standard' French was high on the political agenda from the Revolution onwards.[99] Attitudes vary considerably, in accordance with the varying political beliefs of individual writers. But again the essential tone is fiercely ironic. Thus, the idea of a normative language dictating or controlling the terms of political discussion is savaged by Stendhal, in the fatuous banalities of the style of conversation represented by the de la Mole salon in the Restoration world of *Le Rouge et le Noir* (to which should be added the constant link in Stendhal's critical thinking between literary conservatism and political repression). Alternatively, there is Louis-Philippe, the bourgeois king of the July Monarchy, the ruler described by Hugo in *Les Misérables* (though Hugo's own attitude here is evasive) as acquainted with 'tous les langages de tous les intérêts, et les parlant'.[100] Louis-Philippe, and then later Louis-Napoleon, as empty ciphers, all things to all men, are the perfect parody of the maxim that to master the city you must master its langages; they embody the monologue of power disguised in apparent ability to speak all the languages while being committed to none (other, of course, than to that of the ecumenical confidence-trick whereby real differences are concealed to serve the interests of a ruling class).

Conversely, the language of political revolution (or rather its literary representation) is in principle directed towards turning the sphere of public discourse into a democratic forum, indeed making of language, and the question of language, one of the issues and forms of political contestation. Hugo will emphasize this notion in linking the idioms of the 'peuple' to the revolutionary project, although it is not until Vallès's novel of the Commune, *L'Insurgé*, that the use of demotic is actively mobilized by the narrative voice of the text itself in and as opposition to the neutralizing decorum of established political discourse. On the other hand, in the great nineteenth-century novel of urban insurrection, Flaubert's *L'Education sentimentale*, the language of revolution (specifically of 1848) is presented as a language whose histrionic bravado scarcely conceals its perceived and affirmed emptiness, its status as inert repetition of the inherited slogans of 1789 (Marx will level similiar criticisms at the discursive rituals of 1848).

One point bearing on questions of both method and substance which emerges from the examples I have given of this *mise en scène* and criticism of the languages of the city is that, from the point of view of literary genre, the novel bulks exceedingly large, perhaps disproportionately so. This reproduces itself in most of the following chapters, and I should briefly explain that emphasis. Apart from a side glance at Dumas *fils's La Dame aux camélias*, I say nothing about Second Empire drama. In a larger enterprise, it should certainly have a place, as a symptomatic expression of the contradictions of a bourgeoisie anxious about the uncontrolled circulation of forces (mainly money and sex) that its own spectacular success has brought into being. But it is precisely because it is merely symptomatic literature, hopelessly caught up in the bad faith of the class it serves, that there is very little of sustained interest one can say about it: its plots and characters function largely to produce the formulae whereby the middle class is permitted to keep both its wealth and its morality intact.

A more serious issue is the relatively minor place that – with the exception of the work of Baudelaire and, in the concluding chapter, an account of Laforgue's extraordinary text, 'Grande Complainte de la Ville de Paris' – I have given to poetry. There is but a passing glance at Lautréamont, the briefest mention of Verlaine and a cursory account of some of Rimbaud's townscapes. There is nothing on Tristan Corbière, or the worker poet, Pierre Dupont. There is nothing on Mallarmé, despite the interesting and complex relations between his poetry and the contemporary commodity culture, at once replicated in a certain language of 'manner' and cancelled in the stunningly derisory negations of 'furnished' space in the great sonnets.[101] This is important not just because it is above all certain forms of nineteenth-century poetry which register the more intimate and nervous structures of feeling that, on Simmel's account, characterize the modern urban sensibility. More generally, if, as Michael Riffaterre has argued,[102] it is properly the task of poetry to unsettle clichés, to re-cast 'normal' ways of describing reality, then it is pre-eminently to the language of nineteenth-century urban poetry that we should look for the deepest critical questioning of the given languages of the city. Benjamin has shown us some of the terms in which that might be done in ways that illuminate a more general cultural history, and it is, of course, no accident that it is the provocative images and idioms of Baudelaire which command his attention. If in general nineteenth-century poetry is under-represented here, conversely, Baudelaire is the writer whom I consider in the greatest detail; not only does he recur throughout the book (appearing centrally in four of the chapters), he is also the subject of by far the longest chapter. Indeed, that chapter – on Baudelaire and the prose poem – I consider to be the very heart of the book.

There are many reasons for this concentration of focus on Baudelaire. It is not just that Baudelaire's aesthetics of 'shock' brings us into contact with a whole new range of urban themes; it is also an aesthetics directed at the structure of the poetic lexicon itself, challenging the 'canonical' vocabulary of poetry, or rather the assumption of its own canonical status. If Hugo proclaims the necessity of 'democratizing' the language of poetry, Baudelaire puts it into practice (without being himself a democrat by political conviction). Moreover, whereas Hugo envisages a peaceful coexistence of idioms in the republic of verse, Baudelaire's stance is more aggressive: words coexist uneasily, jostle, clash, bounce off each other. His technique is what Benjamin has imaginatively described as the linguistic equivalent of the *putsch*, a series of raids on the centres of poetic authority.[103] This has profound consequences for the development of both Baudelaire's writings and modern poetry as a whole. In particular, it works to undermine what elsewhere

Baudelaire himself proposes as the very foundation of the poetic impulse – the drive towards 'harmony'. Gathering up the fragments of experience and memory into a harmonious whole situated beyond division and loss is for Baudelaire the *raison d'être* of poetry. But, confronted with the discords and dissonances of the modern city, that project comes under serious pressure, and at certain points simply cracks, as the tension between the poetic endeavour and the recalcitrance of the urban reality with which it engages becomes increasingly more apparent. While the traces of that tension are already there in the verse poetry of the *Fleurs du Mal* (Benjamin's main preoccupation), I shall seek to show how it is above all in the multiple and often conflicting linguistic and stylistic registers of the prose poems that it is most urgently felt.

In the book as a whole, I have, however, given pride of place to the novel, and for essentially three reasons (apart from its obvious value as a fictional archive of scenes from Parisian life). First, the novel is commonly seen as a genre at once distinctively urban and culturally 'democratic'. This is not just because of its external conditions of production and reception – the role of the novel in the social extension of the reading public in the nineteenth century; the growth of city-based forms of publication and distribution ensuring the primacy of the novel in the development of what Sainte-Beuve, from the point of view of an alarmed cultural elite, called 'littérature industrielle'.[104] It has to do with the structure of the form itself, its openness to multiple voice and point of view, its tendency towards inclusiveness and its respect for differences. In particular, the novel might be seen as a point of resistance to that political-administrative ideology coming out of the French Revolution which sought, if only in theory, to impose a normative language ('standard French') on all the speaking subjects of the nation-state. In these terms, the novel is instinctively 'democratic' by virtue of its hospitality to heterogeneous forms of speech, and more specifically, by virtue of the developing interest – from Balzac, Hugo and Sue through to the Goncourt brothers, Zola, Vallès and Huysmans – in the 'deviant' idioms of demotic, slang and popular speech.[105]

On the other hand, this respect for linguistic diversity, especially for the speech styles of the *bas-fonds* of the city, should not be exaggerated. The perspective from which they are represented and discussed is almost invariably that of 'educated' French and its corresponding social and cultural values. If the Revolution produced the dream of a uniform national language, the actual practice of linguistic and literary pedagogy in the nineteenth-century schools was, as Renée Balibar has shown, to produce two languages and two nations divided broadly along hierarchical class lines (as well as regional ones).[106] That hierarchy remains fundamental to the linguistic economy of the novel, as an internally stratified system mirroring or reproducing the divisions of the real social world. Thus Sue, in the preface to *Les Mystères de Paris*, will offer to his readers samples of underworld speech as if they were specimens from a subhuman zoo. Hugo, in his account of popular slang in *Les Misérables*, will plead for linguistic tolerance on the argument that languages should be allowed to proliferate in accordance with a 'natural' order of social difference, but without disturbing the hierarchy in which educated French remains dominant. Above all, the narrative discourse tends to keep its distance from the spoken 'dialects' it reports. The former is the 'literary', and the literary is almost invariably a version of the polite, the language of a sophisticated and essentially metropolitan elite. It is true that Zola's work will start to blur that dividing line, through its extended use of *style indirect libre*. But it is not until we arrive in Joyce's Dublin and Céline's Paris that narrative discourse will show itself fully porous to the heterogeneous flow of social speech.

The second reason for concentrating on the novel is that the city is often represented *as* a novel, as (in the now consecrated phrase) the 'already-written'. For if the city produces writing, there is also an important (though strictly limited) sense in which writing produces the city. The city may live by remembering, but at what point do its memories and records start to become stories and fictions, generating the images through which we construct the city to ourselves? 'Living by the record and for the record', writes Mumford, 'became one of the great stigmata of urban existence; indeed life as recorded – with all its temptations to overdramatisation, illusory inflation and deliberate falsification – tended often to become more important than life as lived.'[107] Or, alternatively, life as lived in the city itself gets modelled on the 'inflationary' fictions of the city. Let us say that cities and narratives have at least one thing in common: they are both desire-producing machines. Rousseau denounces the city for creating an endless multiplication of desires and a correspondingly restless quest for impossible gratification (this is also an important theme in Mercier's *Tableau de Paris*[108]). Similarly, desire in narrative and desire for narrative are what keeps narrative going and what keeps our reading of narrative going.

These two trajectories can be said to cross when the object of desire becomes, precisely, desire for the narrativized city, for its fictional images. Paris will be compared to many other cities in nineteenth-century literature – Athens, Rome, Venice, Baghdad, Babylon, Sodom and Gomorrah. But the most active literary image of this kind for Paris is 'Paris', that is, the Paris of previous narrative incarnations. Several of the novels I shall be looking at re-write, or un-write, the already-written Paris of the novel, principally the Paris of Balzac.[109] Balzac described Paris as 'la ville aux cent mille romans',[110] of which the most prodigious and exciting is none other than his own; as Franco Moretti points out, in Balzac's novels urban life is *already* novelistic.[111] Balzac's Paris will certainly exercise an enduring fascination on those who come after him. The major source of that fascination will be *Le Père Goriot*, the saga of Rastignac's conquest of the city. In Flaubert's *L'Education sentimentale*, the two heroes will preface their entry into the Parisian arena by fantasizing it on the model of Rastignac's adventures: 'Tu réussiras, j'en suis sûr. Rappelle-toi Rastignac dans *La Comédie humaine!*'[112] In Barrès's *Les Déracinés*, Rastignac's famous 'A nous deux maintenant'[113] from the heights of Père-Lachaise is the narrative image inhabited by his characters for their own hopes and projects in the capital.[114] But there is a difference between the two references to Balzac, two opposed forms of intertextual relation. Although sometimes critical of sentimental appropriations of Balzac, Barrès himself is caught up in the Balzacian dream, seeing in the *énergie* of the Balzacian (as well as the Stendhalian) hero the formula for rescuing a degenerate and exhausted city, for regenerating it in terms of the programme of the 'roman de l'énergie nationale' (the subtitle of *Les Déracinés*). Where Barrès seeks to re-create Balzac in the city, Flaubert, on the other hand, seeks to evacuate him, to expose in his own fiction the fiction of Balzac's Paris; Flaubert rewrites the story of Rastignac in the mode of an ironic deconstruction, playing off the heroes' novelistic expectations against the derisory order of reality.

This brings me to the third, and final, reason for concentrating on the novel. Lukács argues that irony is constitutive of the structure of the novel.[115] The novel is built on an ironic exploration of the gap between aspiration and actuality, the hero's projections and the poverty of the available forms of social reality. In terms of narrative plots, this gap is typically elaborated as a story of arrival and discovery: the hero of the great nineteenth-century French novels arrives in Paris from the provinces to discover a wasteland. It is the plot of what Lukács calls the novel of apprenticeship, or the education novel. This resurrects once more the ancient association of the city with the ideal of *humanitas*, the city as a centre of learning, good manners, civilization, culture. The heroes of the novels of Balzac, Stendhal, Flaubert, Zola, Maupassant will excitedly bring that sort of notion to their anticipation of life in Paris, the notion of 'education' as a leading out from the relatively uncouth into the sophisticated. But they will also receive another sort of education: the university of Rastignac, the archetypal student, is less the Sorbonne than the university of adversity and false values, a learning of what the text calls the 'ultima ratio mundi'.[116]

Learning the ways of the world will produce various narrative resolutions: accommodations (in Balzac, Zola and Maupassant), rejections (in Stendhal), fadings (in Flaubert). 'Resolution' is, however, not really the right word here, and certainly not in connection with Flaubert. As has often been remarked, the education of *L'Education sentimentale* is a kind of anti-education, a non-learning as well as an unlearning. *L'Education sentimentale*, we should remember, begins with the city draped in mist, its great monumental sights (Notre-Dame, etc.) removed from clear visibility. It also begins with a leave-taking (the hero, Frédéric Moreau, is on a boat travelling to Nogent); we enter Flaubert's Paris by exiting from it, in an inaugural movement that wilfully reverses the literal and symbolic movements towards the city which characterize the essentially appropriative energies of the earlier narrative tradition. Moreover, when, narratively, we return to it, entry into the city is fraught with obstacle, detour and general disorientation. In *L'Education sentimentale*, Paris is no longer up for grabs or, if so, it often seems as if there is nothing to take hold of, no point of purchase.

This implication in fact describes a complex and unstable figure in Flaubert's novel. We have already seen the ideological uses to which the notion of the 'unseizable' nature of the city can be put. If Flaubert's practice weakens the confident assumption of the knowability of the city we often find in Balzac, Flaubert himself also remains alert to the potential complacencies of a fog-bound scepticism proclaiming its impotence to see or understand anything, since he parodies precisely the latter attitude in the rhetorical question, clearly intended as fatuous, of his fictional painter, Pellerin – 'Qu'est-ce que cela veut dire, la réalité?'[117] Nevertheless, one of the lessons of the nineteenth-century novel, even in its most expansive phases, is the impossibility of a fully settled knowledge of the reality of the city. If the city remains an object of desire, and crucially of the desire for social and intellectual mastery, it can never be finally mastered, either by the hero or by the language of the novelist. Even as it strives for encapsulation and closure, the novel tells us of that supremely important and immensely complicated truth: that the great cities of modernity never close.

It is, however, time to enter the city ourselves. Entrances were an obsession with Benjamin, the arcade, the shop, the Métro, the railway station, the catacombs constituted so many points of entry into the 'labyrinth' of the city and its dream-world (its 'phantasmagoria').[118] I shall return later to some of the problematical implications of the image of the 'labyrinth' (it should not simply be taken for granted). For the moment, however, I want to effect an entry into the topic of nineteenth-century Paris by way of two sites of vision, the window and the panorama. This, of course, risks precisely that prioritizing and privileging of the *visual* against which I previously warned, as well as – in connection with the first of these two sites – that all too easy adaptation of Henry James's pluralistic metaphor of the house of fiction. In the terms of Benjamin's account, it is a move which can skirt close to the fetishizing stratagems of the *flâneur* as pure spectator ('the spectator of the market' in whom 'the joy of watching is triumphant'[119]). If, however, I start with two visual constructions of the city, it is not in order to give special emphasis to the relation of looking, but in order to set the stage, via the visible, for the whole problematic of the possibility of knowledge of the city.

2

Framing the City:
Two Parisian Windows

I

As the wild, hallucinatory itinerary through nocturnal Paris of Lautréamont's poem-novel, *Les Chants de Maldoror*, reaches its climax, we are, bizarrely, invited for a moment to window-shop: 'Les magasins de la rue Vivienne étalent leurs richesses aux yeux émerveillés. Eclairés par de nombreux becs de gaz, les coffrets d'acajou et les montres en or répandent à travers les vitrines les gerbes de lumière éblouissante.'[1] Lautréamont's text here echoes, and even self-consciously quotes from, what by the time of *Les Chants de Maldoror* has become a routine topic in the discourse of 'Paris'. Here, for example, is Jules Lemer ten years earlier on the delights of Paris by gaslight: 'tout est magasins brillants, pompeux étalages, cafés dorés, illumination permanente; de la rue Louis-le-Grand à la rue Richelieu, le flot de lumière qui jaillit des boutiques vous permettrait de lire votre journal en vous promenant.'[2] In Lautréamont's version of this, however, we are not dazzled for long. Abruptly, the lights go out, not just the shop lights, but all the lights of the city, in dramatic and ironic negation of a recurring nineteenth-century theme – Paris as 'spectacle'.[3]

The idea of Paris as an endless adventure and feast for the eyes, a vast and inexhaustibly interesting catalogue of *choses vues* (in the title of Hugo's collection of notebooks), is basic to the more optimistic side of the nineteenth-century urban imagination. Spectacle, in this context, meant several things, but it was rarely far from fascination with the commodity. Indeed the presence of light itself, both natural and artificial (at first the gas lamps, later electric light), came to be seen as one of the most precious commodities in the city. The provision of ever more lighting in public places was one of Haussmann's more cherished ambitions in the project of transforming a dark and dangerous *vieux Paris* into a fully spectacularized

31

and efficiently policed centre of imperial civilization. The relation, both practical and symbolic, between the lighting and the policing of the city had a long history.[4] Mercier's *Tableau de Paris* records that the street torch-bearers of eighteenth-century Paris were often, or often believed to be, police spies and informers; beneath the 'réverbères' of Baudelaire's 'Vin des chiffonniers' we see the 'mouchards' of the regime; Sébillot's ambitious and unrealized scheme for the construction of a huge Sun Tower (Eiffel won the competition with the proposal for his tower) flooding the city with light was explicitly associated with a strategy of anti-revolutionary surveillance.[5] Indeed, lantern smashing became from 1830 onwards a standard aspect of insurrectionary behaviour in the city, often culminating in the replacement of 'reactionary' light by revolutionary light in the form of great festive firework displays. Garnier-Pagès records the street-light smashing of 1848 and the demand, in the euphoric days of February, once the rioting was over, for all citizens to celebrate revolutionary victory by lighting all the lamps in their homes.[6] The practice was so deeply ingrained by 1848 that the symbolic ended by taking precedence over the practical: the smashed gaslights, by releasing large flames into the air, produced even more light than before and thus helped rather than hindered the efforts of the authorities to keep track of things.[7]

The gradual displacement of oil lighting by gas lighting represented a major change in the nineteenth-century urban environment from several points of view. In the 1830s gaslight was a novelty; by the 1850s 3000 new gas lamps had been installed on the streets, along with the practice of all-night lighting.[8] On its public surface Paris seemed altered beyond recognition, supplying at once the promise of excitement and the reassurance of security, as the place where it was safe to look at, and for, what you wanted. More lights meant more tourists and less crime; it also meant better value for money (the prostitutes could – in theory – be seen with greater clarity). In more allegorical mode, the public provision of light represented a triumph over social and cultural 'darkness'; light meant *lumières* in more than one sense; the project of the illuminated city was connected with, and even captured, the older idea of the enlightened city.[9]

The urban experiment with light generated a whole minor literature, from the learned monograph and inspector's report to that specialized version of the memoir and the guidebook, the observations and musings of the nocturnal *flâneur*. It also entered decisively into the inspiration of many of the major forms of nineteenth-century art and literature. At the end of the century, the Symbolist poet, Gustave Kahn, will describe the lights of the Parisian street as producing a veritable symphony of polychromatic colour: 'La rue actuelle, la Polychromie de la rue par les couleurs de façades, les affiches et les lumières'.[10] This account, of course, rehearses the terms of Impressionism, the conjunction of the urban theme and the techniques of *plein-air* around the Impressionist painters' interest in the play of light. The famous street scenes of Monet, Pissarro and Renoir emphasize airiness and luminosity, the blending of natural and artificial light, often in contexts celebrating urban sociability and festivity (as, for example, in Pissarro's *Boulevard Montmartre, La Nuit* (plate 1), where the street lights are represented as twinkling star lights). This search for the lyric tone, however, was not the only response. Manet's great painting, the *Rue Mosnier. Les Paveurs* (plate 2), is great because of the way the lyric harmony of its representation of light is checked, and challenged, by its representation of urban labour in the foreground of the picture; whatever the light means to the 'paveurs', it is not as an object of aesthetic pleasure or as focus of pastoral fantasy. Similarly the brilliant electric light shed on the scene of *Un Bar aux Folies-Bergère*, with its glittering reflections in the mirror behind the counter, is refused all connotation of innocent conviviality by virtue of the complete absence of light in the neutral, distancing gaze of the serving girl's eyes.[11] Manet's pictorial ironies and dissonances also have their poetic equivalent in Baudelaire, for example, in his macabrely ironic version of that traditional poetic topos, dawn over the city. In 'Crépuscule du matin', we are a long way from the purifying and unifying light that comes with daybreak over Wordsworth's London in 'Westminster Bridge'. The natural light that appears over Baudelaire's Paris is from the start poisoned by its passage through the artificial light of the gas lamps, the light of Evil rendered in the dramatically violent image of the bleeding eye ('Où, comme un œil sanglant qui palpite et qui bouge / La lampe sur le jour fait une tache rouge'[12]).

Light (and its absence) clearly meant different things to different people. It depended, of course, on where exactly you went, and, more importantly, where exactly you lived. Many of the urban poor saw very little of it, especially the natural sort. As the contemporary reports of Villermé and others make clear, the cellars and ground-floor dwellings in the narrow streets inhabited by the destitute of the city rarely, if ever, saw the light of day, and in the descriptive literature regularly produced the analogy of an 'underground' population resembling a race of primeval cave dwellers.[13] It is not surprising that the painters of modern life do not, to my knowledge, seek to represent the typical interiors of the urban poor. They furnished little or no possibility for the effect of sunlight pouring through the window into enclosed domestic space that is the hallmark of the seventeenth-century Dutch painters (famously, Vermeer's 'patch of yellow') rediscovered in the later nineteenth century. Without light, painting has nowhere to go, especially when the commitment is to the methods of *plein-air*. Literature, on the other hand, will take us there, notably in the descriptions of the urban slum in the novels of Hugo, Sue and, later, Zola. The physical absence of light will, moreover, generate a counter-symbolism of protest. In Hugo the theme of light will be the focus of an intertwining of republican ideology and

Christian eschatology serving a vision of social and spiritual 'redemption'. Light, both literal and figurative, will also play a part in the utopian imagining of the alternative city as the site of progress and justice – from, say, Fourier's dream of the future *cité ouvrière* and Duveyrier's Saint-Simonian 'ville nouvelle' (with its plan for a huge temple in the centre from which would issue a great flood of light[14]) to the prophetic visions of urban harmony in Zola's late novel, *Paris*, and the brilliantly illuminated 'underground city' deep in the coal mine of Jules Verne's *Les Indes noires*.[15]

But, in terms of urban actuality, the essential preoccupation remained with light in its artificial rather than its natural or symbolic forms. The lights of the city are linked to the lure of the city, the beckoning signs of what is deceptively promised by the new and fast-growing leisure and pleasure culture. Paris as illuminated 'spectacle' is Paris offered for consumption, and nowhere, of course, did gas and electric lighting more directly contribute to the function of the city as dream-machine than in the glitter it conferred on the commodity. This took the form of both private and public display. The ostentatiously lighted interiors of Balzac's Birotteau and Crevel signify, awkwardly and crudely, the acquisition of wealth, as will later the invention of electroplating, designed to give a fake aura of luxury to the household utensils of the bourgeoise.[16] These were attempts at 'spectacle' on a small scale, enclosed and privatized. Its more dramatic manifestations occurred in public space – in the construction of those super-windows on the commodity, the huge glass edifices of the Exposition Universelle, or in the exploitation of the large shop window in the new department store during the Second Empire.

Boucicaut, the inventor of the Bon Marché, quickly grasped the commercial advantages of saturating merchandise with all manner of lighting, subtle or strong. The introduction of sheet glass and electric lighting for the ground-floor displays not only enticed potential purchasers (mainly women) into the store; it made window-shopping along the boulevards a standard form of Parisian *flânerie*: 'On se promène, on flâne dans toutes ces rues où le commerce entretient tous les soirs une illumination splendide,' wrote Lemer.[17] The lighting systems of the boulevards and the department stores instituted a whole new relation between the gaze and the commodity, the spectacularizing and fetishizing relation bound up with what Rachel Bowlby has called 'just looking'.[18] That specular relation was magnified beyond measure by the Great Exhibitions (Georg Simmel brought the latter and the store together when he spoke of 'the shop-like quality of things that is evoked by exhibitions'[19]). This involved not only the use of new technology for the display of the commodity but the display of the technology itself *as* commodity. The decisive development here was the large-scale use of electricity: the 'phantasmagoria' of the commodity culture came finally to be represented as pure 'fairyland' by means of the great fin-de-siècle light shows – the 'luminous fountains' introduced, along with the completion of the Tour Eiffel, in the 1889 Exhibition and, at the end of the century, the overwhelmingly impressive productions staged by the Palais de l'Electricité in the 1890 Exposition Universelle.[20]

The new systems appear to have entranced nearly everyone, including critics from the left. An index of their power over the urban imagination is given by the response of none other than that fiercest of critics of contemporary capitalism, Jules Vallès. Here is Vallès's Aladdin's cave version of the city lights:

> Pas une ville au monde n'offre le spectacle de ces boulevards parisiens, surtout à certaines heures. Le soir, quand le gaz s'allume, quand théâtres, cafés-concerts, grands bazars, estaminets dorés ou pauvres, allument leurs enseignes et leurs candélabres, quand les fenêtres des grands cercles flambent, quand sur le pavé les trainées d'électricité font comme des rivières d'argent, qui parlera des *a giorno* de Venise et des illuminations de l'Orient![21]

And specifically on the windows of the department store: 'Toute l'actualité frissonne le long de ces tonnelles de verre, bariolées de réclames joyeuses.'[22]

An important term in this description is the word *bariolées*. It is difficult to translate, but broadly connotes a multiple and mobile play of colour. It is a key term in the perceptual vocabulary of the later nineteenth-century literary equivalents of Impressionism, from Rimbaud to Zola, and a complex nodal word in the representational economy of the nineteenth-century urban imaginaion. In Rimbaud's prose poetry (for example, 'Ornières') it is linked to the experience of perceptual unhinging entailed by the programme of systematic 'dérèglement', a term for the flux and movement dissolving the illusion of the integrated ego.[23] In Zola, on the other hand, a characteristic, though by no means exclusive, context for the term is commercial, notably in the novel of the department store, *Au Bonheur des Dames*, where it designates the swirl of perception and desire around the 'colourful' article for sale, its staging as *objet d'art*.[24] This is the context for the *bariolage* of the window displays that so excites Vallès. It is also the context for Lautréamont's spectacular annihilation of spectacle when the lights go out in *Les Chants de Maldoror*. Lautréamont's window darkens and disappears, and with it the arresting power of the commodities it displays. But let us now consider, in more detail, what happens to spectacle with, or through, two other literary windows, in Baudelaire's prose poem, 'Les Yeux des pauvres', and Zola's novel, *La Curée*.

II

Baudelaire is fascinated by the urban window, almost as much as he is by the human eye; indeed, in one of the verse poems, the former becomes a figure for the latter ('Tes yeux, illuminés commes des boutiques'[25]). The window, whether of the private dwelling or the shop, is a key staging-post in the itinerary of the Baudelairian *flâneur*. One of the earliest entries in the notebooks which record Baudelaire's self-imposed exile from 1864 in the detested Brussels laments the absence of a supreme Parisian pleasure – 'La flânerie devant les boutiques, cette jouissance'.[26] The window, like the eye, is an invitation to a journey, a voyage of the imagination. In 'Les Fenêtres' the act of looking through a candle-lit window from the street generates a veritable proliferation of some of the major terms of Baudelaire's poetic lexicon: 'Il n'est pas d'objet plus profond, plus mystérieux, plus fécond, plus ténébreux, plus éblouissant qu'une fenêtre éclairée d'une chandelle.'[27] The window is fertile ('fécond') in that it opens a space for the productivity of the imagination, supplies a passage from vision into reverie and a release from self into otherness.

Yet the assumed fertility of the encounter between poet's gaze and window proves to be potentially deceptive, and is hedged about in the text by various uncertainties. Through another window, seen from a distance in the rooftops of Paris, the poet glimpses a woman, poor and ageing ('une femme mûre, ridée déjà, pauvre'). The poet constructs a whole life behind the window, the sad 'story' of the woman: 'Avec son visage, avec son vêtement, avec son geste, avec presque rien j'ai refait l'histoire de cette femme, ou plutôt sa légende, et quelquefois je me la raconte à moi-même en pleurant.' But in its concluding moment the poem turns against and equivocates its own expansive imaginative claims. The 'story' appears ultimately as self-referring rather than other-referring, and the glass pane less a window than a mirror reflecting back not the 'truth' of the other but an enabling fiction for the self: 'Peut-être me direz-vous: "Es-tu sûr que cette légende soit la vraie?" Que m'importe ce que peut-être la réalité placée hors de moi, si elle m'a aidé à vivre, à sentir que je suis et ce que je suis?' Baudelaire here says that the collapsing of other into self, of story into fiction ('légende'), does not matter ('Que m'importe'). But of course it matters; knowledge of the (ethical) distinction between self and other is as important as knowing the (cognitive) distinction between what, in 'La Corde', is called 'illusion' and 'le fait tel qu'il existe en dehors de nous'.[28] The concluding declaration of the poem thus seems more a piece of rhetorical bravado masking an anxiety and a failure – the failure to pass through the window, to connect the inward imperatives of the imagination with the outward forms of the real.

'Les Fenêtres' tells us, then, of the ambivalent and unstable relation between self and other in Baudelaire's city poetry, and in particular of those critical moments of resistance and breakdown experienced by the Baudelairian psyche in its efforts to project out into the alien flux of contemporary urban life. The gaze through the window is but one inflection of this complex psychic and social drama. It is, however, a privileged one, in that it directly implicates the figure of the poet himself and the very act of writing poetry about, or against, the city. The window may invite a fertile transaction between the poet and the city, but more often it serves to open up a gap between subject and object, to bring about cleavage rather than communication. This is the scene of Baudelaire's great prose poem, 'Les Yeux des pauvres'.[29]

The setting of 'Les Yeux des pauvres' is a café on one of Haussmann's new boulevards still in process of construction ('un café neuf qui formait le coin d'un boulevard neuf, encore tout plein de gravois et montrant déjà ses splendeurs inachevées'). The two protagonists of the poem – the narrator and his beloved – sit by the café window on the pavement terrace; the narrator's attention is drawn by the dazzling lights and decorations of the café's interior:

> Le café étincelait. Le gaz lui-même y déployait toute l'ardeur d'un début, et éclairait de toutes ses forces les murs aveuglants de blancheur, les nappes éblouissantes des miroirs, les ors des baguettes et des corniches, les pages aux joues rebondies trainés par les chiens en laisse, les dames riant au faucon perché sur leur poing, les nymphes et les déesses portant sur leur tête des fruits, des pâtés et du gibier, les Hébés et les Ganymèdes présentant à bras tendu la petite amphore à bavaroises ou l'obélisque bicolore des glaces panachées; toute l'histoire et toute la mythologie mises au service de la goinfrerie.

This extraordinary sequence, generated by the simple sentence 'Le café étincelait', is, on the surface, testimony to the narrator's condition of dazed enchantment. But behind the ingenuous narrator there is Baudelaire the ironist, whose relentless itemizing of the terms of 'spectacle' is already the latter's undoing. In its accumulation of the fake, the vulgar and the in-coherent, this proliferating description is reminiscent of Flaubert's account of the grotesque structure of Emma Bovary's wedding cake. Like Flaubert's cake, this too is pure confection, a spectacle proposed literally for consumption ('goinfrerie'), both physical and emotional. What is seen through the window is the dream-machine in action, presenting the terms on which the city entices into a fantasy of comfort, luxury and gratification. More specifically here, the café offers an equivalent of the décor of the edenesque love affair, the recovery through urban artifices of a paradisiac image of lovers' happiness; the café scene prolongs a previously formed illusion of communion and harmony ('Nous nous étions bien promis que toutes nos pensées nous seraient communes à l'un et à l'autre, et que nos deux âmes désormais n'en feraient plus qu'une').

Abruptly, however, the illusion snaps, in a characteristic instance of the Baudelairian tactic of poetic 'shock'. The text works structurally as a kind of extended zeugma, the incongruous yoking of clashing worlds: on the one hand, the self-absorbed world of the lovers, on the other hand, an intruding public world. Suddenly, the lovers become aware of the presence on the pavement of a poor family, a father and his two children, all in rags ('tous en guenilles'), looking in mute amazement through the café window:

> Droit devant nous, sur la chaussée, était planté un brave homme d'une quarantaine d'années, au visage fatigué, à la barbe grisonnante, tenant d'une main un petit garçon et portant sur l'autre bras un petit être trop faible pour marcher. Il remplissait l'office de bonne et faisait prendre à ses enfants l'air du soir. Tous en guenilles. Ces trois visages étaient extraordinairement sérieux, et ces six yeux contemplaient fixement le café nouveau avec une admiration égale, mais nuancée diversement par l'âge.

This, in another idiom, is again Paris as 'spectacle', but no longer from the point of view of the consumer or the happy *flâneur*. What the eyes of the poor see, and what they say, is that the poor are excluded, that spectacle and the pleasures it promises are a matter of class. They do not say this insistently; Baudelaire's text does not, either here or elsewhere in the prose poems, deal in a polemically contrived image of 'class', but in the brute reality of class, simply there, obdurate, intractable, as that which will not go away. The poor do not protest, they disrupt by virtue of their sheer presence. In particular, their stupefied gaze distracts, and destroys, the mutually communicating gaze of the lovers. Understanding becomes conflict, harmony is converted into dissonance. Confronted with the poor, the poet feels uncomfortable, guilty, moved to humanitarian sentiment ('attendri par cette famille d'yeux . . . un peu honteux de nos verres et de nos carafes, plus grands que notre soif'). He looks into his partner's eyes for signs that his own stirring of conscience is shared, but is immediately repulsed: 'Ces gens-là me sont insupportables avec leurs yeux ouverts comme des portes cochères! Ne pourriez-vous pas prier le maître du café de les éloigner d'ici?'

The twin motifs of the window and the gaze have by now acquired quite different connotations. For the lovers the window initially frames a scene of urban pastoral;[30] for the poor it is a barrier. From the clash of those two meanings of the window, the relations of looking and seeing issue in a splintering of the images the narrator-lover wishes to find and have confirmed. For the lover, the eyes of his mistress refuse reciprocity.[31] For the woman, the eyes of the poor usurp what is not properly theirs. In this respect, one is particularly struck by the comparison of their eyes with 'portes cochères'. The expression 'des yeux comme des portes cochères' was a perfectly standard idiom for the wide-eyed in the nineteenth century, and from the narrator's mistress almost certainly 'means' no more than its given idiomatic sense. The wider context of the woman's use of the analogy, however, arguably reactivates the literal sense of 'porte cochère' (as the main gate of an aristocratic or bourgeois 'hôtel', through which a carriage could be driven) and hence realizes, if only unconsciously, an ironic meaning: just as the poor are excluded from the scene their gaping eyes seek to take in, so they will never pass through the gates of the city's great houses (Baudelaire will pick up on this theme again in the figure of the poor boy looking through the railings of the rich boy's house in 'Le Joujou du pauvre'); the poor do not belong in such worlds, they belong rather where servants and tradesmen belong, at the margin and behind the scenes, in the area of both the unseen and the non-seeing, entering, if at all, by the 'porte de service'.

The poem ends with one of Baudelaire's typically deceptive maxims, secure in the inherited authority of its form, but ambiguous as to its exact target: 'Tant il est difficile de s'entendre, mon cher ange, et tant la pensée est incommunicable même entre gens qui s'aiment.' This is not just another piece of Baudelairian misogyny, the scarcely veiled violence of aggressive feeling directed towards the feminine (what at the beginning of the poem is identified as a case of 'l'imperméabilité féminine'). Or rather it is, except that the violence has to be relativized to its particular context and occasion of utterance. It is of course a poem about the life and death of male desire, the transformation of love into hate at a failure of reciprocity. The maxims seek to represent that failure as a matter of universal psychology. But the poem's psychological concerns are inseparable from its social concerns, and it is that inseparability which wrenches loose the ostensibly secure framing of the text by the narrator's generalizations. The man's aggression derives less from moral outrage at the woman's indifference than from being reminded by her reaction of what he would rather ignore: that guilt is a pointless self-indulgence and that charitable sentiments change nothing. The real objection, masked by the generalizing 'wisdom' of the maxims, is to the woman's refusal to play the game, her blunt refusal to be for the man a mirror reflecting back, either in her eyes or in her words, the image he wants. The woman's callousness is therefore irreducible to the psychologizing claims of the narrator's discourse, and has a precise ironic function in relation to the poem's wider theme of social division. It undoes one of the great fictions of Second Empire Paris: that the culture of the boulevard has been fully democratized, and that the city of pleasure is available to all. In her heartless way, the woman says it how it is, that the poor have no place where the lovers are; and, if the man comes to hate her, it is because her

words expose the bad faith involved in trying to combine incompatibles –
physical and emotional well-being with a good conscience.

There is here, then, a politics of urban pleasure and pain, traced out in
the fractured intimacy of a personal exchange. While it is doubtless excessively reductive to see in the reactions of the man and the woman a representation of political positions (the man standing for the 'liberal left' and
the woman for 'the right, the Party of Order'[32]), it is quite wrong to say
that this poem evades and defuses the politics of class by displacing attention
away from the situation of the poor on to a lovers' private quarrel.[33] The
point is precisely their conjunction. In his city poetry, Baudelaire is the
great artist of the intermeshing of the public and the private, those moments
at which the most delicate kinds of personal feeling – generally the sexual
– are deeply affected and mediated by the social history of the city as a
whole. The window of 'Les Yeux des pauvres' is a site of exactly that kind
of mediation.

III

The other window on nineteenth-century Paris that I want to look at,
or through, is from a passage in that remarkable novel of appropriations
and expropriations (from real estate to bodies), Zola's *La Curée*.[34] Like
Baudelaire's, Zola's window involves a café scene, a pair of lovers and a
problematic construction of 'spectacle': it is the window of the private
dining room in the Café Riche, through which the semi-incestuous lovers,
Renée and Maxime, look out on to the boulevard below. What initially they
see, or rather what initially is presented through their point of view is, in
the terms of Zola's more elaborate and detailed prose, very similar to Vallès's
account of the city lights as evoking a kind of magical fairyland (later in the
passage, the play of light and colour is described as a 'tohu-bohu féerique'):
the exotic comparison of the newspaper kiosks with Venetian lanterns, and
its further qualification by the important adjective 'bariolées'; the blaze of
the gas lamps on the café tables; the perceptual trick whereby the night
lights of the shop fronts create the illusion of daylight.[35] But if Zola's own
discourse here recapitulates the myth of the illuminated city, it also distances and ambiguates the myth by relativizing the perspective on the
boulevard to a specific point of view – at first, that of the two lovers, and,
in the subsequent development of the passage, the trajectory of Renée's
gaze. What we are invited to notice is essentially what she notices ('Renée
remarqua' . . . 'la jeune femme les suivait du regard' . . . 'Renée crut' . . . 'Elle
entendait' . . . 'Elle s'arrêta aux annonces d'un kiosque'). Renée's way of
looking at the boulevard is interested, mobile, it flickers from one object to
the next, but at the same time it is blanked out, detached from the flow of
life it witnesses.

This marks an important difference from Baudelaire's method. In Baudelaire's poem, looking in and at the city is revealed as a dangerous business: the eye has to be on its guard, constantly wary, screening out unwelcome information, and yet permanently vulnerable to sudden interventions in a visual field it cannot ultimately control (as in the poem 'A une passante', centrally about a play of looks and glances in which it is nothing less than the poet's identity that is under threat). One way of putting this might be to talk of a tension in Baudelaire between the gaze and the glance.[36] The gaze, fixating and fetishizing, seeks to hold the objects of the urban environment in a safe relation to the subject's desires, to confer meaning and 'depth' on the appropriated visual material. The glance entails a quite different kind of attention to the life of the city; it picks up on what the gaze excludes, restores the primacy of the ever-changing surface over the illusion of depth, permits the random irruption of the real into the otherwise censored space of vision. The enactment of this tension is moreover naturally suited to the medium of the prose poem: its economy and speed make for abrupt and ironic switches of thematic direction, forms of ellipsis through which the unexpected suddenly comes into focus (in 'Les Yeux des pauvres' the poor are brought into view without narrative warning, in the elliptical movement between the end of one paragraph and the beginning of the next).

Zola's text also has its strategies for the ironic undoing of the settled gaze, the perspective of mastery on the city. But, because it is a novel, these work more by processes of accumulation and delay than by unanticipated local reversals of perception. Renée's encounter with the boulevard does not run the same risks as those experienced by Baudelaire's lovers. The latter are on the pavement, sitting on the café terrace, uncomfortably close to the action of the street. Renée is inside, and moreover high up; from the refuge of the private dining room (refuge not only of illicit lovers but also of the rich), the window supplies access to 'spectacle', but protects and inures against what might be demanding or threatening in the spectacle. What Renée sees is at once a lot and a little. Her eyes take in the whole of the boulevard from one end to the other ('allant d'un bout du boulevard à l'autre'); she notices the kiosks, the shop windows, the café tables, the drinkers, the pedestrians, the omnibus, the ticket collector, the hatter's advertisement. But, if she is passively receptive to diverse bits of information, it is information neutralized in the relative indifference of her gaze. Intensely present to the eye, the bright and mobile forms of the city finally produce a 'blur' in the consciousness of the observer, merge into the condition of the indistinct and the undifferentiated: the further reaches of the avenue appear as 'tumultueux et confus'; the crowd of pedestrians becomes an anonymous swirl, a black swarm ('un grouillement noir'), a crowd without identity-distinctions ('étrangement mêlé, et toujours le même'); and then, in the gathering of people at the omnibus station, a collection of mechanical dolls ('l'éternelle procession de petites poupées mécaniques'). Renée's gaze, a sequence of largely disconnected observations, has no way of making sense of the artefacts and forms of life it meets; as information, it does not pass into reflection, translate into knowledge. If this is Paris as 'spectacle', it is also Paris effectively de-realized, seen as in a dream, resistant to sense. In the sequence, there is no point of purchase from which the eye might construct a meaningful whole. All the gaze can do is to focus momentarily on contingent particulars, and then move on, as in the shift of attention – this time effected through the distancing medium of the binoculars ('ayant pris son binocle') – from the omnibus station to the hatter's advertisement ('qu'elle ne comprit pas').

Duranty, the high priest of the aesthetic of the new 'realism', claimed that the view from the window was the gaze of 'modernity' *par excellence*, detached, disengaged, neutral.[37] Following Duranty, we might then wish to say that Renée's gaze is a case in point and moreover that it announces or prefigures the alienated perspective of 'modernism', the existentially estranged viewpoint on the city characteristic of a great deal of twentieth-century literature. On the other hand – and this is surely the point of Zola's text – the conditions of Renée's estrangement are socially specific, the privilege of wealth and class, alienation *tout confort*. What the view from the Café Riche tells us is that being released from the demands of sense-making is a luxury. And, although the blur in Renée's perceptions necessarily implicates the prose which dramatizes her point of view, it does not entirely obliterate its potential critical force. Zola distinguishes himself from Renée precisely by sustaining distinctions and oppositions which her way of looking tends to collapse, he recovers sense from blur by way of essentially three contrasts. In the first place, the brightness of the lights may follow a consecrated late nineteenth-century motif in the evocation of a 'fairyland', but it also serves to throw into relief the exhausted pallor on the faces of the people who actually live and work in the city ('et c'était surtout au centre de cet ardent foyer qu'ils voyaient les faces blêmes et les rires pâles des passants'). The contrast turns again on questions of class and money.

The opposition is further marked by a more specific contrast at the level of sex: in the teeming crowd, what Renée particularly notices is the women, especially the prostitutes plying their trade and taking a drink. (In other circumstances they would not be seen at all; one of the interesting features of the social history of the Parisian window is that, whereas it was crucial to the soliciting force of one sort of commodity (in the shops), it was proposed to ban it for the display of the sexual sort; according to the recommended regulations for the policing of prostitution, 'the windows of a brothel under police supervision must remain closed'[38]). Here, then, we have a woman looking at other women. As Griselda Pollock has noted, in nineteenth-century representations of the city, the woman is rarely in the position of the subject of looking.[39] Zola's Renée is an exception. She does not of course take the customary place of the male viewer, namely the place of the *flâneur*. She does not have the freedom of the street;[40] she is in a room, an interior, moreover a private room within public space (the private dining room in the restaurant usually hired by rich illicit lovers or by wealthy client and prostitute). The situation thus implies a certain connection between the woman of the café and the women of the street, the common involvement in the circuit of sexual exchange (Renée 'bought' by her wealthy husband and shortly to become the lover of her stepson).

But, if there is a common condition here, there is also a separation, a barrier that cannot be crossed. Renée, as subject of the gaze, is separated from its objects by virtue of the relation of class. The window thus intersects another division: between inside and outside, the elegant woman in the dining room and the women who belong to the street, *les filles*, wearing 'showy dresses' and 'making loud remarks'; or the woman sitting alone, in her dress garnished with white *guipure*, sipping a glass of beer 'd'un air d'attente lourde et résignée', reminiscent of the crushed and vacant look on the face of Degas's absinthe drinker or those of the waitresses, shop-girls and prostitutes in Manet's bar pictures. Although the sight of the women 'interests' Renée ('elles intéressaient'), it does not really engage her; she can be curious about their lives but she can never know those lives, nor does she make any effort to do so. Questions of class and gender thus cross here, but, if only for the purposes of this particular narrative scene, the more powerfully determining category is class and its divisions.

This aspect of the text is further accentuated by the third contrast it draws, namely the extraordinary closing moment of the passage when, as the omnibus passes the café, inside and outside briefly meet though the window, in a strange reversal of the terms of 'spectacle': the men on the omnibus raise their tired faces, 'et les regardaient, elle et Maxime, du regard curieux des affamés mettant l'œil à la serrure'. This is a culminating moment in a complex series of visual transactions. Subject/object relations are here reversed, as Renée (along with Maxime) becomes the object of the men's look. But it would make no sense to gloss that reversal in the way we would read, say, a corresponding reversal in Mary Cassatt's painting, *At the Opera* (plate 3). Cassatt's picture should be considered alongside another, exactly contemporary picture, Caillebotte's *Jeune homme à sa fenêtre* (plate 4). In the latter, Caillebotte depicts, with a matter-of-fact yet disturbing neutrality, a man staring out of the window at a solitary woman crossing the street, a gaze she does not see and we do not see (we see the man from the back). Cassatt's picture adds another dimension: in the foreground there is a woman looking towards the stage through a pair of opera glasses (like Renée looking with a 'binocle'), but in the background to the left there is a man looking, also through opera glasses, at the woman looking. The Cassatt picture thus places the woman as both subject and object. It is a complex and unstable placing, compositionally emphasizing the autonomy of the woman by placing her in the foreground, but then – in the eye's journey from foreground to background – qualifying that emphasis in the shock-effect of discovering a second, male, subject of vision, who makes the woman a term of his voyeurism. The closing moment of the Zola passage cannot, however, be construed in this way. Zola's interests and priorities in this passage are different, less subtle but no less urgent; the male gaze here is not a mode of domination but a sign of disempowerment and dispossession, and if it is a case of 'voyeurism' it is the voyeurism of the poor, the look of the famished briefly turned on the well-fed, through the window not as private but as social keyhole.

Zola's way with the window on the world of the city replays in micro-cosm a central ambiguity in nineteenth-century representations of the city, especially those of the later nineteenth century. Through Renée's point of view there is staged a loss of the perspective of meaning; Renée's gaze is not one that can hold the diverse aspects of the urban scene in clear and coherent focus. This implies a particular version of the city: that it is too fluid and amorphous to be reduced to the sets of oppositions and distinctions from which meaning is produced; there are so many differences (particulars, contingencies, 'individuals') that Difference no longer counts for much; the heterogeneous proliferates, but at the same time is absorbed into the homogeneous, the 'black swarm' of the faceless crowd.[41] It is a view arguably like the dots and blobs to which the urban population is reduced in Monet's views over the Boulevard des Capucines (plate 5) or indeed Zola's own description of the urban crowd in *L'Œuvre* as so many 'points noirs' and 'taches sombres'.[42] On the other hand, the text of *La Curée* also places Renée's view, shows that removal of the perspective of sense and the principle of differentiation is accomplished at a price. If the construction of an in-telligible, discriminating image confers an 'identity' on the city by shutting out the anomalies which threaten the coherence of that image, then not making sense also involves a shutting out; the view of the city as unintelligible, as having *no* distinct identity, conveniently overlooks what Zola's text does not here forget: that, behind the abstract faces in the deceptively uniform crowd ('strangely mixed and always alike'), there are important distinctions, and that to represent the city as a perceptual blur is to lose sight of real social structures of difference and division, presumably only too clear to those who, as rich and poor, elegant and vulgar, hungry and replete, inhabited different points within them. Along with Baudelaire's prose poem, it reminds us of some of the things involved in 'knowing any real city'.[43] Together these two texts also frame, or are framed by, the category of the 'knowable' as such, and thus serve to remind us of what is crucially lost in the counter-emphases of some of our currently fashionable orthodoxies on the idea of the city as the space of the unknowable *par excellence*.

3

The High View:
Three Cityscapes

I

In 1799 the engineer Robert Fulton brought the panorama from England to France, and it enjoyed an active, if intermittent, life in everyday urban culture throughout the nineteenth century.[1] It was widely held to have educational functions as well as entertainment value; late in the century, Francisque Sarcey wrote that 'l'instruction par les yeux ne saurait être trop encouragée' and that 'le panorama était un moyen d'éducation populaire'.[2] As an instrument of popular instruction, it was never far from propaganda, and it is perhaps no accident that the heyday of the panorama phenomenon was during the Third Republic (one commentator spoke in 1881 of 'la Panoramanie'[3]), since this was the period in which the idea that mass education had an important role in fostering a sense of common social purpose and national 'identity' was particularly strong. Not surprisingly, the panorama regularly dealt in images of historical continuity and political unity. Much of its staple diet consisted of pictorial re-creations and celebrations of the great Napoleonic campaigns, while in 1889 Gervex and Stevens designed a *Panorama de l'histoire du siècle* in which many of the great figures of French history, from Louis XIV to MacMahon, were wheeled on stage in an image of ecumenical national fraternity across time and difference.

But if history, and in particular military history, dominated the repertoire of the panorama, the latter also specialized in spectacular topographical reproductions, notably of the city. The first French panorama was in fact a view of Paris (*Vue de Paris, du pavillon central des Tuileries*), and there were also representations of London, Rome, Amsterdam and Naples (later supplemented with the daguerrotype and the aerial photograph). The panorama had a profound effect on the psychological and ideological forms of urban visuality, on the conditions under which the city was both perceived and fantasized. The great panorama painter, Edouard Detaille, wrote in his notebooks that 'le panorama est un peu comme le théâtre, il faut faire gros et lisible pour tous.'[4] This principle of a universally accessible and instantly legible image encouraged what Michel de Certeau has described as the function of the panorama in generating 'la fiction . . . qui mue en lisibilité la complexité de la ville et fige en un texte transparent son opaque mobilité'.[5] The city seen from the point of view of the panorama was the city evacuated of obstructive challenges to understanding, the city perceived from a position of mastery, confirming an 'identity' at once of the viewing subject and the object viewed. Thus, if, as I have suggested in the previous chapter, there is an ideological dimension to the notion of the city as unintelligible, this does not by any means enable us to recover some unproblematical, ideologically 'pure' perspective of intelligibility; no sooner have we encountered the limits of the former than we are re-confronted with the limits of the latter, especially where the assumed point of vision and apprehension positions the subject in such a way as to foster the illusion of a mastering totalization.

This was precisely the perspective of the panorama and was indeed sometimes explicitly advertised in its accompanying prospectuses. For example, the 'Notice historique et explicative' accompanying the patent for the *Panorama voyageur, vue de Paris* of 1828 specified the position to be occupied by the spectator in the following terms: 'De cette place, la vue embrasse tout l'horizon à plusieurs lieues de distance, et plonge en même temps sur la capitale, au centre de laquelle on est placé. Le choix de cette position n'est pas arbitraire; il a été fait avec intention, et pour mettre le curieux au centre même de la ville qu'il veut connaître.'[6] On this account, the viewing subject is 'centred' in a vision of a city itself characteristically taken in the nineteenth century to be the centre of modern civilization; or in the terms of de Certeau's account, the panorama transformed the spectator into a 'dieu voyeur'.[7] From there it is, of course, but a step to associating the panorama with the contemporary model of Bentham's panopticon, and hence with the ideologico-institutional apparatuses of *haute surveillance*[8] (in the case of the *Vue de Paris, du pavillon central des Tuileries*, we should remember that for much of the nineteenth century the Tuileries pavilion was not a politically neutral space or innocent point of vision; it betokened the centralizing gaze of power, the perspective of the ruler over the ruled).

Nevertheless, we should perhaps avoid too neat an assimilation of the panorama to our new-historicist paradigms of *savoir-pouvoir*. That connection is almost certainly an element – and a powerful element – in the cultural and fantasmatic life of the panoramic image. For the most part, however, the city as panorama was essentially a matter of the pleasures of spectacle, a form of 'sight-seeing'.[9] In addition, we should also not overlook the ostensible 'democratic' inspiration of the panorama, as affording a view in which theoretically all citizens might participate. In so far as a political fantasy of the modern city underlies the development of the panorama, it is as much about utopian projects of political community and civic belonging as about repressive stratagems of social control. Michel Chevalier, the Saint-Simonian who dreamt up one of the plans for the great urban Temple, saw it as housing 'les panoramas et les dioramas qui réuniraient en un seul point tout l'espace et tout le temps'.[10] This, of course, is utopian architectural planning run riot in socio-metaphysical extravaganza. But it tells us that the idea and image of the panorama connected with many aspects of the nineteenth-century social imagination, and in particular with that aspect of it concerned less with techniques of policing than with the values of the polis, the dream of recovering for Paris something of the city of antiquity, and in particular, in a recurring analogy, the notion of Paris as a new Athens.[11]

Aristotle claimed that the ideal city was one that 'can be taken in at a single view'. His model was not in fact Athens. But, from the idealizing retrospects the nineteenth century brought to the ancient world, Athens, as both physical space and political community, would have appeared the natural reference and the corresponding view the unexampled one from the Acropolis, at once down and up – down to the agora, the place of transaction and exchange, the conflict and negotiation of secular interests; up by the Parthenon to the sky and man's relation to the gods. From the summit of the Acropolis, the vertical sweep of the gaze appeared to actualize or confirm in physical space a conception of the city in which the sense of 'belonging', of identity and wholeness, identity *as* felt wholeness, was reflected in a living public reality that was also a site of contact between the human and the divine. The Acropolis, wrote Renan in his *Prière à l'Acropole*, was 'un lieu où la perfection existe ... c'était l'idéal cristallisé en marbre pentélique qui se montrait à moi.'[12]

The same claims could scarcely be made on behalf of nineteenth-century Paris. But in one relatively neutral respect the comparison carried over: in however reduced a form morally and symbolically, there were physical equivalents for Paris of the view from the Acropolis. It was generally agreed in the nineteenth century that the best point from which to contemplate Paris was the point which enabled it to be taken in 'at a single view', to be seen, and comprehended, as a totality. Paris, wrote Alexis Martin in 1890, was 'conçu sur un plan assez clair pour permettre au même coup d'œil d'en embrasser l'ensemble et d'en percevoir les détails'.[13] There was less agreement, however, as to the exact point that would yield maximum perceptual and intellectual grasp of the complex unity of the city (assuming it existed at all; in both the literature and the painting of the period, the assumption is as much contested as affirmed). The obvious candidate was, of course, the high point, the elevated view, especially in 1890, the year after the Eiffel Tower opened to the public. Maxime du Camp, in his massive description of contemporary Paris, disagreed (while nevertheless retaining the analogy with Athens). In the view from on high, he argued, the city and the visible landmarks of its history are blotted out by domestic and industrial smoke (this will become an important consideration in respect of Impressionist painting): 'La brume de fumée bleuâtre incessament poussée par les cinq cent mille cheminées plane au-dessus des toits, enveloppe la ville dans une atmosphère indécise, noie les détails, déforme les édifices et produit une inextricable confusion.'[14] Maxime du Camp's ideal point is rather the 'terre-plein' of the Pont-Neuf, from which 'le panorama est net et précis, la perspective garde des plans distincts qui conservent dans l'éloignement des proportions exactes; tout est clair, s'explique et se fait comprendre.'[15]

Unlike du Camp, however, the majority of writers and painters chose to locate the site of the panoramic view on the high ground. The site, of course, varied, as did the nature of the 'totalizing' vision it served, in accordance with the changing topography and technology of the city. By 1890 (the year of Martin's commentary), all the earlier vantage points had been eclipsed by the spectacular vista from the top platform of the Eiffel Tower; opened to the public in 1889, the Tower literally transformed the 'cultural conditions of seeing';[16] it enabled the city to be seen for the first time as abstract map, thus inaugurating a perspective that will run through modern art to Mondrian's flat and frontal representations of New York (and, more ominously, to the 'abstracted' inhumanity of the gaze from the ferris wheel over devastated post-war Vienna in Carol Reed's *The Third Man*). But, before technology came to furnish these extraordinary inventions and constructions, there were many other sitings for the high view over the city. Balzac favours the view from Père-Lachaise, at least in the most famous climax of the *Comédie humaine*: Rastignac contemplating Paris from the scene of Goriot's funeral, in a moment of understanding that is the prelude to a project of conquest. Hugo celebrates the view from Notre-Dame, in a historical retrospective emphasizing both the cultural continuities and the discontinuities of the city from the Middle Ages onwards. Nadar leaves the city entirely, exploiting the resources of the hot-air balloon in order to conduct the first experiments in aerial photography. This will have its counterpart in painting, for example, in the odd cartographic picture by Victor Navlet, *Vue générale de Paris en 1855, prise d'un ballon* (plate 6) – the city planner's picture *par excellence*, strong on streets and weak on people, precise, meticulous and dead. The Goncourt brothers give us the view from the *belvédère* of the Jardin des Plantes ('Paris était sous eux, à droite, à gauche, partout'[17]). Zola and the novelists of his generation prefer the view from Montmartre; Zola indeed will return obsessively to the steps of Sacré-Cœur, either to dramatize the projections of the acquisitive gaze directed towards the city and its real estate by the property speculator (Saccard in *La Curée*), or to affirm the values of reconciliation and harmony (the affirmative overview at the end of *Paris*). The Impressionist painters will also patronize the view from Montmartre, though in contradictory ways; if some of them use it to stress the spirit of urban festivity and solidarity, then others, notably Manet and Van Gogh, will ambiguate or even negate its claims to coherence by surrounding it with various kinds of pictorial irony and uncertainty. Huysmans goes a stage further; in *Croquis parisiens*, he deals the death-blow to the grander aspirations of the panoramic view by displacing the perspective from the historic city centre and its skyline of touristic sights to the desolate industrial landscape of the Plaine Saint-Denis:

> Du haut des remparts, l'on aperçoit la merveilleuse et terrible vue des plaines qui se couchent, harassées, aux pieds de la ville. A l'horizon, sur le ciel, de longues cheminées rondes et carrées de briques vomissent dans les nuages des bouillons de suie, tandis que plus bas, dépassant à peine les toitures plates des ateliers couverts de toiles bituminées et de tôle, des jets de vapeur blanche s'échappent, en sifflant, de minces tuyaux de fonte.[18]

There is little here to recall the view from the Acropolis, although throughout the century there will be intermittent attempts to retrieve the analogy, especially by Hugo, trying to keep alive the revolutionary notion of the republic as a reinvention of the ancient polis. When Hugo, in *Les Misérables* and elsewhere,[19] compares nineteenth-century Paris to the ancient city, he is inspired in large measure by his republican beliefs and the memory of 1789. Indeed Hugo himself, or rather his death, will come to incarnate that analogy and the fantasized possibility of its cultural realization. In *Les Déracinés* Barrès makes of the funeral procession accompanying Hugo's remains to the Pantheon the occasion of a reminder and a prophecy: that the French have a collective identity and a collective destiny. Hugo's legacy is nothing less than 'le trésor et toute l'âme de notre race',[20] and his burial in the Pantheon (symbol of national unity) its public validation. From the high ground of the Pantheon, Paris is seen as a whole, not just topographically but spiritually, its divisions imagined as healed in the re-creation of a common culture; beyond individualism and fragmentation, Paris and its people discover what Hugo allegedly embodied: 'le génie de notre race'.[21]

In the late nineteenth century there will be other versions, proposed from a similar physical outlook on the city, of this utopian dream of urban communality (notably in the messianic themes of rebirth and harvest stimulated by the view over Paris from Sacré-Cœur at the end of Zola's novel, *Paris*). But the language of Barrès shows how far, at least in certain quarters, the dream has moved from its original source in the comparisons with republican antiquity. The dominant term in Barrès's mystical musings is, of course, the alarming term 'race'. The notion of the *res publica* has here become entirely absorbed by the legitimating rhetoric of right-wing nationalism; and Paris redeemed is Paris cleansed of foreign bodies, the 'degenerate' cosmopolitan mix of the modern boulevard (its paradigm in *Les Déracinés* is the Latin Quarter). This does not so much look back to earlier republicanism as look forward to Action Française and to a rather different mythology of 'regeneration'.

In fact, for the most part in the nineteenth century the city of antiquity appeared less as a plausible model for a project of political and social reconstruction than as an irrecoverable object of nostalgia, an unrepeatable happy moment of history. In the late eighteenth century Mercier could describe Paris as a 'Nouvelle Athènes' (it is one of the chapter titles of the *Tableau de Paris*), but throughout the nineteenth century the analogy survives for the most part only in negative form. In the long didactic poem entitled 'L'Indifférence' that Auguste Barbier wrote as his contribution to *Le Diable à Paris*, Paris is compared to Athens but as a 'triste et pâle copie'.[22] Later in the century, Renan will address his *Prière à l'Acropole*, but from the point of view of irretrievable postlapsarian loss (the 'miracle grec' is 'une chose qui n'a existé qu'une fois ... qui ne se reverra plus'[23]). The great conservative historian, Fustel de Coulanges (forerunner of Durkheim), will argue in his major work, *La Cité antique*, that the foundation stone and integrating principle of community in the ancient city was religion; and that in an increasingly secularized urban civil society the bonds which might unify its members were fractured probably beyond repair. Zola too will contrast Athens and Paris as an opposition between forms of settled life and culture and the self-consuming frenzy of modernity.[24]

Here, then, is one context for the widespread nineteenth-century theme of the fractured, or fallen, city. Take, for example, Rimbaud's parodic reinvention of ancient Athens. Rimbaud's modern Acropolis ('L'Acropole officielle' of the prose poem 'Villes') is not only a hideous travesty of its ancient counterpart but also, in both its architectural reference (perhaps a Great Exhibition-style building[25]) and its urban setting, radically indeterminate. Scholarship has claimed both London and Stockholm, but the text is more probably a collage of perceptions and memories of different cities (including Paris), in which it is precisely the principle of determinate reference that has been scrambled. The Rimbaldian city is one you cannot scan; there is no position, no fixed point, for either the subject or the object of perception; space and depth, relations of above and below, centre and circumference, do not so much converge on the Acropolis as disperse around it: 'j'ai cru juger la profondeur de la ville! C'est le prodige dont je n'ai pu me rendre compte: quels sont les niveaux des autres quartiers sur ou sous l'acropole?'[26] This is the polis in bits and pieces. Alternatively, the analogy with Athens gets overlaid with or displaced by the biblical analogy, the vision of Paris as the whore of Babylon (in the lists of nineteenth-century comparisons with ancient cities, Babylon is prominent[27]). Gautier, for example, will imagine Paris as a Babylon destroyed by the rats of Montfaucon.[28] More famously, there is the implied Babylonian analogy proposed by Baudelaire from the heights of his anti-Acropolis, in the 'Epilogue' to Le Spleen de Paris:

> Le cœur content, je suis monté sur la montagne
> D'où l'on peut contempler la ville en son ampleur,
> Hôpital, lupanar, purgatoire, enfer, bagne,
>
> Où toute énormité fleurit comme une fleur.[29]

On this analogy, the available equivalents for nineteenth-century Paris of the view from the Acropolis – Père-Lachaise, the Pantheon, Montmartre, the Buttes-Chaumont and later the Eiffel Tower – invite us to look down, but rarely up (or, if so, it is in order to take leave of the city, to bid one's farewell to the agora and its machinations). From the high view one looks down as upon a fallen world, sometimes in amazement, even in the hope of redeeming it, but more often to despise it, possess it, manipulate it or escape from it. Let us, however, now move in a little closer to the terms and forms of the high view, by way of three introductory texts, three beginnings – the opening pages of Balzac's La Fille aux yeux d'or, the first poem of the 'Tableaux parisiens' section of Baudelaire's Les Fleurs du Mal and the initial sequence of Zola's Le Ventre de Paris. It is significant that all three texts are beginnings, inaugural visions that are also opening moves which attempt structurally to hold and frame the city as coherent space while, as we shall see, at the same time disclosing the forces which make the effort problematic or even impossible.

II

Balzac detested the panorama,[30] and yet it is difficult to imagine a novelistic enterprise, in both its general conception and its specific technique, more systematically geared to the comprehensive, totalizing overview. Consider, for instance, the opening pages of La Fille aux yeux d'or;[31] as Georges Poulet has observed, they furnish one of the exemplary entry points to the whole of the Comédie humaine.[32] Although the story itself – the lurid tale of a brother and sister competing for the body of the beautiful Paquita Valdès – takes place for the most part in the enclosed intimacy of a private boudoir,

it is inaugurated and contextualized by a vision of Paris and modern life as
vast as Dante's vision of Inferno. The reference to Dante is in fact explicit:
'Nous voici donc amenés au troisième cercle de cet enfer qui aura un jour
son Dante.' The reference will lead in many directions, most obviously of
course to the idea of Paris – Baudelairian *avant la lettre* – as a modern version
of hell ('ce n'est pas par plaisanterie que Paris a été nommé un enfer. Tenez
ce mot pour vrai'). It also, and relatedly, links with a topic I shall discuss
in detail in a later chapter – the theme of Paris underground. For the
moment, however, let us stay with another connotation of the analogy: the
sense of Paris as a 'total' system, like Dante's circles, an ordered, stratified
and intelligible whole. If the story is private and particular, its context is
public and general; it is the 'aspect général' of a whole population ('la
population parisienne') grasped as a hierarchical structure of five 'classes':
in ascending order, the worker (Balzac also uses the term 'prolétaire'), the
'commerçant' and petit-bourgeois, the liberal professions and the haute
bourgeoisie, the artist, and the aristocracy.

Within this confident taxonomy differences are mapped, but the classes
are also alleged to have something in common, which, paradoxically, is the
exact reverse or parody of the idea of 'community'. What binds them all,
what gives the terms of a collective 'identity', is the common pursuit of 'l'or
et le plaisir': 'Que veulent-ils? De l'or ou du plaisir?' The intellectual focus
is thus reductive: it frames the differentiated, heterogenous social terrain
as a unified picture, or – in yet another modulation of this key term – as
'spectacle'. The latter is precisely the relevant, the commanding term: it is
the story's opening noun ('Un des spectacles . . .'). This again has multiple
connotations beyond those we have already considered in the previous
chapter. They include the assimilation of urban space to the idea of the
theatre, thus opening on to the motifs of artifice and *maquillage* (to which
I shall return). It also implies the positioning of the observing subject at
a point sufficiently distant from its object for it to be taken in as a whole,
at a 'single view'. The exact location of this point is not specified by the
narrator; it remains physically indeterminate, but logically it has to be the
point of the famous quasi-demiurgic Balzacian gaze, looking out, over and
down – the universe seen from the point of view of the universe. Although
the focus of the writing will move in to close-up as the description develops
(just as Dante will himself descend into hell as a character in the drama),
the implied dominant position is outside and high up, the position of
mastery.

Mastery, for Balzac, means subjugating the material in the field of vision
to the authority of a generalizing and naturalizing rhetoric of analysis and
explanation: the city is insistently compared to nature ('comme la nature,
cette nature sociale . . .') and the discourse of the narrative to the explana-
tory language of the natural sciences (although, like the material it surveys,

the writing actually consists of a highly unstable mix of different idioms). Given the central emphasis on social 'stratification', one might have expected here an allusion to the scientific model of geology, a model which elsewhere in the period is something of a commonplace. For instance, in the collection of essays by diverse hands (of which Balzac's was one), *La Grande Ville*, the preface characterizes Paris as a set of 'couches superposées' analogous to the system of geological strata in the physical world.[33] The naturalizing potential of that metaphor for ideological ends was, of course, considerable; the metaphor helped to shift attention from the morally problematic, because man-made and strife-ridden, history of class to the more reassuring terms of an account of social formation as natural formation, innocently free of relations of power and exploitation, simply and naturally 'layered'. The notorious example of this adaptation was to be Gambetta's strategically ecumenical speech during the Third Republic implicitly inviting the nation to bury the memory of class conflict on the barricades of the Commune and to construe the task of republican 'radicalism' as concerned not with the provocative term 'class' but with the changes in society entailed by the emergence of 'les nouvelles *couches* sociales'.[34]

Balzac, in fact, on one occasion in the opening pages of *La Fille aux yeux d'or*, uses the word 'class' (but whether deployed as a term drawn from the vocabulary of eighteenth-century scientific taxonomy or in the sense we would now associate with a materialist account of society is unclear). The major terms, however, remain the Dantesque images of 'spheres' and 'circles'; and in any case the prestige of science is invoked not by way of geology but in the various references to zoology, physiology and physiognomics: 'quelques observations sur l'âme de Paris peuvent expliquer les causes de sa physionomie cadavéreuse'; 'Peu de mots suffiront pour justifier physiologiquement . . .'; 'Peut-être avant d'analyser les causes qui font une physionomie speciale à chaque tribu . . . doit-on signaler la cause générale.' Science thus provides a language of both classification and explanation. Yet if the appeal to the power of science carries the promise of intelligibility, in practice there is more promise than delivery: the projected scientific 'justification' of the picture may require 'peu de mots', but curiously their arrival remains largely deferred. The text hesitates on the threshold of stating in scientific terms the ultimate 'cause', but, as we wait for that statement, the writing spins off elsewhere, caught in a rapid, hectically garrulous movement through a flux of verbal registers and figures in which the framing and taming claims of science are left far behind, decisively routed by the sheer pressure on the text of the subject matter it seeks to master.[35]

The closer Balzac takes us to his object, the less secure the anchoring perspective of the panoramic view becomes. One reason why this is so is that the 'cause générale', the founding categories of the description, are not inscribed in nature at all; the motor which drives the city and its population, 'l'or et le plaisir', is social in origin. Gold is not sought in the state of nature. Similarly, the concept of 'pleasure' has to be understood in the strong neo-Rousseauist sense of something cerebrally induced under the conditions of urban civilization; it is the product of what Balzac elsewhere calls the destructive operations of 'intelligence', and is represented here in the metaphor of a 'poison' secreted less by the body than by the mind ('les pores de l'esprit'). The name of the poison is Desire ('les posions, les désirs qui ont engrossi leurs cerveaux'). In a more strictly historical perspective, the motor, the driving force behind the city and its pursuits, is the great 'atelier de jouissances', the impossible dialectic of desire and gratification bound up with the economy of production and consumption characteristic of a developing urban capitalism.

If this is like the natural world, it is so only in the loose and generalized sense of nature's self-undoing and self-renewing movements, its resistance to fixity and stable form ('Cette nature sociale toujours en fusion semble se dire après chaque œuvre finie: – A une autre! comme se le dit la nature elle-même'). There is an attempt to develop this association through the image of nature's ephemera (the insects and the flowers). But the real pull of the writing is towards cancellation of the analogy. If Balzac's Paris is a world in perpetual motion, ceaselessly dispersing its resources, it is not movement in accordance with the rhythms of nature, the cycle of the seasons or any other 'pastoral' motif. Nature does in fact appear as much under the sign of pastoral as under that of science, notably in the comparison of Paris to a 'field' yielding up its 'harvest'. But the pastoral figure breaks down in the very sentence which introduces it: 'Paris n'est-il pas un vaste champ incessamment remué par une tempête d'intérêts sous laquelle tourbillonne une moisson d'hommes que la mort fauche plus souvent qu'ailleurs et qui renaissent toujours aussi serrés, dont les visages contournés, tordus, rendent par tous les pores de l'esprit, les désirs, les poisons dont sont engrossés leurs cerveaux . . .?'

The 'field' is thus swept not by rain, wind and sun, but by the 'storm' of social 'interests' ('une tempête d'intérêts'), whose 'harvest' moreover is the harvest of exhaustion and death – less the cyclical renewal of a world than its constant etiolation and running-down, the image of a world 'consumed'. Whence the further connotations generated from the text's initial term 'spectacle': on the stage of Paris, we see not the face of nature but the face of artifice and deception, the mask ('non pas des visages, mais bien des masques: masques de faiblesse, masques de force, masques de misère, masques de joie, masques d'hypocrisie, tous exténués, tous empreints des signes ineffaçables d'une haletante avidité'). The effect of the mask-image is to prohibit the proposed marriage of urban and pastoral. The mask discloses not the heliotropic instinct of nature, the turning towards the sun, but the opposite, the perverse turning towards the dark; the mask reveals 'la teinte presque infernale des figures parisiennes'.[36] We are not here in the countryside (and it should be remembered that in the early nineteenth century the boundary between city and country, especially when seen from the panoramic viewpoint, was not at all clear-cut[37]); we are in hell, consumed by fire: 'Là, tout fume, tout brûle, tout brille, tout bouillonne, tout flambe, s'évapore, s'éteint, se rallume, étincelle, pétille et se consume.'

This – one of the most flamboyant sentences of the *Comédie humaine* – is the moment at which we experience the full force of Balzac's appropriation of Dante to his vision of the modern city. I shall return shortly to some of the further implications of the metaphor of burning. But one thing that is certainly burnt here, ravaged by the intensities of the writing itself, is the project of a settled and coherent 'scientific' representation of the city undertaken from some serene point above and beyond, and hence untouched by, the frenzy of the scene represented. It is not just that, from a moral point of view – the point of view of what Proust called Balzac's incorrigible 'vulgarity'[38] – the narrator is so visibly fascinated by the social dynamics he records that the dividing line between high critical distance (the Olympian perspective Proust grants to Tolstoy, but not to Balzac) and excited complicity is compromised. The issue concerns less any claim to moral rectitude than the intellectual claim that the text will subdue and hold its endlessly mobile and self-dispersing object in a fixed structure of intelligibility. The text is as turbulent as the city it describes, veers towards its own kind of riotous behaviour. If this, in the name of the 'law' of science, is supposed to be the literary equivalent of a form of symbolic 'policing', then Balzac the policeman himself needs arresting for suspected dereliction of representational duty.

For what, in formal and stylistic terms, characterizes the writing of the city is what characterizes the city itself, its restless, agitated movement. Just as the city 'tourbillonne', so too does the text, turning like a machine that generates and scatters its energies in a re-enactment of the very rhythms of production and consumption which govern the 'vaste atelier' to which Paris is compared ('cette capitale, vaste atelier de jouissances'). Sound, syntax and trope collaborate in a dialectic of creation and destruction; words enter the space of the text 'en fusion' and 'restent à s'y déformer'. In the sentence – 'Là, tout fume, tout brûle, tout brille, tout bouillonne, tout flambe, s'évapore, s'éteint, se rallume, étincelle, pétille et se consume' – the sound of one word suggests the next: the vowel sound of 'fume' is picked up by 'brûle', itself deformed into 'brille'; the 'b' and 'll' of 'brille' are echoed in 'bouillonne'; 'tout flambe' marks a crescendo; then the repeated 'tout' is dropped for the decrescendo, but is followed by a renewed burst of energy – first, in the series of three reflexive verbs ('s'évapore, s'éteint, se rallume'), the last of these not only 're-igniting' the sentence but also restoring the vowel sound of 'fume' and 'brûle'; secondly, in the pair 'étincelle, pétille'

56

(which also play on sound similarity) – only to fade in the closing verb 'se consume', a verb which structurally as well as semantically spells the 'death' of the sentence, while at the same time, at the level of sound, also recalling the inaugural verb 'fume'. The sequence has thus come full circle, its end and beginning are in each other; the sentence folds back upon itself, its consummation a gesture of self-consumption.

This sort of textual movement could be described as the synonymic equivalent of what Barthes called 'la métonymie déréglée',[39] a generation of terms which severally and collectively are supposed to refer back to the sense of a whole, a 'totality', but which in fact, in their very proliferation, postpone the moment of totalization. Similarly, the syntax of the long rhetorical question which dominates the first paragraph ('Paris n'est-il pas . . .?') continually refers ahead, in a sustained proleptic movement. The writing here works at the surface of Paris, its 'face', but the face becomes a mask (a surface on a surface), which in turn has to be read ('tous empreints de signes ineffaçables'); and the sentence which discloses this information – in its elaborate self-extension through units of synonymic qualification, repetition and subordination – follows the same trajectory of delay, displacing as it solicits 'interpretation'. Like the masks, the syntactic units are elements in a deferring chain, without a final term that would resume them all.

In short, the text tries to delineate the 'face' of Paris, to assign it identity, by proliferating predicates, activating the resources of nomenclature. The image of the face is itself rendered variously as 'aspect', 'visage', 'masque', 'physionomie', 'figure', but the accumulation of synonyms succeeds only in returning us to a basic facelessness. The words are abundant but at the same time redundant. The text resembles its object which 'semble se dire après chaque œuvre finie: – A une autre!' A word or phrase is completed, and immediately another is produced, but the new term often does little to further meaning; it simply comes into being in order to be superseded, like the 'moisson d'hommes' of Paris, superfluous beings which nevertheless spring up again as soon as they are cut down. Paris, we are told, concerns itself with things that do not last, and 'jette aussi feu et flamme par son éternel cratère'. But if there is any difference between 'feu' and 'flamme', the latter cannot be said to add anything substantial to the former by way of extending the sense of the image. The pair is an instance of the figure of speech that saturates the opening pages of *La Fille aux yeux d'or*, the figure of hendiadys ('two in one'), one of the figures of redundancy. The text, permanently on the move, is, in important respects, always the same; like the city, it is given over to pointless excess, as productive capacity issuing in superfluity.

Alternatively, if it produces variety, it is variety without a relay back to a 'centre'; again like the city, the writing supplies only the illusion of a centre:

in reality there is no fixed central point around which its constituent parts are rallied. The thematic heart of the text ('l'or et le plaisir') is represented figurally as a 'poison' that swells the brain. By the same token, the text too swells from its prodigious figural input, and finally bursts, spilling over into a potentially uncontrollable flux of terms which threatens to swamp the capacity of the text to hold its object in a stable order of representation. Metaphor is eclectically chosen and promiscuously mixed, its movement centrifugal rather than centripetal: Paris as field, then as theatre (the motif of the mask), then as workshop, then as hell, then as volcano. There is a pretence of continuity in the repetition of the adjective 'vaste' to qualify two of the separated metaphorical terms ('vaste champ'/'vaste atelier') but the repetition is arbitrary and mechanical: field and workshop, pastoral and urban cannot be combined; they are discontinuous and contradictory, and, however much the borrowed 'scientific' discourse invites us to compare the city to nature, it is not a comparison that can be sustained in and by the metaphorical texture of the writing. Given its abrupt switches and redirections, the last thing we can say about metaphor here is that it is 'organic', in the senses of either natural science ('physiologie') or literary criticism.

In fact, towards the end of the 'overture' to *La Fille aux yeux d'or*, we are explicitly taken out of the sphere of the organic, the natural, into that of the mechanical and the man-made. At this closing moment, the writing will change metaphorical tack once again. In one of Balzac's more baroque imaginings, the text places us on the high seas: Paris is elaborately compared to a ship and, in the initial moment of the figure, to its engine ('la chaudière motrice de ces magnifiques pyroscaphes que vous admirez fendre les ondes'). The city as vessel repeats the familiar allegorical motif of the journey, the idea of Paris and its history as an adventurous, discovery-laden voyage. The city as engine, however, has more interesting implications. The engine ('la chaudière motrice') is, of course, a steam-engine, and it is an image that Balzac will use on more than one occasion in the *Comédie humaine* as an analogy for modern society.[40] Science thus returns in the form of technology, but if there is a relevant scientific 'law' in play here, we are perhaps more likely to think of the second law of thermodynamics – the law of 'entropy', stipulating the tendency of all energy-producing systems to run down, to move towards a state of terminal disorder and inertia. Lévi-Strauss once distinguished two main kinds of society (the traditional and the modern) by means of the contrasting images of the 'clock' and the 'steam-engine': the clock society simply ticks over, it is a 'cold' society; the steam-engine society, on the other hand, is a 'hot' society, generating vast amounts of energy, but high on entropy, always at risk of seizing up or burning out.[41]

Balzac's Paris is such a society. The fires which consume it are not just the hell-fires of Dante; the drift of the metaphor is as much secular as theological. It is often, and rightly, said that Balzac's vision of the modern city is the vision of a world in process of constructing its own reality, all exuberance, vitality, *élan*. As the narrator looks down from the high point, he sees the world-historical ship swaying and rolling on the turbulent waves, but also moving confidently forwards, in the vanguard of civilization: 'Paris n'est-il pas un sublime vaisseau chargé d'intelligence? Oui ... Cette nauf a bien son tangage et son roulis, mais elle sillonne le monde ... , crie du haut de ses huniers par la voix de ses savants et de ses artistes: "En avant, marchez! suivez-moi!" ' Once again, the metaphors get confusingly mixed (how does one *walk* in the trace of a ship?). But more important than this local, if symptomatic, incoherence is the larger point that, from the terms of the writing itself, the grounds for Balzac's confident, forward-looking view are deeply insecure; the image of the city articulated in these pages gives us no clear sense that there is anywhere in particular for the ship to go other than towards its own self-consumption and disintegration.

We will find similar disintegrative imaginings projected on to the city elsewhere in the literature of the period (according to Benjamin, imagining the end of the city is the nightmare version of the great urban 'phantasmagoria'): for instance, in the nightmare of entrapment in a disintegrating building recorded by Baudelaire in his notebooks ('J'habite pour toujours un bâtiment qui va crouler, un bâtiment travaillé par une maladie secrète'[42]), and in the many narrative images of collapsing buildings and institutions in the work of Zola (the tenement in *L'Assommoir*, the bank in *L'Argent*). The high view might then be read in part as an attempt to check that imagined collapsing, to hold, order and stabilize. Moreover, it specifically implicates the attempts of the *artist* to hold the city within a secure and unifying frame of vision. What happens when the proposed frames of the high view are explicitly aesthetic in character is the topic of the texts I now wish to consider, in a return to the examples of Baudelaire and Zola.

III

Paysage

Je veux, pour composer chastement mes églogues,
Me coucher auprès du ciel, comme les astrologues,
Et, voisin des clochers, écouter en rêvant
Leurs hymnes solonnels emportés par le vent.
Les deux mains au menton, du haut de ma mansarde,
Je verrai l'atelier qui chante et qui bavarde;
Les tuyaux, les clochers, ces mâts de la cité,
Et les grands ciels qui font rêver d'éternité.

Il est doux, à travers les brumes, de voir naître
L'étoile dans l'azur, la lampe à la fenêtre,
Les fleuves de charbon monter au firmament
Et la lune verser son pâle enchantement.
Je verrai les printemps, les étés, les automnes;
Et quand viendra l'hiver aux neiges monotones,
Je fermerai partout portières et volets
Pour bâtir dans la nuit mes féeriques palais.
Alors je rêverai des horizons bleuâtres,
Des jardins, des jets d'eau pleurant dans les albâtres,
Des baisers, des oiseaux chantant soir et matin,
Et tout ce que l'Idylle a de plus enfantin.
L'Emeute, tempêtant vainement à ma vitre,
Ne fera pas lever mon front de mon pupitre;
Car je serai plongé dans cette volupté
D'évoquer le Printemps avec ma volonté,
De tirer un soleil de mon cœur, et de faire
De mes pensers brûlants une tiède atmosphère.

Baudelaire's 'Paysage' is the opening poem of the section explicitly devoted to the city ('Tableaux parisiens') in *Les Fleurs du Mal*. It works from, but also transforms, a stereotype: the view over the rooftops of Paris from the poet's garret. The attic and the rooftops had been a staple of the literature of the city from the 1830s onwards (in the 1830 uprising they had been used as arsenals and look-outs; it was not long before these revolutionary uses were forgotten in the taming conversion into the terms of the 'charming' or indeed as a point of refusal of the political[43]). Gautier will be found recycling it enthusiastically in the late addition of 'La Mansarde' to the 1872 edition of *Emaux et camées* (though his treatment is arguably not without an element of ironic playfulness). In more straightforwardly journalistic mode, the attic and the perspectives on the city it affords form one of the topics treated at length in Paul de Kock's contribution to *La Grande Ville*.[44] This is a version of the elevated view more restricted and more intimate than the grand panoramic sweep, more hospitable to the idiom of the picturesque and the sentimental. The attic is the place of dream and promise, of youthful awakenings to the potential of the city, and, in the specific association with the artist, the site of struggling creativity; the view from the attic is less the perspective of the demiurge than the high view *à la bohème*.

Baudelaire reproduces the stereotype in the second sentence of the first stanza, and appears to do so without even a trace of ironic self-consciousness:

Les deux mains au menton, du haut de ma mansarde,
Je verrai l'atelier qui chante et qui bavarde.

This is both the classic place and the classic posture of the poet contemplating the city in a relation of happy communion. There is nothing here to disturb the nervous system, to obstruct the subject's access to the pleasures of reverie (the 'dreams of eternity' with which the stanza ends). The specifically urban element of the couplet – the 'atelier' – is absorbed into the mood with an ease that verges on the saccharine; the hideous din of the city's activities, elsewhere posed by Baudelaire as a threat to the autonomy of the psyche and the conditions of poetry, has been softened to the images of song and chatter: 'l'atelier qui chante et qui bavarde' (perhaps as an echo of Hugo's famous 'ville qui chante' in the panoramic description of medieval Paris in *Notre-Dame de Paris* [45]). Noise is thus rendered as at once sociable and harmonious, as is the relation between the poet and his surroundings (the relation of unity binding the two enacted in the rhyme of 'mansarde' and 'bavarde'). This is industry as picturesque 'landscape', and it is not difficult to see why the workshop could be perceived in this way; it does not necessarily menace or equivocate the received notions of landscape in the way that the factory will. The Parisian 'atelier' was part of an inherited and customary urban culture, integral to the traditions of the old working-class *quartier*. When Haussmann set about trying to destroy much of that culture, a substantial literature of protest grew up. It took different forms and served different interests, depending on whether or not one actually lived and worked in the *quartier*. But a major form was quite openly sentimental; attachment to the world of the 'atelier' found a natural home in the literature of nostalgia concerned about a disappearing *vieux Paris*.

The ultimate point of Baudelaire's poem, as of the 'Tableaux parisiens' sequence in general, will be to show the price that has to be paid in order to sustain this sort of imagery, as well as the pressures that induce its breakdown. For the idealization can, of course, work only if much of the reality of the city is edited out of the picture. Indeed the opening sentence of the first stanza might well lead us to believe that the city has been edited out entirely. The initial 'Je veux' both marks and asserts a discourse of mastery, further reflected in the relative syntactic complexity of the whole sentence: from its commanding position, the subject weaves a pattern with discrete elements drawn from the domains of poetry, science, religion and nature. On the other hand, mastery also entails a self-absenting from the immediate urban scene. In the first sentence we could be anywhere other than in the city; the gaze looks up and away, towards the sky ('auprès du ciel') and heavenly matters (the 'grands ciels' of the last line opening on to metaphysical reverie).

If we are in any determinate place at all, then the reference to the Virgilian eclogue is more likely to conjure up Arcadia ('pour composer chastement mes églogues'). The poem begins by speaking of poetry, but in terms of a poetic genre known to celebrate flight from the city. The urban is thus paradoxically encountered by the poet in terms of pastoral; the cityscape is there to be constructed as, precisely, landscape, *paysage* according to a consecrated literary model (the original title of the poem was 'Paysage parisien', later truncated to the more indeterminate 'Paysage'[46]). This is quite different from Balzac's way with the pastoral motif; there, as we saw, the use of pastoral is casual and opportunistic, without sustained commitment, and rapidly displaced by other tropes. In Baudelaire's poem, the determination behind 'Je veux' seems to be to re-route the city systematically into the idiom of pastoral, to exploit the view from the attic in order to reinvent the eclogue in and for a modern context. It is only in the second half of the stanza, with the reference to the 'atelier' and the 'tuyaux' (the chimney pots), that we realize that the context is an urban one. And even here the references are immediately returned metaphorically to the sphere of nature: the chimney pots and the church steeples become masts ('ces mâts de la cité'), thus evoking the favoured themes of Baudelairian exotic, the sea and the journey, the voyage *là-bas*, elsewhere, beyond the confines of the given world, beyond the corruption of the city, place *par excellence* of orginal sin and fallen man, and towards a site of recovered natural innocence.

This process of overlaying urban artefact and activity with the assumed 'naïvety' of pastoral is further developed in the first part of the second stanza:

> Il est doux, à travers les brumes, de voir naître
> L'étoile dans l'azur, la lampe à la fenêtre,
> Les fleuves de charbon monter au firmament
> Et la lune verser son pâle enchantement.

The gaze is still turned skywards, passing without resistance, pleasurably ('il est doux . . . de voir'), through 'les brumes' (quite different from the opaque and nightmarish 'brouillard' of the other poems in the 'Tableaux parisiens'). The window light, the star, the smoke and the moon are fused not only thematically but prosodically, in the use of the articulated 'e' (in 'brumes', 'étoile', 'fleuves' and 'lune') to sustain a connecting rhythm.[47] The chimney smoke – for Maxime du Camp, we recall, an insurmountable obstacle to the construction of Paris as coherent landscape – blends effortlessly with the natural elements of star and moon;[48] the stock image of the '*fleuves* de charbon' is perhaps given renewed life by the link back with 'mâts', and, in the connotation of the journey, arguably summons up an allusion to the great poet of the 'naïve', Homer, whose Odysseus recognizes his home from the coil of smoke rising into the sky.

At this juncture, however, the vulnerability of the poem's efforts to hold its diverse elements together in harmonious relationship starts to become apparent. Pastoral and urban cannot be successfully mixed, and the chimney smoke is in fact the last we shall see of the city from the poet's garret (apart from the negative reference to the excluded 'Emeute' in the last section of the poem). To maintain the notion of 'landscape', the text has to shut out the city. The next line evokes the cycle of the seasons (bar winter) as the object of the contented gaze. The predicted arrival of winter, however, marks the moment of willed exclusion and withdrawal; with winter the cityscape becomes a deathscape. Baudelaire's 'neiges monotones', like the snow-covered Paris at the end of Zola's *Une Page d'amour* or in some of the Impressionists' winter scenes, signify a numbing of sensibility, a loss of the élan which elsewhere characterizes Baudelaire's affective attachment to the colour and movement of the city; Paris blanketed by snow is Paris as source of emotional blank.[49]

The pivot of the poem is just this gesture of shutting out and turning away:[50] the window on the world is closed ('Je fermerai partout portières et volets') in favour of an opening on to pure inwardness ('Pour bâtir dans la nuit mes féeriques palais'). Landscape becomes fairy-tale, idyll, the constituents of which are furnished entirely by the poetic imagination. Here we are no longer in the city, but in a garden, a neo-classical version of the garden of Eden, where it is not the 'atelier' that sings, but birds accompanied by the sound of fountain water falling on alabaster and kisses – in short, the various clichés bound up with a particular literary version of 'tout ce que l'Idylle a de plus enfantin'. This turn of the text is thus visibly regressive, a desired movement back to childhood and the paradise of lost innocence, to what later in the poem is allegorized in 'Printemps', and elsewhere in *Les Fleurs du Mal* represented as the 'paradis parfumé . . . le vert paradis des amours enfantines', in opposition to the 'noir océan de l'immonde cité'.[51]

What we make of this regressive movement is open to interpretation and evaluation. 'Paysage' has been described as 'aggressively archaicizing' and as 'properly infantile because profoundly anti-historical'.[52] Certainly, 'enfantin' can be read critically as connoting self-indulgent collapse into the childish as well as a search for the innocence of the childlike. On the other hand, it is also possible to read both the manner and the placing of 'Paysage' in quite different terms, less as a capitulation to immature fantasy than as a complex ironic statement about the tension between a 'modern' subject matter and a 'traditional' conception of the functions of poetry. The last section of the poem (added to the earlier versions only with the definitive version of 1861) reads ambiguously. Continuous with its previous gestures of rejection and withdrawal, it can be seen as triumphally asserting the power of the individual creative will over the social and historical world, as a celebration of pure narcissism, notably in the opposition of 'Emeute' and 'volupté', the private pleasures of the writing of fantasy set against engagement with the public sphere of insurrection and violence in the streets. But the link, both phonic and thematic, between 'volupté' and 'volonté' suggests another, more critical equation, whereby the former ('volupté') is identified as the product of a mere conjuring trick of the imagination.

'Volonté' is, of course, for the most part a positively valued term in the Baudelairian lexicon, famously in the definition of artistic genius as 'l'enfance retrouvée à volonté'.[53] But, in the context of 'Paysage', its affirmative status is less secure: if 'enfantin' can be said to hover ambivalently between the senses of childlike and childish, so 'volonté' slides uneasily between the connotations of the willed and the wilful. It is as if the poem, in retreating into inwardness, knows the arbitrariness of the purely subjective act it seeks to accomplish, as if, in constructing its fictions, it also recognizes and declares them as fictions. It should also be noted that the value of 'volonté' is indissociable from the ambiguities of its grammatical representation in the future tense. 'Volonté' echoes the masterful 'Je veux' of the first line, but it is more properly connected with the future tense that holds exclusively throughout the second half of the poem, where the opening tense of desire is transformed to the more uncertain tense of as yet unfulfilled (and perhaps unfulfillable) project.

Finally, the poem seems also to signal the impossibility of reinventing simply by means of a subjective act of will the condition of childlike naïvety to which it ostensibly aspires. 'Paysage' is not, and could not be, a naïve poem; rather it is a knowing allegory of the Naïve, in the strong sense – at once psychological, cultural and historical – given to that category by Friedrich Schiller (in his great essay *On Naïve and Sentimental Poetry*[54]), which, precisely as *category*, haunts the modern mind. According to Schiller, the naïve is what belongs as spontaneous experience to the culture of the ancients, whereas the Naïve as abstract category of thought is what characterizes the nostalgia of the moderns for what has been irretrievably lost. The nineteenth century often thought it could simply recover that allegedly lost condition, and one of its literary modes for attempting that recovery was, as Schiller pointed out, the genre of the Idyll.[55] But the use of capitals here, for both the Naïve and the Idyll, already indicates the move into allegory and hence into separation from the condition that is the object of the allegory. Baudelaire's use of capitals seems to tell the same sort of story; the poem evokes not an idyll but the genre of the 'Idylle', just as it produces not the atmosphere of spring but the dead abstraction, Spring.

Sandwiched between the capitalized 'Idylle' and 'Printemps', there is the third capitalized term, 'Emeute' (uncapitalized in the 1857 version). It would indeed be plausible to read that capital letter – along with the indeterminacy of specific historical reference it entails – as the sign of a flight from the pressures of contemporary urban political reality.[56] This seems to correspond exactly to what the ideology of the panorama sought to exclude from its image of the city – division, conflict, insurrection – in order to promote the illusion of an unproblematic unified whole. But, if, as has been suggested, 'Paysage' is to be taken as evidence that in 1861 Baudelaire wished to make his peace with the Second Empire regime by presenting his work as blandly a-political or even anti-political, the juxtaposition of 'Emeute' with 'Idylle' speaks of a particular form of ironic literary self-consciousness. 'Emeute' suggests quotation, specifically from that other inaugural poem which constructs the poet's 'mansarde' as private box wilfully closing off history from its view, namely the preface-poem of Gautier's *Emaux et camées*:

> Sans prendre garde à l'ouragan
> Qui fouettait mes vitres fermées
> Moi, j'ai fait *Emaux et camées*.[57]

However, while Baudelaire's capital letter looks like an intensified reprise of Gautier's anti-political aesthetic, it could also be taken to imply a perspective of distance, marked at the very least by the knowledge of coming belatedly to what is now the cliché of rejecting history in the name of poetry; the capital may well imply that the gesture of bracketing insurrection as an abstraction that is not the business of the 'poet' had long since hardened into stereotype in nineteenth-century poetry. In the same way – though in a much longer historical perspective – the abstract reference to the 'Idylle' as literary genre also hints at a sense of the poet's relation of belatedness to the tradition of pastoral. If the reference to the 'eclogue' is caught up in a fantasy of innocence, a desire to write 'chastely' ('chastement'), the very idea of the chaste presumes its opposite, knowledge of what divides man from nature and the impossible paradox of trying to recapture innocence from the point of view of experience; the spirit of the Virgilian eclogue – itself moreover an extremely sophisticated product of cultural belatedness – is precisely what the modern cannot have other than as the artifice of 'literature'.

This way of reading these elements of Baudelaire's poem thus suggests a possible self-ironizing intention, an awareness of the infantile absurdity of the temptations to which it is subject, and from which the poet must free himself if the 'paysage' in question is to be truly a 'paysage *parisien*'. It is of course odd that the section of *Les Fleurs du Mal* most committed to demonstrating Baudelaire's aesthetic of modernity should begin with a text which seems to represent the exact opposite of those commitments, actively turning away from and negating its object, the modern city. But, as liminal poem,[58] it is perhaps to be read as a poem of farewell to a traditional conception of lyric, as a point of transition from the old to the new. 'Paysage' is not so much about the city as about a literary attitude to the city. Its relation to that attitude is ambiguous: the poem rehearses, even affirms, its terms, but at the same time equivocates them. The poem stands on the threshold of a leave-taking and of a descent, from the high view to ground level, the scene of the urban street which will be the locale and inspiration of most of the succeeding poems of the 'Tableaux parisiens' section.

The high view will in fact return in this section, interestingly in the terminal poem, 'Crépuscule du matin'. But here the intellectual and moral perspective is entirely different. The poem works from the motif of dawn over the city, but in order to invert and destroy the idiom of pastoral: Dawn arrives not as glorious rebirth (of both the new day and new life), but shivering, clad in threadbare dress ('L'aurore grelottante en robe rose et verte'[59]). This reduction of dawn connects with the poem's explicit theme of reduced forms of life in the city; dawn rises over a landscape of desolation, pain and horror, a panorama of life devoured by cold, hunger, sickness and death. The poem ends with an image of continuing life, but of life continuing against the odds. It closes not with a pastoral image but with a class image – the city as labourer, the 'vieillard laborieux' awakening from sleep, reaching for his tools to embark on another day's exhausting work. The city goes on, just. Furthermore, the representation of dawn shivering in her dress takes us back to 'Paysage' by way of an implicitly ironic statement about poetry itself and its problematic relation to the experience of the city. The metaphor of 'dress' often serves in traditional accounts of rhetoric as a figure for poetic metaphor itself (metaphor as the 'garb', often ornate and sumptuous, put by poetry on nature). Baudelaire will play with this analogy in the third poem of 'Tableaux parisiens', 'A une mendiante rousse', at first 'dressing' the beggar girl in the elaborate metaphorical clothing bequeathed by poetic tradition (mainly sixteenth-century) only to 'strip' her of all the false ornament concealing her 'maigre nudité'.[60] By the same token, the implied threadbare quality of dawn's dress in 'Crépuscule du matin' suggests that the very act of translating the city into the terms of poetic metaphor, especially the pastoral metaphor of Dawn, has itself grown threadbare. The relation between art and life has become tense, awkward.[61] We will find similiar tensions at work in Baudelaire's prose poems (which I discuss in a later chapter), and also in that other representation of the shift from night into day over Paris to which I now want to turn, Zola's magnificent depiction of Les Halles at the beginning of *Le Ventre de Paris*.

IV

About a third of the way into *Le Ventre de Paris*, the central character, Pierre Florent, after a substantial dinner followed by coffee in the local bar, looks out from the balcony of his attic apartment to enjoy the view offered by the site of the newly constructed central market, Les Halles. The view, under these conditions, is expansive, lyrical even; in contrast to the narrow streets of the city, the clearing made for the redevelopment permits access to a large stretch of sky, and – in a manner reminiscent of the more lyrical conversions of Impressionist painting – the play of light transforms the urban landscape into seascape:

> Il jouissait du grand morceau de ciel qu'il avait en face de lui, de cet immense développement des Halles qui lui donnait, au milieu des rues étranglées de Paris, la vision vague d'un bord de mer, avec les eaux mortes et ardoisées d'une baie, à peine frissonnante du roulement lointain de la houle.[62]

It is, in the terms of the novel itself, not at all a trivial condition of this view being possible that the viewer has dined well, in contrast to his famished condition in the opening pages. *Le Ventre de Paris* is about food, and the lack of food. The 'belly' is, of course, Les Halles, which, later in the novel, Florent represents to himself as 'la bête satisfaite et digérante, Paris entripaillé, cuvant sa graisse, appuyant sourdement l'empire'.[63] Perhaps only Zola could moralize fruit and vegetables into an allegory of a corrupted Second Empire Paris. But, as well as acting as a (somewhat implausible) moral symbol, food also, and more interestingly, serves in the novel as a focus for an exploration of the problematical relation between 'art' and modern life. Food here brings together both the high view on the city and the artist's view, in a manner which – because of the presence of a third term, the point of view of a hungry man – places a question mark before both.

For *Le Ventre de Paris* is also about the painting of food, and indeed the writing of food, about produce as an object of artistic attention, including that of Zola himself. The book has been described as more of a prose poem than a novel, partly because of its weakly organized plot (a feeble tale of political conspiracy), but also because of the intensity of Zola's effort to give to verbal matter something of the quality of painting. If, from his balcony, Florent sees Les Halles in the way an Impressionist painter might, this is of course because Zola writes it like that; the perceptions are dramatized as Florent's but the prose style is Zola's. It is also the style for much of Zola's way with food itself; for instance, the image of the sea makes an earlier appearance in the opening sequence, as a term in a description of market produce that is clearly designed as a bravura literary equivalent of the conventions of still life:

> Autour de lui le soleil enflammait les légumes. Il ne reconnaissait plus l'aquarelle tendre des pâleurs de l'aube. Les cœurs élargis des salades

brûlaient, la gamme du vert éclatait en vigueurs superbes, les carottes saignaient, les navets devenaient incandescents, dans ce brasier triomphal.[64]

The text here not only mimes painterly conventions, but, as its own metaphors of colour indicate, also declares that this is what it is doing: from the explicit analogy of watercolour for the displays of produce in the earlier light of dawn ('l'aquarelle tendre des pâleurs de l'aube'), the description implicitly passes, in the full light of the sun, to the equivalent of an incandescent oil painting (one critic has called this aspect of Zola's descriptive style an exercise in 'chromatic riot'[65]). However, if this is a sample of the virtuoso poetry of Zola's verbal impressionism, we should not overlook how the passage continues and concludes. Whereas the later view from the balcony is the view of a well-fed man, here Florent, surrounded by food in overwhelming abundance, is himself in an agony of hunger ('son estomac, tordu, tenaillé comme par un fer rouge'). The pictorial frame of the description thus cracks; the perception of merchandise as still life cannot be sustained – either physically by Florent or morally by Zola – on an empty stomach, and the 'sea' now enters the picture only to drown it.:

> La mer continuait à monter. . . . Aveugle, noyé, les oreilles sonnantes, l'estomac écrasé par tout ce qu'il avait vu, devinant de nouvelles et incessantes profondeurs de nourriture, il demanda grâce, et une douleur folle le prit, de mourir ainsi de faim, dans Paris gorgé, dans ce réveil fulgurant des Halles. De grosses larmes chaudes jaillirent de ses yeux.[66]

These lines are the last in what is effectively a long introductory sequence, recapitulating that opening move of so much nineteenth-century French fiction – the arrival of the hero in the capital (in this case, Florent is returning secretly from post-1848 political exile). But, as the novel brings its main character into Paris on a wagon laden with vegetables, its focus also sweeps outwards and upwards, towards the night sky and its transformation into day, and the corresponding play of artificial and natural light on that vast metallic structure, Les Halles. This too is a characteristic Zolaesque move. Zola is pre-eminently the novelist of the sweeping view over Paris, from the snow-covered landscape at the end of *Une Page d'amour* to the exultantly prophetic vision associated with sunrise over the rooftops in the late novel, *Paris*.[67] In Zola's work, the panoramic gaze or what Philippe Hamon has called the *discours du parcours*[68] becomes something of a literary signature, a structuring device which – especially when placed at both opening and close of the novel – serves to hold the teeming life the novels record in an ordered artistic representation. On the other hand, Zola – like Baudelaire – is also aware that the artistic advantages of the device are often secured at a cost. The transcendent view can easily become the comfortable view, excluding, in the interests of 'art', the messy complexities and contradictions encountered by the immanent view or the close-up focus, the experience of actually living in the city. These issues are crucially the preoccupation of the opening pages of *Le Ventre de Paris*, and above all in the passage I now wish to consider in some detail.[69]

The passage stages three points of view: that of an impersonal, anonymous narrator who supplies the bird's-eye view of the market and the *quartier*; that of Florent, half crazed by hunger; and that of the painter Claude Lantier whom Florent meets immediately upon arrival in the capital.[70] The fact that a painter occupies a position of some prominence here (and indeed throughout the whole novel) is perhaps not surprising in view of what we have already seen as the strong painterly interests of Zola's own, or, more accurately, his narrator's prose style. Yet that convergence of narrator-painter and character-painter raises exactly the problem that is also an issue for the novel. For Lantier the market and its produce are primarily aesthetic spectacle ('Claude battait des mains, à ce spectacle'), a 'sublime' profusion of forms and colours, whose sublimity indeed provides the terms of a wholly 'modern' conception of painting;[71] earlier we find Lantier looking at the piles of food and dreaming of 'des natures mortes colossales', while seeing in the similarly colossal iron structures of the market building ('ce colosse de fonte') the very emblem of aesthetic modernity: 'toute l'époque était là. . . . Puis Claude déblatera contre le romantisme; il préférait ses tas de choux aux guenilles du moyen âge. . . . On devait flanquer les vieilles canebuses par terre et faire du moderne.'

This is, of course, in part a way of looking at the world that we associate with the enterprise of Impressionism, or at least that side of the Impressionist imagination for which 'faire du moderne' often meant waxing lyrical over the artefacts of the new industrial and commercial era, and notably those great cast-iron constructions, the railway stations, the halls of the Exposition Universelle, the Eiffel Tower. The latter also captivated Zola both in his critical writings[72] and in his guise as amateur photographer; and the rooftop perspective he adopted for his photographs of the 1900 Exposition Universelle, while probably inspired by Nadar's aerial photography, also echoed the example of the Impressionist overview of the city.[73] For the most part, the panoramic view in Impressionist painting was relaxed, cheerful, celebratory; it preferred to look down on a Paris festooned with the flags of public holidays, to dwell on the symbols of prosperity and 'progress' or the signs of the elegantly leisured life. The boulevard vistas of Monet and Renoir have been appropriately described as exercises in 'boulevard pastoral',[74] all carriages, smart women, top hats and umbrellas bathed in a happy luminosity. Or the Impressionist high view exploited its physical distance from the scene on the ground to promote another kind of 'distance', a detachment whereby the city becomes but pretext for 'art' and its experiments. Pissarro, for instance, said of *Le Boulevard des Italiens, Paris, matin, effet de soleil* that his purpose was to capture 'l'impression d'ensemble', to 'faire tout ensemble, en posant des tons partout'.[75] The concern here with pure technique, with a 'modern' method for achieving harmonies in paint, appears relatively indifferent to the differentiated urban material for which the method is devised, and prompts the question whether the method also produces another, more ideological kind of 'impression d'ensemble': namely, a view of the Parisian boulevard as emptied of any of the 'dissonant' elements which might threaten the proposed painterly harmonics.

We have already seen how Zola disturbs this kind of boulevard imagery in *La Curée* (the view from the Café Riche is elevated as well as closeted). In *Le Ventre de Paris* the question of point of view is a more open and ambiguous one, by virtue of the apparent convergence of the aestheticizing attitude of the painter, Lantier, and the literary interests of Zola himself. In the 'Ebauche' for the novel Zola wrote that 'Le côté artistique est les Halles modernes, les gigantesques natures mortes des pavillons, l'éboulement de nourriture qui se fait chaque matin au milieu de Paris.'[76] The conception of les Halles as 'gigantic still life' thus belongs as much to Zola himself as to his painter, and, in the opening descriptions, that alignment is reflected not only in the style of the description but also in the partial blurring of the point of view from which it is conducted. At one level, the description seems to be Lantier's, as he steps on to the bench ('Mais Claude était monté debout sur le banc, d'enthousiasme'). But what is then described far exceeds what could plausibly be seen from Lantier's position. The sweeping gaze – from the 'traditional' stone of the Saint-Eustache church to the 'modern' metal of the market pavilions,[77] along the rue des Halles out to the crossroads at either end, into the rue Rambuteau, and finally up into some unidentified position in the sky – cannot be exclusively Lantier's. A narrator's transcendent perspective has been smuggled into the character's; the view from the bench has become a kind of surrogate panorama. Again, 'C'était une mer' are arguably Lantier's words in the mode of *style indirect libre*, while the extraordinary proliferation of images in the rest of the passage could be relativized to Lantier's 'enthousiasme', as could the continuation of painterly terms ('aquarelle', 'gamme'). But, in its detail and intensity, most, if not all, of this is of course Zola himself, in a *tour de force* of synaesthetic description, a shimmering *bariolage* that is the literary equivalent of the colourful 'bariolage' to which the text itself refers. It makes literal and specific the aesthetic notion of food which earlier Lantier represents in the cliché of a feast for the eyes ('Puis je déjeune ici, par les yeux au moins').

This, however, is said to Florent, who 'l'écoutait, le ventre serré'; and whereas, in these opening pages, for Lantier (and Zola) the image of the 'sea' conjures up an extended tone-poem, with Florent it works only to articulate the sense of a mind and body drowning in a flux of sensation around an unsatisfied need ('il ne fut plus qu'une chose battue, roulée, au fond de la mer montante'). It has been claimed that the Florent–Lantier relation exemplifies a technique of perspectival doubling, commonly employed in the *Rougon-Macquart* to accentuate the aesthetic force of the Zolaesque 'tableau'.[78] This, however, loses not only the contrast between the excited gaze of the artist and the delirious view of the famished man, but also its value as one of the key opening moves of the novel. Indeed the contrast can be said to carry implications of a more general sort for the later nineteenth-century way, both Naturalist and Impressionist, with contemporary Paris. In theory, the Naturalist project aimed at an exhaustive cataloguing and mapping of the city, mastering the material by means of its complete transcription. The *discours du parcours* serves that end by supplying a point from which the material can be observed and ordered free of the threat of being submerged ('drowned') by its proliferating abundance. The panoramic view thus goes hand in hand with the aestheticizing perspective; both are intent on making wholes out of parts, stitching fragments, 'slices' and 'tableaux' into coherent patterns.

However, Florent's experience (and the weight Zola accords it) is there to undercut that project. His view is less the exhaustive than the exhausted one, burning out rather than adding up; against the heat of the sun and the blaze of colours ('ce brasier triomphal'), there is the hunger-induced burning inside his body ('un feu ardent le brûlait de nouveau au creux de la poitrine'). There is also the other sense of burn-out conveyed by the 'thermodynamic' image with which, in the passage under consideration, Zola renders Florent's perception of Les Halles itself: as he watches the iron buildings emerge from the shadows of the night into the sunlight, he is struck by their machine-like quality, the resemblance to a monstrous boiler or steam-engine ('elles apparurent comme une machine moderne, hors de toute mesure, quelque machine à vapeur, quelque chaudière destinée à la digestion d'un peuple'). This retrieves the 'chaudière' image already deployed by Balzac to figure the idea of a self-consuming urban society, and here, of course, is applied literally to the means and processes of 'consumption' ('la digestion d'un peuple'[79]).

The image, however, also has another context of reference and association, to which Michel Serres has drawn our attention in his remarkable study of Zola, *Feux et signaux de brume*:[80] the steam-engine as emblem of a tendency in Zola's own writing to terminal seize-up. The energy of its descriptive efforts carries with it a high quotient of entropy; the more detailed (and hence in principle the more exhaustive) the descriptions become, the more difficult they are to visualize or to hold within a stable visual frame, and the more we rely less on the information provided than on generalized and preconceived notions of 'Paris' to find our way in the text.

Matter in Zola's world, and above all in Zola's city, is always at risk of exceeding the effort of the writing to subjugate it; translated into the terms of the thermodynamic analogy, the text is a kind of literary 'machine à vapeur' for generating signs but whose consequence more often than not is a certain vaporization of the sign, a loss of focus, a blur akin to the 'brume' which so often hangs over Zola's Paris. Clarity of representation, otherwise so fundamental to Zola's undertaking (for reasons partly explored in the previous chapter), is also problematic; and often we are left not with the sense of an achieved descriptive plenitude but with the sense of an emptiness, a blank at the heart of the city.

This effect may also be related to another set of images, in a logic of association leading from steam back to water. In the opening pages, water imagery includes not only the sea but also the river and the rain: 'ce fleuve de verdure qui semblait couler dans l'encaissement de la chaussée, pareil à la débâcle des pluies d'automne'. It frequently rains in the Naturalist novel, as it does in the Impressionist picture, but, whereas in the latter this is for the most part a reflection of its own aesthetic play with reflections, in the former it is just as often the occasion of a real 'débâcle' of representation, the evocation of an urban scene whose 'identity' has been blanked out by grey skies and muddy pools.[81] Yet this contrast between novel and painting is too neat, and, if the city seen from Florent's point of view implies Zola's partial disavowal of that side of the Impressionist imagination embodied in Lantier, we must not forget some of its more questioning and even disturbing performances. For example, Morisot's spacious views of Paris from the Trocadéro, while they appear to rhyme indulgently fashionable modernity and historic monumentality, also speak of exclusion: the elegantly dressed woman in *Vue de Paris du Trocadéro* (plate 7) who, with the pretty girl, looks out at the city is also excluded from it, from a history and an arena made essentially by men for men.[82] Manet will, of course, accentuate that sense of exclusion in his own *Balcon*, which has Berthe Morisot herself staring out with a strange intensity of self-abstraction on a street scene absent from the picture.

Then there are the ironies of Manet's disconcerting vistas, most famously the *Exposition Universelle de 1867* (plate 8) which shows us Paris viewed by a group of strollers from the heights of the Buttes-Chaumont. The painting is comedy, pantomime, a parodic echo of the 'totalizing' endeavour. Centred on an absence of significant relation, a disconnectedness between viewers and city and between the viewers themselves, this is Paris seen panoramically, but without commitment to the presuppositions and aspirations of the panoramic view; it is the city seen non-committally, with indifference, as a place which doesn't add up, which doesn't *mean* much any more.[83] There is also Manet's provocative funeral picture, *L'Enterrement* (plate 9), less a panoramic view than a mockery of the panoramic view and its cultural pretensions: at the foot of the Buttes Mouffetard, and against a background taking in the Observatoire, the Val-de-Grâce church, the Pantheon, the steeple of Saint-Etienne-du-Mont and the Tour Clovis, we see, under a stormy sky, a handful of people accompanying a funeral hearse; some say it is Baudelaire's, and it has all the casual inconsequentiality of a pauper's burial, contrasting ironically with the monumentality of the Pantheon, at once resting-place of the consecrated thinkers and poets of France and (as we have seen) privileged point from which the city can be represented as a unity. Manet's image is the exact reverse of what Barrès will later do with Hugo's burial at the Pantheon and the corresponding view from the Montagne Sainte-Geneviève; if it is Baudelaire here, the great poet of the modern city goes to his grave unnoticed, and, of course, when Banville delivered his graveside oration, it rained.

But perhaps most compelling of all is that extraordinary cancellation of the panoramic view, Van Gogh's *La Terrasse du Moulin le Blute-fin à Montmartre* (1886) (plate 10). What we might call *montmartrisme* was in full swing by the mid-1880s, producing the stereotypes destined for the countless postcards and chocolate boxes of the twentieth century. Van Gogh's picture gives us five figures, what appears to be an old woman seated and two couples, one of which is sitting on a tall wooden structure. All have their backs turned to the viewer; they are looking out over the city. But what they are looking at is a blank; the city has disappeared and the content of the panorama been reduced to a vacant *grisaille*. Once again, the analogy with the sea presents itself, and art criticism has been quick to praise the lyrically 'marine'-like quality of the painting.[84] But it is just as likely to be the urban landscape washed out by rain. Certainly, this is no equivalent to a leisurely stroll along the sea-front promenade. It is desolate smudges of people forlornly staring out into space emptied of meaning, memory, history, any sense of 'belonging'; they have about them the air of homeless people. The cultural life of the panorama-image thus ends here in a visual space that is at once vast expanse and dead-end, its fictions of a common belonging within the unified 'family' of the nation in ruins. Whoever the city and its views belong to, it is clearly not to these people.

4

Paris Underground

I

In 1879 Manet intriguingly submitted a proposal to do five paintings of 'la vie publique et commerciale de nos jours' as mural decorations for the new Hôtel de Ville (reconstructed after its destruction during the Commune).[1] The list of subjects suggests a continuity in the forms of public urban imagination from the Second Empire to the Third Republic; it reads like a roll-call of Haussmannian topoi, not only as a recapitulation of the elements of the baron's programme of urban renewal, but also as a listing of the very symbols of the latter's particular conception of urban 'modernity': 'J'aurais Paris-Halles, Paris-Chemins de fer, Paris-Ponts, Paris-Souterrain, Paris-Courses et Jardins.'[2] For a variety of political and administrative reasons the proposal came to nothing (the murals were not decided until after Manet's death). But, in respect of the majority of the suggested subjects, we can make some reasonable guesses as to what the murals might have looked like from the example of some of Manet's other paintings (notably, of the railways, the bridges, the racetracks and the gardens). Such comparisons would of course imply a characteristically ambiguous contribution to the efforts of the refurbished Hôtel de Ville to celebrate the modern city; if, as Antonin Proust records, Manet's purpose was 'peindre la vie de Paris dans la maison de Paris',[3] it is nevertheless unlikely that he would have commemorated the municipal achievements of the later nineteenth century without his particular brand of deadpan equivocation. What guesses, however, might we make in respect of the apparent odd man out, the true joker in the pack – 'Paris-Souterrain'? What did Manet propose to paint, why would he have seen it as an appropriate inclusion in a project of this sort, and how might he have painted it?

If all we can do is guess at the painterly answers Manet might have given to these questions, we can nevertheless do so from the rich variety of sources available to us as testimony to a continuing obsession with Paris underground, as both reality and metaphor, throughout the whole of the nineteenth century in the minds of administrators, politicians, engineers, writers, artists and photographers.[4] It was an obsession articulated across essentially three, often interrelated, areas of practical life – the cemeteries, the sewers and, in the later part of the century, the underground railway; and it typically took one of two forms, either as an anxiety-laden sense of subterranean forces threatening the health, both physical and moral, of the overground city, or as a passionate belief in the power of the scientific and technological imagination to master the city's problems. The 'problems' were largely those of managing bodies. From the point of view of the nineteenth-century urban 'planner', human bodies, both alive and dead, must have been minimally a nuisance, and more often a nightmare. Mass migration into the city (in the first half of the century the population of Paris doubled) produced what is bureaucratically and euphemistically re-ferred to as 'overcrowding', and – in the far less muted terms of Louis Chevalier's magisterial account – a corresponding increase in the symptoms of urban 'disorder' (malnutrition, cholera epidemics, rising infant mortality, murder, mental breakdown, suicide, etc.). Excess bodies meant housing shortages, traffic congestion and the creation of more rubbish than the circuits of evacuation could handle. In addition they continued to be a nuisance even when they were dead: if the systems were inadequate to transporting bodies about the city and removing waste from the city, arrangements also proved unsatisfactory when the body itself became waste (what, in connection with Dickens and Victorian London, Catherine Gallagher has aptly called 'garbage-bodies'[5]); the cemeteries, like the cess-pools and the sewers, were becoming clogged to the point of constituting a menace to public health.

But, as well as providing the phenomenologist of nineteenth-century urban life with the terms of an obsession (from the bureaucratic to the poetic), the cemetery, the sewer and the underground railway also furnish the historian with a framing device for a fable of beginnings and endings. For the historian with an eye to the importance of the symbolic and a flexible view of the matter of dates, 'nineteenth-century' Paris could be said neither to begin nor to end in the nineteenth century. By this I do not simply have in mind those currently influential theoretical notions which make of the very categories of beginnings and endings in history arbitrary and ultimately unlocatable affairs, but a more precise alternative history that takes us not only out of the nineteenth century but also out of the city or, more exactly, beneath it. In 1782 a collection of illustrious scientists from the Académie Royale des Sciences and the Société Royale de Médecine gathered around the cesspool of the Hôtel de la Grenade to experiment with a new antimephitic substance, whose inventor had claimed that it was capable of containing and destroying miasmic emanations. Unhappily one of the cleaners fell into the cesspool. M. Verville, an inspector of ventilators, tried to save the asphyxiated victim by means of artificial respiration, but immediately recoiled, crying 'je suis mort!', prematurely but not implausibly (Verville recovered from inhaling the breath of the stricken worker, but the worker himself was mortally afflicted).[6]

To this emblematic anecdote – figuring, among other things, the Canute-like stance of the modern 'expert' before the menace of urban filth – we may add a second and equally suggestive anecdote: according to Philippe Muray, the nineteenth century (or that more abstract entity Muray calls *dixneuvièmeté*) in fact begins in 1786 with the removal, on grounds of public health, of the human remains chaotically buried in the cemetery of the Innocents church to the more salubrious and better-organized resting place of the catacombs.[7] On this view, then, the history of the nineteenth century begins underground, as a story of the depositing and transporting of skeletons. The move was not only a victory for the hygiene reformers (who had long deplored as a municipal scandal the allegedly life-threatening emanations of the Innocents cemetery), but, at a deeper cultural level, the consolidation of a new secular attitude towards the dead. Death was no longer, as in Christian doctrine, a mere matter of passage from one's frail and contingent mortal form to the condition of immortality. The body in death was now less a trifle to be discarded than a problem to be dealt with, essentially a problem of waste, above all in a city increasingly overcrowded with the living; by mid-century, the rationalized cemetery seemed a natural component of the larger dream of the rationalized city. Haussmann, for example, not only completed the systematic removal of remains from the more overburdened cemeteries to the catacombs; he also sponsored a scheme for a network of suburban cemeteries that were to be linked by train to a main terminal at the Montparnasse cemetery. This ultra-technocratic scheme proved, however, to be one of the most controversial and fiercely resisted of Haussmann's proposed 'reforms' (especially that feature of it which recommended an end to all further burials in the Père-Lachaise cemetery). The living wanted their dead to remain within the confines of the city ('il ne saurait y avoir . . . de cités sans cimetières'[8]); the dead represented memory, and their presence in the city was seen as an indispensable token of the continuity of past and present in an urban environment that seemed otherwise intent on obliterating a great deal of the visible traces of its history. The 'cult of the dead' also became, of course, a potent theme in the discourse of 'national identity', in a complex political and ideological history from the construction of the Pantheon to the emergence of Action Française.

But if rationalizing the cemetery system touched a sensitive nerve, both private and political, excess bones nevertheless had to be dealt with, and the catacombs seemed the answer. Equally, the disposal of other kinds of waste, in particular via the city's antiquated and inefficient sewer system, was a constant source of anxiety and reformist zeal. Under Napoleon I the sewers were systematically mapped (mainly by the intrepid inspector, Bruneseau, commemorated by Hugo in *Les Misérables*); during the Restoration they were cleaned (partly as a result of the reports of the great Parent-Duchâtelet[9]); under Louis-Philippe the size of the network was doubled (largely as a consequence of the terrible cholera epidemic of 1832); during the Second Empire the basic system itself was transformed, in terms of both outlets and collection points, under the supervision of Haussmann's engineer, Belgrand (who also wrote a massive five-volume account of his endeavours[10]); and during the Third Republic the network virtually doubled in size yet again. Haussmann's enthusiasms in this particular sphere were not only practical but also rhetorical: he was fond of alluding to the Cloaca Maxima as one of the great achievements of urban planning in ancient Rome, and indeed often used the expression to dignify the description of his own projects for sewer reform in memoranda to the Emperor.[11] He nevertheless stopped short of recommending a system that would dispose of human excrement (the *tout-à-l'égout* was not agreed until 1894); powerful commercial interests were in play here: the value of excrement as commodity was in direct proportion to its solidity, and Haussmann declared himself to be of the non-dilution party.

Renovation of the sewers was in the main a practical response to a practical problem: when in 1848 the Fourierist social critic, Victor Considérant, wrote that 'Paris, c'est un immense atelier de putréfaction',[12] this was no mere metaphorical flourish, but a reflection of real material conditions, especially though by no means exclusively in the poorer districts of the city. But the programme of renovation was also in part a response to a collective cultural phantasm, the widely shared fear of putrid substance and pestilential vapours streaming into a defenceless city through cracks in the pavements, fissures in the walls and even the porosity of, mortar.[13] Perhaps most intolerable of all, from the point of view of everyday urban sensibility particularly in the first half of the century, was the stench. At the end of the eighteenth century Pierre Chauvet wrote in his *Essai sur la propreté de Paris* that Paris, 'centre des sciences, des arts, des modes et du goût', was also 'le centre de la puanteur'.[14] That complaint became a commonplace of nineteenth-century commentary, especially when the north-east wind got up. For well into the nineteenth century, the epicentre of Parisian stench remained Montfaucon, the district of the city's abattoirs as well as the site of the huge cesspools into which went not only the carcasses from the knackers' yards, but also vast amounts of the fecal matter of Paris. When the wind blew from the north-east, the smell, according to numerous contemporary witnesses, was insupportable; and, in one of those curious yet characteristic nineteenth-century mixtures of scientific and popular belief, it was widely held to be a carrier of disease and death (at the level of popular belief, the fact that Montfaucon had also been a site of public hangings reinforced the web of associaton). Parent-Duchâtelet's description of Montfaucon in his survey of 1820 is unforgettably graphic, and effectively raised the inspector's report to the status of a literary genre:

> Qu'on se figure ce que peut produire la décomposition putride de monceaux de chairs et d'intestins abandonnés pendant des semaines ou des mois, en plein air et à l'ardeur du soleil, à la putréfaction spontanée; qu'on y ajoute, par la pensée, la nature des gaz qui peuvent sortir des monceaux de carcasses qui restent garnies de beaucoup de parties molles; qu'on y joigne les émanations que fournit un terrain qui pendant des années, a été imbibé de sang et de liquides animaux; celles qui proviennent de ce sang lui-même qui, dans l'un et dans l'autre clos, reste sur le pavé sans pouvoir s'écouler; celle enfin des ruisseaux des boyauderies et des séchoirs du voisinage; que l'on multiplie autant que l'on voudra les degrés de puanteur, en la comparant à celle que chacun de nous a été à même de sentir, en passant auprès des cadavres d'animaux en décomposition qu'il aura pu rencontrer, et l'on n'aura qu'une faible idée de l'odeur véritablement repoussante qui sort de ce cloaque, le plus infect qu'il soit possible d'imaginer.[15]

But even under more tolerable olfactory conditions the city's smells were a major concern to all kinds of imagination and strands of opinion. Tracking and classifying odours became a serious preoccupation not only for natural scientists but also for social observers from Louis Mercier to Louis Veuillot.[16] Indeed it would be no exaggeration to say – especially in the light of the recent researches of Alain Corbin – that a whole new dimension appéars to have been added in the nineteenth century to the phenomenology of urban sensibility, to the body's way of monitoring its sensory world. At certain moments at least, the primacy traditionally granted to the sense of sight was dislodged from its supremacy by the sense of smell; Parisians became, if not active and persistent sniffers (this was generally left to a small band of specialist fanatics), at least supporters of the view that the sense of smell was an important source of practical urban knowledge. It was not, as Corbin notes, that nineteenth-century Paris had actually become more foul-smelling than before, but rather that thresholds of tolerance had been lowered, as both condition and effect of the new concerns with public health. Once again scientific belief (pre-Pasteurian) and popular superstition collaborated to produce that particular, and powerful, branch of the movement for hygiene reform whose central aim was the comprehensive 'deodorization' of the urban environment. The strictly medical inspiration of this strategy was soon overlaid by a rich and complex fantasmatic layer: deodorization was to be applied to all areas of public and private space, to streets, prisons, hospitals, kitchens, bedrooms, gardens and bodies (especially the bodies of the urban poor and working classes).[17]

Thus emerged the fantasy of the odourless city, ideally sanitized to a zero degree of olfactory disturbance. It was the extreme point of the practical project of cleaning up the city transposed to the realm of the imaginary, to what we might call – untranslatably – an *imaginaire du Propre*, where *propre* is to be understood as signifying not only 'clean' but also 'proper' in the sense of what, at least from the point of view of the propertied classes, properly belongs to the city as constitutive of its *identity*.[18] Cleanliness carried the promise of uniform identity mastering the threat of alien difference, of a homogenized environment keeping dirt – and then by extension 'dirty' people, and then, by further and even more alarming extension, 'polluted' people – as potentially disruptive 'matter out of place' firmly in place, out of sight and smell. In the terms of this fantasy, the city acquired and retained identity in direct proportion to its success in ridding itself of 'impure' matter, on a spectrum from excrement to revolutionaries, perverts and foreigners.

In short, notions of cleanliness were not only practical but moral in their reference, and were directly related to the business of policing the city. Bruneseau, Napoleon's intrepid inspector of sewers, had long before asserted the link between physical and moral 'health' that was at the ideological heart of the movement for public hygiene: 'La salubrité du corps', wrote Bruneseau, 'est l'image de la propreté de l'âme. . . . La propreté d'une ville est l'image de la pureté des mœurs de ses habitants.'[19] In this convergence of preoccupations, beliefs and fears, Paris underground thus appears as not just one topos among many others; it is a key point of articulation for changing conceptions of the city as a whole, precisely for the sense of its 'identity' or, in the terms of Didier Gille's brilliant account of these matters, 'what was at the time presented as a form of medicine has in fact produced the modern meaning of the city.'[20]

II

The dream, even the reality, of the sanitized and deodorized city assumed some strange shapes in the nineteenth century. There is, for example, its oddly paradoxical incarnation in the sewers of Nadar's autobiography *Quand j'étais photographe*, which described them not only as odourless but even as sweet-smelling; the latter, to be sure, was but the contingent result of an underground itinerary that happened, amazingly, to pass beneath a perfumery, but the former was the outcome of a system and its technology (the absence of odour was 'grâce à la ventilation parfaite' governing 'cet exutoire des infinies putridités d'une grande capitale').[21] More important of course are the photographs themselves. In 1861 Nadar, having previously taken aerial photographs of the city (from an air balloon), took his camera underground, into the catacombs and the sewers. His primary purpose appears to have been technical – to explore the possibilities of the patent he had recently taken out for the development of photography by means of electric light – and a great deal of his own account of the venture is concerned with the challenges and difficulties of the adverse conditions he encountered. But beyond their significance for the technical history of photography or as a passive record of visual 'referents', what kind of 'statement' do they make when seen as items in the archive of a kind of photographic urban ethnologist? What do they tell us about the anthropological *imaginaire* of the underground city?

The catacombs were opened to the public in 1809 and rapidly became a popular tourist attraction. They even gave rise to a certain 'literature': a special book was placed in the entrance for those inspired to write elevated verse reflections on Life and Death, suitably dosed with Gothic frisson.[22] During the July Monarchy the Préfet de Police, Rambuteau, took a different view and prohibited visiting the catacombs, on the grounds that 'il y aurait une sorte de provocation d'exposer ainsi aux regards les amas d'ossements, . . . d'offrir à la curiosité publique un pareil spectacle, peu digne d'un peuple civilisé.'[23] Since in his memoir Nadar himself refers wryly, if obliquely, to this prohibition, we might have expected a mildly ironic counter-provocation to the official view of what was properly a matter for public exhibit. And indeed, in this strange encounter of camera, underground and bodily remains, there seems to be much play with the category of 'spectacle'. If, as Roland Barthes has claimed, there is a natural relation between the photographic image and death,[24] in Nadar's underground work that relation is thoroughly literalized in a double gesture enacting both death as spectacle and the death of spectacle. What we look at are heaps of bones, some chaotically heaped, others carefully 'patterned', but in both cases utterly random, gratuitous and absurd, like the redundant and grotesquely self-referring sign of the skull and crossbones built into the middle of the heaps (plate 11). The irony also appears to engage the relation of viewing itself: as we, with Nadar and his camera, look, the skulls and empty sockets 'look' back, as if in some macabre parody of our and the photographer's gaze. Then there is the comedy produced as a (doubtless unintended) effect of the technology: Nadar's lighting gives to some of the skulls a bizarrely polished look. The effect is a comic version of what Barthes called the photographic *punctum* (the element which takes us by surprise, escapes the predictable and instantly readable culture of the *studium*): the polished quality of the skulls could be said to send us, by unexpected association, back into the world of the *grand magasin*, as if the skulls were so many shining spectral commodities placed on display.

This is not the only tacit reminder of the overground city in Nadar's underground. The tiered rows and heaps of skeletal remains (in *Façade de tibias avec ornementation horizontale de crânes* (plate 12)) resemble nothing so much as a ghoulish replica of faces seen during a night at the opera or the theatre. These theatrical connotations are, moreover, strengthened by Nadar's use of dummies in many of the pictures to represent underground workers (no actual worker could be used given the impossibility of standing still for the required exposure time of eighteen minutes). In theory, the use of dummies was designed to enhance the 'natural' realism of the photograph, to generate a certain 'reality effect'. In fact, the dummies confer on the image a further atmosphere of theatrical unreality, and, as themselves ghostly presences, fake living beings engaged in stacking the fragmented remains of the dead, evoke one of the perspectives described by Nadar himself for the interpretation of the photographs – as a modern version of the traditional *vanitas*. Death, the great equalizer, writes Nadar, abolishes all distinctions of history, class, reputation, rich and poor, famous and anonymous: 'Quelle vanité humaine, quel orgueil pourrait tenir devant cette inéluctable promiscuité finale de nos poussières.'[25] Indeed, beyond the skulls and bones themselves, there are several possible allusions to the conventions of the *vanitas* painting: the pokerfaced formality of the title, *Façade de tibias avec ornementation horizontale de crânes*, recalls, in a quite obviously grotesque echo, the seventeenth-century *nature morte*; the bottle in the famous picture of Nadar himself (plate 13), while 'referentially' there as the container of the photographer's chemical materials, connotatively suggests the ubiquitous wine bottle of the still-life repertoire.

Yet, both textually and visually, the rhetoric of the *vanitas* allusion, for all its jokiness, does little more than repeat a generalized romantic commonplace. Moreover, whatever their deliberate or unintended ironies, Nadar's photographs finally present a view of Paris underground that must have been largely congenial to the official view. The principal connotation of the visual denotations is one of efficient mastery of the problem of disposing of bodily detritus. If the skeletal fragments sometimes look as if they are threatening to overwhelm the capacity of the 'system' to organize them, the dominant image is of rows of skulls and bones arranged in neat and tidy patterns; although individual 'identity' has been obliterated in the random anonymity of the pile, the pile itself has the identity of ordered space, clean, coherent and cost-efficient, testimony to the victory of technological modernity over a proliferating disorder.[26]

This implication of order triumphant is even stronger in the photographs of the modernized sewers (plate 14). The autobiographical memoir describes the sewers as 'un enchevêtrement difforme de sentines et boyaux à défier l'imagination de Piranèse'.[27] But, for all the ingenuity of Nadar's *chiaroscuro* effects, the photographs themselves in fact have virtually nothing of the wildness of Piranesian urban phantasmagoria. There is very little here to disturb us; as Shelley Rice has nicely put it, Nadar's sewers come to us 'laundered',[28] in the imagery of organized dynamic space geared to ceaseless and energetic circulation. Above all there is the visual emphasis on the machine, the aestheticizing of the power of technology (it is well known that for Nadar 'progress' and technology were indissociable). Indeed one might say that the true significance of Nadar's photographs is that they record, and celebrate, the encounter of two technologies, the progress of his own demonstrated in its capacity to record progress in the other. It is no accident that the photographs were offered to the Hôtel de Ville in homage to Haussmann's engineer, Belgrand. The light Nadar brought into the sewers and the catacombs was itself continuous with the project of bringing the 'light of Reason',[29] in the particular form of the new technologico-administrative rationality, into the darker places of the city (for someone of psychoanalytical persuasions the imagery of these dark cave-like places, not only illuminated by electric light but also 'penetrated' by pipes, pistons and machines driven by dummy male workers, might plausibly suggest other kinds of fantasmatic investment). As such, Nadar's undertaking may perhaps also be aligned with the operations of a more general cultural logic of urban domestication and *surveillance*, in relation to which what matters is less the content of the photographs than the act of photographing itself; though one view of the police (Rambuteau's) was that what comes from 'below' properly belongs out of sight, the other, and more influential, was that such things are better monitored, recorded and patrolled. The 'eye' of the camera, while mocking notions of identity and identification as it photographs the anonymous remains of the dead in the catacombs, will of course eventually become, along with the technique of fingerprinting, a way of keeping track of the living.

Here, then, we find the motif of Paris 'underground' and the related idea of keeping the city 'clean' shifting into a more strictly metaphorical, and ideological, gear, notably in their metaphorical extension to the representation of certain sections of the urban population: criminals, prostitutes, beggars and the urban poor generally; or, to be more precise, its application to that perceived (and feared) mingling of 'classes laborieuses' and 'classes dangereuses' registered in the collective image of the *bas-fonds*, the lower depths of society. Some of this metaphorical extension was doubtless metonymically motivated, from the memory or experience of the literal uses to which various underground sites in Paris had often been put. The quarries and the catacombs had long been associated with the activities of smugglers, thieves, witches, freemasons, conspirators and secret societies.[30] Montfaucon, we saw, entered the mythology of the nineteenth-century urban imagination in part by virtue of its grim association of cesspool and gibbet, waste and crime; while the historical association of Paris underground with sedition and insurrection runs at least from Babeuf's meetings in the cellars of the Pantheon to the group of insurgents in 1848 who hid themselves in the Montmartre quarry (massacred and left there by Cavaignac's troops) and the anarchist plotters in the cellars of Sacré-Cœur described by Zola in *Paris* (Elie Berthelet's popular novel of the 1850s, *Les Catacombes de Paris*, which went through twenty editions in ten years, based its plot on a secret society descended from the Knights Templar and intent on blowing up the whole city[31]).

But, whatever their origins in social and physical fact, these metaphorical adaptations developed a complex and unstable life of their own in descriptions and representations of the Parisian lower classes. The instability in question was essentially ideological, as the metaphors travelled across reactionary, reformist and even revolutionary accounts alike. I do not mean by this that the common presence of a metaphor and its variants in the relevant accounts obliterates their ideological differences, in the same way that it does not follow that real social differences disappeared in nineteenth-century Paris because of the progressive attenuation of the external marks of difference. Nevertheless the behaviour of the underground metaphor and its associated terms in these otherwise widely divergent contexts recapitulates over and over again a particular move: the move which insists on *separation*, not just – as in traditional emphases – the separation of polite and plebeian society, but a structure of separation within the 'lower' orders themselves. The world of the criminal, the prostitute, the ragpicker, the absolutely destitute was to be repeatedly represented as, in the words of Lachaise summarizing the *bas-fonds* in 1822, 'une cité particulièrement distincte des autres quartiers de la capitale',[32] and above all apart from the respectable, industrious and law-abiding sections of the working class (what Frégier called 'la masse des ouvriers honnêtes et laborieux'[33]). To some extent this simply reflected actual topographical and social arrangements in the city: the concentration of the *bas-fonds* in certain of the faubourgs and *barrières* (some districts both in the heart of the city and on its outskirts were effectively no-go areas). But it also nourished, and was in turn nourished by, an ideological desire to enforce, in both actuality and representation, a system of distinctions and separations that would minimize contact between the (respectable) labouring classes and the dangerous classes. While there was a counter-discourse emphasizing contact and mixing in terms of class solidarity, mixture and coagulation were predominantly linked to a fear of 'diseased' matter surging up out of the depths to infect the healthy parts of the social body. They were also linked, as Chevalier shows, to a worry that violent crime, if not cordoned off as social reality and sociological category, would and did fuel popular violence, riot and revolution (Frégier thought it would be best to place 'sous la rubrique des classes dangereuses des individus qui fomentent les séditions populaires'[34]).

This is of course a move that we customarily attribute to the workings and interests of the conservative political imagination. Thus Thiers, in a famous speech to the Assembly in 1850, reproduced the distinction between the 'people' and the 'multitude' in terms literally designed to refuse *droit de cité* to the latter ('C'est la multitude, ce n'est pas le peuple que nous voulons exclure', where 'multitude' is specified as 'cette multitude de vagabonds dont on ne peut savoir ni le domicile, ni la famille'[35]). This was indeed a programme for keeping the city 'clean', and from there it was but a step to classifying whole sections of the urban population as subhuman, inhabiting an 'underground' world beyond the reach, either educative or repressive, of 'civilization'. But, if the literalization of metaphor along these lines into actual policy became the reflex of a jittery or hysterical post-1848 ruling class, the language of descriptive and symbolic exclusion was by no means monopolized by the party of reaction, either before or after 1848. Consider, for example, the figure of the ragpicker, perhaps the emblematic figure of Parisian pauperism throughout the century. 'The ragpicker fascinated his epoch,' wrote Benjamin (he has also come to 'fascinate' ours, though less as a figure of poverty than as a figure of speech, metaphor for a postmodernist conception of art as rag-bag).[36] There are the images with which we are now generally familiar – the image of intoxicated rebelliousness in Baudelaire's 'Le Vin des chiffonniers' (along with the extraordinary description of the ragpicker in the *Paradis artificiels*[37]), of insolent detachment in Manet's *Le Chiffonnier*, or of mute witness to appalling urban callousness in Lautréamont's *Les Chants de Maldoror*. Less well known, but I think the most haunting, is Seurat's drawing, *Le Chiffonnier* (plate 15). It works as an image of pure dispossession by virtue of the systematic dispossession of the image itself, the removal of all familiar recognition-points, in particular those supplied by the idiom of the *physiologie* and its visual equivalents (during the July Monarchy the ragpicker regularly appeared as a colourful 'type' in journalistic illustration, as, for example, in the work of Traviès[38]). Seurat's image is of a social and physical landscape reduced to cursory black marks, and of a figure so shadowy and insubstantial that its readability *as* figure in the landscape has become problematical.

Against these images there are, however, many others that tell a less obviously provocative or poignant story. The literature of picturesque (in a tradition going back to Mercier[39]) survived well into the century, and along with it the emphasis on the ragpicker as embodying a form of grimy yet amiable bohemianism. Victor Fournel, for example, described the ragpickers as inhabiting a kind of aristocratic marginality. But he also described them as 'savages' encamped within the city ('en campement dans Paris') and

1. Camille Pissarro, *Boulevard Montmartre, effet de nuit*, 1897, oil on canvas, 53.3 × 64.8 cm. (Reproduced by Courtesy of the Trustees, The National Gallery, London)

2. Edouard Manet, *La rue Mosnier. Les Paveurs*, 1878. (Private Collection, Chicago; photo: Ets Bulloz, Paris)

3. Mary Stevenson Cassatt,
At the Opera, 1879, oil on
canvas, 80 × 64.8 cm. (The
Hayden Collection, Courtesy,
Museum of Fine Arts, Boston)

4. Gustave Caillebotte, *Jeune
homme à sa fenêtre*, 1875. (Private
Collection) (Author)

5. Claude Monet, *Boulevard des Capucines*, 1873. (Pushkin Museum, Moscow) (Author)

6. Victor Navlet, *Vue générale de Paris*. (Musée d'Orsay. © photo: Réunion des Musées Nationaux)

7. Berthe Morisot, *Vue de Paris des hauteurs du Trocadéro*, 1872–3, oil on canvas, 45 × 81 cm. (Collection of the Santa Barbara Museum of Art, Gift of Mrs. Hugh N. Kirkland)

8. Edouard Manet, *L'Exposition universelle de 1867*, 1867, oil on canvas, 108 × 196.5 cm. (© Nasjonalgalleriet, Oslo; photo: Jacques Lathion)

9. Edouard Manet, *L'Enterrement*, 72.7 × 90.5 cm. (The Metropolitan Museum of Art, Wolfe Fund, 1909 [10.36].)

10. Vincent Van Gogh, *La Terrasse du Moulin le Blute-fin à Montmartre*, c.1886, oil on canvas mounted on pressboard, 43.6 × 33 cm. (Helen Birch Bartlett Memorial Collection, 1926.202. Photograph © 1991, The Art Institute of Chicago)

11. Félix Nadar, *Façade avec ornementation de tibias et de crânes*. Reproduced by kind permission of Caisse Nationale des Monuments Historiques et des Sites © ADAGP, Paris and DACS, London 1992)

12. Félix Nadar, *Façade de tibias avec ornementation horizontale de crânes.* Reproduced by kind permission of Caisse Nationale des Monuments Historiques et des Sites © ADAGP, Paris and DACS, London 1992)

13. Félix Nadar, *Félix Nadar: autoportrait dans les Catacombes.* (Reproduced by kind permission of Caisse Nationale des Monuments Historiques et des Sites © ADAGP, Paris and DACS, London 1992)

14. Félix Nadar, *Egout sous la rue de Chateaudun.* (Reproduced by kind permission of Caisse Nationale des Monuments Historiques et des Sites © ADAGP, Paris and DACS, London 1992)

15. Georges Seurat, *Le Chiffonnier.* (Private Collection) (Author)

16. Adolphe Leleux, *Le Mot de passe*. (Musée de Versailles. © photo: Réunion des Musées Nationaux)

17. Jean-Louis Meissonnier, *La Barricade*, 1848. (Musée d'Orsay © photo: Réunion des Musées Nationaux)

inspiring 'une peur instinctive au digne citadin, qui les regarde comme une famille de réprouvés et de maudits'.[40] Here, then, we find – in a mutually reinforcing interplay of the literal and the ideological – the crucial stress on apartness, on the idea of a city within the city. These are also the terms of Privat d'Anglemont, friend of Nerval (who himself mythologized Paris underground as the site of an Orphic journey into Hades[41]) and literary anthropologist of *Paris-inconnu*; in a language mixing the fascinated and the horrified, Privat d'Anglemont's account of the ragpickers' world takes us – under the heading of 'Le Camp des Barbares à Paris' – to a *quartier* that is scarcely recognizable as such, a 'faubourg impossible', an indeterminate and perhaps unnameable *là-bas*:

> Là-bas, bien loin, au fond d'un faubourg impossible . . . dans un quartier où personne n'a jamais passé, il existe quelque chose d'incroyable, de curieux, d'affreux, de charmant, de désolant, d'admirable. . . . C'est une ville dans une ville, c'est un peuple égaré au milieu d'un autre peuple.[42]

This kind of writing suggests not only a population at the edge of the city's acknowledged spaces but – in the confused medley of epithets and corresponding lack of a coherent view that characterize the prose – a problem of representation as such. This indeed was something of a nineteenth-century commonplace. Much earlier in the century, the moralizing 're-former', Frégier, in his investigative book, *Les Classes dangereuses*, had hesitated over classifying the ragpicker in the dangerous classes or labouring classes. This was not just some innocent question for the taxonomist grappling with unmanageably 'heterogeneous' material. It reflects an anxiety of knowledge and naming that is allied to a desire for control (an index of its intensity is the fact that in 1822 the ragpicker was the object of no fewer than *seventeen* reports to the Conseil de Salubrité[43]). Frégier solved his problem by opting for the former classification, the consequence of which, in the terms of Frégier's general social thinking, was to isolate the ragpicker from a notional common 'humanity'.[44] Jules Janin tried to remove the ragpicker from the map of 'civilized' urban life altogether, locating him in 'le moment où la nation souterraine se met en marche' and describing him as setting forth each night 'cherchant sa fortune parmi ces haillons affreux qui n'ont plus de nom dans aucune langue';[45] by an effect of contiguity, the namelessness of the filthy rags turns back on the ragpicker himself, implicitly menaced with removal from the community of language.

We see here the seeds of the horrified conservative Janin was to become. But it is a view in many ways not only consistent with the left-humanitarian positions of Fournel and Privat d'Anglemont. In a somewhat more surprising alignment, the ragpicker is also menaced with excommunication, at least from the language of mainstream social description, in Marx's *Eighteenth Brumaire*. Marx instances the ragpicker in his long list of the diverse members of the 'bohème' or *Lumpenproletariat* ('the whole amorphous, disintegrated mass the French call *la bohème*'). Figured as belonging to the 'scum', 'offal' and 'refuse of all classes', the ragpicker is thus disposed of as so much taxonomic waste matter; situated at the ragged edge of the categorial system Marx uses to describe modern society (*Lumpen* itself, of course, means 'rags'), he represents a kind of tear in the otherwise well-stitched, even seamless fabric of Marx's language of class representation.[46] Much has been made of this in recent criticism as a moment of semiotic rupture or 'scandal' in the otherwise self-assured functioning of the Marxist account of class society in nineteenth-century France.[47] But it probably makes more sense of this aspect of *The Eighteenth Brumaire* to see it less as a moment of modernist 'excess' *avant la lettre* than as the trace of a characteristic nineteenth-century obsession with a proper order of things; it is a 'left' version of the middle-class desire to keep not only the city but also the order of its representations as 'clean' as possible.[48]

From that desire came the shape of a discourse that, whatever the political 'intentions' of its users, implicated both left and right, though of course in varying ways and degrees, in a common identification of the *bas-fonds* as radically other, alien, a subculture below the threshold of the human. It is a discourse that was active from the late 1820s, finding its first major statement in Cassagnac's *Histoire des classes ouvrières et des classes bourgeoises* (which, in Benjamin's telling summary, 'claimed to give the origin of the proletarians' as 'a class of subhumans which has come into being by crossing robbers with prostitutes'[49]), and survived well into the late nineteenth-century social-psychological formulations of 'mob' theory in the work of LeBon and others. Janin referred to 'une population grouillante et suintante à laquelle on ne peut rien comparer'; Delphine de Girardin stood aghast before 'une ville souterraine' whose inhabitants lived 'comme des reptiles dans un marais'; Proudhon talked of 'cette immense voirie, ce pays de maîtres et de valets, de voleurs et de prostituées'; the left-wing poet, Auguste Barbier, described lower-class Paris as 'cet égout du monde' and its population as 'des races sauvages parmi cette population si active, si spirituelle, si parée, si polie'; Louis Blanc (citing Frégier in *L'Organisation du travail*) remarked that 'les visages qu'on y rencontre n'ont rien que de farouche et de bestial'; Buret claimed (as a title for one of the sections of his *De la misère des classes laborieuses en Angleterre et en France*) that 'l'extrême misère est une rechute en sauvagerie'; Considérant captured what this looked like from the point of view of the fears of the bourgeoisie: 'la bourgeoisie l'a parfaitement reconnu, quand elle s'est écriée, tout effrayée: "les barbares sont à nos portes."'[50]

The barbarian at the gate, or the reptile in primeval mud, these are the

tropes with which the discourse closed off the lower depths, in a naturalizing and regressive reduction to the animal and the primitive, even where
the intention was of a protesting or meliorist kind. They are, for example,
the tropes which frame and determine much of the writing in the work that,
probably more than any other in nineteenth-century France, caught the
collective imagination as a cry of protest against the degrading conditions
of the urban poor, Sue's serial novel, *Les Mystères de Paris*. Sue's preface (in
the form of a letter to the readers of the *Journal des débats* where the novel
was first published in serial form) introduced his fictional world as the
equivalent of a human zoo into which the reader is pruriently invited on an
exotic, if frightening, literary inspection tour:

> Nous allons essayer de mettre sous les yeux du lecteur quelques épisodes
> de la vie d'autres barbares aussi en dehors de la civilisation que les
> sauvages peuplades si bien peintes par Cooper. Seulement les barbares
> dont nous parlons sont au milieu de nous. . . . Ces hommes ont des
> mœurs à eux, des femmes à eux, un langage à eux, langage mystérieux,
> rempli d'images funestes, de métaphores dégouttantes de sang.[51]

The opening lines of the novel itself (a description of the rue de Fèves in
the Ile de la Cité where much of the narrative is located) have its hero
'plunge' ('s'enfonça') into a 'dédale de rues obscures, étroites, tortueuses',
elaborated as a nightmarish underground world, dark, muddy, fetid, reeking
of filth and putrefaction, but at the same time – as a sign of reassurance to
a suitably appalled reader – circumscribed and watched over ('très circonscrit,
très surveillé') by the police and the law courts (the Palais de Justice borders
the *quartier*).[52]

These motifs reflect only the terms of Sue's initial conception of *Les Mystères
de Paris*, and not those of the various changes it underwent (broadly from
novel of the criminal classes to novel of working-class life). Yet, even in its
more developed phases and critical aspects, these terms are never really
dropped; they return in one guise or another throughout the novel in the
form of a narrative which continually reproduces and reinforces those stratagems of separation, enclosure and surveillance that allowed the bourgeois
reader to wax philanthropic with a good conscience and to sleep at night
in the belief that the city was, after all, well policed. The real provocations
to this comfortable divorce of worlds and languages came from the major
novelists and poets. In *Le Père Goriot*, for example, Balzac worked the mud
and filth of the Parisian streets into both a metaphor ('Paris est un bourbier'[53])
and a structural device for the forging of a plot of 'connections' binding all
classes, high and low, to the moral implications of the metaphor. Zola too
will make both a plot and a (perhaps slightly strained) metaphor out of the
motif of domestic garbage in the novel *Pot-Bouille*, from the deceptive

contrast of the respectable façade of the middle-class apartment house and the disgusting backyard into which the household slops are thrown.

Above all there is the poetic example of Baudelaire and Lautréamont. Mallarmé, in his homage to Baudelaire, placed the latter's poetic vision underground, in a memorably condensed conjunction of grave and sewer, mud and death ('la bouche / Sépulcrale d'égout bavant boue et rubis').[54] And in *Les Fleurs du Mal* the city's trash comes to serve as both means and motto of a certain conception of poetic *modernité*; the appearance of the language of rubbish (for example, the term 'voirie' in the poem 'Le Cygne') is, as Benjamin notes,[55] one of Baudelaire's ways of rubbishing the poetic tradition; its mere presence in the linguistic environment of the poem, as neighbour to its more poetically settled and consecrated terms, yokes together in tense and unhappy co-existence ideas and associations which the culture would have preferred to keep apart. Finally, there is the 'underground' Paris of Lautréamont's *Les Chants de Maldoror* which brings together, in an extraordinary proto-surrealist patchwork of images and incidents, virtually all the motifs we have touched on – cemetery, catacombs, excrement, brothel, crime, poverty, abjection and bourgeoisie – beginning with the hurtling omnibus that appears 'comme s'il sortait de dessous terre', carrying a respectable but glazed-eyed citizenry ('l'œil immobile comme celui d'un poisson mort'), blind to the deprivations of the overground city – blind to the abandoned child in the street, to the observing ragpicker (who picks up the child with 'plus de cœur que dans tous ses pareils de l'omnibus'), and of course to the filth and horror of Maldoror's insane itinerary.[56] But it is now time to turn to the classic literary text of Paris underground, the great novel of the sewers, Hugo's *Les Misérables*.

III

Les Misérables has been called a 'roman déambulatoire',[57] and it is certainly true that in it one walks a lot; in the company of bourgeois, criminals, policemen, prostitutes, street urchins or students, the reader manages to cover most of the terrain of early nineteenth-century Paris. But the key, climactic actions of the novel occur in essentially two places, on the barricades of Les Halles and underground, in the city's sewers. 'Aujourd'hui', writes Hugo in *Les Misérables*, 'l'égout est propre, droit, froid, correct . . . la fange s'y comporte décemment.'[58] This echoes Nadar's imagery, but is not intended as a compliment to Belgrand's endeavours (although praise is heaped on his intrepid predecessor, Bruneseau). For the great novel of the Parisian sewers, wild muck is to be preferred to domesticated muck, if only by virtue of supplying greater narrative value; what is arguably the most exciting sequence in the whole of nineteenth-century French fiction is unimaginable in the sanitized and regimented sewers of the Second Empire (it is of course set in the July Monarchy). Here, however, we encounter a paradox that will take us to the heart of Hugo's underground world and, from there, perhaps to a more general complexity in representations of nineteenth-century Paris. If Hugo prefers the wild, he detests the wasted; refuse is there to be *used* (or, in the multiple senses of the term that reverberates throughout the novel, 'redeemed'), whether narratively, commercially or archaeologically. The famous historical account of the Parisian sewers begins with a poetically excited celebration of the economic value of excrement (on Hugo's calculations, worth 25 million francs per annum to the city's inhabitants). In addition, the sewer and its contents possess, at least to the appropriately trained eye, a strictly intellectual value; as a kind of alternative archive, the sewer contains the traces of the city's secret moral history:

> L'histoire des hommes se reflète dans l'histoire des cloaques. . . . L'égout de Paris a été une vieille chose formidable. Il a été sépulcre, il a été asile. Le crime, l'intelligence, la protestation sociale, la liberté de conscience, la pensée, le viol, tout ce que les lois humaines poursuivent ou ont poursuivi, s'est caché dans ce trou. (pp. 1309–10)

Two things flow from this version of the material and symbolic value of refuse. The first is that Paris underground is seen as an extension of Paris overground; and this emphasis on relations of extension and continuity will be an insistent theme of *Les Misérables* (crucially in the parallel, at once temporal and thematic, between the story of Valjean's odyssey through the sewers and the insurrection on the barricades of the rue de la Chanvrerie). The second is that, consulted as a kind of archive or document, the sewer can be made to disclose an order of intelligibility and knowledge. The wild can thus be tamed by way of its intellectual use-value; into the hidden archive and the lawlessness it records Hugo will bring the 'light' of understanding and the 'law' of representation. The novelist as 'observateur social' or as philosopher-detective will read off the secret history of the city from the detritus of the sewer, as a sustained exercise in inference from physical remains and traces: 'Avec le cloaque, elle [la philosophie] refait la ville. . . . Elle retrouve dans ce qui reste ce qui a été, le bien, le mal, le faux, le vrai' (p. 1312). What, then, are these relations of extension and continuity above and below ground, what kind of knowledge is at stake, and to what sort of image of the city in general do they contribute?

As a site of traces and signs, the sewers reflect a variegated Parisian history, but pre-eminently they house the residual annals of urban crime and insurrection. This in turn connects back figuratively to Hugo's description of the *bas-fonds* of the city (or, as Hugo himself puts it, echoing Cicero, the *fex urbis*, p. 1218). The literal underworld of filth and excrement becomes a metaphor for the 'dregs' of the city, and the corresponding chapters of the secret moral history are thus written as social pathology ('le cloaque est la maladie de Paris. L'égout est le vice que la ville a dans le sang', p. 1323). This way with the sewer as metaphor echoes what we have already seen to be one of the standard tropes with which the collective (essentially middle-class[59]) imagination of the period sought to order dangerous and recalcitrant social 'matter'. Indeed the novel first refers to the sewers when introducing what it appears to construe as an unregenerate criminal class, represented by the gang called the 'Patron-Minette' ('*Patron-Minette*, tel était le nom qu'on donnait dans la circulation souterraine à l'association de ces quatre hommes'). The sphere occupied by the Patron-Minette Hugo describes as the 'troisième dessous' of the social underground, in turn elaborated as the 'fosse des ténèbres', the 'cave des aveugles', the limboid world of 'ignorance et misère', of 'prostitution, meurtre et assassinat' (pp. 757–65). This, it will be clear, is the rhetoric of symbolic exclusion in full flight. As Louis Chevalier argues,[60] Hugo's novel here reproduces the categories of an older literature of criminality, combining the registers of the picturesque and the melodramatic and performing the familiar classificatory gesture of separation and enclosure: the *bas-fonds* as monstrous aberration and unsalvageable waste matter, the unredeemable *part maudite* of the social body. There is a limit beyond or rather 'beneath' which recognizable humanity ceases; and, interestingly, that boundary will be defined in part by the liminal figures of the sewer cleaner and the ragpicker ('l'égoutier qui balaie la boue et le chiffonnier qui ramasse les guenilles', p. 634).

Yet the presence of the word 'misère' in the description of the Patron-Minette also points to the terms in which this older conception of urban crime and its corresponding modes of literary representation are overlaid in the novel by the new awareness of the imbrication of crime with the conditions of modern urban poverty. The great fact of *Les Misérables* – as Chevalier again suggests – is the process whereby it came to acquire its title, or rather how the title itself came to acquire its more contemporary range of meaning and reference (in particular, that semantic shift whereby the term *misérable* moved from denoting a criminal to denoting the destitute condition which produces crime).[61] In this context, the knowledge of the city embodied in Hugo's use of the underground metaphor gathers into itself a whole social formation and a matching politics of contestation: what finally comes from 'below', or from the 'belly' of the city, is the People in the state of high revolutionary ferment: 'au plus profond des cavités insondables de ce vieux Paris misérable qui disparaît sous la splendeur du Paris heureux et opulent, on entendait gronder sourdement la sombre voix du peuple' (p. 1171).

In Hugo's underground, then, we are invited not only to read a history but also to hear a voice, or the rumbling of a potential social explosion;

amongst other things, muck is 'la substance du peuple' and its circuits the originating site of possible utopias ('les utopies cheminent sous terre dans les conduits', p. 757). The grafting of the revolutionary theme on to the topos of the sewer gives to *Les Misérables* a greater richness of conception and design than that informing any of the other comparable texts of the period (Sue's novel, written shortly before Hugo began his, cannot get much further than the claim that the answer to the social 'problem' is for the rich to be made aware of what, blamelessly, they do not know – how the other half, or rather nine-tenths, lives). On Hugo's account, Paris and revolution are often inseparable; 'Paris', quite simply, *is* revolutionary Paris. The wider context of Hugo's imagery of revolutionary Paris is the subject of the next chapter, and I shall therefore not dwell on it here. Its interpretation is moreover complicated by the fact that the boldness of Hugo's figurative and symbolic meshings (of the cloacal, the popular and the insurrectionary) is weakened by some deep-seated confusions; these bear directly on the fundamental logic of the narrative and, more particularly, on the actual sewer sequence itself (namely, the story of Valjean's flight with the wounded revolutionary student, Marius Pontmercy).

Many of these confusions can be tracked in lexical terms, especially across the vocabularies Hugo mobilizes to describe both the 'peuple' and the language the 'peuple' itself uses. Hugo always seems to have had problems with the relevant field of collocationary terms, although we should beware here of getting caught up in endless niceties (in the same way that prolonged immersion in what is often referred to as Hugo's 'social thought' is for the most part time ill spent). But some of Hugo's own terminological equivocations shed light on the more problematical aspects of *Les Misérables*, and – as we shall see – notably that aspect of it which accords primacy to the image of Light itself. Thus, in an important speech to the National Assembly in 1849, Hugo stumbled hopelessly over the key word 'misère': asked to clarify what he meant by it, the best he could come up with was that he didn't really know but believed that, whatever it was, it need not be around for ever.[62] Several years previously in his *Discours de réception* on election to the Academy he spoke of the 'populace' (in French a pejorative term close to 'rabble'); and when later reproached by the worker journalist, Vinçard, he fumblingly replied that he did not say 'populace' but 'populaces', adding that 'dans ma pensée, ce pluriel est important.' The importance of the plural, however, appeared to consist entirely in the assertion that there is an upper-class 'populace' ('une populace dorée') as well as 'une populace déguenillée'.[63] In other words, the 'vices' are not exclusive to the lower order; there are rotten apples at all levels of society – which may well be true but as such is a proposition that does little to advance the cause of a usefully precise language of social explanation.

This kind of ideological blurring is often also a property of the uneasily shifting political lexicon of *Les Misérables* itself. 'Populace' (along with cognate terms, 'gueux', 'canaille', 'ochlocratie') will reappear, at one moment in contradistinction to the consecrated republican category of the 'peuple', but then at another moment redefined as the bearer of authentic revolutionary aspiration (pp. 1217–8). Similarly, Hugo's presentation of the language of the *bas-fonds* (in the famous account of Parisian argot) turns on the difficult coexistence of contrary identifications. On the one hand, it is the language of protest and potential transformation; on the other hand, when seen, as for the most part it is, from the point of view of 'standard' French ('la langue française, la grande langue humaine'), it is scarcely a 'language' at all, or, in the pertinent analogy, it is the rubbish dump and cesspool of human speech: argot is not just 'la langue de la misère', it is also 'cet idiome abject qui ruisselle de fange', 'ce vocabulaire pustuleux', 'une sorte d'horrible bête faite pour la nuit qu'on vient d'arracher de son cloaque'. Although there is an attempt to classify the varieties of popular speech according to the principle of the *métiers*, the former, like its speakers, is ultimately beyond classification; in the familiar gesture of exclusion, it is outside the community of human speech, more noise than information ('plus voisin du hurlement que de la parole') and, in the corresponding reduction to the terms of the 'animal', indelibly marked by 'on ne sait quelle bestialité fantastique' (pp. 1026–33).[64]

This, one might say, is a form of literary slumming, the equivalent of viewing and sniffing the masses with a perfume-soaked handkerchief in one's hand. Whatever Hugo's alleged 'democratic' values (and notably on the question of literary language), it is the view *de haut en bas*. As such it is also the perspective in which enlightenment and salvation are proposed (when, significantly, lower-class characters accede to the purer feelings, they intuitively and miraculously reach for the language of middle-class French). Seen 'à la lumière de la pensée', the language of the social gutter is 'l'inintelligible dans le ténébreux' (p. 1027). Thus, just as the narrator brings light into darkness by translating the terms of argot into the terms of his educated reader, so the narrative also proposes history as the stage on which a filthy and disorderly *populace* can attain to the dignity of that entirely discursive and self-validating category, the *peuple*, only by means of a helping hand; in the recurring message from *Les Misérables* to *Quatrevingt-treize*, revolutionary action itself leads on a downward spiral into the baseness of evil 'matter', and accordingly the benighted masses can transcend their condition only when shown the way by middle-class leaders or converted aristocrats or poets, the latter the delegates of an authority that is ultimately divine.[65] The naked form of this view of the redemption of the lower orders is to be found in the manuscript version of *Les Misérables*. Here Hugo sketches an episode of underground encounter between the revolutionary students and a band of criminals in an abandoned quarry. The student leader, Enjolras, cheeringly greets the latter with 'Vous êtes la maladie sociale ... nous voulons vous guérir'; and to the more elaborated version of this medico-moralized address the criminals respond with both alacrity and gratitude: 'Bravo! cria le groupe sombre. Merci! dit celui qui semblait être le chef.' 'Merci', we shall see, crops up in other unpalatable forms; but even Hugo, whose taste for certain kinds of sentimentality often seems boundless, decided against including this in the final version.[66]

Nevertheless, showing the way, curing diseased souls, bringing light into darkness, translating the unintelligible into the knowable, and transforming the base into the spiritual (converting 'la boue' into 'l'âme', in the title of the last sections of the novel) – these are key themes of the actual sewer sequence in *Les Misérables*, and they all converge on the moral 'redemption' of its central character, the ex-criminal, Jean Valjean. 'Qu'est-ce que les convulsions d'une ville auprès des émeutes de l'âme?' (p. 1197), asks Hugo, and the answer of course is very little, though the convulsions and the mutinies share a common destiny in their exposure to the taming and transfiguring power of a 'great light'. In the very depths of the sewer, Valjean's soul is invaded by 'une étrange clarté' (p. 1346). This is the moment when Valjean begins his upward interior journey to the superior realm of moral self-understanding. For the most part, however, Valjean in the sewers is, in the various relevant senses, a man lost and blind. The 'prodigieux réseau ténébreux' doubles the topography of Parisian streets ('Le tracé des égouts répercute, pour ainsi dire, le tracé des rues qui lui est supérieur', p. 1327), but, as mirror image, also magnifies the 'labyrinthine' qualities attributed to the city. The sewers – like the streets of the criminal 'underworld' in Sue's *Les Mystères de Paris* – are 'dédaléens' (p. 1328); they constitute a 'labyrinthe qui a pour fil sa pente' (p. 1309); they are like a strange script ('quelque bizarre alphabet d'orient', p. 1309) or a Chinese puzzle ('casse-tête chinois', p. 1328). It is then no wonder that Valjean wanders helplessly 'de zigzag en zigzag' (p. 1328), and that around his disorientated figure should gather the phantasms of being blinded, drowned and buried alive.

But where Valjean gets lost in the labyrinth the Hugolian narrator provides a map, both literal and figurative. For Valjean all is 'brouillard, miasme, opacité, noirceur' (p. 1327), but for the narrator intelligibility is always to hand. This involves three kinds or levels of knowledge. The first is simply knowledge of the physical lay-out of the sewers; for Valjean to find his way 'il eût fallu connaître à fond, et dans toutes ses ramifications et dans toutes ses percées, l'énorme madrépore de l'égout. Or, nous devons y insister, il ne savait rien de cette voirie effrayante où il cheminait' (p. 1338). One wonders, however, about the insistence here ('nous devons y insister'). It of course emphasizes the narrator's superior knowledge of the underground network ('Si Jean Valjean eût eu quelque notion de tout ce que nous indiquons ici', pp. 1328–9). But the insistence also resonates into other, more strictly symbolic areas of the novel. If Valjean doesn't know where he is going, the narrator does, and in more than one sense.

One such sense – the second kind of knowledge – concerns the knowledge of narrative outcomes, access to the terms of what Barthes called the operations of the 'hermeneutic code' (the code for the posing and unravelling of enigmas). 'Il marchait dans une énigme' (p. 1329) is one of the figures for Valjean's stumbling in the sewers, where the enigma is in part a matter of explicitly marked narrative suspense: 'Trouverait-il une issue? Le trouverait-il à temps?' (p. 1329), asks the narrator in the slightly breathless rhetorical style of the contemporary serial novel and its promissory convention of *suite à venir*. Hugo of course knows what neither Valjean nor the reader knows, that Valjean's journey will indeed find an 'issue', out of the sewer into the arms of a waiting policeman. But the terms of this resolution are not just a matter of satisfying the plot requirements of the hermeneutic code. The narrative conjunction of coming into the light of day and into the clutches of the law indicates the third perspective of knowledge and mastery that is brought to bear on Valjean's underground adventure. This is not, however, the banal endorsement of the policeman's version of 'order' (as so often in nineteenth-century popular fiction). The light brought by the police into the sewer is the self-cancelling, oxymoronic kind reflected in the metaphors of the 'astre horrible' and the 'sombre étoile de la police' (p. 1330). Javert, the obsessional and merciless embodiment of human law, is a perversion of the true law and an obscuring of the true light – the light which comes from the eye of God and penetrates the human conscience. As Valjean wanders in the dark of the sewer, seeing nothing, knowing nothing, Hugo detects in what Valjean mistakes for pure chaos the shape of a providential design: 'Il allait devant lui ... ne voyant rien, ne sachant rien, plongé dans le hasard, c'est-à-dire englouti dans la providence' (p. 1329). This will later also be Valjean's realization: on his death-bed he contrasts Cosette's wonderful good luck with her mother's dreadful bad luck as basically the consequence of a divine deal of the cards: 'Ce sont les partages de Dieu. Il est là-haut, il nous voit tous, et il sait ce qu'il fait au milieu de ses étoiles' (p. 1509).

Beyond the frailties of earthly policemen there is, then, a divine policeman, over-seer of all, whose perspective the text itself proposes as its own (Cocteau once quipped that Victor Hugo was a madman who thought he was Victor Hugo, one reason perhaps being that 'Victor Hugo' saw himself, in Sartre's memorable phrase, as 'l'interviewer favori de Dieu'[67]). The motif of the all-seeing eye pervades *Les Misérables*. It is, for example, remarkable that, given the extraordinary richness of Hugo's sensory vocabulary, very little attention is paid in the sewer sequence to the sense of smell and a preponderant weight given to the sense of sight (George Piroué described Hugo as a writer with 'un œil dans chacune de ses narines'[68]). 'Le regard du drame doit être présent partout' (p. 1266), observes the narrator somewhat redundantly, since in the reading of *Les Misérables* we are rarely allowed to forget the ubiquity of that presence. In Valjean's transfiguration, the eye has to turn inwards to obtain redemption. This is entirely consistent with the various programmes, both practical and literary, in the nineteenth century for the spiritual and social 'correction' of malefactors. Sue has the hero of *Les Mystères de Paris* tear out the eyes of the master criminal before placing him in solitary confinement. In his involvement with the penal reform movement, Sue also recommended blinding as a substitute for capital punishment; the idea was that removing vision of the normal sort would encourage the virtues of inward, self-cleansing vision turned upon the sewer of the soul.

Cleaning up is also the narrative business of the concluding moments of *Les Misérables*. Valjean not only has to undergo spiritual purification; he also has to vacate the scene, to make way for the forms of 'order' necessary to securing a respectable future for his adoptive daughter, Cosette. In his journey through the sewer, Valjean, as he carries within the burden of a contaminated soul, carries without the instrument of his own ultimate effacement, the wounded body of Marius. In the local context, Valjean carries Marius to escape the forces of order closing in upon the revolutionaries. In terms of the broader narrative and ideological design of the novel, the real purpose is to effect his delivery to Cosette so as to ensure the replacement of the fake father by the true husband, thus making the narrative safe for the legalities of marriage and property. The less said about Hugo's presentation of the Cosette–Marius relationship the better. Its place in the climax of the novel is to contribute to the establishing of a proper economy of positions and identities. This crucially involves money matters, the reduction of the language of 'redemption' to that of the legal document and commercial transaction, in Valjean's attempt to convince the upstanding Marius of the 'innocence' of Cosette's dowry. But, instinctive gentleman that he is, Marius smells a rat, a sewer rat, we are tempted to say. For, although legally acquired by Valjean in his disguise as the middle-class factory owner, M. Madeleine ('C'est de l'argent honnête. Vous pouvez être riches tranquillement' (p. 1508), he pathetically pleads with the young couple on his death-bed), it is a fortune nevertheless tainted by the masked origins of its owner. Marius knows, when the chips are down, that God's law is the law of clean property: 'Il était évident que Marius avait des doutes sur l'origine de ces six cent mille francs, qu'il craignait de quelque source non pure' (p. 1471).

Valjean's supreme gift therefore has to be his own exposure, followed by his erasure. 'Etre une fausse signature en chair et en os' (p. 1445) is Valjean's dying worry, and this just about sums up the terms of the novel's closing preoccupations. Questions of names, signatures and identities turn on an anxiety about the usurping of the authentic by the false or the adulteration of the proper by admixture with the improper; they are questions about people being in their properly ordained place, both socially and sexually. Nothing is more of a threat both in and to the narrative order instituted by *Les Misérables* than the blurring of the distinctions and oppositions from which a stable order of social and sexual relations is constituted; and that threat is seen as coming primarily from 'below'. Thus, Marius's brief sojourn in the world of 'la vraie misère' (or what, in an absolute give-away, Hugo also calls the world of 'le mauvais pauvre', pp. 766 ff.) brings him horror-struck before what the text – echoing the terms used by the contemporary inspectors' reports on the 'brutish' sexual life of the urban poor[69] – calls 'cette brumeuse promiscuité des sexes' (p. 781). Valjean in his guise as Monsieur Madeleine would be the first to share this sense of alarm; he maximizes output in his factory by organizing the workers on the principle of the strict segregation of the sexes.

Similarly, the finale of the novel argues the need for moral and social clarity by restoring the distinctions blurred in the narrative of disguises and concealed identities. Valjean declares his name as if he were in the confessional, and in order to hand over Cosette to another, far more important name, the name Pontmercy. Much has been made of the latter's allegorical meanings,[70] though surely the essential point is their embarrassing obviousness. Through his surname Marius evokes both the 'mercy' with which to temper the rigours of the law, and a 'bridge' across which Cosette can walk from her dead guardian to her new and more respectable protector. But Marius is a bridge in another and wider sense: as the son of the heroic Napoleonic officer, Colonel Pontmercy, Marius brings into fiction a new kind of ideological pedigree (in the conventional popular novel of the nineteenth century the young hero is normally revealed as an aristocrat), a legitimacy enabling him to serve both in and for the novel as a symbolic bridge between what otherwise will remain divided. Whether on the Napoleonic battlefield or the revolutionary barricade or in the Parisian slums or the lawyer's office, the name Pontmercy is impeccably *French*, and its bearer a point of potential reconciliation for nearly all the major interests and shades of opinion of nineteenth-century France; in Marius's person, everything truly *patriotic* is safe, the revolutionary heritage of 1789 (but not 1793), the Napoleonic legacy, religion, marriage, property, the law, philanthropy, in short everything that flows into the creation of a certain image of the modern French nation-state and civil society. In his blind, desperate itinerary through the city's underground, Valjean carries on his back not only a future husband for Cosette but a myth, an idealized image of the future of France.

In this account of *Les Misérables* I have been wilfully flippant, and the nature of the account is such as to attract one last, and seemingly conclusive, flippant rhetorical gesture: as the novel closes by evacuating from its circuits the muck of problematical origins, so we might be tempted to treat the novel itself as so much ideological garbage, best consigned to the literary rubbish bin (Baudelaire, it should be recalled, while praising *Les Misérables* in public, in private said that 'ce livre est *immonde*'[71]). But this is to approach the novel in roughly the same spirit as that of its own more palpably objectionable aspects; it is to describe *Les Misérables* condescendingly, from the assumption of our own superiority, in the way the novel itself so often describes what, in the nineteenth-century social world, it sees as lying 'beneath' it. In brief, it is to reproduce the patronizing view *de haut en bas*. Of course, to say that *Les Misérables* is saturated through and through with the more sentimental and evasive forms of bourgeois ideology is to say something importantly true about it. And it is also true that the critical effort to 'save' Hugo's novel by 'modernizing' it, by rewriting its quintessentially nineteenth-century terms on the grid of some modern critical paradigm, does not finally dispose of these difficulties. For example, one of the more favoured contemporary approaches has been by way of the category of the 'mythopoetic', along with some associated notions of literature as bound up with 'psycho-history' and 'historical psychodrama'.[72] But, whatever the interest of this approach for certain kinds of literary understanding, in relation to 'history' understood as something more than simply a network of private obsessions, it has to be said that the 'myths' spawned or sponsored by *Les Misérables* arguably do not so much enhance as blunt the edge of what incisive vision it otherwise possesses. Hugo's way with the intractable in history is finally to move out of history altogether. The ultimate aspiration is towards transcendence, towards exit from conflict-ridden history into metaphysical harmony and reconciliation, where contradictions miraculously evaporate, into the sphere of pure Light.

In particular, Hugo's 'politics', especially in their bearing on the novel's modes of ending and resolution, are a very poor affair indeed. It has often been noted that the politics house 'tragic contradictions', but, while there can be no doubt about the contradictions, it is extremely doubtful that anything is usefully gained by representing them as 'tragic'. They are more accurately described as incoherent, where incoherence has a function: that of fudging the essential issues the novel confronts. Thus 'socialism' is to be taken seriously but provided, in this novel of the sewer and excrement, it is not of the 'intestinal' kind (i.e. less devoted to spiritual transfiguration than to economic emancipation).[73] Again, in theory the project and the prospect of revolutionary emancipation are offered as central to the novel's meaning (in a letter to Lacroix Hugo claimed the image of the barricade as the 'heart' of the novel and the key to its 'dénouement'[74]). In practice, however, revolution is fine, provided it never actually succeeds, or provided no revolution succeeds after the great one of 1789; in one of Hugo's more torturedly incoherent formulations, the point of 1789 is to serve as a 'vaccine', its purpose being to 'inoculate' progress against further progress ('une vaccine qui inocule le progrès et qui préserve des révolutions').[75] The Revolution that will preserve, not revolution, but *from* revolution: this – in so far as we can make sense of it at all – is the outlook of pure political Thermidorianism, the revolution made to the specifications of the property-owning bourgeoisie, and the city ordered to protect its interests.

Yet, when we have, relevantly but condescendingly, said all this about Hugo's novel, there is still more to be said. And the deepest critical embarrassment is not knowing how to say it. For neither is it a matter of 'saving' *Les Misérables* by cutting it up and extracting the 'good' from the 'bad'. The problem nearly always with Hugo is that he has to be taken more or less whole. What we might see as the strengths of his work stems from the same source as does what we also see as its weaknesses, broadly a taste, sometimes fatal and sometimes inimitable, for the dramatic stroke of simplification. This aspect of the Hugolian imagination can indeed produce a type of 'mythopoetic' image that is neither evasive nor saccharine, in *Les Misérables* crucially its images of absolute destitution, abjection and abandonment. Valjean making his way through the filth of the sewer like an animal tracked and hunted is the unforgettable image of *Les Misérables* (quite unlike the sentimental stereotypes invested in the creation of the novel's 'unforgettable characters', above all perhaps Gavroche).

In this respect, Valjean's underground journey does not so much produce as challenge a 'myth' (to which in other ways, as we have seen, Hugo himself was deeply wedded), the myth of the modern city, and especially nineteenth-century Paris, as the locus of enlightenment, as polis, the natural home of the 'political' understood as man's effort to replace the rule of anarchy with that of justice.[76] No nineteenth-century French writer can forge this sort of troubling image as Hugo does, and it is quite impossible for the modern self-conscious temper to manage the writing with any degree of critical poise. It has a directness and a force beyond our now routine cultivation of complexity, but is also entirely unlike the sententious maxims and *faux-naïf* pieties which – as in the presentation of Gavroche – disingenuously tug at our heartstrings. Something of its kind can be seen in the following sentence describing Valjean in the sewers prior to the arrival of cleansing and redeeming light: 'Il ressemblait aux êtres de nuit tâtonnant dans l'invisible et souterrainement perdus dans les veines de l'ombre' (p. 1327). It is an extraodinary moment: the ex-criminal, 'false' father to the daughter of a dead prostitute, carrying the wounded body of a revolutionary student, lost in the night-world of the underground city or, more exactly, in the 'veins of darkness'. That last metaphor is, of course, the brilliant touch of Hugo the incomparable wordsmith: the immediate association is with another underground image, with 'seams' of coal, the blackness of the telluric. But the more distant association of 'veines' is with the bodily sense, and hence with another kind of 'circulation', conjoining filth and blood, the disease-bearing sewer and the 'healthy' body (the body politic), and thus decisively blurring the very distinctions – physical, moral, political – which the various discourses of the 'hygienic' city sought to maintain.

The bodily meaning of 'veines' also includes, of course, the notion of 'arteries' and so, by metaphorical extension (or circuitous return), sends us back to that other space of circulation which Hugo explicitly poses as a site for the analogy between sewer and city: the palimpsest-like relation between the underground network of tunnels and the overground network of streets (though it is only with Haussmann's scheme that the principle of an arterial grid becomes a critically determining consideration in urban planning). From the dual sense of 'arterial', we may well be tempted into seeing and activating further potential in this moment of Hugo's text beyond its immediately local connotations. Indeed we have here a new semantic trajectory that also leads towards a fitting conclusion to the history of the nineteenth-century obsession with Paris underground, specifically by way of that historical fable of endings to which I earlier alluded. If, following Muray, we effectively begin a certain adventure of the 'nineteenth century' in the catacombs of the late eighteenth century, then the adventure might be deemed to end with entry into the twentieth century in the form of another underground experience: the triumphal opening in 1900 of the Métropolitain railway, suitably decorated with Guimard's art nouveau designs.

The introduction of the underground railway proved an immensely controversial affair and was the object of much anxiety and intense debate. For example, it furnished the theme of a most remarkable speech by the republican deputy Madier de Montjau on the civic and political dangers of the project: 'Le métropolitain est antinational, antimunicipal, antipatriotique et attentoire à la gloire de Paris.'[77] The fears here were multiple, but were based on a generalized dislike of a version of 'modernization': the Métro would involve tearing up the fabric of the city once more; travelling underground would carry considerable physical risk; there was also the old fear of 'miasmic' infection associated with unhealthy 'emanations'. This, however, was but one view of the matter; on the other side of the debate, the Métro was prized as the very symbol of 'modernity', as a key development in the production of the fully rationalized city. As such, the opening of the Métro not only ends the story of nineteenth-century imaginings of the underground city but, in the ambiguity of social perception which accompanied its introduction, it can also be held to sum up much of the general significance of that story.

The ambiguity of the Métro turned precisely on the relation, at once literal and analogical, with the network of streets. As both replication and extension of the overground system of transport, the underground railway was understood and defended by its supporters in terms of the more general project of constructing the city as cleanly ordered and efficiently functioning space. At the level of social imagination and literary representation, the latter, as we have seen, was reflected in basically two symbolic operations: a gesture of separation and a gesture of connection. The first sought to reinforce a static conception of the social order of the city; it aimed at keeping people and things in their 'proper' place and feared circulation as carrying the risk of 'contamination' (it emphasized the separateness of the *quartier* rather than the mobility of the street). The second operation was, however, more dynamic in character, stressing relatedness rather than separation, the city as interlocking grid for the purposes of travel, evacuation, exchange and so forth. It is largely from the latter association that the Métro occupied such an unstable position in public consciousness and debate. As a 'network' of interconnecting lines modelled on the streets, it signified the increasingly managed and controlled urban movement of bodies, a vital aid to disciplined and utilitarian movement between work and home. But the dynamic principle of connectedness could also evoke unexpected crossings and encounters and thus rapidly slide over into the sense of a growing loss of control, a fluid and messy transgression of boundaries, a disruption of the cleanly arranged whereby the hidden and the repressed come into dangerous contact with the mainstream, as a release of feared energy or problematic desire.

At the level of the street, this concern manifested itself in anxieties at once political and sexual. As we shall see in the next chapter, managing the street as a system of circulation was in part bound up with minimizing circulation of the insurrectional sort. In terms of sexuality it was of course related to the question of policing prostitution. Prostitution, as we have also seen, was commonly figured via the analogy of the sewer. In addition, we might perhaps have expected, via the whole imaginary of the cloacal, some allusion, if only unspoken, to the heavily tabooed area of the anal-erotic and so to the theme of homosexuality. The association is vaguely there, for instance, in Balzac's representation of the underworld: through the character of Vautrin, both criminal and homosexual (referred to as 'tante' in *Splendeurs et misères des courtisanes*), the notion of the 'underworld' may well drift towards a realm of forbidden erotic desire associated with the image of the underground. This, in any case, is exactly the point at which the Métro will enter twentieth-century literature as disreputable locale, no longer the image of the modernized city but as the place of its hidden and prohibited transactions. I am, of course, thinking here principally of Proust, though, in a final, interesting twist of the interconnected metaphorical knot, Proust's term of comparison is not the sewer but the catacombs. In a somewhat implausible, though irresistible, hypothesis, Montjau's worst fears would undoubtedly have been realized *après-coup*, had he been around, and disposed, to read Proust's conjunction of underground railway and catacomb in his imagining of the erotic uses of the Métro as bomb shelter during the First World War: while apocalypse rages above ground, furtive orgy takes place below 'dans les couloirs du métro, noirs comme des catacombes'.[78]

5

Insurrection

Ah! Ces révolutions!

Flaubert, *L'Education sentimentale*

Flânons, mais flânons en patriotes.

Le Flâneur, journal populaire, 3 May 1848

I

'Frédéric prenait la Maréchale à son bras; et ils flânaient ensemble dans les rues.'[1] This sentence from Flaubert's *L'Education sentimentale* records a stroll by the hero of the novel, Frédéric Moreau, and his mistress, Rosanette, during the February days of the 1848 insurrections. Its flatly ironic narration of casual *flânerie* following upon violent uprising is entirely characteristic of Flaubert's deadpan style. Taken at face value, it simply registers a fact of the historical experience in question, the euphoric honeymoon period which succeeded the barricades and the bloodshed (although the latter was of course as nothing compared to what was to come in June).[2] This was indeed a time for strolling in the streets of Paris, the moment of that short-lived illusion when it seemed that revolution had actualized the ideal of fraternity and the city had been given over to 'carnival' ('On avait une gaieté de carnaval . . . rien ne fut amusant comme l'aspect de Paris, les premiers jours').[3]

In Flaubert, however, face values are often misleading, and his sentence can be construed in other, less straightforwardly referential ways. Both written and read from a position of hindsight (minimally, from the knowledge of June and its aftermath), it resonates with obvious ironies. Furthermore, in the immediate narrative juxtaposition of violence and *flânerie* (the latter had become, by the time of the writing of *L'Education sentimentale*, a settled term in the received discourse of 'Paris' and arguably a candidate for entry in the *Dictionnaire des idées reçues*), the sentence also touches an issue in the wider political and cultural history of nineteenth-century Paris and its representations. In its deceptively simple shorthand, it can be said to reflect some of the terms of a developing conflict over claims, both formal and informal, official and popular, to the symbolism of the street. By the 1860s

102

the street was no longer simply a literary 'topic', as it had largely been in Balzac's time (in, for example, the genre of the *physiologie* to which Balzac himself contributed with his *Histoire et physiologie des boulevards de Paris*). Behind the tongue-in-cheek blandness of Flaubert's sentence, there is perhaps a question: to whom and to what is the street now supposed to 'belong', to the leisured bourgeois stroller or the 'people' exercising the right of resistance?[4] And behind this question was the even larger, and fiercely contested, question: what were the political terms on which the history of modern Paris was to be written and exhibited?

Haussmannization was in part a sustained practical answer to this question. As we know from his memoirs, one of Haussmann's considerations in proposing the plan for the renovation of Paris was how to secure the city against future riots and insurrections (though just how weighty a consideration remains controversial[5]). But, in addition to the scheme for breaking real barricades, there was probably also a desire to break a symbolic association. The wide boulevards and monumental vistas installed in Second Empire Paris, as well as making it seem easier to control and defeat a rebellious population, sponsored an official view of Parisian public space as a site of leisure and an embodiment of social peace. Cleaning up the city meant in part cleaning out the signs of a history (and is perhaps one reason why, in writing most of *Les Misérables* from a position of exiled opposition to Louis-Napoleon's regime, Hugo stresses the recoverability of that history in the underground of Paris). Certainly, for Hugo, whatever the incoherences and evasions of his view of revolution, the streets of Paris, especially those of the faubourgs,[6] are saturated with the signs of their revolutionary heritage; and in *Paris* he proposed an unqualified identification of the city with its revolutionary history: 'Qu'a donc Paris? La révolution.'[7]

Indeed 'Hugo', as distinctive idiom, will itself become both cause and form of the continuing life of this identification, notably during the Commune and in the writings of Jules Vallès. Already during the Second Empire Vallès had taken the street as a major theme of his journalistic writing. In 1866 he collected in book form a series of pieces with the title *La Rue* (and the following year became editor-in-chief of a newspaper bearing the same name). In *La Rue* Vallès coined a new term: *rualisme*.[8] His purpose was to play on an implied connection with the neologism's phonetic neighbour, *réalisme*, thus implying a new way with the description of the Parisian street, one that would get beyond both the inherited stereotypes and the official slogans (especially those justifying and celebrating Haussmann's 'redevelopment'). But, while critical of the latter, the criticism is for the most part conducted within the terms of the former. The 'realism' of Vallès's version of the street and its culture was not very different from – though less sentimental than – Victor Fournel's *Ce qu'on voit dans les rues de Paris*; the focus is on the street as 'pittoresque et populaire', the world of artisans and trades, street artists and fairs (Vallès was particularly attached to the tradition of the 'saltimbanque'), in short, the standard elements of a nostalgic mythology of *vieux Paris*, much of which by the late 1860s no longer existed. The notion of *rualisme* is, therefore, better understood not in the implied association with some straightforward principle of 'realism', but as the making, from diverse mixes of myth and reality, of a counter-cultural discourse of the 'street', attacking and displacing Haussmann's monumentalism but often in terms that are themselves immersed in the pieties of nostalgia. During the Commune and after, the mix changed, but it was still a mix; more fully politicized, the story of the street was unbreakably linked to revolution, but essentially as a story filtered through the language and imagery of the Hugolian revolutionary city, which – despite what Hugo himself said about the Commune ('Je suis pour la Commune en principe, et contre la Commune dans l'application'[9]) – remained a constant source of inspiration in the Communard newspapers and broadsheets.[10] For example, Vallès, in both *Le Cri du peuple* and *L'Insurgé*, returned again and again to the figure of Gavroche, and his description of Paris as the 'cité du salut, bivouac de la Révolution' is arguably pure Hugo.[11]

Yet the appropriation of Hugo's style to a cause Hugo himself did not support raises a further question: if the character of the city is centrally tied to revolution, what more particular meanings lie behind this blanket identification? Or, to put this another way, which revolutions and which aspects of which revolutions supply the key terms on which the city's past and present were to be understood? For if there was a conflict between revolutionary and anti-revolutionary discourses for the 'meaning' of the city, there were also disputes and divergences *within* the former, in that long, complex insurrectionary history of Paris from 1789 through 1848 to 1871. For instance, in Hugo's equation of Paris and 'la révolution', is the latter to be read as '*la* Révolution', the italics and the capital letter signifying of course 1789 and its (contested) legacy? Certainly 1789 was decisive for the creation of Paris as a modern capital (the Revolution, it will be recalled, brought the capital back to Paris from Versailles). 'Sans . . . 89,' wrote Hugo 'la suprématie de Paris est une énigme.'[12] Although written to provoke the imperial regime of Louis-Napoleon, this is not as radical as it sounds. Back in 1830, even Louis-Philippe accommodated this view by agreeing to the construction of the commemorative monument on the Place de la Bastille which proposed a continuity linking the storming of the Bastille and the *trois glorieuses* of the 1830 uprising.

From the regime's point of view, however, this was, as Agulhon has suggested, an act of 'iconographical imprudence'[13] (the regime was iconographically somewhat more prudent in connection with Delacroix's great picture, *Liberté guidant le peuple*, purchasing it only to hide it from public view). Moreover, in the matter of public symbolism, as well as operational ideology, the important reference in the acknowledged links to the revolutionary past was to 1789 (and not 1792 and still less 1793, all signs of which had long been erased from the public face of the capital). It is all the more curious, then, that the July Monarchy, in its early fit of ecumenical generosity, also tolerated the completion of Rude's decorative sculpture for the Arc de Triomphe, *Le Départ des volontaires*. For this piece (also known as the *Marseillaise*), commemorating the departure of the soldiers to the wars of 1792 and thus interpretable as an image of patriotic and nationalist fervour directed against the foreign enemy, was also, if by date alone, necessarily associated with the declaration of the First Republic. There was certainly nothing here to suggest the link between two constitutional monarchies – and hence a version of 'acceptable' revolution as a moderate and reasonable affair – that was implied by the monument erected on the Place de la Bastille.[14]

These confusions surrounding both political values and their expression in the symbolic repertory of nineteenth-century Paris overflowed in 1848. In this respect, as in so many others, 1848 was a watershed, a point of convergence, collision and splitting of different notions, both old and new, concerning the revolutionary legacy. How Paris in 1848 related to its revolutionary past (and laid down terms for its revolutionary future) is a complicated, fast-moving and often incoherent affair. It depended to a large extent on which side of the barricade you chose and what side you were on when (February or June); whether your priority was political (establishing and defending the 'Republic') or the 'social question' (the economic needs and interests of the working class). The dominant initial view accompanying the formation of the Second Republic and its Provisional Government was that 1848 represented the delayed moment of entering into full possession of the legacy of 1789, or rather of the period from 1789 to 1792, now grasped as a teleological process geared to the emergence, despite imperial and monarchical interruption, of the law-governed Republic. Daniel Stern spoke for many in defining the revolution (of February) as 'la manifestation extrême, la plus complète jusqu'ici de ce mouvement organique qui ... s'efforce depuis 1789 ... de substituer au *droit divin* le *droit humain*'.[15]

This was also the view of Lamartine, effective head of the Provisional Government and, in his historical memoir of 1848, spokesman for the broadly *girondiste* version of the revolution as 'une continuation de la première avec des éléments de désordre de moins et des éléments de progrès de plus. Dans l'une et dans l'autre c'est une idée morale qui fait explosion dans le monde. Cette idée, c'est le peuple.'[16] By 1848 the 'peuple' had become so abstract and rhetorical a category as to attract all manner of descriptions, according to the shifting play of interests and allegiances (as we shall see, Michelet will try, against the odds, to breathe new life into it in the writing of *Historie de la Révolution française*). But, whatever and whomever Lamartine meant by the word, it clearly did not include the insurrectionary Parisian proletariat. In order to run the analogy with 1789, the June insurrectionaries had to be edited out of the space of the 'peuple'; they represented a 'mouvement de plèbe et non de peuple',[17] an echo of the Commune and the *sans-culottes* of 1793 and a recipe for bloodshed, chaos and anarchy ('les excès de l'anarchie'[18]). This view probably explains some further editing operations at the level of Lamartine's historical narrative. The June days appear to be unworthy of serious narrative attention ('Je ne raconterai pas les différents combats de ces journées'[19]), and accordingly get short shrift, a mere few pages in a text that runs to well over six hundred.

Unfair though the analogy must sound, Lamartine's way with revolution was not unlike Haussmann's way with the Paris streets. His idea was to keep things as clean as possible; if revolutions come from 'below', they acquire genuine moral and political worth only once they have been sanitized by an overground culture speaking the respectable language, and representing the prudent interests, with which Lamartine himself was aligned.[20] Indeed on the matter of language Lamartine also diverged from Hugo (although on so many of the substantive political issues they were more or less of a common mind[21]). For instance, Lamartine, lover of the 'peuple', had little time for popular speech; he objected both to General Cambronne's famous 'Merde!' as he faced defeat at Waterloo and its inclusion in the Waterloo episode of *Les Misérables*, taking the view that the verbally noisy – and specifically obscene – way with death on the battlefield was unbecoming to a gentleman ('Mieux valait mourir en silence!').[22] More generally, he also deplored what he called the 'saletés' of Hugo's language, specifically in that narrative nexus of the text binding the themes of the sewer, excrement, demotic and insurrection (in a note for *Les Misérables*, Hugo described 'merde' as the 'misérable des mots'[23]).

Lamartine's linguistic fastidiousness would seem to have been on a par with his social and political caution, and it comes perhaps as no surprise that his famed 'eloquence' ends up as a term in the ironic citational space of Flaubert's *L'Education sentimentale*, specifically – as a kind of drastically truncated anthology piece – the famous set speech about the 'drapeau rouge, etc.' (the 'etc.' is, of course, Flaubert's).[24] But so too will most of the other discourses of 'revolution' that were in circulation in 1848. It would appear, from Flaubert's manuscript notes for *L'Education sentimentale*, that the question of language was of paramount importance in determining the novel's approach to its historical and political interests: 'Langage' is the generic heading under which he lists the various topics he proposes to treat in these sections of the novel.[25] Some of the specimens in the great discursive exhibition mounted by *L'Education sentimentale* I will come back to later, as one of the major forms of a new way of dealing with the established imagery of the revolutionary city. One of the exhibits – though appearing in tacit, oblique and, finally, complex fashion – was Michelet's *Histoire de la Révolution française* (which I wish here to compare and contrast with Flaubert's novel, as two exemplary moments of the nineteenth-century construction of the revolutionary city).

Michelet was also deeply concerned with revolution and its representation as a question and a problem of language, but in terms entirely different from those of Lamartine's diffidence and Flaubert's detachment. Michelet rather was caught up in a problematic of intellectual and political engagement which centred on the gap between writing (the writing of the historian, educated, professional, erudite) and speech (the speech of the common 'people'). This problematic had two interrelated aspects. The first involved the notion of a project of writing that would also be a speaking, namely a speaking for and to the 'people' in the hour of its direst need. This is how Michelet put it to Béranger in the dark days of June 1848 (recorded in a text, *Nos Fils*, published in the same year as *L'Education sentimentale*): 'Après l'horrible et ténébreuse affaire du 24 juin 48, courbé, accablé de douleurs, je dis à Béranger: "Oh! qui saura parler au peuple? . . . Sans cela nous mourrons."'[26] The *Histoire de la Révolution française* was in part Michelet's answer to that question. The first volume appeared in 1847, and throughout 1848 Michelet continued writing frenetically, precisely as a desperate effort to keep alive in and for 1848 the memory of 1789.[27] On the other hand, it was not an answer to Michelet's question in so far as the desired closing of the gap between writing and speech was in fact impossible. For the ideal was not only to speak to and for the 'people' but also to do so in the language *of* the people: 'Je suis né peuple, j'avais le peuple dans le cœur. . . . Mais sa langue, sa langue, elle m'était inaccessible. Je n'ai pu le faire parler.'[28]

Michelet's relation to the language in which the story of revolution was to be told was thus a matter of passionately felt commitments and hopelessly anguished defeats. It was no wonder that he reacted coldly to what he saw as the 'coldness' of Flaubert's account of 1848, noting in his diary: 'Je parcourus Flaubert, *Education sentimentale* ou histoire d'un jeune homme. Froid et indécis. . . . Emeutes de 48, très froides.'[29] The respective versions of the revolutionary history of Paris to be found in Michelet and Flaubert therefore make for instructive comparison and contrast. By virtue of the intensity of his identification with his subject, matched by a corresponding narrative and rhetorical energy, Michelet's *Histoire de la Révolution française* offers, more than any other comparable nineteenth-century text, novelistic or historiographical (the distinction here matters little), a paradigm of a certain nineteenth-century way with the revolutionary tradition, precisely the paradigm which Michelet sought to keep alive in 1848 and which Flaubert's fiction, as an account of 1848, will take apart as 'fiction' (although, as we shall see, in a manner more complicated than that of a simple ironic negation). Where Michelet writes about 1789 in the hope that it might continue to be a living model for 1848, Flaubert writes about 1848 as if 1789 were indeed the model, but dead rather than alive. This contrast I want now to explore and illustrate in some detail by way of two moments in the respective texts of Michelet and Flaubert, one from the chapter in *Histoire de la Révolution française* devoted to the storming of the Bastille, the other from the narrative of February 1848 from the beginning of Part 3 of *L'Education sentimentale*.[30] They will help us focus both the changing terms of historical imagination in the nineteenth century and the rhetorical form of those terms (which is one reason why, for the purposes of this analysis, the distinction between fiction and historiography is not of great importance[31]).

II

Both passages deal with popular insurrection, and as representations of revolutionary crisis they have one thing in common: there is in both a stress on the theme of anonymity, on the absence of precisely locatable cause or origin which sets the chain of events in motion. But each respectively makes of that absence the overarching sign of two quite different narrative strategies. In Michelet's text it serves a particular idiom, broadly the idiom of epic commemoration, in which the storming of the Bastille is represented as grand *archè*, the founding moment of a world-historical event, the pure embodiment of a world-shattering and world-creating inauguration; that is to say, where the theme of the absence of determinate origin is directly linked to a quasi-metaphysical view of the Revolution as itself the incarnation of pure Origin (as, in François Furet's words, that form of 'commémoration révolutionnaire où l'accent est mis sur la dynamique de l'événement fondateur, et ses pouvoirs d'avenir').[32]

The chapter begins with a rhetorical move, the antithetical play of two metonymies:

> Versailles, avec un gouvernement organisé, un roi, des ministres, un général, une armée, n'était qu' hésitation, doute, incertitude, dans la plus complète anarchie morale.
>
> Paris, bouleversé, délaissé de toute autorité légale, dans un désordre apparent, atteignit, le quatorze juillet, ce qui moralement est l'ordre le plus profond, l'unanimité des esprits.

'Paris' and 'Versailles' are thus not just geographical references but also rhetorical terms charged with certain symbolic meanings. Paris is not just the theatre of the action but also its protagonist, as Versailles is the antagonist; although both are marked by a certain 'disorder', in the case of the latter it is the symptom of a disabling moral affliction ('la plus complète anarchie morale'), while in the case of the former it is but 'apparent', a deceptive surface beneath which is gathered all the energy of a common moral purpose ('ce qui moralement est l'ordre le plus profond, l'unanimité des esprits'). The figure of antithesis will be deployed throughout the whole passage, but its most immediate and dramatic function will be to cast the inaugural moment of the Revolution in the mould of an apocalyptic story of revelation and rebirth, tacitly saturated through and through with echoes of the Bible (it will be remembered that the inaugural moment of the book itself, its founding and framing question – which 'historiquement, logiquement, précède toute autre'[33] – concerns the relationship between the Revolution and Christianity).[34] In particular, the opposition of night and day, the shift from physical to metaphorical light ('une lumière dans les esprits, et dans chaque cœur une voix: "Va, et tu prendras la Bastille!"'), implies an analogy between the emancipatory project of the Enlightenment and the biblical injunction 'Let there be light!' This modelling of secular narrative on biblical narrative is further intensified by stylistic devices such as the resonant paratactic sentence 'Et cela se fit'; at the level of denotation this is a pure tautology (what happened happened), but it also carries a connotation: an allusion to a form of biblical utterance, thus signifying a miracle of collective human action seen as a secular version of divine action. In short, if the story of Genesis tells us that in the beginning God made the world and made man in his own image, Michelet is telling us that 14 July 1789 is the moment of a second Historical Coming, the moment when man remakes the world in the image of the Revolution.

It is thus already clear how rhetorical figure, allusion, tacit quotation are being used to shape this particular story as a piece of literature, and specifically of course as a piece of epic literature. The epic transformation of the raw historical 'data' is nowhere more active than in the representation of the agent of the historical process, namely, that resonant and loaded category, 'le Peuple'.[35] Michelet takes great pains to stress that the beginnings of the French Revolution have nothing to do with the projects and decisions of particular individuals, for example the politicians and parliamentarians. The question who started the process receives the answer, moreover insistently repeated, 'personne': 'Personne ne proposa. . . . Personne, je le répète . . .' But the negative or 'empty' pronoun 'personne' is posed only for its instant transformation into the 'full' category 'tous', the grammatical marker of oneness, of an experience of collective historical solidarity: 'Mais tous crurent et tous agirent.' In other words, this episode is not the property of individuals, still less of the great names of the revolutionary story; the emphasis falls rather on anonymity but an anonymity that has a clear moral and political identity – the unified collective will of the People intent on ushering in the reign of universal liberty and justice. As Michelet put it in the preface to *Histoire de la Révolution française*, 'l'acteur principal est le peuple.'[36]

This is clearly history as epic poem, and indeed, as the chapter unfolds, the text moves away from straight historical narrative into pure commemorative celebration. The turning point in this respect (perhaps generated by the preceding appearance of the word 'peuple') is the paragraph in which the narrative perspective is aligned with the retrospective point of view of the 'vieillards' ('Les vieillards qui ont eu le bonheur et le malheur de voir tout ce qui s'est fait dans ce demi-siècle unique . . . déclarent . . . que le seul 14 juillet fut le jour du peuple entier'). Here we move from the world of action into the world of memory via a figure (the 'vieillard') who occupies both, once an actor in the events and now a witness, a narrator, of them. We have therefore a kind of narration-within-a-narration, the rhetorical function of which is to effect another kind of solidarity, between the tale and its telling and its tellers. One might even say that the tacit solidarities proposed by Michelet's effort to stage the 'voice' of his witness-participants is a rhetorical equivalent, or compensation, for the impossible dream of a written history moulded to the rhythms of popular speech, a history told by the 'people' as well as a history of the people. Certainly, the rhetorical move has a strong legitimating function. As the voice of experience, knowledge and wisdom, the point of view of the 'vieillards' serves to authenticate and guarantee the meanings invested by Michelet himself in the episode recounted, and hence to justify the dramatic shift of literary gear towards the end of the passage, namely the shift into exhortatory apostrophe affirming yet another solidarity – the universalizing identification of 14 July 1789 with the whole of mankind and the whole of human history: 'Qu'il reste donc, ce grand jour, qu'il reste une des fêtes éternelles du genre humain, non seulement pour avoir été le premier de la délivrance, mais pour avoir été le plus haut dans la concorde!'

Apostrophe of this sort is not a figure we would normally associate with the responsibilities of 'scientific' history-writing; and indeed Michelet's style seems at this point to become entirely severed from the conventions of ordinary historical report. 'On sait ce qui se fit au Palais-Royal,' he remarks laconically. The 'on' of that simple statement appears to signify at least two things. First, it is another rhetorical looping of narrative into narration; actor, narrator and reader are all here assumed to participate in shared knowledge (of the sort corresponding to one dimension of what Barthes called the operation of the 'cultural code' in narrative). Secondly, the implication of common knowledge legitimizes the text's apparent loss of interest in the factual record. Let us not bother with the facts, Michelet appears to be saying. Let us instead devote all our imaginative energies to the business of empathetic identification with the heroic actors of the episode. What exactly happened is common knowledge; how it happened is a mystery beyond rational understanding. It can be comprehended only by an act of intuitive apprehension which is far closer – and here Michelet reveals the influence of Vico and Herder – to poetic insight than to rational analysis. 'On sait ce qui se fit au Palais-Royal, à l'Hôtel de Ville; mais ce qui se passa au foyer du peuple, c'est là ce qu'il faudrait savoir. Là pourtant, on le devine.' *Deviner* is indeed the key verb, representing a form of hermeneutic guessing, a leap across time in the effort to recapture intuitively what for Michelet must have been in the minds of the revolutionary protagonists. And what, for Michelet, was in their minds is once again the biblical model, the model of the Last Judgement. History, in the perspective of the People, is transformed into a Court, a court delivering 'le jugement dernier du passé' in the name of the law of universal justice ('l'immuable Droit').

This court is constructed rhetorically from the combination of two figures – once again apostrophe (to the 'hommes forts' of the Revolution) and personification, or more precisely and more interestingly, the form of personification called prosopopoeia (in the particular sense of that complex figure which involves the giving of speech to the mute, whether as natural object, man-made artefact or abstraction).[37] History (along with Right – 'le Droit'), hitherto the object of Michelet's discourse, now becomes figuratively the subject of discourse, the grand narrator of its own story and the prime speaker in its own courtroom: 'L'avenir et le passé faisaient tous deux la même réponse; tous deux ils dirent: "Va!"' In the figure of prosopopoeia, history is thus enabled, God-like, to see itself whole and to speak its own meaning; past, present and future converge in a perspective at once inside time and outside time ('hors du temps'), at once immanent and transcendent, describing a teleological pattern in which the meaning of the 'end' (the reign of universal justice) is already inscribed and seized in the beginning.[38]

III

To move from Michelet's account of popular insurrection to Flaubert's at the beginning of Part 3 of *L'Education sentimentale* is to move between radically discontinuous narrative worlds. It is to move from an image of heroic collective purpose whose moral meaning is wholly unambiguous to an image of historical process from which nearly all sense of visible purpose and meaning has been removed; from a narrative striving for maxium integration (around the themes of unity, solidarity, etc.) to a narrative which systematically fragments as it recounts, which refuses not only the epic register, but also the very idea of a 'history' that could be represented as a coherent and intelligible whole. Flaubert's account of the February days begins by installing us in a particular perspective, the point of view of the

111

hero, Frédéric Moreau. It is a very different point of view from that which informs Michelet's narrative, where we have either the God-like view of the narrator to whom the meaning of the historical drama is entirely transparent, or the point of view, both immanent and retrospective, of the main historical protagonist, the 'Peuple'.

Frédéric's stance is essentially that of the detached witness, the passive bystander. It is classically the perspective of alienation, of disconnection. Take, for instance, what Frédéric first sees in the street – the start of the construction of a barricade (that prestigious emblem of nineteenth-century revolutionary discourse and iconography): 'Plus loin, il remarqua trois pavés au milieu de la voie, le commencement d'une barricade, sans doute.' Frédéric thus perceives the construction of a barricade, but it is a perception immediately weakened by the equivocating 'sans doute'; it is probably the start of a barricade, but nothing is clearly enough perceived for that to be certain; it may in fact be just the contingent detail of a random disorder.

This sense of history fractured into the random will recur throughout the whole sequence.[39] It is immediately reinforced by the very next clause: 'quand tout à coup s'élança de la ruelle un grand jeune homme pâle, dont les cheveux noirs flottaient sur les épaules, prises dans une espèce de maillot à pois de couleur. Il tenait un long fusil de soldat, et courait sur la pointe de ses pantoufles, avec l'air d'un somnambule et leste comme un tigre.' That clause and that sentence are quintessentially Flaubertian. First, there is the deceptive syntax marked by the semicolon which ends the preceding clause; the semicolon is conventionally a marker of continuity (what succeeds the semicolon will, however tentatively, be in some way connected with what precedes). Here, however, the emphasis falls instead on an idea of abrupt discontinuity (the sudden appearance of the pale young man). Secondly, there are the curiously indeterminate and ill-fitting terms of the description of the young man himself. He is unidentified; we do not know who he is, nor on what side he is fighting. His person, moreover, resembles a kind of bizarre collage of incongruously related items, a collection of signs that sit alongside each other in the description but which do not quite match. The motifs 'young', 'pale', 'long black hair' and the 'soldier's rifle' evoke the stereotype of the Revolutionary Student, and there is perhaps here a tacit allusion to the figure of the heroic student in Hugo's account of the barricades of 1832 in *Les Misérables*, or to the student in Delacroix's *Liberté guidant le Peuple*.[40]

The parallel with Hugo may in fact be made more precise, if we consider the following sentence from the insurrectionary chapters of *Les Misérables*: 'A la barricade de la rue des Ménétriers . . . un jeune homme blond, sans cravate, allait d'une barricade à l'autre portant des mots d'ordre.'[41] But the phrase 'mots d'ordre' implies precisely an 'order', a determinacy and coherence of purpose we do not find in Flaubert's account. If Flaubert's 'jeune homme' is an echo of Hugo's, it is an echo surrounded, equivocated and dissolved by the jarringly ironic effect of the details of his description: the gratuitous notation of the 'maillot à pois de couleur' (a descriptive detail that seems to be without thematic function or connotative force); the odd juxtaposition of the emblem of revolutionary zeal (the rifle) and the prosaic precision of the emblem of private life (the 'pantoufles'); and, finally, the even more incongruous syntactic link between the image of the somnambulist and the analogy with the tiger. This is the writing of history as collage, a kind of stylistic bric-à-brac or, in rhetorical terms, an extended zeugma; where Michelet at once integrates and idealizes by means of prosopopoeia, Flaubert integrates ('yokes') ironically by means of the figure of zeugma (the figure which conjoins incongruities). Above all, of course, there is the sheer evanescence of the moment: the young man randomly appears and just as randomly disappears, as the text effects yet another discontinuous leap into the next sentence: 'On entendait, par intervalles, une détonation.'

This sentence, and in particular its subject pronoun, brings us to the heart of Flaubert's vision of modern history. The pronoun 'on', along with the noun phrase 'des hommes', is the most common designator in the passage of the human subject and of the relation of agent to action. It contrasts sharply with pronominal usage in Michelet, and gives a quite different view of the nature of agency and identity in revolutionary process. Michelet's usage, as we have seen, stresses impersonality or rather trans-individuality: the agents of the revolution are not isolated individuals but a collective entity. Flaubert's 'on' is very different: it cannot be filled with determinate identity and purpose; it is rather the marker of a dispersal of agency into anonymity and indeterminacy. If the 'on' of the earlier 'on avait arraché les grilles de l'Assomption' must refer, although even there also somewhat indeterminately, to the insurrectionaries constructing the barricade, it is certainly quite unclear to whom the 'on' in 'on entendait' refers, who the subject of the action of 'hearing' is – is it other insurrectionaries, Frédéric, bystanders including an unidentified narrator-witness?[42]

That focus, or rather lack of focus, becomes particularly pointed at exactly the moment the word 'insurrection' first appears in the text: 'et, pendant qu'aux Tuileries les aides de camp se succédaient, et que M. Molé, en train de faire un cabinet nouveau, ne revenait pas, et que M. Thiers tâchait d'en composer un autre, et que le Roi chicanait, hésitait, puis donnait à Bugeaud le commandement général pour l'empêcher de s'en servir, l'insurrection, comme dirigé par un seul bras, s'organisait formidablement.' This whole sequence calls for extended comment, especially in respect of the characteristic forms and functions of syntax in the passage. Structurally, the syntax of this sequence of clauses articulates an antithesis, on the face of it not unlike the opening antithesis between Versailles and Paris in Michelet's text. On the one hand, there is the disarray of the Authorities, represented in a syntax that itself conveys confusion and incompetence: the irony of the repeated form 'pendant que ... et que ... et que ... et que', suggestive of an accumulating frenetic activity which is leading precisely nowhere, which goes around in circles or collapses into negation and paradox ('M. Molé ... ne revenait pas', 'le Roi ... donnait à Bugeaud le commandement général pour l'empêcher de s'en servir').

On the other hand, there is the representation of the insurgents in a clause whose shape connotes the opposite – simple, direct, suggestive of unity, solidarity and power: 'l'insurrection, comme dirigé par un seul bras, s'organisait formidablement.' Decontextualized, this could well be Michelet's prose, and indeed might even be a kind of submerged echo of Michelet or of Hugo ('L'émeute se comportait selon la plus savante tactique militaire'[43]). But, if so, it is, yet again, as ironic echo, the ironic perspective supplied by the recontextualization of that clause in what immediately follows it. For what follows is less an image of 'organization' than the account of a shambles – a flux of meaningless discourse ('des hommes d'une éloquence frénétique haranguaient la foule') coupled with a sequence of chaotic actions (once more governed by the pronoun 'on'), issuing, at the end of the sentence, in a now completely devalued restatement of the key revolutionary image of the Barricade ('Paris, le matin, était couvert de barricades'). This is the moment of the triumph of the 'people', its dramatic seizure of power and the equally dramatic dissolution of the institution of monarchy ('le peuple ... possédait les points stratégiques les plus sûrs ... la monarchie se fondait dans une dissolution rapide'). History, for a moment, looks as if it wears the face of purposive agency. But once more any such implication is abruptly checked; in what is almost certainly an allusion to the legendary narrative of the storming of the Bastille,[44] the 'peuple' becomes once more the anonymous 'on', engaged in the futile enterprise of emptying a prison that has no one in it: 'et on attaquait maintenant la poste du Château-d'Eau pour délivrer cinquante prisonniers qui n'y étaient pas.'

The image of the Barricade is, moreoever, at the centre of the last paragraph of the passage: 'Une barricade énorme bouchait la rue du Valois.' What happens around this barricade is once more cast in the idiom of radical confusion and pervasive indeterminacy. Take, for instance, the sentence that follows: 'La fumée qui se balançait à sa crête s'entr'ouvrit, des hommes couraient dessus en faisant de grands gestes, ils disparurent.' In both content and structure, that sentence may be said to resume the whole Flaubert story of 1848. First, there is the motif of smoke blotting out visibility and, by implication, threatening conventions of historical and narrative intelligibility. Secondly, there is the momentary glimpse of human action through the smoke, undone and dispersed at the very moment it comes into vision: on the one hand, the 'full' image of the 'grands gestes' (connoting heroic action), on the other hand, its abrupt displacement into the 'empty' image of disappearance, its cancellation by the absolute finality of that melancholic past historic, 'ils disparurent' – a verb which, from both its meaning and its tense, negates any potential for narrative development in the preceding clause. Flaubert's use of the past historic here is arguably the exact opposite of the teleological function Barthes assigned to it in *Le Degré zéro de l'écriture*. Barthes described the past historic as the term of narrative mastery, one of the grammatical means for converting 'life' into 'destiny', for ordering the past as meaningful pattern from a position of masterful retrospect.[45] Flaubert's practice is quite otherwise; what 'disappears' in the obliterating finality of Flaubert's 'disparurent' is, precisely, the finality ('finalité') of *telos*.

Closing down on narrative potential, on the sense that history can be made to tell a coherent story, is also the essential move of the closing lines of this passage. The battle continues ('la fusillade recommença'), but in a context which evacuates the scene of all identifiable humanity: 'Le poste y répondait sans qu'on vît personne à l'intérieur.' There is the sound and fury of battle but no accompanying or at least visible human agency; moreover, not only is there no one to be seen inside the 'poste', there is also – once again by virtue of the indeterminate pronoun 'on' – doubt as to who the subject of that (non-)seeing might be. Everything here is swallowed up into a kind of fog (not unlike the smoke on the barricade). The sense is precisely that of history as caught in a fog, without distinct contour, or as a sort of 'blur'. That notion of 'blur' might also help to account for what is perhaps one of the strangest effects of the passage – the description of the bullets hitting the wall of the monument: 'et le monument avec ses deux étapes, ses deux ailes, sa fontaine au premier et sa petite porte au milieu, commençait à se moucheter de taches blanches sous le heurt des balles.' The phrase 'moucheter de taches blanches' implies a perspective of quite extraordinary distance and estrangement from what is taking place, the conversion of the violence of history into a purely abstract visual object. 'Taches blanches' is almost a painterly image, and in particular perhaps reminiscent of the Impressionist painterly image. The tracery of bullets on the wall of a monument thus appears as a swarm of white dots on the historical canvas, analogous to the blurred traces of paint on the Impressionist canvas. But, whereas with the Impressionist picture what close up appears to be a blur can be reconstituted as a visually readable image once you stand back, in Flaubert's text the blur seems more chronically pervasive, the sign of a more radical illegibility;[46] the blur is at the very centre of the historical process, it defines it; or rather there is no centre, no site from which coherent sense can be produced.[47] The centre is occupied by the negative, by absence, emptiness; and it is then perhaps significant that the narrative elaboration of the image ends with the adjective 'vide' ('Son perron de trois marches restait vide').

IV

Raymond Williams suggested that there are essentially two literary modes for the representation of revolution, the epic and the tragic, depending on whether the point of view on events was immanent (tragic) or retrospective (epic).[48] One can easily see how these categories – especially the latter – apply to Michelet's account. But from the example of Flaubert, from, precisely, the systematic dissolution in *L'Education sentimentale* of the terms of Michelet's grand narrative, we would have to add a third category: the 'ironic' would be the obvious if weakly generalized term;[49] better perhaps would be Flaubert's own phrase for the outlook that underlay his writing in general, what he called the *grotesque triste*.[50] The latter is difficult to characterize exactly, but covers a complex range of negative attitude on a spectrum from the satiric to the melancholic. Something of both the sense of the phrase and its relevance to the text of *L'Education sentimentale* can be had from the following deadpan concatenation of the utterly incongruous:

> Des bandes nouvelles de peuple arrivaient toujours poussant les combattants sur le poste. La fusillade devenait plus pressée. Les marchands de vin étaient ouverts; on allait de temps à autre y fumer une pipe, boire une chope, puis on retournait se battre. Un chien perdu hurlait. Cela faisait rire.[51]

'Cela faisait rire . . .' Revolution in these terms is history revealed as farce, in the double sense of both theatrical routine and pointless gesture, history as joke ('farce, and 'blague' are central, though – as we shall see – also problematical, terms in the political lexicon of *L'Education sentimentale*). More precisely, 1848 is the 'empty' recapitulation of the myths and symbols of 1789, simulacrum without content, repetition as travesty (the opposite of Michelet's dream of an active transforming repetition).[52] Deslauriers, who predicts 'un nouveau 89',[53] fantasizes himself as a 'futur Mirabeau';[54] Sénécal plays at Fouquier-Tinville;[55] Frédéric imagines himself in a new incarnation of the Convention; indeed – in a perspective of double removal from the original model – the game of imitation becomes so derivative as to be imitation of an imitation: in the proceedings of the Club de l'Intelligence, Sénécal copies Blanqui who copies Robespierre ('et, comme chaque personnage se réglait alors sur un modèle, l'un copiant Saint-Just, l'autre Danton, l'autre Marat, lui, il tâchait de ressembler à Blanqui, lequel imitait Robespierre'[56]).

The denunciation of 1848 as empty ritual aping of 1789 (or – with reference to the June days – as dangerous echo of 1793) was, of course, something of an *idée reçue* in the period. Marx famously attacked 1848 as the shadow of 1789 without the substance,[57] while Tocqueville, writing of the invasion of the Assembly, described the events as pure theatrical charade, more a 'literary' mimicking of the Great Revolution than a development of it.[58] Then there was the painting (which I mention for a special set of reasons to which I shall come shortly): alongside the official iconography of the Republic, its immediate questioning or demystification in the counter-imagery of Daumier, Courbet, Millet, Leleux, Rethel and Meissonnier, the sense of the revolution and its publicly endorsed imagery as dead replicas of an exhausted tradition of history painting.[59] If Flaubert's tracery of bullets on a wall conjures up the Impressionist image, those bullets are already, and literally, there in the blank neutrality of Leleux's *Le Mot de passe* (1849), (plate 16), as a sign signifying nothing in particular, a mark from which meaning has been drained away.[60] Meissonnier's *La Barricade* (1849) (plate 17) displays the same deadpan matter-of-factness, while also sharing with Rethel's wood cut, *New Dance of Death* (1848), a sense of fractured space, a resistance to given models of thematic coherence and closure. Above all, there is the idiom of ferocious burlesque, in particular the comic reworkings of the canonical nineteenth-century image of revolution, Delacroix's *Liberty* (plate 18). This bore less on Delacroix's commemoration of the 1830 revolution itself; for, against the grain of its strong, dramatically articulated pictorial organization, there is in it arguably considerable uncertainty over the ideological terms on which it can be read as a coherent political image celebrating the *trois glorieuses*. It was more a question of the assembly-line reproduction of 'Delacroix' during the Second Republic, Delacroix congealed into painterly doxa.[61] Daumier's *Le Gamin aux Tuileries* (1848) (plate 19) and Millet's *Liberté aux barricades* (c. 1848) are openly declared and instantly recognizable parodies; Leleux is more oblique and low-key, though his *gamin* in *Le Mot de passe* is clearly a restatement of Delacroix's minus the by now mythical streetwise insolence.

Much of this resembles the tone and emphasis of Flaubert's account of 1848 (an account which, through the figure of Pellerin, includes the involvement of painters and painting[62]). 'Delacroix', moreover, seems to have entered deeply into contemporary writing about the revolution, nourishing a wide range of transactions between image and text. For instance, a (possibly unconscious) memory of Delacroix may well be at work in the pictorial analogies with which Tocqueville presents 1848 as a failed re-run not only of 1789 but also of 1830, perhaps imagined as a peculiarly perverse case of 'life' imitating art in the form of recycled Delacroix: 'ces anciens tableaux qu'on veut faire entrer de force dans de nouveaux cadres font toujours un mauvais effet' is Tocqueville's remark on the parallel between 1848 and 1830.[63] The Delacroix doxa also seems to have been a significant reference for Flaubert; not only is he mentioned, but allusions to *Liberty* appear throughout the text of *L'Education sentimentale* as a kind of running yet broken leitmotif, the elements of the painting literally scattered across the novel in a sustained ironic dispersal. Thus, the *gamin* reappears on the barricade, wrapped in the *tricolore*, but this time on the opposite side to the fervent though bamboozled republican, Dussardier.[64] The figure of the Polytechnicien turns up twice, once as model for the preposterous Regimbart (who 'se faisait habiller par le tailleur de l'Ecole polytechnique'[65]) and once in the flesh, as imbecile ('Frédéric s'engagea à s'interposer. Le Polytechnicien ne comprit pas, semblait imbécile, d'ailleurs'[66]). Finally, Liberty herself (commonly perceived as gross and repulsive by hostile critics when Delacroix first exhibited the painting) is here unambiguously parodied in the figure of the common prostitute posing as Liberty on the throne during the sack of the Tuileries.[67] All this adds up to a Delacroix that no longer adds up, Delacroix in bits, disintegrated into derisory and degraded fragments.

The point of referring to the painterly dimension of the topic is not, however, merely to draw up a list of correspondences, parallels and echoes (it is not even clear what the term 'echo' might usefully mean here). It is rather a question of reconstituting, in schematic outline, a set of terms spaced over some twenty years which come to challenge and even displace a previous set of dominant terms for the representation of the insurrectionary city. On this account, Flaubert does not inaugurate the relevant terms; they are already in place some twenty years earlier in the painting of the revolutionary period itself. Flaubert thus comes to these terms belatedly and hence, if only as a consequence of historical timing, is himself arguably caught up in a paradox: Flaubert contests a prior doxography of revolution from within what, by the time of *L'Education sentimentale*, is already a new doxa, the routine notion, virtually the cliché, of history and revolution as a sad and sorry joke.[68] If 1848 is, by virtue of belatedness, an empty simulacrum of 1789, what are we to make of Flaubert's own relation of belatedness to that very idea?

The question certainly has implications for how we ourselves might make political sense out of this way of seeing. The critical work by the painters of 1848 was clearly also a work of protest, a refusal to be taken in by the slogans and a determination to keep visible the gap between the wilfully self-serving blindness of the stereotypes and the ghastly mess of the reality. But a necessary disillusion can, and often did, turn to an easy cynicism, entailing a somewhat different kind of politics; as Benjamin remarked in connection with Baudelaire, the politics of the joke, of the cult of the *blague*, are historically linked to the politics of the extreme right.[69] This is likely to be all the more so when the view of history as pointless joke and meaningless farce has itself, by dint of repetition, become something of a tired joke. Sartre had something like this in mind when characterizing Flaubert's version of revolution as profoundly reactionary. It is certainly clear that, as Sartre says, 1848 broke Flaubert's life in two;[70] it appears to come as the equivalent of an irremediable catastrophe, doubly confirmed by the later experience of the Commune. From this point on, when the façade of ironic detachment cracks, most of Flaubert's comments on contemporary politics (chiefly in the *Correspondance*) are resolutely, and sometimes hysterically, anti-democratic.

Yet *ad hoc* remarks are not necessarily reliable guides to the reading of *L'Education sentimentale* itself. By this I do not mean simply the way the novel, secure in the possession of its Olympian neutrality, indifferently pours scorn on the parties on both sides of the barricades; that is entirely compatible with the strategy of reducing history to the insignificance of the joke. It is rather the complex subtlety with which this very strategy is at once rehearsed and exposed within the novel itself, restaged as, precisely, joke. For not only is the language of the *blague* given a certain prominence in the array of discursive styles put on exhibition by *L'Education sentimentale* around the themes of politics and revolution; it is also a language marked by considerable instability and undergoes some curious and even bewildering migrations in the text from character to character and context to context, in ways that question and devalue its possible status as a touchstone for Flaubert's own point of view.

We first meet it in the mouth of the cynical journalist, Hussonnet.[71] 'Quelle bonne farce!' is the latter's comment on a disturbance in the Latin Quarter to the newly arrived Frédéric.[72] Seven years later, the chaos on the barricades and around the Tuileries elicits from Hussonnet a virtually identical remark, again to Frédéric: 'Voilà une bonne farce!' Inside the Tuileries both are witness to the actions of the 'peuple' ('C'était le peuple'), shortly afterwards modified by the narrative discourse itself to 'foule', then the unambiguously contemptuous 'canaille' and finally the derogatory 'populace'. Frédéric, though entirely uncommitted, is seized by a sudden burst of enthusiasm and finds himself speaking in the register of Michelet: 'moi, je trouve le peuple sublime.' Hussonnet, on the other hand, mocks the idea of the heroic ('les héros ne sentent pas bon') and the myth of the sovereign people ('Quel mythe! ... Voilà le peuple souverain').[73] In the play of positions here, it would seem fairly clear where Flaubert himself 'stands'; the vocabulary of his own narrative, in the shift from 'peuple' to 'foule', 'canaille' and finally 'populace', implies a strong alignment with the jaundiced attitude of Hussonnet.

Yet, as so often in Flaubert, that apparent alignment is strictly unsustainable. Fixity of position buckles and clarity of view gets blurred, as the terms in question start to migrate to other contexts. If we think the text has given us a secure vantage point from which to interpret and evaluate events, we are mistaken. More particularly, if the category of the 'political' looks as if it has been wiped out in the withering contempt of the joke we find that this very gesture is itself seen as having a distinctive political function, in the service of particular interests. For example, 'blague', along with the talismanic Flaubertian word 'bêtise', reappears in the reaction to the February days offered by Regimbart, the 'Citoyen' who says much but does nothing; for whom the joke serves as rationalization of that form of grumbling inaction which demands the revolution in principle but always finds reasons for rejecting it in practice: '"Quelle bêtise!" grommela une voix dans la foule. "Toujours des blagues! Rien de fort!"'[74]

More important, however, is the relativizing of the joke to its social and political uses in the conversational gambits of M. Dambreuse's salon. *L'Education sentimentale* impresses upon us the view that in 1848 the 'revolution' has been inflated by a certain discursive excess. But so also do the reactionaries who gather around M. Dambreuse: '"N'importe", remarqua tout haut un monsieur. "On s'occupe trop de la Révolution; on publie là-dessus un tas d'histoires, de livres!"' (the reference is almost certainly to Michelet).[75] Revolution, observes Martinon in self-serving agreement, should not be taken so seriously ('"il y a peut-être des sujets d'étude plus sérieux"').[76] This is the bluster of a class which, although it has not yet lost its nerve, is rattled and requires its jesters for reassurance. It provides perfect terrain for the opportunistic Hussonnet, who reappears 'défendant les intérêts d'un cercle réactionnaire . . . en blaguant les principes de '89'.[77] Here, however, the relevant terms do not simply travel from one context to another, they start to slip and slide in quite unpredictable ways. Hussonnet places his demystifying wit in the service of the political right. But if, against that self-interested accommodation, we wish to affirm that revolution is no joking matter, then this position too we find pre-empted by members of the party of order once the June days are upon them: 'Ce n'était pas le moment de plaisanter, du reste; Nonancourt le dit, en rappelant la mort de Monseigneur Affre et celle du général Bréa.'[78] Revolution is, after all, a serious business, but from the point of view of a frightened bourgeoisie. Finally – in one last migration, or twist, of the textual knife – Hussonnet, having played court jester to the Dambreuse milieu, later avails himself of the graveside orations at Dambreuse's funeral as matter for a series of humorous newspaper articles: 'Hussonnet, qui devait rendre compte de l'enterrement dans les journaux, reprit même, en blague, tous les discours.'[79]

This looks like a case of having the last laugh. But that would be a plausible interpretation only if there were reasons for respecting Hussonnet's point of view, and also if there were sound reasons for believing that, in the swirl of shifting terms, positions and alignments, we could locate a point of view for Flaubert himself. In fact, there is no last laugh, no meta-joke overarching all the others. Flaubert's purpose in fact seems less to endorse the cult of the joke than to *place* it, to pose it as being not above politics, transcendent to history, but as deeply complicit with worldly interests, opportunistic calculations and capitulations. Being above it all is indeed one of the vantage points for seeing history as joke, and is famously such in

Flaubert's reference to seeing the things of this world 'au point de vue d'une blague supérieure, c'est-à-dire comme Dieu les voit, d'en haut'.[80] But this position too is critically distanced by virtue of its transference to the words and thoughts of his characters. Thus Hussonnet, who derides not only the disturbances of the Latin Quarter as 'une bonne farce' but also the alarmism of the authorities as 'une vieille blague du Gouvernement pour épouvanter les bourgeois',[81] appears, in his even-handed detachment, as a pure caricature of the stance of transcendent dispassionateness. This, however, does not prevent the 'republican' industrialist, Arnoux, from laying claim to a very similiar position of disengagement, though the paradoxical knot tightens here in that the context of the claim is nothing other than an attack on the 'cretin', Hussonnet: 'Ce crétin-là me fatigue! Quant à desservir une opinion, le plus équitable, selon moi, et le plus fort, c'est de n'en avoir aucune.'[82]

In this swirl of mutually cancelling perspectives, it becomes thus less a question of making a joke out of revolution than of making a joke out of those who, like Hussonnet, make a joke out of revolution. Here, of course, the spin of terms, like the proliferation of points of view on points of view, becomes radical and potentially unstoppable, opening on to the regresses with which we are familiar from Flaubert's obsession with the paradoxes of *bêtise*. In their transposition to the idiom of the joke, these paradoxes would require us, for example, to try to make sense of any inclusion of Flaubert himself in the description of 'Artistes' given in one of the versions of the *Dictionnaire des idées reçues*: 'Il faut rire de tout ce qu'ils disent. Tous farceurs.'[83] However, as we spin away into exitless epistemological circles, we should perhaps remember that in *L'Education sentimentale* the last occasion of the cynical joke, properly speaking, is in fact given to the 'people' (or rather its pronominal surrogate, the anonymous 'on') at the time of Louis-Napoleon's *coup d'état*: 'On parlait librement, on vociférait contre les troupes des plaisanteries et des injures, sans rien de plus.'[84]

We make of this what we may. The joking crowd is indeed history as joke, but here the whirl of terms takes us towards an idea of the joke less as a method of demystification than as a symptom of political impotence ('sans rien de plus'). On the other hand, it may also generate another, and entirely different, association – with Hugo's emphasis on popular laughter as a contestatory political force.[85] Such a convergence might seem implausible, given the systematic divergence of Hugo and Flaubert at the level of their stated political opinions. Certainly, in Flaubert's version the sentimental-utopian constituent of the Hugolian version disappears into a perspective of exhaustion; the point is precisely that jokes won't dislodge either the Emperor-to-be or his troops.

There is, however, perhaps something else here that remains once the critical view has been fully taken into account, a trace of another view and of another – greatly more complex – convergence. If Flaubert detested the whole baggage of 'democratic' notions which for Hugo, and Michelet, gave meaning to the revolutionary traditions of Paris (equality, universal suffrage, etc.), he seems to have shared with them a view of the people as a 'force': we read in *L'Education sentimentale*, 'et l'on sentait dans ses profondeurs une force incalculable, et comme l'énergie d'un élément.'[86] Both this view itself and the fact of its sharing are ambiguous entities. In many important respects, they are readily identifiable as indicating reactionary positions. For example, all three writers, along with very many others in the nineteenth century, will compare the revolutionary crowd to an elemental and irresistible 'force' of nature, often the turbulent river or the storm-tossed sea; from the comparison with elemental nature, it is but a step to what, in the previous chapter, we have seen to be the characteristic naturalization of the Parisian masses by way of the notion of 'mob' regression to a condition of un-controllable animality – the crowd as inarticulate and violent beast, or as 'bête' in that double sense of both animality and stupidity which particularly exercised Flaubert.[87]

Yet we should also remember that, although muteness and 'bêtise' often go together, the latter in Flaubert is essentially a property of discourse; in Flaubert's world being dumb may be a sign of being stupid, but his characters are never more stupid than when they claim to be intelligent speakers (as in the political speech of the absurdly named revolutionary Club de l'Intelligence). And if, against the idealizing slogans reproduced in the empty talk, the reality of the crowd is represented as brute force, the idea of 'force' can be made to carry another sense and correspondingly suggest another respect in which Flaubert can be said to converge with Michelet and Hugo. Michelet's grand subject of revolutionary history, the 'Peuple', becomes of course an object of the parodic work of Flaubert's novel. But once again the ground moves beneath our feet. For here is the 'anti-democratic' Flaubert giving voice to a view which – albeit with some rather severe editing – could easily be taken for Michelet: 'Cependant il faut respecter la masse, si inepte qu'elle soit, parce qu'elle contient des germes d'une fécondité incalculable. Donnez-lui la liberté, mais non le pouvoir.'[88] Take out 'inepte' and pos-sibly, though less obviously, the back-handed concession of the second sentence (for 'pouvoir' here refers to the right of universal suffrage, thus rendering problematic the political sense of 'liberté'), and here, in the metaphors of 'generation' and 'fecundity', we re-find the imagery of one major dimension of Michelet's approach to politics and history.

How we might return this to the analysis of *L'Education sentimentale* is not at all clear. It would be evidently absurd to assign to such a self-aware text any central place for some romantic-intuitionist notion of unreflective 'doing' in opposition to the incurably mediated and derivative culture of speech, and even more absurd to make of Flaubert an enthusiast for the

June days and a champion of proletarian revolution. It is clear that for the most part the 'political' in *L'Education sentimentale* (as in *Bouvard et Pécuchet*[89]) represents Flaubert's secular version of the Fall. Innocence is what comes 'first' in the novel (in the brothel scene recalled in the closing pages by Frédéric and Deslauriers); the political is what comes after, as one of the major contexts for the loss of that innocence. The brothel scene is in fact importantly related to the themes of laughter and the joke. For, if in the novel there is no last laugh in the sense of some meta-joke overarching all the others, the last *laugh* in the chronological sense belongs to the brothel; it is the laugh of the prostitutes at the embarrassment of the two adolescents: 'Toutes riaient, joyeuses de son embarras; croyant qu'on s'en moquait, il (Frédéric) s'enfuit.'[90] This, however, is not the laugh of the worldly joke: Frédéric takes it for mockery but Flaubert's adjective is 'joyeuses' and Frédéric's 'croyant' carries the strong implication of mistaken belief; the prostitutes' laugh is an innocent laugh, entirely devoid of cynicism, the laugh before the Fall into knowledge and betrayal.

There is, however, in all this perhaps another, more tantalizing joke. The brothel scene is paradoxical not only thematically (as the site of innocence) but also structurally, in giving us a 'beginning' only at the end. It also – in a typical, category-confounding Flaubertian 'echo' – sends us back to the novel's actual beginning and another laugh, this time Frédéric and Deslauriers laughing in allusion to the very brothel incident we learn about only in the novel's closing moments ('Cette allusion à une aventure commune les mit en joie. Ils riaient très haut, dans les rues'[91]). The formal play here with conventions of prospect and retrospect may be said to carry some interesting implications for the political and historical pessimism of the novel. If there is a Fall here, it is not straightforwardly into the easy knowledge, the closure of the point of view implied by the idea of history as a 'farce'. As both genre and ideology, farce works as retrospect, or rather it is, so to speak, proleptically retrospective (and as such the exact opposite of the paradoxical 'beginning' given at the end of *L'Education sentimentale*).[92] Its 'surprises' assured in advance, farce predicts, and even secures, outcomes by way of a jaundiced relationship to the past, and as such can be said to stage an expanded version of the dictum *plus ça change, plus c'est la même chose*. Farce, in this sense, is the *reductio* of the world seen from the point of view of the 'blague supérieure'; and since the latter is (roughly) the point of view of – a doubtless world-weary – God, it is therefore perhaps no accident if Flaubert also says that the knowledge of beginnings and endings is reserved for the deity (mere mortals know only middles).[93]

Although centrally about 'repetition' and its mechanical gestures, *L'Education sentimentale*, as a narrative form, does not itself merely repeat the predictive, teleological structures of a knowledge secured in advance (and we should remember here that teleology is not uniquely a property of optimistic notions of history; absolute historical pessimism is based on a negative *telos*).[94] Flaubert once wrote – as an adolescent – that 'l'histoire du monde, c'est une farce.'[95] One of Flaubert's biographers (Gille Henry) has suggested that, because Flaubert thought this as a very young man, he must have thought it all his life. Henry himself certainly thinks it should command all the representation of that life, since – in a perfect example of a pure *telos* of writing – the quotation is to be found both on the cover page (as the biography's title) and on the last page, as the biography's closing sentence.[96] Happily Flaubert's novels resist such simple framings. Unlike farce, the form of *L'Education sentimentale* remains open to an unknown and unknowable future. For while the lives of its two heroes fade out, into a future that is no future but mere unending sameness, that particular outcome of those particular lives is not necessarily offered as a generalized model of 'ending'. If, therefore, it is correct to speak of narrative indeterminacy as the major principle of plotting in *L'Education sentimentale*, it is equally important to emphasize that in the novel there are different kinds of indeterminacy bearing different implications. It may then be possible to return to the chaotic indeterminacy on the barricades and to give it a different meaning from the conventionally ascribed one, a different inflection to the non-visibility of history through the smoke. The 'blur' here concerns the future as much as the present.

We should also not forget that in the manuscript version of *L'Education sentimentale* Flaubert momentarily committed himself to the view that 1848 was not in fact pure repetition of a model, a pale shadow of an 'original' event, but that it was itself absolutely original ('Jamais rien de pareil n'avait eu lieu à Paris').[97] And one is, of course, struck by the recurrence, in the passages from the novel and the correspondence, of the adjective 'incalculable' ('une force incalculable', 'une fécondité incalculable'). These are not mere rhetorical flourishes, fragments of an *idée reçue*, with tacit quotation marks around them. Flaubert here speaks of effects that cannot be calculated, hence not evaluated, which in turn suggests that the meanings of the nouns ('force' and 'fécondité') the adjective qualifies, their implications both within and beyond the novel, cannot be readily determined and circumscribed. Indeed the weight of the term 'incalculable' is itself in many ways incalculable (it has become something of a hot potato in some current debates about the so-called 'politics' of deconstruction[98]). In the relevant nineteenth-century context, however, as Paul Virilio reminds us, the sense of the 'incalculable' was at the very heart of ruling-class perceptions and fears of the revolutionary situation, where the 'incalculable' meant above all the difficulty of the state machine and the fortress-city in controlling speed of movement, 'circulation', in the streets of the city of its non-sedentary inhabitants, the population without *domicile fixe* – casual labour, the unemployed, vagabonds, 'nomads'.[99] What the term might then be held to signify

124

in Flaubert, whatever scenarios of political possibility or impossibility it might be said to open on to, the latter are clearly beyond a joke, although it is, I suppose, a typically and perhaps unmanageably disorientating touch on Flaubert's part that the character who actually uses this expression is, of course, Hussonnet (on, of all things, the subject of prostitutes and works of art): 'Car enfin, voyons, pas de blagues!'[100]

6

Noisy and Hysterical Scenes:
Poetry in the City

I

In its more confident moods, modernism can have its cheerful, even lyrical, way with urban noise. Apollinaire pastoralizes – though not without a certain irony – the sound of traffic crossing the Seine by comparing it to the bleating of sheep, watched over by the Eiffel Tower figured as a shepherd ('Bergère o tour Eiffel le troupeau des ponts bêle ce matin'[1]). Joyce's Stephen Dedalus walks across Dublin, 'passing on his way amid the squalor and noise and sloth of the city, fearlessly and with a light heart'.[2] Proust's narrator awakens to the street noises of Paris as if to a morning symphony, or rather to the strains of Gregorian chants.[3] This retrieves an association once rooted in social fact (the street cries of medieval Paris mingling with and echoing the liturgy of the neighbouring churches[4]). But it is not just a question of Proust's miraculously intuitive historical imagination. It is also a matter of the narrator's privileged capacity – socially as well as aesthetically – for making subjective magic out of his sensory environment (it was of course entirely otherwise for Proust in real life, protected against the intrusion of the city's 'music' in the famous cork-lined room overlooking the Boulevard Haussmann).

Waking up to the din of the city going about its business in, for example, the rue de la Folie-Méricourt or the rue Saint-Denis must have been a quite different auditory experience. Speaking of the latter around the middle of the nineteenth century, Paul de Kock tried to turn the experience into a picturesque joke: 'le bruit qu'on y entend sans cesse doit servir de réveil-matin.'[5] Victor Fournel, indefatigable, and hopelessly sentimental, *physiologiste* of urban street cries, adapted the idiom of picturesque to a veritable semiotic: to the expert ear, the 'discordante et criarde mélopée des mille cris de Paris' can be made to yield a whole social taxonomy; discordant yet intelligible,

126

the human sounds of the street are a reliable guide to the varieties of trades, professions and ranks, a kind of aural map of a naturalized social order.[6] This, however, is Fournel looking back nostalgically to an allegedly lost Paris, the raucous yet agreeable 'concert' of a city on the human scale, the Paris of the old, settled *quartier* culture where the street cries signify a world of everyday transactions at once 'naturally' differentiated and 'harmoniously' orchestrated (Fournel cites approvingly the testimony of Madame de Genlis, who claimed in her *Mémoires* that the street cries of pre-revolutionary Paris were a 'chant' sung 'en ton majeur', whereas those she hears on her return to post-revolutionary Paris were 'à peine intelligibles, excessivement tristes et lugubres, et presque tous en ton mineur'[7]). Fournel's own complaint is that, in the Paris of Haussmann, there is no more song at all, in either major or minor key: the Haussmannized street, according to Fournel, is the desolate street, morose, emptied of the vital idioms and rhythms of the *petits métiers*. George Sand, buoyantly optimistic as ever, thought otherwise: 'Il y a dans l'air, dans l'aspect, dans le *son* de Paris, je ne sais quelle influence particulière qui ne se retrouve ailleurs'; and to her ear, even in Haussmann's Paris, city noise softens and blends into harmony ('sa sonorité confuse où tout s'harmonise'[8]).

In the literature of picturesque cacophony there is little sense of the aggressive onslaught on the ear of urban noise, and in particular scarce reference to what is central to the Baudelairian phenomenology of the discordant city, the noise of traffic, what, as early as 1830, Amédée de Tissot had called 'l'insupportable bruit que font nuit et jour vingt mille voitures particulières dans les rues de Paris'.[9] The centrality of that experience to Baudelaire is also at the centre of this chapter, and indeed of the argument of the book as a whole, in so far as it reflects a point of maximum tension and complexity in the relation between the nineteenth-century city and its representation in literature. It is an experience that penetrates deeply and disruptively into Baudelaire's imaginative encounters with the Parisian street and its inhabitants, and is of major consequence for his conception of what 'poetry' is and what it might be in the modern world.

In 'Les Petites Vieilles', for example, not only are the deformed bodies of the old women shown 'frémissant au fracas roulant des omnibus', but the shuddering reaction to the 'fracas' passes metaphorically into the depiction of the physical deformity itself ('à l'aspect de ces membres *discords*'[10]). Noise is thus damagingly inscribed in the body as well as in the psyche. Naturally, there is a countervailing instinct of self-preservation, ways of containing and deflecting damage. The most obvious is to switch off, the imperative of 'Crépuscule du soir' ('Et ferme ton oreille à ce rugissement'[11]). Another is to leave, either literally or figuratively; from a distance, the aggressive roar of the city can be muted, silenced or transformed. In a letter to Desnoyers accompanying the text of 'Crépuscule du soir', Baudelaire speaks of the 'prodigieuse musique' of 'nos étonnantes villes', but it is an urban music significantly heard from afar ('Dans le fond des bois, enfermé sous ces voûtes semblables à celles des sacristies et des cathédrales'[12]). As we have seen, the elevating view from the attic in 'Paysage' has its aural counterpart, in the conversion of industrial noise into song ('l'atelier qui chante'). 'Rêve parisien' evacuates noise entirely, though the silence of the alternative dream city is as much a source of terror as of peace (a perfection whose price is severance from communication and community). In the prose version of 'Crépuscule du soir', the 'cris discordants' of the city (specifically of the insane) travel upwards into a space of poetic reverie where they are trans-formed into 'une harmonie lugubre'.[13] When literally absent from Paris (as during his stay in the detested Brussels), memory softens reality by way of euphonious alliterative play in Baudelaire's prose: 'Bruxelles, ville plus bruyante que Paris. . . . Paris , infiniment plus grand et plus occupé, ne donne qu'un bourdonnement vaste et vague, velouté, pour ainsi dire.'[14]

'Pour ainsi dire' . . . But this is not saying it how it really was for Baudelaire *in situ*. This, famously, is what it is like to step into the street of Baudelaire's city poetry:

La rue assourdissante autour de moi hurlait.[15]

This line from 'A une passante' repays close analytical attention; its inter-action of sound, metre and syntax places us on the threshold of poetic 'modernity' and its intricate relation to the modern city. Technically, the line is a perfectly regular alexandrine, with caesura after 'assourdissante'. But 'assourdissante' weighs heavily on the line, dominates it – not, however, as is sometimes claimed, by virtue of some 'onomatopoeic' relation between its phonic properties and the deafening roar of the city, but by virtue of its length, sibilance and structural prominence. Indeed, one possible scansion of the line produces the following distribution of stresses:

La rue assourdissante\\ autour de mòi hurlàit.

In this reading, the voice moves breathlessly through the first hemistich towards the single accented sixth syllable, gathering up the stress of the city in the most stressful word of the line. In addition, 'La rue' and 'hur-lait' echo each other, the latter a near-inversion of the former, as quasi-palindrome proposing an identification of street and noise precisely at the level of sound itself. They relate moreover in terms of the line's syntax, as framing terms of the adverbial phrase 'autour de moi', literally *autour*, enclosing the self as at once object of aggressive bombardment and subject insulating itself against invasion. Finally, there is the strategic use of hiatus, not once but twice (*rue/assourdissante* and *moi/hurlait*). The double use of

128

hiatus, spaced between the two hemistiches, halts the smooth progress of the reading voice or the scanning ear. It is as if the din of the city, or rather the attempt to represent its effect in poetry, is putting pressure on poetry itself, threatening to damage the integrity of the line at a fundamental level of its constitution, its rhythm.[16]

I. A. Richards remarked that the level of noise generated by modern systems of urban transport placed almost intolerable strain on our responsiveness to the rhythms of poetry: 'No one at all sensitive to rhythm, for example, will doubt that the new pervasive, almost ceaseless, mutter or roar of modern transport, replacing the rhythm of the footstep or of horses' hoofs, is capable of interfering in many ways with our reading of verse. Thus it is no matter of surprise if we find ourselves often unable to respond in any relevant or coherent fashion.'[17] There is, of course, in this notion of the proper social and material conditions for the reading of poetry, an element of idealizing nostalgia for a lost 'organic' community whose rhythms of life are in natural harmony with the rhythms of verse. But there is a real issue here. It also seems to have been an issue for Baudelaire in the writing of poetry.[18] The dissonances of the city strike at what for Baudelaire is the very heart of verse, the principle of *harmony*. Baudelaire shares Poe's view of (lyric) poetry as 'the Rhythmical Creation of Beauty',[19] and would almost certainly have endorsed Coleridge's claim that 'metre' is 'the proper form of poetry', the expression of 'the high spiritual instinct of the human being impelling us to seek unity by harmonious adjustment'.[20] Poetry, according to Baudelaire, embodies the 'instinct immortel du Beau', itself connected with the desire to attain to the realm of 'harmonie universelle'.[21] Through its regularities of sound and rhythm, verse binds together, integrates, resolves or at least holds in equilibrated tension the scattered and fragmentary bits and pieces of experience. It is the conception of lyric poetry ('la vraie poésie') represented, for example, in Baudelaire's essay on Théophile Gautier: 'C'est, du reste, le caractère de la vraie poésie d'avoir le flot régulier, comme les grands fleuves qui s'approchent de la mer, leur mort et leur infini, et d'éviter la précipitation et la saccade. La poésie lyrique s'élance, mais toujours d'un mouvement élastique et ondulé. Tout ce qui est brusque et cassé lui déplaît.'[22]

This, of course, is an idealist and arguably regressive view of lyric, and its limits are searchingly tested when the bits and pieces prove radically recalcitrant to the endeavour of poetic integration. For Baudelaire, the city is the scene *par excellence* of that resistance. As the city fractures experience, so it also 'disfigures' what, in a traditional conception, is understood as 'poetry'. This explains in some measure the general shift in Baudelaire from verse to the genre of the prose poem, although the term 'genre' begs questions in so far as a presupposition of genre is a set of relatively settled conventions, and it is precisely part of the meaning of the prose poem to put that presupposition into question.[23] The pressure of urban experience subjects Baudelairian poetry to what Barbara Johnson has described as a process of 'défiguration'[24] – essentially, the move from the unifying power of poetic metaphor to a language of heterogeneous metonymies vainly gesturing towards a whole in a context where it is precisely the sense of 'wholeness' that is lacking. I do not, of course, mean by this (and neither does Johnson) to imply some absolute stylistic break between the verse poetry and the prose poetry.[25] As the use of hiatus in the opening line from 'A une passante' shows (and one could multiply the examples), dislocated rhythm is often a property of *Les Fleurs du Mal*, especially in the 'Tableaux parisiens' section.[26] Conversely, *Le Spleen de Paris* does not entirely jettison the aesthetic of harmony. The latter is active not only in the dreamscape prose poems of exotic displacement ('Une hemisphère dans une chevelure', etc.), but in some of the city-based poems as well.

There is, for example, the attempted poetic transfiguration of the artists's hovel in 'La Chambre double' (pp. 233–5) . 'La Chambre double' seeks to convert the ugliness and 'discordances' of the real into the harmonies of art ('Ici, tout a la suffisante clarté et la délicieuse obscurité de l'harmonie') by means of a language of metaphorical correspondences: 'Les étoffes parlent une langue muette, comme les fleurs, comme les ciels, comme les soleils couchants.' In its use of the language of mystic harmony for the attempted transfiguration of the disordered squalor of urban space, the text draws upon the ideas of the verse poem 'Correspondances'. This is no idle fantasy, though it turns out to be an empty one. The principle of *correspondances* is fundamental to Baudelaire's conception of lyric as possessing a unifying, identity-protecting power; in Benjamin's words, *correspondances*, as both doctrine and literary practice, represented for Baudelaire an attempt to cast experience in a 'crisis-proof form'.[27] Yet in 'La Chambre double' the se-ductive dream of the crisis-proof, or at least crisis-relieving, condition (figured in the notion of the soul taking 'un bain de paresse, aromatisé par le regret et le désir') comes out finally as non-sustainable reverie, the mere effect of an illusory analogical 'magic' dissolved and dispersed as the reality of the urban slum dwelling returns to shatter the poem's lyrical aspirations. Indeed the dream is revealed as empty not just thematically but also rhetorically, within the terms of the 'analogical' play of the text itself, and as such echoes the poem 'Correspondances' in another, more disconcerting way: just as, in the latter, the genuinely analogical, and thus integrating, function of the term 'comme' is collapsed into its inertly enumerative use in the final ter-cet,[28] so in 'La Chambre double' the 'comme' in 'comme les fleurs, comme les ciels, comme les soleils couchants' is simply the grammatically elliptical term (for 'comme font') of a list rather than the pivot of a poetic synthesis.

There can, then, be no hard and fast distinction between the verse poetry and the prose poems. In both, similar ambitions and similar doubts are played out. Yet in the prose poems the tension has arguably become more acute, more difficult to sustain and more liable to collapse. The tension has indeed become constitutive, structural, and has important implications for Baudelaire's general conception of the prose poem itself. Consider, for instance, the strangely ambivalent description of the project of the prose poem in the well-known letter to Arsène Houssaye, which normally serves now as a preface to the collection. Here Baudelaire explicitly links the ideal of the prose poem to the experience of the city: 'C'est surtout de la fréquentation des villes énormes, c'est du croisement de leurs innombrables rapports que naît cet idéal obsédant.' The heterogeneity of the city (its 'innombrables rapports') demands a new mode of poetic representation:

> Quel est celui de nous qui n'a pas, dans ses jours d'ambition, rêvé le miracle d'une prose poétique, musicale sans rhythme et sans rime, assez souple et assez heurtée pour s'adapter aux mouvements lyriques de l'âme, aux ondulations de la rêverie, aux soubresauts de la conscience?[29]

This passage appears in virtually all discussions of the prose poem but what is rarely pointed out is its deceptive syntax.[30] What in their juxtaposition look like synonyms or collocationary terms ('mouvements lyriques de l'âme', 'ondulations de la rêverie', 'soubresauts de la conscience') are in fact terms that pull in opposite directions. The first two phrases are entirely consonant with the aesthetic of harmony sketched in the essay on Gautier, as the terms of a project permitting the unhindered flow of mobile desiring fantasy through the life of the city ('ondulations de la rêverie' of course echoes 'un mouvement plastique et ondulé'). The third ('soubresauts de la conscience'), however, suggests, along with the word 'heurtée', the sudden starts and turns which check the easy rhythms of lyricism and reverie, the points where consciousness encounters the city as hard-edged, brittle, un-yielding, and where poetry therefore is called upon to open itself to 'la saccade', the 'brusque' and the 'cassé' definitionally closed off from the space of poetry in the account of Gautier. More exactly, the main terms of the description in the letter to Houssaye are internally discontinuous with each other. They themselves clash, and so both suggest and, more in-terestingly, enact an idea of the prose poem as a space of clashing items, as a 'music' whose rhythms are jerky and nervous, staccato rather than harmo-nious. Forsaking or modifying the ideal of harmony seems therefore to have been the only way Baudelaire could stay poetically in the city, though the drive to resistance, withdrawal and escape will also remain strong. That tension, moreover, tells us that the flexibilities of the prose poem are not to be seen simply as a *solution* to the problem of keeping poetry in the city. It is not, as is sometimes suggested, that the prose poem furnishes a style 'adequate' to the modern city. The question behind the experiment with the prose poem is whether there are *any* adequate, fully workable forms for the poetic representation of urban life, or whether the latter is so refractory that it puts the idea of poetry itself into crisis.

II

The wilfully low-key nonchalance of the letter to Houssaye, of course, encourages us to believe that there is no problem. This, however, may be as much mask as anything else, one of the many self-protective disguises in which Baudelaire presents himself to the world. The energetic commitment to what, in 'Les Bons Chiens' (pp. 806–10), Baudelaire lauds as the 'muse citadine' – as against the dead forms of the 'muse académique' – conceals potential contradictions; in the former expression, noun and adjective do not just happily coexist as the collaborative terms of the experimental verve of *modernité*; between the two there is a gap, a space of potential conflict. One occupant of that space is noise. Another, and related, source of the antagonism between muse and city is velocity, especially the speed of traffic on the streets and the boulevards. In 'Perte d'auréole' (pp. 299–300), the symbol of the muse, the poet's halo, falls in the street mire as the narrator stumbles in his effort to avoid the hurtling traffic: 'Tout à l'heure, comme je traversais le boulevard en grande hâte, et que je sautillais dans la boue, à travers ce chaos mouvant où la mort arrive au galop de tous les côtés à la fois, mon auréole, dans un mouvement brusque, a glissé de ma tête dans la fange du macadam.'[31] The tone here is awkward – an odd melange of the flippantly anecdotal and the ponderously allegorical. But the awkwardness itself reflects the problem of finding an appropriate voice for the transaction of the poet with the city; just as the 'auréole' slips, so the voice 'slips', moves uncertainly between stylistic registers.

Moreover, the image of the stumbling poet undoes abruptly ('dans un mouvement brusque') two other privileged figures through which Baudelaire attempts to sustain the fiction of a poetically engaged and controlled encounter with the urban environment. First, the grotesque spectacle of the poet hopping in the mud ('je sautillais dans la boue') implicitly ridicules the image with which Baudelaire elsewhere presents both the city and the prose poem as a free field for the play of the imagination – the image of the dance. In the letter to Houssaye, Baudelaire says that the collection of prose poems resembles a 'serpent' that can be chopped up in any way one likes ('Nous pouvons couper où nous voulons, moi ma rêverie, vous le manuscrit, le lecteur sa lecture'[32]). This remarkable analogy conjures up various notions. I shall argue later that, if the image of the 'knife' leads us towards these texts and the ways in which we might read them, its aggressive connotations are not ultimately compatible with the easy acceptance of the principle of 'fragmentation' implied here. In addition, however, the analogy with the snake recalls the verse poem 'Le Serpent qui danse'[33] as well as the figure of the 'dance' in the prose poem often taken as the explicit allegory of the collection as a whole ('Le Thyrse'). But, if the metaphor of the dance appears to retrieve for the prose poem the notion of 'rhythm' partially lost in the eclipse of the musical idea of 'harmony', it does not do so unequivocally. The strangely violent comparison of the writing and reading of the prose poem to the arbitrary hacking to pieces of the serpent scarcely suggests the steps of a sinuous yet measured choreography. It implies not only a series of improvised movements, open to the unpredictable mobilities of the city, but also the writhing movements of a body in pain, or a kind of *danse macabre*, like that of the 'petites vieilles' of *Les Fleurs du Mal* who 'dansent, sans vouloir danser, pauvres sonnettes / Où se pend un Démon sans pitié!' Or it evokes a choreography of madness, of movement running destructively out of control, a frenzy of directionless energy comparable to the 'chaos mouvant' of the city street, as in the poet's reaction to the 'cortège infernal' of old men at the end of 'Les Sept Vieillards':

> Et mon âme dansait, dansait, vieille gabarre,
> Sans mâts, sur une mer monstrueuse et sans bords.[34]

The second figure undone or parodied by the image of the helplessly stumbling poet in 'Perte d'auréole' is the one we have come to see, largely from the influence of Benjamin's seminal study, as being at the very heart of the articulation of the urban theme in Baudelaire's writings, the figure of the *flâneur*.[35] 'La flânerie, si chère aux peuples doués d'imagination,' writes Baudelaire in *La Pauvre Belgique!*,[36] here simply repeating – doubtless from the exile's feelings of loss and nostalgia – what for decades had been the standard view of *flânerie* (the *Livre des Cent-et-un* had described it as 'la plus haute expression de la civilisation moderne'[37]). This amiable equation of strolling and imagining also underlies one of Baudelaire's descriptions of the prose poems; in a letter to Sainte-Beuve, he refers to the dreaming hero of the latter's text, *Joseph Delorme*, as an analogue for the poetic subject of the prose poems ('un nouveau Joseph Delorme accrochant sa pensée rhapsodique à chaque accident de la flânerie'[38]). Furthermore, not only does this echo Sainte-Beuve in terms of the given representations of *flânerie*, it also recapitulates in a new urban context the Rousseauist topos of the solitary 'promeneur' culling from the natural world the materials of self-sustaining reverie (one of the originally projected titles for the collection was *Le Promeneur solitaire*[39]). Unpacking what lies buried or anaesthetized in these easy equations and analogies is one of the main purposes of Benjamin's account (though his own interests are directed to the verse poems rather than to the prose poetry). In particular, Benjamin shows that *flânerie* was not just an urban custom, but that it also supplied the terms of an *attitude*; or, as we might say nowadays, it was not just a social practice, but a practice generating, and in turn inflected by, a discourse with ideological claims to its object, the city.

Like the panoramic view, the discourse of *flânerie* aims at a perspective of mastery.[40] Although its incarnations are various, in Benjamin's account it is commanded by essentially two figures (the *physiologiste* and the detective), and has a double objective: to make the city comfortable and to make it intelligible. The *flâneur* as physiologist is someone who, in Benjamin's striking phrase, 'goes botanizing on the asphalt';[41] he makes the city safe and innocuous by classifying its population in the form of picturesque character sketches, giving a picture of Paris as 'harmless and of perfect bonhomie'.[42] The *flâneur* as detective has a more heightened sense of the city as disquieting and dangerous, but brings to danger a capacity to interpret its signs quickly and surely; the language of *flânerie* and the emerging form of the detective novel have in common a 'criminological sagacity'[43] which both acknowledges and yet subdues what threatens the 'identity' of the city, in both the social and the intellectual senses of the term.

There is, however, a third figure in Benjamin's description, under which the previous two can be subsumed, namely the idea of the *flâneur* as 'connoisseur'.[44] In this guise, the *flâneur* is above all a skilful agent, an expert at converting the city into a fund of interesting 'sensations'; *flânerie*, on this view, is what Edmond Texier in his *Tableau de Paris* calls 'cette flânerie féconde, instructive, piquante, animée, riche d'émotions, de souvenirs et d'enseignements'.[45] Although, as Benjamin says (following some remarks of Baudelaire on the significance of the dandy), the *flâneur*, as typically a man of means and leisure, is in some respects the antithesis of the expert, a point of resistance to 'specialization' in a culture based on an increasingly rationalized system of the division of labour, in his most important aspect he in fact reproduces the terms of the system he apparently rejects and transcends.[46] Much of the minor literature of nineteenth-century *flânerie* is devoted to discriminating kinds of urban strollers according to the degree of skill they bring to their pursuits. The basic distinction is between the *flâneur* and the *badaud*. Sometimes the terms are used interchangeably, but more often to distinguish between the knowledgeable and the ignorant, the expert and the incompetent. Victor Fournel will move bewilderingly between the two uses.[47] Louis Huart's *Physiologie du flâneur*, on the other hand, proposes – largely in humorous vein – a rigorous codification based on discriminations between the *flâneur*, the *badaud*, the *musard* and the *batteur de pavé*. The *badaud* is the gawker, who sees but without intelligence (there are in fact two sorts of *badaud* – the *badaud étranger*, the tourist, who sees only once and who therefore lacks all intimate knowledge of the city, and the *badaud indigène*, who sees routinely but passively); the *musard*, who sees nothing, who sniffs the city but – to anticipate a later reference – does not know how to 'savour' it; the *batteur de pavé* is the lowest of the low, the parasite or street hustler (close to the category of the *mendiant*[48]).

In contrast to all these stands the authentic *flâneur* whose 'esprit mobile'[49] displays the mentality of the connoisseur in a new form of sophisticated attention to the city, based on informed, directed and dominant 'looking'; the city is there 'pour occuper ses yeux, provoquer ses réflexions, animer son existence de mouvement loin duquel sa pensée s'alanguit'.[50] The objects attracting the attention of the *flâneur* can vary in direct proportion to the 'variety' (normally assumed as innocently given) of the city itself. Nevertheless, empirical diversity of interest does not mean the absence of a set of inclusions and exclusions from which a 'discourse' is characteristically constructed. Theoretically, the discourse of the *flâneur* is porous to everything the life of the city can present. In practice, of course, it is not, and Baudelaire himself will play havoc with its conventions, precisely by bringing into the field of vision and representation objects and events generally screened off by it. In the majority of the relevant texts, *flânerie* as an exercise in connoisseurship, in expert 'looking', is governed by the play, and often the mixture, of two idioms – the idiom of science and the idiom of pleasure. The skill or expertise of the *flâneur* consists essentially in monitoring the urban scene with a view either to dominating it through an act of understanding (normally in a classification) or to exploiting it as a vein of sophisticated pleasures.

Although in several contexts the two idioms are indissociable, for the purposes of the present argument it is the latter emphasis – on the city as a field of pleasure – that I wish to retain. Its most succinct formulation is perhaps Balzac's in *La Fille aux yeux d'or*, when he describes the Paris of the *flâneur* as a kind of a box of poetic delights, endlessly available for degustation: 'l'heureuse et molle espèce de flâneurs, les seuls gens réellement heureux à Paris, et qui en dégustent à chaque heure les mouvantes poésies'.[51] *Flânerie* as connoisseurship thus implies as much the notion of 'tasting' Paris as of seeing it. And, as I have previously noted, in nineteenth-century literature, the theme of gustatory pleasure is rarely far from the theme of erotic pleasure. The representation of the 'jouissance' of the city stroller in the terms of sexual feeling and metaphor recurs throughout the period. To stay with our two main examples, Huart sketches the adventures of the *flâneur* as a veritable erotics of the street, while Fournel tames what is potentially dangerous in that association by describing *flânerie* as a repeated return to the pleasures of first love ('Quelle bonne et douce chose que la flânerie. . . . Quiconque en a goûté une fois ne s'en peut rassasier, et y revient sans cesse, comme on revient, dit-on, à ses premiers amours'[52]).

This is, of course, anodyne stuff, in particular domesticating and conceal-

135

ing the most obvious analogical source for the sexualization of *flânerie* – the almost endless possibility of encounter with the prostitute in the public spaces of Paris. But if, on the whole, the minor literature of agreeable picturesque edits out the figure of the prostitute (like the guidebook maintaining decorous silence on the sites and occasions of indecorous pleasure in the city), elsewhere the preoccupation with the 'place' of the prostitute in the economy, both material and symbolic, of Paris verges on the obsessive. In novels, plays, operas, paintings, cartoons, newspaper articles, scientific publications, inspectors' reports, political speeches, police dossiers, the prostitute is everywhere to be found, or rather the attempt, often baffled and contradictory, to establish a set of terms, a space of representation, for the prostitute within the social order.[53] Both the details and the significance of that obsession have been much discussed by other commentators.[54] The specific feature of this discursive abundance I am concerned with here concerns the way in which these terms get transferred to the representation of the city itself, the way in which the prostitute becomes a metaphor *for* Paris.[55] This, as we shall see, is central, though in extremely complex form, to Baudelaire's articulation of the figure of the *flâneur*, notably in the prose poems.

Balzac, as early as *Ferragus*, describes Paris as 'cette grande courtisane',[56] and, as the century unfolds, the analogy will become insistent and ubiquitous. In itself, there is nothing unusual about this rhetorical move; the metaphorical association of city and prostitute has a lineage stretching back to the literature of antiquity, and its appearances in nineteenth-century literature very often have an air of sheer routineness to them (what, after all, more 'natural' comparison than that of the city with its oldest profession, etc.?). Furthermore, 'courtisane' is not the same as prostitute. This is not just a matter of semantics but also of ideology, of the categories in which social reality is thought and maintained. The analogy with the 'courtisane' is in part a moralized image, an expression of anxiety. But it is also an image connoting glamour, excitement, the great cosmetic game of leisure and pleasure in the modern city, part of the normal apparatus of civilized 'commerce'. If the category of the courtesan served to convert the transaction between money and sex into an amiable fiction, then its analogical transfer to the city itself was likely to produce a similar set of connotations. On the other hand, the sense of anxiety also ran deep, and developed with a new intensity from the late 1840s into the Second Empire and the Third Republic, as the place of prostitution in the city's economy of sex became more visible. The characteristic expression of that anxiety in literature was through the medicalized imagery of 'disease'. Balzac's late novel, *La Cousine Bette*, uses the diseased body of Valérie Marneffe (the prostitute disguised as the respectable woman) to organize a whole vision of a corrupted, self-prostituting urban society;

and this motif will recur in different guises in the nineteenth-century novel through to Zola's *Nana*.[57]

It has been said of nineteenth-century literature that in it 'woman' – in particular the transgressing, adulterous woman – is always the site of a sexual and social trouble, a trouble of classification, a problem of *identity*.[58] The diseased prostitute, or prostitution as source of disease, is fundamental to the structure of that anxiety. Its most famous, though instructively softened, instance is Dumas *fils*'s *La Dame aux camélias*. Dumas was arguably the Second Empire writer in whose work the obsession with the idea of prostitution as pervading and destroying the whole social 'organism' was most active. In *La Dame aux camélias*, Marguerite dies of tuberculosis, a convenient euphemism essential to maintaining the romantic ingredients of the plot. The plot, however, demands her death, because its ideology (reflected in the humane yet firm 'reasonableness' of Armand's father) demands that her desire be sacrificed to ensure the proper functioning of society, proper 'circulation' (including the circulation of women). Marguerite does not threaten anything for so long as she remains as available 'courtisane' in the shadowy zone of the *demi-monde*. Once she steps out of that world, exceeds the assigned role and its accompanying illusions, there is a danger of 'contamination', of a loss of control.

Regulation of prostitution, in function of a primary division of sexual labour between women for men, is of course the name of the game. Projects to control prostitution in the city proliferate in direct proportion to the increase in anxiety over loss of control. Parent-Duchâtelet sought to devise an ingenious system of signs whereby prostitutes would be recognized by men, specifically potential clients, but not by respectable women;[59] for the male *flâneur* the streets must be furnished with appropriate means for recognizing the sexual goods on sale, but not so obviously that the streets could not be felt as safe and clean by wives and daughters. It was simply a matter of getting the categories right, and installing the signs of those categories in the right places. Many had a shot at this. In a literary mode, Dumas *père* – more relaxed about this sort of thing than his agitated son – was assigned for his contribution to *La Grande Ville, Tableau de Paris* the task of descriptively classifying the city's population of prostitutes. He has little difficulty with *courtisane* ('la reine de toutes les civilisations') and with *fille publique* ('cet être dégradé'), but comes unstuck with *lorette* ('qu'on ne pouvait classer dans aucun des genres connus').[60] The specific difficulty does not matter, and certainly the urbane Dumas is not particularly bothered by his taxonomic problem. Its value as example is rather of a symptomatic character. The nomenclature is predicated on a desire to impose order: master the varieties of whore and you are close to mastering the variety of the city itself; classifying is an activity strictly cognate with the logic of policing prostitution in terms of the distinction between the registered and the non-registered (the *insoumise*). But as the nomenclature expands, tries but fails to keep up with its own proliferating distinctions, the whole category system is endangered by what exceeds it, just as in reality the *police de mœurs* could never really succeed, in an increasingly opaque and fluid urban reality, in keeping track of the identities and movements of the *fille insoumise*.

The literature and painting of the period that are resistant to the demands of the official ideology invite us precisely into that experience where 'margin' and 'middle', 'high' and 'low' cannot be held apart, where categories and signs are dislodged from their rightful place. One thinks of Balzac's great plots of 'connection' (especially *Splendeurs et misères des courtisanes*) bringing high and low – harlots, pimps, criminals, society ladies, judges, policemen, bankers, politicians – into intimate relation in ways that inflict severe damage on the society's self-image; or of Flaubert's internalizing of that blurred dividing line through the psychology of his hero, Frédéric Moreau, which mirrors the social category system by separating female objects of desire into sacred and profane, madonna and whore, but which also has those separations collapse back into one another; or of Zola's great, if excessively schematic, set-piece in *Nana*, reversing the high/low distinction in the scene where the prostitute rides horseback on the humiliated aristocrat, Muffat. Above all, there is Manet, his provocative mixtures of the respectable and the *louche* in *Bal masqué à l'Opéra* and *La Musique aux Tuileries*, and the dramatization of that mix in the implied relation between male viewer and naked woman in *Olympia*. This picture – in recent times perhaps more discussed than any other nineteenth-century painting – quotes from the social vocabulary of the Courtesan and the pictorial vocabulary of the Nude, but only in order to equivocate them both, forcing a recognition that the body of the woman in the painting cannot be recuperated into the comfortable space of either; reminding the male viewer that he had, in his own primitive way, actually got the point he wished to ignore when, in his guise as nineteenth-century art critic, he described that body as 'dirty', 'unwashed', 'greasy': namely, that Olympia comes from the streets, and that the happy charade prettifying the money/sex exchange could be accomplished only by a retreat into bad faith, by literally averting one's eyes.[61]

III

What, then, from this sort of context, does it mean to compare the city, or, even more intriguingly, *oneself* in the city, to the figure of the prostitute? What questions of 'identity' are raised – as both the identity of the city and the identity of the self – in that comparison? These questions are of some considerable importance for understanding the Baudelairian version of *flânerie*. Baudelaire is the writer *par excellence* in whose work the theme of the 'streetwalker' brings together both the prostitute and the *flâneur*.[62] This is not just a matter of the fraternity of *la bohème* (a stock theme of the period). Nor does it turn solely on Benjamin's point about the implication of the poet in the venalities of commercial exchange. In comparing poet and prostitute in the terms of hawking their respective wares around the market-place, Baudelaire is repeating another commonplace (which Balzac had already used as an organizing metaphor for literary life in *Illusions perdues*). Yet Baudelaire does not simply repeat the commonplace; he also transforms it (a great deal of Baudelaire's city poetry can be read as a transformation of the repertoire of city clichés, the stock of *parisianismes* deposited in the *physiologies* and suchlike). The analogy with the prostitute Baudelaire makes uniquely his own, as one of the key terms of a complex and ambivalent erotics of urban space.

The incarnations of the Baudelairian *flâneur* are multiple – prince, dandy, detective, connoisseur and so on – but they frequently include a staging of the poet/city relation as amorous encounter, notably in the representation of the poet's relation to the urban crowd. In the essay, *Le Peintre de la vie moderne* and the prose poem 'Les Foules', the city is dramatized as a scene of attraction and seduction, in which the crowd appears variously as mistress, wife and harlot, and the artist as husband, lover and client taking possession of a malleable and receptive female body. In *Le Peintre de la vie moderne*, the artist (specifically Constantin Guys) is seen as the 'amoureux de la foule' whose 'passion' is to 'marry' the crowd (*'épouser la foule'*[63]). The same motif is both repeated in the prose poem, 'Les Foules' ('celui-là qui épouse facilement la foule connaît des jouissances fiévreuses'), and developed in a language of mounting excitement centred on ideas of entering, possessing, enjoying, fertilizing, whose climactic moment will be the conversion of the image of 'jouissance' into the wilder image of 'orgie' and the corresponding image of 'marriage' into that of 'prostitution' ('cette ineffable orgie, . . . cette sainte prostitution de l'âme', pp. 243–4). This might be said to give a model of the prose poem in general as a series of unexpected and illicit 'couplings', an extension of Baudelaire's conception of the stylistic project of *Les Fleurs du Mal* as based on 'l'*accouplement* de tel substantif avec tel adjectif, analogue ou contraire'.[64]

Here, however, the text – true, in its own movements, to the intercommunicating mobilities of which it speaks – effects a number of reversals and displacements. The poem begins by placing the poet-*flâneur* in a position of mastery, as the lover for whom all is open, who is free to 'enter' the city at will: 'Comme ces âmes errantes qui cherchent un corps, il entre, quand il veut, dans le personnage de chacun. Pour lui seul, tout est vacant.'

But the position of mastery is also dislodged, turned upside-down, so to speak, as the idea of losing the self through entry into non-self ('à sa guise être lui-même et autrui') is meshed with the contrary idea of being entered oneself, putting oneself in the place of the 'woman'.[65] Active/passive, entering/entered, giving/receiving – these terms, and the antithetical relations they normally hold in place, are allowed to become fluid, convertible, in the same way as the terms 'multitude, solitude: termes égaux et convertibles pour le poète actif et fécond'. This gives the context for a further reversal, or rather a recovery. The phrase 'sainte prostitution de l'âme' not only refers to the poet (it is the poet, not the city crowd, who is figured as the prostitute), it also recovers a sense of the term 'prostitution' which in certain respects is the exact opposite of the usual connotation of venal transaction. This is the old, semi-sacred sense of prostitution as a freely promiscuous giving out of oneself, a destruction of identity-barriers in the form of what Baudelaire here calls the intoxication of universal communion: 'Le promeneur solitaire et pensif tire une singulière ivresse de cette universelle communion.'

This recalls yet again Rousseau's *Rêveries*, suggesting a view of the urban *flâneur* as a transformation of Rousseau's *promeneur*, who, in a state of permanently receptive openness, both acquires and loses the sense of self through a movement out of self into harmonious communion with nature. Yet, if there is an allusion here to Rousseau, Baudelaire's city is not, and can never be, the same as Rousseau's nature; indeed a precondition of the latter's affirmed equilibrium of self and non-self is precisely flight from the city, as compensation for what cannot be had from normal social intercourse. Rousseau is in fact present in the prose poems in a variety of ways, but supremely, as Starobinski has shown, as the *irréparable*, as a presence, a set of values and aspirations, damaged beyond possible repair.[66] A neo-Rousseauist reading of the 'promeneur' of 'Les Foules' thus rapidly comes up against the conditions of its own impossibility. It may be, as Nathaniel Wing has suggested, that 'Les Foules' can be read as putting into circulation a series of 'libidinal exchanges which disrupt oppositions' around a 'plural object of desire', as a happy enactment of polymorphous desiring fantasy in which fixed subject–object relations and stable markers of identity are dispersed into fragmented yet interchangeable multiplicity.[67] But, if so, the concluding point of such a reading would have to be that this is an enactment which is strictly non-sustainable. There are essentially two reasons why this is so. First, the logic of this description would require the indefinite prolongation of the fantasy, its deferral of any moment of arrest or closure. But the poem does close, not just in the banal technical sense, but as a sudden, ironic switch of direction, an abrupt turning back on or cancellation of its initial energies:

Il est bon d'apprendre quelquefois aux heureux de ce monde, ne fût-ce que pour humilier un instant leur sot orgueil, qu'il est des bonheurs supérieurs au leur, plus vastes et plus raffinés. Les fondateurs de colonies, les pasteurs de peuples, les prêtres missionnaires exilés au bout du monde, connaissent sans doute quelque chose de ces mystérieuses ivresses; et, au sein de la vaste famille que leur génie s'est faite, ils doivent rire quelquefois de ceux qui les plaignent pour leur fortune si agitée et pour leur vie si chaste.

Closure of this kind is one of the distinctive formal characteristics of the prose poems as a whole, and it generates an instability, a *vertige* radically different from the self-dissolving vertigo of *jouissance*. Many of the prose poems – and *all* those dealing with subjects taken from the city – close in a manner that suggests withdrawal from, or at least equivocation of, some prior commitment (though the move is often concealed in an ironic tone so deadpan as to be virtually impenetrable). Wing himself takes note of the odd ending of 'Les Foules' – its relocation of the experience of 'ivresse' in the creative power of male celibacy – but wants it to serve precisely as prolongation of the earlier ideas of the poem: this time as the 'neuter' defined as another space or mark of the non-hierarchical play of differences.[68] However, it is difficult to concede the plausibility of that reading. The male figures of the last paragraph are not 'neuters', and scarcely 'neutral'; they are essentially figures of ascesis, renouncing the libidinal (other than in the form of 'creative' sublimation). They are also figures that belong to an elsewhere, the Baudelairian *là-bas*, out of the crowd and away from the city. In other words, what is restored here appears to be a perspective of mastery, one of whose conditions is a self-distancing from the city and a retreat from emotional involvement with otherness.

The moment of closure is thus also a moment of leave-taking. Yet it is a leave-taking which, in its very denial of its point of departure, returns us to it, that is, to the question of the city as an *issue* for the poem. This brings me to the second reason why the account I have rehearsed might be deemed unsatisfactory. Psycho-literary descriptions of the prose poems, turning on analogies between the sexual and the textual, risk eliding, or at least relegating, the specifically social and historical dimension of what is being described – here precisely the reality of nineteenth-century Paris. Although sexualized through and through in its metaphorical representations, 'Les Foules' is not primarily about a project of sexual mastery subsequently deconstructed into free interchange between male and female identities. I do not mean by this that questions of sexual difference are irrelevant to this poem; indeed it may be that Baudelaire's physical and emotional experience of the city is finally reducible to a drama of libidinal attachment and disengagement around the 'feminine' other, that the metaphors count for more than the referent. But, even on those (debatable) assumptions, the referent should not be allowed simply to disappear from view: the poem is 'about' the individual in the modern urban crowd, and the point about the crowd is that, however much it is personalized and sexualized, it is fundamentally impersonal, abstract and alienated; its social nature is inimical to anything we might understand as 'communion', and, as such, quite beyond imaginative appropriation as an object of identification.

Indeed, even if we stay within the terms of a sexualized figurative reading, the switch to the motif of celibacy in the last paragraph could just as plausibly be interpreted according to the figure of 'castration'. The city does not 'penetrate' and occupy consciousness as pleasure, but rather as wounding incision, as a painful 'cutting' into the psyche, and thus gives the lie to – or reveals the other side of – the image of the chopped-up serpent nonchalantly proposed in the letter to Houssaye as signifying the easy openness of the world of the prose poems, unproblematically hospitable 'aux mouvements lyriques de l'âme, aux ondulations de la rêverie'. In Baudelaire's Paris, consciousness does not dance, it bleeds. We should not forget that in the prose poems there is a whole thematics of the *knife* – notably, the bloody surgical instruments which obsess the deranged Mlle Bistouri in the poem of that name, or, in the poem which brings hell into Paris ('Les Tentations, ou Eros, Plutus et la Gloire', pp. 259–62), the 'brillants couteaux' and the 'instruments de chirurgerie' which Satan wears around his waist (the belt, incidentally, consists of a live serpent placed around a body described as 'd'un sexe ambigu', two quite different modalities of the sinuous and the sexually indeterminate).

To be open to the city is to invite a potential mutilation, a maiming of human and poetic impulse against which various strategies of self-defence have to be devised, and is one reason why Benjamin attaches so much importance to the image of the 'fencer' in Baudelaire's work, as an image for the attempt to parry and deflect the blows the city would inflict on the mind.[69] In this version of Paris, the city does not activate an ecstatic undoing of identity on the model of *jouissance*; it does not release subjectivity from fixity into movement, propelling the self into an embrace of 'fraternal' union with others; if that were so, we might well find Baudelaire's erotic metaphors, once unpacked, on the side of a particular ideology of modern urban experience – endorsing the fiction of Second Empire Paris as a pleasurama available to all, without distinction of wealth and class, above all in those strangely amorphous gatherings and assemblages on the boulevards, in the streets and cafés, called the 'crowd'.

On the contrary, for Baudelaire the city menaces what might remain, in however residual a form, of the sense of identity. 'Baudelaire, l'homme des foules,' wrote Sartre, 'est aussi celui qui a le plus peur des foules.'[70] Fear of the crowd can have many sources and take many forms, and I shall return at a later point to the terms of Sartre's own psycho-existential account. But one major source of threatened identity for Baudelaire was the presence in the crowd of the *unpredictable*. If the city crowd is the opposite of 'community', this is not just because, as in Benjamin's account, the crowd is mere 'statistical existence', anonymous numbers;[71] it is also because, in the absence of the relatively secure framework of a customary culture, the self has far fewer points of orientation. In the flow of urban masses through the city, the psyche becomes accident-prone, subject to the dislocating vagaries of pure chance. The theme of chance, of random experience, is in fact one of the cherished preoccupations of the literature of *flânerie*. Time and again, we are complacently invited to construe the 'charm' of *flânerie* as the pleasures of the unexpected: 'le plus grand charme de la flânerie, c'est d'être imprévue,' says Huart; the ideal urban stroll is the one 'suivant la volonté du hasard'.[72] 'Promenons-nous donc au hasard' is Paul de Kock's invitation.[73] These texts were written in the 1830s and 1840s; we are still in what Edmond de Goncourt calls 'the world of Balzac'. By the time we enter Baudelaire's Paris – essentially the Paris of the Second Empire – this sort of claim about the city will be contested, largely in the context of the debate about Haussmannization. Goncourt will lament the passing of an old Paris on the grounds that Haussmann's city is a place from which chance has been abolished ('Je suis étranger à ce qui vient, à ce qui est, comme à ces boulevards nouveaux sans tournant, sans aventures de perspective, implacables de ligne droite, qui ne sentent plus le monde de Balzac'[74]). Others, however, will perpetuate the affable conception of randomized *flânerie* by cultivating – in suitably edited form – what seems in fact to have been closer to the truth of the matter: that, however regimented a shape the city might appear to be acquiring, its social texture was more hospitable than ever to the *jeu du hasard*. The new street, according to Feyruet, was the street 'prodigue de surprises'.[75]

But, whether lamented as loss or promoted as actuality, the view of Paris as place of surprise much preoccupied the contemporary imagination. The attractions of risk are at the heart of the ideology of the modern city. It is a notion doubtless rooted in the many different forms of nineteenth-century urban mobility, notably in the emergence of a social formation increasingly commanded by the movement of speculative capital and the corresponding dream of the quick killing on the Stock Exchange. Already in Balzac the *Bourse* serves as analogy for the workings of the city in general, in both its material and its mental transactions; and many of Balzac's urban plots will turn on chance events and coincidences for which the explicit model will often be the risky investment or the random spin of the gaming table. Speed in nineteenth-century Paris was not just a matter of the traffic. It included the speed with which fortunes could be won or lost. It also included that other form of fast transaction, the quick pick-up. The metaphor of one commentator unwittingly joins the two in the description of Paris as offering 'des surprises, des séductions'.[76] Into that bland juxtaposition can be inserted what Edmond de Goncourt – in brutal qualification of his view of the rigidly planned city – says about the prostitute/client encounter in *La Fille Elisa*: 'D'ordinaire à Paris, c'est la montée au hasard . . . d'un escalier bâillant dans la nuit . . . le contact colère . . . de deux corps qui ne se retrouveront jamais.'[77] The settings of the quick killing and the quick pick-up will also be subjects for painting, for example, in the whispered dealings represented in Degas's *A la Bourse* and the innumerable images of ambiguous private exchange between men and women in the work of some of the Impressionists. Despite the dissenting voices, which mistook the rationalized physical layout of the city centre for the lived social reality itself (all lines and demarcations), Haussmann's Paris engendered in most observers a quite new sense of randomness, although in what it consisted and whether it was to be welcomed depended on one's point of view and, more importantly, one's perceived interests; those who welcomed it as giving a new kind of 'freedom' presumably gave little thought to the mass of the city's working population, those 'slaves of chance' dependent for employment on the apparently uncontrollable play of market forces.[78]

We know that Baudelaire was fascinated by chance, as a mechanism for the delivery of invigorating and illuminating 'shock' to the psychic system and the poetic imagination, and that the urban landscape seemed to him the obvious environment for experiences of this kind. In its most affirmative aspect, it furnishes one of the fundamental principles of the aesthetic of *modernité*, a conception of modern art based on the excited cultivation of the unknown, the sudden and the strange ('cet élément inattendu, *l'étrangeté*, qui est comme le condiment indispensable de toute beauté', as Baudelaire puts it in the 'Notes nouvelles sur Edgar Poe',[79] or, in the remark from *Fusées*, 'l'irrégularité, c'est-à-dire l'inattendu, la surprise, l'étonnement sont une partie essentielle et caractéristique de la beauté'[80]). Chance bulks large in Baudelaire's version of 'making it new', and the rapid flow of unpredictable stimulus provided by the city seemed its natural source, as supplier of the experiences for the project of unsettling inherited literary clichés. In the verse poem, 'Le Soleil', a novel adaptation of the olfactory theme of 'sniffing' Paris brings chance event and the search for poetic inspiration into direct relation ('Flairant dans tous les coins les hasards de la rime'[81]). In 'Les Foules', the giving of self to the city expressed in the image of prostitution is elaborated as 'l'âme qui se donne tout entière, poésie et charité, à l'imprévu qui se montre, à l'inconnu qui passe'. The same emphasis characterizes the description of 'l'homme de la foule' in *Le Peintre de la vie moderne*: 'il se précipite à travers la foule à la recherche d'un inconnu dont la physionomie entrevue l'a, en un clin d'œil, fasciné.'[82]

This, of course, recalls the famous moment of 'A une passante', the sudden flash of intense perception, as the woman comes into view against the background of street and crowd. In this poem, the appearance of the woman is described precisely as a flash ('un éclair'). And that in turn might bring us back to another term of *Le Peintre de la vie moderne*, the image of electricity: 'Ainsi l'amoureux de la vie universelle entre dans la foule comme dans un immense réservoir d'électricité.'[83] This is one context for the Baudelairian aesthetic of 'shock', as being in tension with the 'static', dislocating fixed and habitualized frames of perception. In 'A une passante' it is also linked with a notion of rebirth, an epiphany of potential resurrection from deadened sensibility ('Fugitive beauté / Dont le regard m'a fait soudainement renaître'[84]). Chance experience is thus potentially fertile, and fertility is another of the figures that Baudelaire will use to represent both the city and the poet's relation to it. In the 1846 Salon, it appears in what looks like a declaration of a new poetic programme: 'La vie parisienne est féconde en sujets poétiques et merveilleux.'[85] 'Fecundity' is an image that will recur in a number of the prose poems: in 'Les Fenêtres', it will be recalled, the glimpse through the window is described as 'fécond'; the poet in 'Les Foules' is 'le poète actif et fécond'; and in 'Les Projets' (pp. 265–6) the tavern randomly encountered during a stroll through the city is the 'auberge du hasard, si féconde en voluptés' (the material of its window curtains, moreover, attracting the significant term 'bariolée').

'Les Projets' is perhaps the prose poem in which Baudelaire gets closest to establishing an equilibrium between consciousness and the city, the text in which project and actuality, inner and outer worlds, urban landscape and landscape of the mind, merge as one. But, as the occasion of the fully achieved delights of *flânerie*, it stands virtually alone. If, for Baudelaire, the random electrifies the mind, the experience is more commonly painful than pleasurable, less a switching on than a potential electrocution. The 'shock' of the contingent and the aleatory is, as Benjamin suggests, more appropriately thought of on the model of 'traumatic' event, threatening to overwhelm both the poise and the pose of the adventure-seeking *flâneur*.[86] Chance appears here rather as 'le hasard méchant' of 'Les Sept Vieillards', as a violence done to the mind rather than a release from routine into exhilarating perceptual freedom. The promised moment of epiphany becomes its opposite, the moment not of heightened awareness but of a fall into the meaninglessness of discontinuous, fragmented life. It speaks to us not just of the risk-taking heroism of the architect of modernism who, in Harold Rosenberg's revealing metaphor, 'gambles his judgment',[87] but also of the degraded temporality of, precisely, the gambler, the risk-taker of Baudelaire's gaming house ('Le Jeu'), for whom exposure to pure chance entails the disintegration of experience into autonomous moments, spaced disconnectedly between the euphoria of winning, the anguish of losing and the emptiness of waiting.

We simplify the contradictions and tensions of Baudelaire's work if we see it as being merely an audacious prefiguring of the modernist aesthetic of *étonnement*. If part of the meaning of Baudelaire's notion of the 'heroism of modern life' has to do with strength, the capacity to survive and transform invasion by dangerous stimulus (the 'chocs et conflits quotidiens de la civilisation'[88]), this makes sense only if we also remember the extreme fragility of the Baudelairian psyche and the extent to which it found exposure to a rapidly changing and uncontrollable urban environment to be quite intolerable. Sometimes it becomes so intolerable as to veer towards madness. Benjamin's most brilliant insight, in my view, is the moment when he draws attention to the full semantic resonance of the line in 'A une passante' where the poet describes the 'shock' of seeing the woman in the street: 'Moi, je buvais, crispé comme un extravagant.' Benjamin reminds us that the body contracting in spasm expresses 'the kind of sexual shock that can beset a lonely man' in the big city, but he also reactivates what might otherwise lie buried in the word 'extravagant', namely its connotation of being on the edge, close to breakdown.[89] This is scarcely an example of 'ecstasy-producing shock'[90] melting self into other; it is rather loss of the sense of self, pressure on 'identity', of an intensely distressing kind. It suggests shock as trauma or, perhaps better, as hysteria.

Here indeed is Baudelaire taking the place of the 'woman', but in terms of that formulation classically applied in the nineteenth century from Charcot to Freud to female sexual disorder, the identity-confusion of woman in the state described as 'hysterical'. The word is important for Baudelaire in both his poetry and his critical writing. On the one hand, it is effectively placed in quotation marks, as the term of a questioned or rejected medical discourse ('cette humeur, hystérique selon les médecins, satanique selon ceux qui pensent un peu mieux que les médecins').[91] Or it is provocatively stretched across the boundaries within which nineteenth-century scientific and popular opinion sought to confine it. The genius of the article on *Madame Bovary*, for example, derives in large measure from Baudelaire's intuitive grasp of the intimate transfer between author and heroine of 'male' and 'female' attributes. Hysteria is seen as belonging crucially to this shifting psychological ground, as designating a problem of identity that travels across the boundaries of gender: 'L'Hystérie! . . . ce mystère . . . qui, s'exprimant dans les femmes par une boule ascendante et asphyxiante (je ne parle que du symptôme principal), se traduit chez les hommes nerveux par toutes les impuissances et aussi par l'aptitude à tous les excès.'[92] It is also applied both to Baudelaire himself ('J'ai cultivé mon hystérie avec jouissance et terreur'[93]) and to the poet's persona, in the prose poem 'Le Vieux Saltimbanque' (pp. 247–9). The isolated street artist, standing apart from the festive crowd, is one of the many pariah figures in the prose poems who serve as allegory for the poet himself. But more important than inert allegorical appropriation (for appropriation is what it is) is the intensity of the poet's emotional reaction to his perceived double: 'Je sentis ma gorge serrée par la main terrible de l'hystérie.' If this is a case of identification, it is one in which the category of identity itself has become problematic, caught in that tightening of the throat which symptomatically presages strangled confusion of utterance, a crisis of self-expression which, in connection with women, the doctors labelled 'hysteria'.

IV

Baudelaire wrote in *Le Peintre de la vie moderne* that 'toute pensée sublime est accompagnée d'une secousse nerveuse, plus ou moins forte, qui retentit jusque dans le cervelet.'[94] This is entirely consistent with the tradition of the Sublime, but it also registers something more urgent, a translation into the discourse of physiology of a new, and peculiarly vulnerable, form of modern sensibility. The echo in the cerebellum of the 'sublime thought' more often bounces against the walls of the mind in ways so taxing that it is ultimately best to try to silence it; the cerebellum can take only so much. Keeping out what Baudelaire calls 'the projectiles of chance' is the self-protective, though futile, move enjoined on the 'chosen spirits' in that hymn of praise to Baudelaire's hero of agitated imagination, Edgar Allan Poe: 'Vainement elles [les âmes de choix] se débattent, vainement elles se forment au monde, à ses prévoyances, à ses ruses; elles perfectionneront la prudence, boucheront toutes les issues, matelasseront les fenêtres contre les projectiles du hasard; mais le Diable entrera par une serrure.'[95]

The attempt to maximize self-protection by sealing all the points of entry and exit could serve as a perfect description of one major strategy of the prose poems. As in the Poe text, the Devil does, of course, get in, literally in 'Les Tentations, ou Eros, Plutus et la Gloire' and 'Le Joueur généreux' (pp. 274–7). In the first he gets into the poet's dream world; in the second he accosts the poet while strolling on the boulevard and escorts him into an underground habitat ('une demeure souterraine, éblouissante, où éclatait un luxe dont aucune des habitations supérieures de Paris ne pourrait fournir un exemple approchant'). The Devil's underground apartment thus surpasses anything Haussmann's overground world could come up with. This is the scenario of Faustian temptation brought into the city, but in an oddly, disconcertingly humorous way, half serious, half joke. If, on the serious view, the Devil stands for the devil in our desires,[96] exacerbated by the soliciting force of new Parisian *luxe*, then the bizarrely paradoxical spectacle at the end of 'Le Joueur généreux' – of the poet praying to God not to protect him against temptation, but to ensure that the Devil keeps his promises – pushes the poem towards parody and burlesque. This is a way of keeping the Devil out at the very moment he gets in, in the sense of keeping at a distance the potential seriousness of the poem's moral and emotional drama. On the other hand, as a joke, a *blague*, it resembles the 'plaisanteries nerveuses' of 'Le Mauvais Vitrier', jokes which 'ne sont pas sans péril', dangerous in their own right, at once designed to protect the nervous system from danger, while at the same time symptomatically declaring it to be at the very edge of crisis.

This sort of equivocating, self-undoing irony is, as we shall see, constitutive of the stylistic reality of the prose poem. It is the main element of the poet's armour, his means of sealing the exits. The prose poems have been correctly described as enacting a 'withdrawal of affect from the world'.[97] The 'world' here is essentially the world of the city, as object of hatred and disgust. Withdrawal (the opposite of the metaphors of entering and penetrating) is a recurring theme in *Le Spleen de Paris*. In 'A une heure du matin' (pp. 240–1), the generalized exclamation 'Horrible vie!' is quickly particularized to 'Horrible ville!', and prefaced by a transformation of the 'bain de multitude' of 'Les Foules' into 'un bain de ténèbres', the retreat into darkness and solitude as cleansing and soothing antidote to the self-loathing produced from daily contact with the life of the city: 'Enfin! il m'est donc permis de me délasser dans un bain de ténèbres! D'abord, un double tour à la serrure. Il me semble que ce tour de clef augmentera ma solitude et fortifiera les barricades qui me séparent actuellement du monde.'

The turning of the key in the lock recalls the closing of the window on the 'émeutes' of the streets in 'Paysage', as does the displacement of 'barricades' from the public language of revolution to the language of inwardness. A similar movement of retreat characterizes 'La Solitude' (pp. 263–5). It concludes with two quotations from La Bruyère and Pascal (respectively, 'Ce grand malheur de ne pouvoir être seul!'; 'Presque tous nos malheurs nous viennent de n'avoir pas su rester dans notre chambre'), and explicitly deploys the latter in ironic repudiation of the vocabulary of 'openness' at work in 'Les Foules': the virtue of Pascal's maxim is that it reminds us 'dans la cellule du recueillement' of 'tous ces affolés qui cherchent le bonheur dans le mouvement et dans une prostitution que je pourrais appeler *fraternitaire*, si je voulais parler la belle langue de mon siècle'.

This is the Baudelairian prose poem as private box, excluding and self-sealing, the text as *cellule* (whether as the place of meditating priest or penitent transgressor is left open). There is nevertheless something odd about the ponderous use of maxims taken from the tradition of the seventeenth-century *moralistes* (however much Baudelaire's developing flirtation with the ideas of de Maistre might have brought him back to Pascal). As with the *idée reçue* in the novels of Flaubert, so the status of maxims in Baudelaire's prose poems is often ambiguous, especially when the maxim is coined by Baudelaire himself. They seem to be less apodictic utterances than provisional, and frail, gestures at self-defence, the parrying moves of the poet as 'fencer'. Their formal authority confers a specious aura of detachment, of intellectual 'connoisseurship', the stance of the dandy as worldly-wise and world-weary. Here, then, we find the 'observateur passionné' – the description of the Parisian *flâneur* in *Le Peintre de la vie moderne* [98] – reduced to being just an *observateur*, lucid, cynical, uncommitted, in whom 'passion' is replaced by the more detached and anti-libidinal Baudelairian value of 'curiosité'. It is the curiosity which approaches the ugly, the violent, the irrational as if these were interesting yet matter-of-fact, the 'natural' properties, as it were, of the city landscape. It is the 'regard curieux' directed towards urban misery in 'Les Veuves', the experimental curiosity linked to *ennui* and issuing in cruelty in 'Le Mauvais Vitrier'.

Alternatively, the maxim, we might say, in this context is the intellectual equivalent of a certain sadism, a manifestation of what, adapting a term from psychoanalytical theory, has been termed the 'sado-dispassionate'.[99] It corresponds to what Sartre refers to as Baudelaire's 'coldness', the acting out in his poetic practice of the proposition that is the exact reverse of the other-orientated sexual images and energies of 'Les Foules', the famous maxim-like proposition in *Mon cœur mis à nu*: 'Foutre, c'est aspirer à entrer dans un autre, et l'artiste ne sort jamais de lui-même.'[100] However, I am less concerned here with Sartre's existential account of Baudelairian *froideur* as stemming from some primal 'choice', a kind of a priori refusal of the Other, than with the social conditions which arguably determine, at least in part, that refusal. Similarly, the difficulty we have in interpreting ('penetrating') some of Baudelaire's pronouncements, deciding whether or not they are ironic and, if the former, what the target of the irony is, may well be an index of Baudelaire's refusal of penetration. But the psychological explanation of Baudelairian diffidence as 'resistance' to the mobilities of desire seems to me substantially under-determined unless it also takes centrally into account the deforming effect on desire of the threatening randomness of the city. Wandering the streets of Paris *au hasard*, allowing the eye to roam randomly across the urban scene, permanently risked encounter with the unbearable, the flotsam and jetsam of the city, its specimens of irreparably crippled life, in ways that threatened in turn to cripple the movement of the desiring poetic consciousness towards the world.

Baudelaire does not seem to have had much resource for coping with this, including the kind of resource for thinking hard about how the unbearable might be removed. I am more or less persuaded that Sartre was devastatingly right about Baudelaire's 'politics': that 'il s'est un peu agité en 1848: mais il n'a manifesté aucun intérêt sincère pour la Révolution. Il voulait simplement qu'on mît le feu à la maison du général Aupick.'[101] Certainly by the Second Empire Baudelaire has given up the political ghost altogether, and, in so far as he subscribed to the values of dandyism and the new boulevard culture, these were, as Kracauer points out, the values of political reaction.[102] On the other hand, Baudelaire, unlike the true dandy whom Baudelaire himself describes as aspiring to the condition of absolute 'insensibilité',[103] could not pretend that the unbearable was not there; nor could he allow himself the luxury of that recurring form of nineteenth-century bad faith which anaesthetized the horrors of the city by means of the sentimental pieties of easy compassion and charitable relief. Taking the knife to the soft underbelly of the discourse of *bienfaisance* is part of the action of the prose poems, notably in 'Le Joujou du pauvre', 'La Fausse Monnaie' and 'Assommons les pauvres!'. In 'Le Joujou du pauvre' (pp. 255–6), for example, we meet the *flâneur* in a variety of assumed guises from connoisseur to philanthropist, a kind of benign Father Christmas setting out on his morning stroll armed with little toys to distribute to the children of the poor:

> Quand vous sortirez le matin avec l'intention décidée de flâner sur les grandes routes, remplissez vos poches de petites inventions à un sol – telles que le polichinelle plat mû par un seul fil, les forgerons qui battent l'enclume, le cavalier et son cheval dont la queue est un sifflet – et le long des cabarets, au pied des arbres, faites-en hommage aux enfants inconnus et pauvres que vous rencontrerez.

Here we have a metaphor of the city as playground virtually literalized, and, in that literalization, ironically undone. Yet there is here an unsettling obliqueness, a resistance to clear focus, an enigma of tone. The scrupulous attention to the detail of the toys, and the sheer elaborateness of the sentence in which the description is embedded, jointly enact a ritual of literary formality which obscures its ironic target, and in which the force of the key term 'pauvres' is partially lost or neutralized in the lexical and syntactic accumulations of the whole. Furthermore, the story which the text relates leaves us guessing as to its point: the philanthropist comes across two boys, one rich, one poor, playing respectively in a garden and in a street separated by iron railings. Both, but especially the poor boy, are described from the distanced point of view of the urban connoisseur, the specialist in aesthetic observation and sensation, in a 'painterly' language anticipating the manner of the narrator in 'La Corde'; the poor boy is 'un de ces marmots-parias dont un œil impartial découvrirait la beauté, si, comme l'œil du connaisseur devine une peinture idéale sous un vernis de carrossier, il le nettoyait de la répugnante patine de la misère'.[104] This tone carries through to the narrator's concluding observation on the central feature of his narrative. On one side of the railings the rich boy, having abandoned his own 'joujou splendide', stands transfixed by the poor boy's toy, a live rat in a box: 'Et les deux enfants se riaient l'un à l'autre fraternellement, avec des dents d'une *égale* blancheur.'

This is the poem's concluding sentence, and it is another instance of uncertain Baudelairian closure. Given the cross between compassionate philanthropist and detached connoisseur in which the figure of the narrator is cast, it is difficult to know how to construe the sentence. The italicized *égale*, alongside the adverb 'fraternellement', of course alerts us to its derivative status as quotation, but, displaced to the whiteness of teeth, the intended effect of the quotation is unclear. Something is being parodied, but what is not obvious. Is it the rhetorically inflated but politically failed egalitarian project of 1848? Is it an idea of 'progress' defined as social redistribution of material possessions? Is it the nineteenth-century commonplace of a shared 'humanity' beyond class divisions (beyond or across the 'grille' that separates the two boys)? Is it the politically reactionary notion that the equalities conferred by nature (who distributes white teeth regardless of class and wealth) render social difference insignificant? Is 'Le Joujou du pauvre' like one of the ingeniously wrought 'canards' Baudelaire ascribes to Poe, the writer who releases 'à torrents son mépris et son dégoût sur la démocratie, le progrès et la *civilisation*', while also proclaiming his belief in 'la souveraineté humaine'?[105]

The ground on which the 'je' of this poem speaks is thus highly uncertain. To the question – where does Baudelaire 'stand'? – we cannot confidently supply an answer. It looks like a standing off, but whether from urban misery and the class war, or from the pose of the *flâneur* taking his elegant, mannered and cleverly paradoxical distance from these issues, is virtually impossible to say. This is Baudelaire in yet another of his favoured incarnations, travelling around the city incognito: 'L'observateur est un *prince* qui jouit partout de son incognito.'[106] Benjamin interprets this in terms of the theme of the 'mask', as a means of self-concealment.[107] This view can, however, carry the implication that, behind the mask, we find some core of moral identity intact (and from there it is in turn but a step to the platitudes of the full human presence, Baudelaire's underlying 'pity' for the outcasts of the city, and so on). But what it might mean to be, actually or potentially, fully humanly present to the suffering of the city is exactly the problem. In these terms, Baudelaire's enigmatic ironies appear less as an instrument of clever concealment than as the symptom of a series of splits and cleavages and, at the most drastic moments, of incipient disintegration. The self-conscious ironies tell not of an 'identity' secured in an assumed detachment, but of separation, an inability to connect with the sense of a whole, inner or outer. Behind Baudelaire's ironic stance, 'hysteria' is never far away, the sense of self as battered into crisis, splintered into clashing voices, precisely as *dissonance*.

This is very far removed from the easy (and ultimately reactionary) position from which, in Baudelaire's more worldly concessions to the worldliness of Constantin Guys in *Le Peintre de la vie moderne*, he invites us to consider the divinely arranged 'harmony' of the modern city: 'il [Guys] admire l'éternelle beauté et l'étonnante harmonie de la vie dans les capitales, harmonie si providentiellement maintenue dans le tumulte de la liberté humaine.'[108] This is a proposition one can scarcely take seriously and is one reason for seeing substantial portions of *Le Peintre de la vie moderne* as Baudelaire's most unsatisfactory statement of the doctrine of *modernité*.[109] Baudelaire's ironies of course tell another story; if their precise focus is often blurred, they are nevertheless clear in their general and necessary opposition to the fiction of urban harmony. Irony, by definition, is the sign of an absence of fit between self and world, the sign of a relation of discord, the relation described in *Les Fleurs du Mal*:

> Ne suis-je pas un faux accord
> Dans la divine symphonie,
> Grâce à la vorace Ironie
> Qui me secoue et me mord?[110]

But, if the discords of irony check and disrupt the drive towards harmony in the verse poems, they become – as I have already suggested – systematically constitutive of the formal reality of the prose poems, as a space of highly unsettled, conflicting and mutually cancelling terms. How this works can be described only by way of a detailed look at the shifting terms and tones of particular texts. Let us therefore consider what happens in that space by way of a closer look at the different registers used in two of the more 'shocking' of the prose poems, 'La Corde' and 'Mademoiselle Bistouri'.

'La Corde' (pp. 278–81) introduces itself as a cautionary tale on the errors of popular belief and its sustaining maxims, notably the belief in the constancy of maternal love: 'S'il existe un phénomène évident, trivial, toujours semblable, et d'une nature à laquelle il soit impossible de se tromper, c'est l'amour maternel. Il est aussi difficile de supposer une mère sans amour maternel qu'une lumière sans chaleur.' The closed self-evidence of this maxim is what the story of 'La Corde' opens up by means of a wilful exercise in the macabre. Yet *exercise* is precisely the term; the poem is a carefully staged performance in pure deadpan around the absolutely horrific (arguably 'La Corde' is the most horrific in the whole collection). It is no accident that the story is dedicated to Manet and narrated by a painter. This is not just a matter of the circumstantial origins of the story.[111] If the doubling of self in the persona of the painter-narrator is Baudelaire's way of removing himself from emotional involvement in the events recounted, the dedication to Manet appears to be a declaration of solidarity with a certain aesthetic of *modernité*: the horrors of modern life are to be recorded with apparent indifference, with the matter-of-factness that speaks not just of 'a broken desiring self' (as Bersani has it[112]), but also of a broken moral vocabulary, the loss of an available scale of 'appropriate' response to what is recorded.

That loss is primarily inscribed in an uncertainty of tone masked by an apparent analytical detachment and ethical sophistication. The comfortable maxims of maternal love are met by what seem, deceptively, to be equally comfortable counter-maxims: behind the 'illusions' of popular wisdom there is the bracing yet pleasurable knowledge of 'l'être ou le fait tel qu'il existe en dehors de nous', the surprise of the real disrupting the sentimental stereotype, but as 'surprise *agréable* devant la nouveauté, devant le fait réel' (my italics). It is the adjective 'agréable' that should put us on our guard here. In accordance with the proto-modernist doctrine of *étonnement*, the story of 'La Corde' is indeed full of surprises, but they are scarcely agreeable ones. Set in a working-class district of Paris, it is the chilling story of a suicide: a young boy, acquired by the painter from his poverty-stricken parents to serve as model and assistant, hangs himself, for reasons that are unclear, in the painter's studio. Yet the suicide as such is less the central narrative concern than the occasion for testing and exploding what are posited as the myths of maternal love. The mother, impassive before the news of her son's suicide (which the narrator misinterprets according to another maxim – '"Les douleurs les plus terribles sont les douleurs muettes"'), shows an excited interest in the instrument of the suicide. This produces yet another misinterpretation, as a fetish whose form is perverse but whose source is pure: 'elle s'éprenait de tendresse maintenant pour ce qui avait servi d'instrument à la mort de son fils, et le voulait garder comme une horrible et chère relique.' The truth of the matter dawns on the narrator only when he starts to receive letters from his neighbours begging for a piece of the rope: the mother has been doing a brisk trade in the relics of death ('Je compris pourquoi la mère tenait tant à m'arracher la ficelle et par quel commerce elle entendait se consoler').

The point about this grim tale concerns the manner in which it is told. The narrator responds to its various incidents with what appear to be the 'appropriate' emotions, on a spectrum from astonishment to anger and disgust. Yet the way these emotions are distributed between the incidents and, more important, the way they clash with other, far more 'astonishing' reactions suggest that they lack conviction. Like the studiedly ingenuous, or rather disingenuous, misinterpretations of the mother's behaviour, the narrator's emotional reactions seem more like a game of make-believe, a *faux-naïf* feigning of emotion, a dramatizing rhetoric deployed simply to maximize the shock effect of the final revelation. For the narrator is in fact no innocent abroad. His behaviour and attitudes lie exactly parallel to those of the characters. In the first place, his role *in* the narrative is one of unambiguous complicity in the reduction of the boy (whether in life or death) to an object of exchange. The painter acquires the boy for the purposes of 'Art', accompanying the acquisition with a spurious gloss of moral rationalization concerning the boy's welfare ('Cet enfant, débarbouillé, devint charmant, et la vie qu'il menait chez moi lui semblait un paradis, comparativement à celle qu'il aurait subie dans le taudis paternel').

In the second place, there is the curious mismatch of emphasis to event in the narrator's account of the suicide itself. He displays no interest in its possible causes and motives, or rather the contextual information we are given is both slight and oddly inconsequential, hinting at possible explanations but exploring none. We are told that, however 'charmant' the boy becomes in the artist's studio, he nevertheless suffers from 'des crises singulières de tristesse précoce', the bizarre symptom of which is a 'goût immodéré pour le sucre et les liqueurs'; this elicits a reprimand from the painter, which, when the reprimand is ignored, is succeeded by a threat to return the boy to his parents. The suicide follows upon this sequence of events. Inferences can, of course, be drawn fairly easily from the information given, but the narrator himself offers no guidance; he hints at, but – either from indifference or perhaps repressed guilt – also suspends a basic code of narrative verisimilitude.

In addition, there is the reverse form of mismatched narrative and narration in the incongruously accentuated interest shown by the narrator in detail that, in a 'normal' narrative, would be of strictly secondary importance: the fussy quasi-medical attention to the deep incision of the slender cord into the neck and the difficulty of cutting it out from between 'les deux bourrelets de l'enflure'; or, in a piece of pure *macabre grotesque*, the corresponding difficulty of removing the clothes from the rigidified corpse: 'Quand, plus tard, nous eûmes à le déshabiller pour l'ensevelissement, la rigidité cadavérique était telle que, désespérant de fléchir les membres, nous dûmes lacérer et couper les vêtements pour les lui enlever.' This disproportionate attention to minor narrative detail – a technique Baudelaire probably got from Poe – represents a shift from the 'sado-dispassionate' to what might now be called the sado-realist.[113] It at once enhances and distances the horror, produces an image so intensely focused that it overwhelms its context and paradoxically acquires a kind of surreality. In particular, the absurd formality of that last sentence – its carefully crafted structure, its demonstrably precious use of the past historic, its manically precise way with punctuation – is another example of Baudelairian literary 'style' in strangely alienated relationship to its content, notably of course in the preposterous trivialization of the theme of 'despair', the bizarre reversal and displacement of values whereby 'désespérant' over the business of undressing a corpse receives extended and linguistically refined attention, while the 'désespoir' of the bereaved mother is revealed as fake.

The tone also contrasts markedly with the highly informal style adopted elsewhere in the story, above all in connection with the story itself: the latter is referred to in the opening paragraph as 'cette petite histoire'. The narrator is in fact uncommonly fond of the belittling force of the word 'petit'. Not only in life is the boy described as 'ce petit bonhomme', but also in death ('mon petit bonhomme . . . pendu au panneau de cette armoire', 'le petit monstre s'était servi d'une ficelle fort mince'). This is the familiarity of affectionate reference become *unheimlich*, in a disturbingly cruel form, the reduction of tragedy to the idiom of *blague*. It resembles the mother's impassive attitude before the news of her son's death ('la mère fut impassible'), and also the tone of the begging letters sent by the narrator's neighbours ('en style demi-plaisant', the tone of 'apparent badinage'). At its most brutal, the tone of the joke modulates into pure cynicism. The narrator, as yet ignorant of the mother's callousness and notionally appalled at the pain she will suffer on seeing the corpse of her son, remarks: 'Elle voulait, disait-elle, voir le cadavre de son fils. Je ne pouvais pas, en vérité, l'empêcher de *s'enivrer de son malheur* et lui refuser cette suprême et sombre consolation' (my italics). Grief as intoxication, pain as pleasure, here is a reversal of values where we might least expect it, the aesthetic of 'surprise' at work in the borrowed, and apparently secure, language of the *moraliste*, effecting a chiastic displacement of its terms across the oppositions and discriminations with which that language typically makes moral sense of the world.

The parallel between the manner of the narrator and that of the characters is in fact so striking that one is tempted to see the latter as deliberate *mise en abyme* of the former. It represents a particularly 'modern' form of irony, not just in its internally reflexive aspect, but also in its unplaceability, its challenge to interpretation, its refusal of the terms of an identifiable 'position'. This is not invariably the case with Baudelairian irony. Some of it is entirely conventional and fully readable according to a straightforward code of reversibility. Thus, the sentence – 'J'ai négligé de vous dire que j'avais vivement appelé au secours; mais tous mes voisins avaient refusé de me venir en aide, fidèles en cela aux habitudes de l'homme civilisé, qui ne veut jamais, je ne sais pourquoi, se mêler des affaires d'un pendu' – conforms to the 'classical' model of irony, in the mode of, say, Voltaire (whom Baudelaire detested): the syntactically delayed 'affaires d'un pendu' reflects back on and undoes the meanings of 'l'homme civilisé'. There would appear to be no uncertainty of stance here; it pretends to a position of cold detachment but the implied moral criticism of the 'civilized' neighbours is clear.

From this example, it would thus be tempting to see the ironies of 'La Corde' as another variant of the self-protective mask, as protection against the emotional force of a vocabulary which threatens to take over, especially in the second half of the poem ('horreur', 'colère', 'dégoût'). Unbearable outrage and distress have to be kept at a distance if they are not to shatter or 'strangle' the subject; the ironies of high stylistic formality are a protection against incipient hysteria.[114] The terms for such a reading appear to be given by the text itself, in the initial hypothesis couched in the form of a quoted maxim: ' "Les douleurs les plus terribles sont les douleurs muettes." ' But, then, this cannot serve as a reliable model, either in particular or in general. As we have seen, in its relation to the mother's feelings that statement proves to be palpably false. More generally, the maxim and the proverb – privileged forms of the operation of what Barthes called the 'cultural code' in the construction of narrative[115] – are not a reliable guide to anything in Baudelaire's narrative; the point of the latter is to reveal the inadequacy of the former, even when the maxims, invented or quoted, are apparently offered as the very basis of the narrative. In the complex play of meta-language and object-language staged by 'La Corde', its multiple levels of citation and address, there is very little that stays in place for very long, even, perhaps above all, in the relation between narrator and interlocutor, writer and reader. What, finally, gets lost or blurred in this story of 'commerce' is the assumption of a stable language of transaction in the telling of stories.

This, then, suggests that Baudelaire's irony has a literary as well as a psychological function; that it is not simply self-protection against an otherwise intolerable horror, but that it is directed against the story itself, its narrator and its readers. It tacitly puts in question the propriety of taking the boy and his death as object of narrative production and consumption; in dramatizing the problem of its own 'readability', it reproduces, at the level of the story itself, what is disturbing about the painter's acquisition of the boy *in* the story as a 'subject' for his painting. For the painter, the boy is, in life and death, everything but himself: 'Il a posé plus d'une fois pour moi, et je l'ai transformé tantôt en petit bohémien, tantot en ange, tantot en Amour mythologique. Je lui ai fait porter le violon du vagabond, la Couronne d'Epines et les Clous de la Passion, et la Torche d'Eros.' In the context of the story as a whole, this is an attitude that we can scarcely deem to be innocent. On the contrary, it suggests a set of terms for problematizing not only the painting but also the poem. Baudelaire here mobilizes the strategies of irony and artifice against Art itself, proclaims a gap, a point of non-negotiable incommensurability between the stuff of the city and the resources of 'poetry'.

The conflicting tones, and the corresponding instabilities of stance, which characterize 'La Corde' return us finally to the question with which I began – the question of the generic indeterminacy of the prose poem, and the extent to which that question can be addressed from the social context of the modern city to which Baudelaire himself, notably in the letter to Houssaye, ties the form. The clear separation of genres was classically believed to be characteristic of a more or less settled and coherent society, matching an ordered arrangement of the cultural division of labour. The blurring or the crossing of the boundary lines of genre is thus seen as the sign of the declining authority of a normative literary culture. The prose poem is a case in point (as attested by the widespread sceptical, even hostile response to *Le Spleen de Paris* by orthodox critical opinion[116]). Despite various, more or less sophisticated, neo-formalist attempts to 'define' the prose poem as a genre,[117] it is best thought of as a hybrid mix, irreducible to analytical definition, and, on a historical view, reflecting that tendency from the early nineteenth century onwards to break the traditional hierarchy of genre, in particular the distinction between the high 'poetic' and the low 'prosaic'.

The 'prosaic' in this context has normally been understood in terms of the project of 'realism', but in the very limited sense of the incorporation into the space of poetry of quasi-journalistic notations (Claudel described the style of Baudelaire's prose poems as a mixture 'du style racinien et du style journalistique de son temps'[118]). But the relatively inert notion of journalistic transcription of the everyday leaves out of account one of the major formal incarnations of prose writing, its articulation as *narrative*.[119] As we have seen, many of Baudelaire's prose poems tell a story. Yet the manner in which the stories are told, the way in which their various elements – from the horrific to the banal – are accorded more or less equivalent value, departs radically from the way in which the tradition of narrative realism typically works. The latter backgrounds and foregrounds, solicits judgements of relevance and importance. This has implications for the recent efforts to adapt to the analysis of Baudelaire's prose poems Jakobson's model of metaphor and metonymy. If, following Jakobson, realist narrative is governed by the figure of metonymy, it is not in the mode of endless dispersal into fragments; its succession of metonymic details is subject to a *telos*, under which they are gathered up and referred to a meaningful whole, or – in the non-totalizing version of this principle – distributed across the different registers or 'codes' which Barthes identified as controlling and constraining the production of meaning in realist narrative.

Baudelaire's way with narrative, at least in the most disturbing of the prose poems, is entirely different. Although formally complete, there is something lacking. What is lacking is *telos*, the point in semantic space or narrative time which gives meaning to the parts.[120] Consider the case of 'Mademoiselle Bistouri' (pp. 300–3). The title of the poem is Baudelaire's sedulously polite way of referring to an insane woman who accosts the poet in one of the working-class suburbs of Paris, mistakes him for a doctor, invites him back to her slum apartment, where she gives him supper, and shows him two bundles of photographs. The photographs – which have been obtained from a 'bouquiniste' on that sacred site of innocent Parisian *flânerie*, the quayside of the Seine – are the archive of a fetish, a sexual obsession with doctors, operations and surgical instruments: 'Je voudrais qu'il vînt me voir', she says of one of the surgeons, 'avec sa trousse et son tablier, même avec un peu de sang dessus.'

The name 'Mademoiselle Bistouri' is, however, given only once, in the title of the poem, and it should not be read as a conventional sign of respectful *politesse* before the injured and the outcast of the city (in the exchanges between the woman and narrator, the discourse switches from the polite 'vous' to the familiar 'tu'). Rather it is yet again a deceptive sign of emotional distance, a fake detachment of tone in the telling of this bizarrely troubled story. The *bizarre* is another of the collocationary terms in Baudelaire's description of the modernist aesthetic project ('Le Beau est toujours bizarre'[121]). In its application to the story of Mlle Bistouri, it serves to reproduce the stance of the expert *flâneur*, for whom the insane is but another exotic specimen collected in the course of a relaxed urban stroll: 'Quelles bizarreries ne trouve-t-on pas dans une grande ville quand on sait se promener et regarder?'

In this apparent neutralizing of horror, the method of 'Mademoiselle Bistouri' resembles the strategy of 'La Corde'. But, unlike the latter, the method proves unsustainable. As in 'La Corde', tones shift and roles get reversed throughout the text in a continuously destabilizing movement. The narrator adopts the role of the *flâneur*-as-detective ('J'aime passionnément le mystère, parce que j'ai toujours l'espoir de le débrouiller'), but the enigma of Mlle Bistouri's obsession eludes him (to his question about the origins of her obsession she replies, 'Je ne sais pas . . . je ne me souviens pas'[122]). Where she remains uniformly calm, he becomes neurotically agitated and violently angry, verging once more on the 'hysterical'. The self-assured tone is recovered, in, for instance, the bland generalization on the 'bizarreries' of the city. But in the final moment of the story the detached voice cracks completely, into the register of desperate prayer for the perspective that would make sense of the senseless. It is a rare moment in Baudelaire, when the irony fails him, the mask slips, and we see a despair entirely different from the feigned, game-playing 'désespérant' of 'La Corde'.

> Seigneur, mon Dieu! vous, le Créateur, vous le Maître; vous qui avez fait la Loi et la Liberté; vous, le souverain qui laissez faire, vous le juge qui pardonnez; vous qui êtes plein de motifs et de causes, et qui avez peut-être mis dans mon esprit le goût de l'horreur pour convertir mon cœur, comme la guérison au bout d'une lame; Seigneur, ayez pitié, ayez pitié des fous et des folles! O Créateur! peut-il exister des monstres

aux yeux de Celui-là seul qui sait pourquoi ils existent, comment ils *se sont faits* et comment ils auraient pu *ne pas se faire?*

The prayer in 'Mademoiselle Bistouri' is a plea for meaning, for the *telos*, the absent macro-narrative into which this mini-narrative of the 'monstrous' might fit. It gives a sudden glimpse of the anxiety beneath the adopted style of the casual anecdote, the other side of narrative as relaxed and detached *flânerie* through the modern urban scene – the anxiety that these stories of madness and suicide don't add up to anything very much, are merely the product of incomprehensible contingent forces in a world of generalized *anomie*, and that, in respect of their victims, both the question 'comment ils auraient pu *ne pas se faire*' and its converse are not only without answers, but also without meaning. The fear of a complete loss of determinable meaning necessarily puts in question what, all too easily in the letter to Houssaye, Baudelaire invites us to privilege as the organizing principle of the collection as a whole. This, it will be recalled, is the idea captured in the analogy with the serpent 'sans queue ni tête', cut up into 'petits tronçons',[123] thus commending a view of the text and its reading as radically fragmentary, open to multiple entry and without definite closure.

V

Accepting this invitation has started to become something of a routine occasion of modern criticism; the value of the prose poems, on this view, consists in their 'disruption of an ideal of totality'.[124] However, as we busy ourselves making of Baudelaire a kind of postmodernist *avant la lettre*, for whom the 'fragment' opens the royal road to imaginative freedom, we should pause to consider whether in fact the actual practice of the prose poems encourages us to see this as a condition to be unambiguously welcomed.[125] In the first place, Baudelaire's analogy is offered by him as a description only of the whole collection; the individual items within the collection are seen as free-standing, autonomous units ('Hachez-la en nombreux fragments, et vous verrez que chacun peut exister à part'[126]). There is nothing particularly self-fracturing about the narrative design of the individual units. If, therefore, the principle of fragmentation applies here, its level or field of application is less structural than semantic. But is it a case of meaning deferred, in the endlessly pleasurable experience of self-dissolving dissemination, or a case of meaning disturbingly lost? 'La Corde', for instance, is clearly not a simple moral fable generating a single 'meaning' (the signified 'bad mother', the exception to the rule articulated by the maxims of maternal love). On the other hand, it is difficult to see what in this story is compatible with the notion of a happy semantic multiplicity. It is not that there are many meanings, but that there is *no* meaning; there is nothing here that properly makes sense: all the main elements of the story – the boy's suicide, the mother's callousness, the narrator's nonchalance – are portrayed from a position of moral and aesthetic 'indifference', the main effect of which is the collapsing of those elements into a kind of semantic in-difference.

If there is a cultural model for this kind of story-telling, it could well be the sensational *fait-divers* of the newspaper, thus giving a far stronger context to Claudel's reference to the 'journalistic' element in the style of the prose poems. Unlike traditional story-telling (which, according to Benjamin, is a form that 'preserves', carries within it the traces of a link with a community), the newspaper supplies mere 'information' (which 'does not survive the moment in which it was new').[127] It is, in the domain of mass culture, the mode of fragmentation and neutralization *par excellence*, in which the world is represented as de-contextualized and disconnected bits and pieces. The newspaper lives off, but also neutralizes, the sensational story, by virtue both of the unrelated items that lie alongside it on the same page and its abstraction of the story from any wider history; deprived of meaning, the sensational becomes simple 'thrill', immediately forgotten once the effect of novelty has gone. Baudelaire's play with conventions of narrative and literary relevance in the unquestionably sensational story of 'La Corde', the refusal of a hierarchy of significance and the sheer blandness with which the tale is told, could be seen as an ironic miming of the discourse of the newspaper, and hence as an implicit comment on the fate of a certain kind of 'story-telling' in the culture of the modern city.

The Goncourt brothers once sketched an interesting relation between the contemporary novel and the prose poem: 'On pourrait baptiser notre genre présent de romans et ceux que nous rêvons pour plus tard un poème en prose de sensations.'[128] The parallel turns on a notion of the disarticulation of narrative coherence into a flux of pure 'sensations'. This reflects in part the dream of a literary phenomenology approximating as closely as possible to the rhythms of the body. But it also speaks of a severance of the category of 'sensation' from the social, of a tendency to pose sensory experience as essentially 'private', beyond the resources of a shared public discourse.[129] This corresponds to one influential dimension of the later nineteenth-century sense of the nature of the city – the city as a place of fast and fluid sensations, mobile, intense and yet formless. 'Fragmentation', in this context, means the partial eclipse of what is sometimes called an 'orientative competence',[130] the feeling of mind and body adrift in a sea of meaningless stimulus, without significant relation to either a past or a future. This is a recurring Baudelairian theme. In Benjamin's terms, part of Baudelaire's project was to give to the newness and the immediacies of *Erlebnis* something of the continuity of *Erfahrung*; it was to re-find in the atomistic texture of urban life at least

160

some of the remnants of historical community, largely through a preoccupation with 'days of remembrance', the commemorative creation of a personal calendar in a world where significant ritual activity has been 'dropped from the calendar'.[131]

The project, of course, fails, as its privileged signs – church bells,[132] holidays, public concerts – turn into their opposite, the signs of exile and solitude. As Baudelaire looks out on the city, what he finds is not community, but rather a collection of what, in the *Salon de 1846*, he refers to as 'existences flottantes'.[133] But before we rush to convert the reference into the currency of the 'floating signifier', purchasing the adventures of life *à la dérive*, we should remember its context: the 'existences flottantes' are specifically those of the criminal and the prostitute, the groups whose life at the margin and in the 'moment' most vividly dramatizes for Baudelaire the illusion that the city has a 'centre'. Fittingly, the criminal and the prostitute reappear in the 'Epilogue' poem to the *Spleen de Paris* (p. 310), where they are given pride of place in Baudelaire's profoundly ironic restatement of the poet's 'amorous' relation to the city:

> Je t'aime, o capitale infâme! Courtisanes
> Et bandits, tels souvent vous offrez des plaisirs
> Que ne comprennent pas les vulgaires profanes.

The irony here is complex, at once thematic and formal. Baudelaire returns, at the end of the collection of prose poems, to the 'harmonies' of verse, which, along with the adoption of the panoramic view, outside and above the city, appear to offer a more settled perspective, a recovery of the perspective of totality. But yet again form and content strain at each other; the form suggests the effort to see the city from an 'aesthetically soothing distance' (in Michael Hamburger's phrase[134]), a vantage point from which its contradictions are transcended and resolved; but the content – in conscious parody of the official mythology of Paris as the city of pleasure and enlightenment – refuses such complacent resolutions. The conventions of public address, of the ode and the apostrophe ('o capitale'), are undermined from within. The pleasures of Paris, in this poem, are not the pleasures of the harmoniously integrated society; they are the pleasures of *énormité* ('Où toute énormité fleurit comme une fleur'[135]). 'Enormité' recalls the term 'monstre' in 'Mademoiselle Bistouri', and echoes and transforms another *parisianisme*: the cliché of the city as 'monster'.[136] In Baudelaire's development of this idea, we come back once more to the prostitute as the site of a metaphorical transaction, not just a figure in the city but a figure of the city: Paris – the exemplar of the 'villes énormes' of which Baudelaire speaks in the letter to Houssaye as the natural setting of the prose poem – becomes the 'énorme catin', at whose breast the poet seeks the rejuvenation of jaded appetite. 'Enorme' and 'énormité' can mean various things here, from the physically gigantic (something of an obsession in Baudelaire's fantasizing of women) to the psychologically excessive and the morally perverse. Yet it is clear that the figure of the prostitute in this poem does not serve, as it does elsewhere in the literature of the period, as a banal moralized image for the 'excesses' of city. The full irony of 'énorme' is perhaps best grasped by restoring to the word something of its literal force: it is the *é-norme*, that which transgresses and exceeds the norm, not just as subversion of the morally normative, but also as distressingly beyond norms of intelligibility, as that which defeats the sense-making powers of the artist.

The *é-norme* can, of course, also be read in terms of the idea of the artistically liberating, as an occasion and space of 'freedom'. The association of the prose poem with an aesthetic of freedom is indeed regularly found in Baudelaire criticism. He himself described the prose poems in a letter to Troubat as '*Les Fleurs du Mal*, mais avec beaucoup plus de liberté, et de détail, et de raillerie'.[137] But the other two terms of this description ('détail' and 'raillerie') complicate a simple celebration of the first term. Details which proliferate without cohering, which can be 'held' only in the focus of a self-conscious mocking irony ('raillerie'), are in many ways a travesty of the freedom of the artistic imagination to make meaning out of the fragments of modern experience. In fact, the whole question of the relation between freedom and art always remained a complex issue for Baudelaire. In one of his more disparaging moods, he likens the free play of 'fantaisie' (significantly taking prose poetry, along with the novel, as his literary examples) to the domain of 'absolute freedom', in turn compared – revealingly enough – to the figure of the prostitute: 'la fantaisie est d'autant plus dangereuse qu'elle est plus facile et plus ouverte; dangereuse comme la poésie en prose, comme le roman, elle ressemble à l'amour qu'inspire une prostituée et qui tombe bien vite dans la puérilité et la bassesse; dangereuse comme toute liberté absolue.'[138]

This is the sort of Baudelairian remark that one does not really know how to handle. There is much in it that is offensive (notably to prostitutes) and alarming (the voice of de Maistre does not seem far away). But it perhaps also belongs with those many other remarks by Baudelaire directed against the easy individualism that informs certain nineteenth-century versions of the 'freedom' of modern art, what in the *Salon de 1846* he refers to as 'le chaos d'une liberté épuisante et stérile' characteristic of the modern age, the 'liberté anarchique qui glorifie l'individu'.[139] In those terms, the prose poems are less the programme of a free-wheeling imagination, open to multiple adventure ('accrochant sa pensée à chaque accident de la flânerie'), than the record of an awkward, hesitating, 'stumbling' figure, looking for a 'home', whether in the city or the poetic tradition, that is not to be found. Indeed one of the most interesting, and paradoxical, features of that manifesto of *modernité*, the section 'L'Homme des foules' in *Le Peintre de la vie moderne*, concerns, precisely, the theme of the 'home', and its paradoxical character is such as to overturn many of our more entrenched ideas of Baudelaire as the harbinger of the open road.

In the prose poem 'Les Foules', Baudelaire translates the scene of the poet wandering the city streets into a more general image for the exemplary condition of the poet as a condition of exile; 'jouir de la foule' is a capacity enjoyed only by those endowed with 'le goût du travestissement et du masque, la haine du domicile et la passion du voyage'. The corresponding notion in *Le Peintre de la vie moderne* turns out, however, to be somewhat more complicated. We have already seen the terms in which the famous passage built on the idea of *épouser la foule* is customarily discussed, namely those emphasizing the imagined erotic relation between subject and object. The metaphorical texture of Baudelaire's prose is, however, richer than this unidimensional reading acknowledges. 'Marrying' the crowd entails not only the fantasy of sexual possession but also the paradoxical dream of setting up home in what appears as its (ostensibly desired) antithesis and negation: 'élire domicile dans le nombre', 'être hors de chez soi, et pourtant se sentir partout chez soi', 'fait du monde sa famille'.[140] If Baudelaire wrote the great modern poem of homelessness ('Le Cygne'), a condition then celebrated in the opening poem of *Le Spleen de Paris* ('L'Etranger'), he also, in *Mon cœur mis à nu*, diagnosed what he called 'l'horreur du domicile' as 'une grande maladie'.[141] Naturally, the idea of the city as *chez soi* raises further issues, especially where the city-as-home is fantasized as a woman. Is the wife-mistress-harlot then also imaginatively cast in the role of housekeeper? Is it a fantasy whose logic would require leaving the streets altogether, along with the more dangerous forms of 'circulation', in favour of the bourgeois sedentarities of fixed abode? Where these questions might lead is not at all obvious, but my point here is simply that the drift and implications of this aspect of Baudelaire's metaphors, however problematical in other respects, give the lie to any unexamined celebration of the theme of 'exile' and hence of a matching notion of the prose poems as the great text of the unattached poet. The other point is that, if the *chez soi* is what Baudelaire desires, it is crucial to our understanding of his work not only that he desires it but also that, of course, he fails to get it.

7

A Walk in the Park

I then talked to her about the parks, and whether she ever went to them.
'The parks,' she replied in wonder, 'where are they?'
Henry Mayhew, *London Labour and the London Poor*

C'est un champ de bataille, ce Paris, même en temps de trêve.
Jules Vallès, *Le Tableau de Paris*

I

In his notes for further topics of conversation between the two heroes of
Bouvard et Pécuchet, Flaubert sketched a Paris of the future, imagined by an
expansively optimistic Bouvard to counter a morosely defeatist Pécuchet, as
a vast winter garden ('Paris deviendra un jardin d'hiver').[1] Though brief, the
scenario is not short on invention: the Seine will be filtered and warm,
façades will be painted with a phosphorescent substance and thus radiate
light and colour into the streets, and so on. But if this extravaganza reflects
Flaubert's scholar-clowns in delirious overdrive, it is but a logical extension
of a whole range of later nineteenth-century imagery representing Paris as
a kind of endless amusement park. With its physical roots doubtless in the
phenomenon of the open-air café-concert (most famously the Chat Noir),
it is an imagery proposing – and selling – forms of modern urban leisure on
the analogy with the enchanted garden (the classic example was Chéret's
poster, *Le Pays des fées* (plate 20), advertising, in exceedingly un-childlike
terms, the children's park called the Jardin Enchanté, which had been built
close to the site of the 1889 Exposition Universelle). The analogy had in
fact become something of a commonplace as early as the Second Empire.
The newspaper, *Le Siècle*, commenting on Haussmann's new park at the
Buttes-Chaumont, said that it resembled 'un jardin enchanté de la Perse
antique'.[2] The notion of Parisian public space as fairyland even found its
way into official discourse; Alphonse Alphand, Haussmann's lieutenant in
charge of smartening up the boulevards and creating the new parks, wrote
of the Champs-Elysées that it had become the very exemplar of what a
'grande promenade publique' should be by virtue of the fact that everything had been done to give it, especially for evening strollers, 'un air
féerique'.[3]

164

The winter garden and the enchanted garden were the related terms of a manufactured fantasy of release from the strains and tensions of modern city life. More generally, they were terms of the attempt, at once symbolic and practical, to re-enchant the 'disenchanted' new capitalist order within and through the commodity form itself.[4] As the connection with the phenomenon of the Exposition Universelle suggests, there were, of course, powerful commercial interests at work in the making and diffusion of that fantasy. There was also a political interest in marking the garden and the park, or more broadly leisure and festivity in public space, as places and occasions for the bracketing of social conflict, especially in post-1848 and post-Commune Paris by governments anxious to promote a sense of national identity based on the much-trumpeted principle of 'concord'. As Charles Rearick shows in his account of public festivity in late nineteenth-century France, a key symbolic event here was the first official Bastille Day, 14 July 1880.[5] After nearly a decade of nervousness regarding public manifestations, the new republican government instituted Bastille Day not only to commemorate the Revolution but also to foster the notion of social and political reconciliation within the modern national 'family': 'La population tout entière de toutes les classes et de toutes les nuances', claimed the newspaper, *Le Temps,* 'y a pris une part active et joyeuse qui ne s'est traduite sur aucun point par l'excès ou le désordre.'[6]

This was not the only sense given to either Bastille Day in particular or more generally the whole culture of holiday, festivity and leisure, and it would clearly be fatuous to interpret that culture simply as a form of economic manipulation and 'social control' exercised by commercial and political power. If the latter sought to link leisure to patriotism and productivity by way of the *fête nationale,* there were other, counter-cultural forces, in working-class life and radical politics, appropriating what little 'leisure' there actually was for working people to a quite different set of meanings and values. For example, if this was the period which saw the publication of the republican Auguste Montagu's 'disciplinarian' *Manuel politique du citoyen français* ('Le travail ennoblit, l'oisiveté avilit'), it was also the period of Paul Lafargue's *Le Droit à la paresse,* focus of a whole tradition of working-class protest against the values of labour discipline and industriousness commended by both conservatives and republicans.[7] It should also be recalled that the café-concert was regularly identified as a source of 'sedition' by the authorities and was often an object of police scrutiny.[8] Finally, there were those points of pure and explicit resistance to the official propaganda of festival as expression of national solidarity: for example, Vallès argued for 'un jour en République dans la ville' that would be truly popular in its rejection of 'la vie officielle toujours solennelle et déclamatoire',[9] while in the 1890s the paintings and prints of the socialist artist, Steinlen, similarly refused or ironized the given terms of celebration[10] (in a decade, moreover, when, behind the easy *belle-époque* euphoria, May Day was regularly perceived by a terrified establishment as a 'dress rehearsal of a revolution'[11]).

Nevertheless, throughout this whole period, the emphasis on unity and concord remained the keynote in the mainstream accounts of leisured and festive gatherings in public space (Camille Pelletan described Bastille Day as nothing less than 'la résurrection de la France'[12]). Two years previously, that contradiction in terms, the monarchist politicians who for most of the 1870s dominated the Republic, also organized a *fête nationale*, this time to mark the 1878 Exposition Universelle; as an exercise in the symbolic defusing of class antagonisms, it enjoyed considerable, if strictly temporary, success, when – in an extraordinary echo of the *trois glorieuses* of 1830 – 'workers and citizens walked arm in arm along the illuminated boulevards singing Pierre Dupont's *Hymn to Peace*'.[13] There was, moreover, another feature of this particular festival, which returns us to the terms of the fantasy of the city-as-garden. The *fête* was imagined as a distinctly bucolic affair, as analogous to 'a traditional harvest festival';[14] and its great pictorial statement, Monet's *Rue Montorgueil* (plate 21), brought politics and pastoral together in a densely packed, rhythmic composition suggesting the street as field and the flags as foliage (looking back on the event nearly two years later, Pelletan referred to 'un éblouissement de guirlandes et de feuillages, de drapeaux voletant, papillotant au vent . . . comme si je ne sais quel joyeux printemps tricolore avait éclaté sur la ville'[15]).

Importing pastoral into politics by bringing the country into the city was not, however, just a matter of analogies, artistic or journalistic. It also found a direct translation into practical policy, in the programme for the renovation and creation of public parks initiated by Haussmann (with the active support of Louis-Napoleon) and carried out by Alphand. The provision of public parks and gardens in the city was an issue that went back to the urban planning debates of the 1820s and the reports of the Comte de Chabrol, Préfet de la Seine during the Restoration.[16] But it was during the Second Empire that a programme on a grand scale was both conceived and executed, beginning with the systematic transformation of the Bois de Boulogne, followed by extensive work on the Bois de Vincennes, the Parc Monceau, the Tuileries and the Luxembourg Gardens and including the creation of two new parks, Montsouris (completed only in 1878) and the Buttes-Chaumont as well as a very large number of squares and public gardens. These were the innovations that prompted the star-struck reaction of a visitor to Paris in 1869: 'Paris has been developing into Arcadia.'[17] It was a comment presumably directed not just to the scale of the development but also to its style: the 'Arcadian' was at the very heart of the prevailing aesthetic concept of the modern urban park. Edouard André, the city's head gardener, said it all in his contribution to the 1867 *Paris-Guide*, when, in a quite unselfconsciously formulated oxymoron, he referred to the parks of Paris as 'Edens bourgeois'.[18] Louis-Napoleon himself brought to the landscaping of the Bois de Boulogne (he was less interested in the more working-class Bois de Vincennes to the east of the city) particularly active enthusiasms of this sort, encouraging the installation of grottoes, waterfalls and other such features of a pseudo-neoclassical version of the Bucolic. It was for the most part a piece of pure fakery, notably the great waterfall which fell – for technical reasons close to farce – but once a day around about tea-time.[19]

As with most of the Emperor's exercises in the fake, this construction had political as well as recreational uses. The park, as the grafting of soothing Nature on to the turbulence of the City, was a means for proposing and organizing an illusion of social tranquillity. Indeed the park became literally a burial ground for the traces of urban conflict and disorder: the building of the Buttes-Chaumont obliterated not only the former cesspools of Montfaucon but also the site of a notorious gibbet, while the refurbishing of the Parc Monceau during the Third Republic made use of the debris of the Hôtel de Ville, demolished during the Commune, for the bordering of flower-beds.[20] Notwithstanding their artifice, in the Emperor's parks, you were supposed to feel 'free' and 'natural', removed from the demands of 'authority' and the pressures of social strife.[21] In the park, you could both be yourself and be with others as (a version of) Nature intended.

Around this ideal, and ideological, conception of the park there gathered a whole imaginary order, based for the most part on two overlapping images. The first was of the park as a space of retreat, a haven or oasis in which, as Alphand and Ernouf somewhat lamely put it, 'on oublie un instant les préoccupations de la vie quotidienne.'[22] Part of the genius of Paris, wrote Texier, in more strongly lyrical vein, was to have reserved for its inhabitants 'de frais enclos où il [Paris] a réuni toutes les merveilles des champs, les arbres les plus majestueux, les gazons les plus verts, les fleurs les plus riches en couleurs et en parfums'.[23] The politician, Jules Simon, reminiscing in the late 1890s, recalled the Jardin du Luxembourg as the place one went to 'oublier Paris au centre de Paris',[24] while the poet, Théodore de Banville, wrote, again of the Jardin du Luxembourg, that in it 'on était à mille lieues des préoccupations et des niaiseries affairées de la ville'.[25] This image – the park as oasis or retreat – centred on several recurring figures, the *flâneur* lost in reverie, lovers lost in each other, or, perhaps most commonly, mothers and children.

In Texier's account, the presence of women and children is repeatedly mentioned as an index of the quasi-paradisiac character of the park. In the 1840s, Trébuchet, the hygiene reformer, had called for the creation of parks and gardens where 'enfants de toutes les classes' could meet and play.[26] By the 1850s what had previously been a goal of the reformers was now allegedly a matter of established fact: according to Texier, the Tuileries, handed over to the city by a benevolent ruler, has become an Arcadian playground open to children of (virtually) all social classes ('un royaume à partager entre les nombreux enfants de la capitale').[27] Delvau's text interestingly switches to English when it is a question of, precisely, babies: the Parc Monceau is for 'mères de familles et babies', while in the Tuileries we find 'des babies blonds et roses, jouant, sautant'.[28] Jumping babies sounds odd, and, while the use of 'baby' for 'child' was not uncommon in the nineteenth century, one suspects that the adoption of English here may well be unconsciously associated with the widespread notion of the English park itself as an informal, casual and 'free' space (it was one of the models officially favoured by the planning authorities, notably by Louis-Napoleon, whose ideas for the Bois de Boulogne were based on his memories of Hyde Park).[29]

The second of these two dominant images emphasized the park more as a space of easy sociability, for the informal encounter and transaction of city-dwellers otherwise separated by class, occupation and residence. Alphand – doubtless with utter sincerity but also echoing the propaganda of his political masters – stressed on several occasions the 'democratic' inspiration of his project, as 'cette œuvre vraiment démocratique . . . conforme aux tendances de l'esprit moderne et aux justes aspirations de la démocratie.'[30] This meant in part an alleged commitment to providing 'les quartiers les plus pauvres' with greenery and fresh air. But it also implied a notion of the great park spaces of the city as public property, open to all, and thus furnishing the appropriate place for the suspension of social division in the spirit of civil harmony and concord; in the parks people were nice to one another and, more specifically, a potentially menacing rabble became an amiably gentle (and *polite*) 'fraternal' presence. This, for example, is how George Sand put it, in her contribution to the 1867 *Paris-Guide*: 'traversez les jardins publics: tous ces êtres vulgaires et pernicieux forment une foule bienveillante, soumise aux influences générales, une population douce, confiante, polie, on dirait presque fraternelle.'[31]

Ideologically and politically, this second image was a particularly charged one, with a long reach back through the whole history of nineteenth-century Paris. It is often argued that the mixing of social classes in public space was specifically a preoccupation of the later nineteenth century, in at once anxious yet fascinated relation to a certain 'blurring' of the legibility of social identities and relations; the new mobilities, the emergence of 'les nouvelles couches sociales' (in Gambetta's famous phrase), the new leisure culture, the standardized forms of sartorial self-presentation made possible by mass *confection* and the *grand magasin*, all these developments were commonly held to have generated uncertainty, and even confusion, of class identities in the crowded places of the city; nothing was any longer what it seemed or in its 'proper' place; the *calicot* – the standard metonym for these various economic and social novelties – could now ape, more or less suc-cessfully, the gentleman.[32]

Yet, while it is true that these were issues that became particularly press-ing in the second half of the century, they were by no means unique to this period. Michelet, for instance, in *Le Peuple* (1847) explicitly linked the question of mass-produced clothes to the weakening of codes of social affiliation and recognition. Michelet's own attitude to these developments is mixed; on the one hand, he welcomes semiotic change, changes in the signs of class, as a real change in class formation itself, as a real force for greater equality and democracy; on the other hand, he also speaks of a 'mélange rapide et grossier' of social identities, the emergence of 'classes bâtardes' and the new rich masquerading as 'lords'.[33] More generally, the forms and implications of social mingling in public space had been a regular theme in the literature of modern Paris from its beginnings. Mercier's *Tableau de Paris* speaks of a 'foule d'états indéfinissables' circulating in the city, notably in those ritual meeting-places, the Palais-Royal and, especially in Easter week, Longchamp.[34] Indeed, if the café-concert of the 1860s produced its popular song about the *calicot* imitating the baron, this has an exact precedent in Desaugiers's song of 1801 about the great Easter parades at Longchamp, in which the woman perceived as a well-dressed 'ci-devant dame' turns out to be a 'ci-d'vant blanchisseuse'.[35]

The worry about the invasion of public space by the fake and the parvenu thus goes back a long way, and is probably intrinsic to the very constitution of the city as 'a human settlement in which strangers are likely to meet'.[36] In the specific history of nineteenth-century Paris, it seems, however, to have been a worry as much about the *gandin* as about the *calicot*, the former now accruing the sense of the imitation dandy or the fashionable man about town of uncertain or dubious origins (this will be one of the main themes of Balzac's novels; Lucien de Rubempré's first lesson about the arts of appearing to be what you are not is a lesson, acquired in the Jardin des Tuileries, about the value of clothes). And it was of course also, and continuingly throughout the whole century, a worry about 'woman' and the social organization of sexual exchange, around the blurred distinction between the respectable lady and the elegant *cocotte*. Delvau's guide through the Bois de Boulogne of the 1860s enjoins on the unwary the need 'de ne pas prendre ces élégants et ces élégantes pour ce qu'ils ne sont pas, mais bien plutôt pour ce qu'ils sont pour la plupart, des faux dandies et des *femmes de manèges*'.[37] On the other hand, it is unlikely that the unwary were particularly numerous, and, while we should certainly not underestimate the extent of contemporary nervousness over the fluidities of the new social formation, it is doubtful if at any time in the century this actually entailed systematic or even frequent misreadings of class 'identity' (even the *calicot* masquerading as a baron in the song betrays himself by the pair of scissors sticking out of his pocket). Although mistakes and misrecognitions could of course occur, mingling was not at all necessarily the same thing as confusion, and certainly most of the commentators who warn us of the dangers of misperception seem themselves to have retained a confident belief in their own capacity for dependable semiotic monitoring of the terrain.[38]

It is possible therefore to exaggerate the extent to which, even in the later part of the century, the surfaces of everyday Parisian life had become, or had come to be perceived as, ambiguous or opaque (other than by those with a peculiarly intense nostalgia for the allegedly more stable and transparent systems of an earlier epoch). It may be that special considerations apply to the case of the café-concert; if only by virtue of its size, and the consequent effect of 'social dishevelment'[39] that stemmed from cramming lots of people together into a small space, actual contingencies of physical proximity and contact must have struck some observers (such as the Goncourt brothers) as the very image of what was feared as the promiscuously massified, homogenized and hence illegible society of the future.[40] But for the most part this was not the real issue. As the Goncourts retreated to the eighteenth century and associated fictions of educated 'taste', the nineteenth century continued with the business of constructing its own fictions of contemporary urban sociability. The park was at the very heart of that effort. Indeed, if anything, the strictly ideological investment in the idea of the park, as hospitable to the dilution of social difference and conflict, was the converse of the anxious. On the whole, as Alphand's comments on the 'democracy' of the park show, it was welcomed as evidence of the growing neutrality of the city in general towards the marks and hierarchies of class distinction; and from there it was but a step to a larger and profoundly fraudulent implication, the ideological conjuring trick whereby certain (limited) indeterminacies in the codes of social recognition operative in the city were held to signify 'an overall loosening of class ties'.[41] In the promotion of the park as a kind of egalitarian Arcadia, what predominated was less the fear that difference was no longer reliably mappable, than the notion that it no longer existed or at least no longer counted for a great deal.

In this connection, it is also significant that in Alphand's commentary the park is linked to considerations of public health. This had been a recurring theme of park-discourse from the 1820s into the 1840s. Trébuchet argued in the *Annales d'hygiène* that the park should be a place 'où les habitants de tous les âges pourraient aller jouir de l'influence solaire et respirer un air plus pur que dans leurs habitations'.[42] Alphand made similar claims, stressing 'l'importance hygiénique' of his project, and quoting the Emperor on the virtues of clean air, especially for the poorer·classes. Parks, from the point of view of hygiene, were supposed to supply what narrow streets, overcrowding and slum housing choked off; in yet another variation on the theme of 'circulation', the park, according to Alphand, is a place 'où l'air circule plus librement' and for that reason it is 'absolument nécessaire dans l'intérieur des grandes villes sous le rapport de la salubrité'.[43] But, in addition to this laudable concern with the availability of properly circulating air, there was also the Emperor's belief in the moral virtues of the healthy life, more precisely, its alleged potential for effecting 'a revolution in working class morality'.[44] Behind this concern with the link between open spaces, public hygiene and the moral improvement of the working class, there lay distinctly political imperatives. A major focus of anxiety for the regime bore paradoxically on one of the consequences of its own programme of urban renewal: namely, the extension and reinforcement of segregated patterns of residence. In fact, concern about the effects of segregation also pre-dates Haussmannization: in the 1840s we find the municipal councillor, Lanquetin, voicing misgivings over the threat to social tranquillity and public order represented by the growing residential separation of the social classes[45] (not that, as Daumard reminds us,[46] we should exaggerate the degree of social interpenetration in the earlier forms of Parisian 'neighbourhood' culture, that myth of a previous Paris, for example, Balzac's 'Paris en 1831' allegedly characterized by 'la cordiale familiarité qui existe entre tous les habitants de la grande ville, sans distinctions de rang ni de condition'[47]). Segregation, especially when allied with overcrowding, meant, in the eyes of many observers, potentially lethal concentrations of class resentment; it also encouraged 'bad' mixing, the contamination of the working class by criminal 'elements', and, of course, furnished a breeding ground for revolutionary disorder.

One answer, then, was to encourage a form of 'good' mixing, the quasi-bucolic sort. Getting the poor out of the slums and into the parks would not only be good for the lungs but also be good for the order of things: rubbing shoulders with the well-to-do would show the not so well-to-do that Paris was a fairly friendly place after all, and that, in the perspective of a democratized and democratizing Nature, they were all more or less the same anyway. The idea that, on entering the park, one left one's class identity behind, at home, in the workplace or on the street, in order to participate in a socially ecumenical, fraternal get-together was, of course, a preposterous fiction. The reality of the social use of the Paris parks was quite different. When we read Delvau's claim that 'à Paris, les jardins publics ... sont tout aussi fréquentés par les promeneurs de toutes les conditions, de tous les âges et de tous les goûts',[48] we may initially misinterpret this as yet another invocation of the myth of the democratized park, until we realize that he does not in fact mean that strollers of all 'conditions' stroll *together*. His own text, despite its talk of confused minglings and potential perceptual errors, is for the most part a differentiated social mapping of the stroll in the park: the Bois de Boulogne on weekday afternoons as the 'promenade publique d'une bonne moitié de Paris, la plus riche, bien entendu', and on Sundays for the common herd; the Bois de Vincennes, largely empty in the week, filled on Sundays with the 'bourgeois et ouvriers du Faubourg Saint-Antoine'; the Parc Monceau frequented mainly by the 'petits rentiers du quartier' (although Delvau also includes 'petits ménages d'ouvriers'); the Jardin du Luxembourg for 'étudiants', 'grisettes', 'enfants' and 'vieillards'; the Jardin des Tuileries as 'le jardin aristocratique par excellence'; the Champs-Elysées for the 'va-et-vient étourdissant de la *high life*'.[49] The mapping is not necessarily accurate, and is certainly incomplete; the distinctions are too pat, and reflect as much the disposition to neat taxonomies built into the genre of the nineteenth-century Paris guidebook as the results of actual observation. The point nevertheless is that there *is* a map to be drawn; and, however it is drawn, it gives the lie to the myth according to which the purpose of the park was to blur the very social geographies for which such maps existed.

II

These two images of the park will recur throughout a wide range of nineteenth-century artistic sources, both literary and pictorial. Hugo, for example, in *Les Misérables* will exploit both in his representation of the Jardin du Luxembourg as at once 'paradisiac' retreat from the squalor and menace of the city for the two young lovers, Cosette and Marius,[50] and as place of relaxed and garrulous social gathering (significantly, Hugo always takes us to the Luxembourg in springtime[51]). They were also for the most part the characteristic images of the painters. The Impressionists painted the garden and the park from many angles of visual interest, from the high view to the intimate view, in all seasons and weather conditions (Pissarro did a series of six paintings of the Jardin des Tuileries in winter mainly as an attempt at catching variations of light). Yet, as we know, the Impressionist preoccupation with 'light' was not just inquiry into optics and experiment with paint, but also fundamental to a version of 'modernity', and in particular of urban modernity. This does not, however, mean – even in this exceedingly amateurish excursus into art history – some simple mechanical relation whereby one gets directly from brushstrokes to social history. Nevertheless, 'technique' was importantly connected to what Meyer Schapiro called the 'moral aspect' of Impressionism, and in particular that feature of it which Schapiro describes, in somewhat enthusiastic assessment of the painters' engagement with the forms of the contemporary leisure culture, as the painting of 'urban idylls'.[52]

The terms of idyll and pastoral were central to much of Impressionism's way with the theme of the garden and the park, especially in the work of Monet and Renoir. Monet's painterly love affair with the theme begins in the private gardens of the various suburban homes rented in the 1870s.

'Privacy' was indeed the main emphasis of these pictures, and was to remain such even on the return to the city and its public gardens in the late 1870s. *Camille au jardin* (plate 22), *Camille au banc*, *Le Déjeuner* (plate 23) are images of pure enclosure, bordering on the womb-like in their connotation of the arbour as safe haven from the encroachments of 'modernity'.[53] On the other hand, Monet's suburban gardens are also peculiarly worldly representations. If this is an oasis, it is an oasis made to the specifications of a male, middle-class, urban fantasy, a glamorous landscape of pleasure stamped *made in Paris* for private consumption. 'Privacy' in these paintings becomes indistinguishable from a drive towards 'privatization', in the economic sense of the desire to own or, more exactly, to be seen as owner. It is well known that Monet had both Camille and himself appear in these pictures of homes they had rented in the guise of elegant and leisured proprietors.[54] The recurring elements of the garden pictures – the accoutrements of the fancy luncheon, the fashionably dressed women, the pretty children, the parasols and straw hats mixed in with the lawns, trees, flowers and unblemished blue sky – add up to what the critic Théodore Duret rightly identified as Monet's marked taste for 'decorated nature',[55] nature commodified and put on display as something appropriated and possessed.

Much (though not all) of this will, of course, change in the last pictures of Giverny, a garden indeed 'owned' but where, at least in the *Nymphéas* paintings, we are taken to the very edge of a recognizable world and its worldly appropriations, to a point where the idea of 'property', economic, emotional or artistic, simply 'dissolves' into a wake of painterly traces. In the earlier pictures, however, representation seems inseparable from a fantasy of taking possession and a gesture of shutting out (Manet captured something of this in his painting of Monet painting landscape, *Claude Monet et sa femme dans son bateau-atelier*[56]). Similar excluding moves inform the subsequent paintings of the public parks of Paris. For example, Monet painted four panoramic views of the Jardin des Tuileries, but the scope of the 'panorama' is carefully controlled so as to avoid all contact with the ruined parts of the Tuileries palace, in part destroyed during the Commune (plate 24). Thus, while the signs of one sort of history (the towers of Eglise Saint-Clotilde, the Invalides dome, the Pavillon de Flore) are all variously there in the four paintings as the grand reminders of the *patrimoine* enjoyed by the morning strollers, the signs of another, less agreeable history – the Tuileries as the site of recent political conflict – have been bypassed and suppressed.[57] On a more intimate scale, the various paintings Monet did of the Parc Monceau are also governed by a strategy of closing off the terrain from unwanted, potentially blemishing interferences (plates 25 and 26). Monet's characteristic method with the Monceau pictures was to situate the easel in a manner that concentrated on a section of the park as a self-enclosed space; Monet's public garden, like his private garden, comes to resemble a protected, domesticated interior, a kind of pastoral nursery, and it is no accident if its population consists mainly of middle-class mothers, nannies and children as carefully tended as the gorgeous and opulently displayed flower-beds. There are certainly no signs of the 'petits ménages d'ouvriers' mentioned by Delvau as being amongst the park's regular users.

This may appear to be pushing a particularly narrow and uncharitable form of *Ideologiekritik* to breaking point. Mothers, nannies and children were after all major beneficiaries of the new parks and, as we have seen, are a constant reference of the descriptive commentaries; and if the workers are absent this is doubtless because Monet, having chosen to depict the park on a weekday, they were at work (or looking for it). In any case, in the aftermath of extensive residential developments, by the 1870s the Parc Monceau had become, as Zola's descriptions of it in *La Curée* indicate, virtually a middle-class preserve. Yet, as always, if these are some of the 'facts' of the matter, everything depends here on how the facts are met and transposed in representation (starting perhaps with exactly *which* facts are selected in the first place). There are no neutral registrations, particularly in those pictures which, echoing the official myths, wished to present the park *as* neutral, exempt from the tensions and divisions of the city, above all perhaps in the paintings of Renoir.

Renoir was the great lyrical painter of the urban park as an Arcadia in which women and children are supposed to appear as the embodiment of prelapsarian innocence. Renoir himself encouraged an analogy between his own work and the *fête galante* tradition of Watteau, and he also wrote a manifesto defining and defending a view of art as 'utopian' project in implied critique of and opposition to the actualities of work, industry and class. We should perhaps not be too quick to deny the significance of the utopian impulse in Impressionism generally.[58] Yet there is a strict limit on the extent to which we can read Renoir's garden and park pictures in these terms. It has been claimed that the latter create 'their impression of naïve innocence' by virtue of the absence in them of 'fashion and *chic*'.[59] But that is a view which can be maintained only if one passes in silence over a painting such as *La Promenade: femmes et enfants* (plate 27). Texier mentions that wealthy mothers often used a walk in the Tuileries as an occasion for decking out their offspring in all kinds of elaborate finery, parading their children like dolls.[60] Renoir's *Femmes et enfants* is the classic endorsing representation of that practice, the garden of Eden as fashion show, entirely given over to the signs of money and class, promoting a 'feminized' image of the park that is less an implied criticism of the harsh 'male' world outside the park than its confirming reverse image. In this picture one feels it is but a step from the park to the salon, and one is reminded of exactly that analogy in Hippolyte Taine's sharply irritated observation on the uses of the park as an instrument for the socialization of middle-class girls into the culture of the drawing room: 'Les Tuileries sont un salon, un salon en plein air, où les petites filles apprennent les manèges, les gentillesses et les précautions du monde, l'art de coqueter, de minauder et ne pas se compromettre.'[61] Maupassant was even more brutal, picking up the cliché of the park as idyllic mixtures of strollers, mothers, maids and children and ironically recontextualizing it as a rendezvous scene in which the hero of *Bel-Ami* stages the cynical seduction of the prudish Madame Walter.[62]

Against the effortlessly inhabited world produced by Monet and Renoir, there were thus other, less comfortable and comforting images, images which returned to the park what the Arcadian idiom had sought to exclude. In the sphere of painting, the work of Berthe Morisot and Mary Cassatt, for so long confined to the dustier regions of the art-historical archive, has recently been recovered precisely in connection with its own questioning of the terms of a wider and more systematic 'confinement' engaging both – and interrelatedly – the artistic and the social. The park – along with the garden, the kitchen, the bedroom, the veranda, the theatre – was, as Griselda Pollock has argued, one of the consecrated 'spaces of femininity' given to Morisot and Cassatt as both women and working artists.[63] The park, from this point of view, is not only one of the very few forms of public space in the city available to the women artists, it is in any case effectively folded back into the private, as coextensive with the domestic sphere to which women were held properly to belong; in the park, when they are not serving as objects of display, women perform the kind of activities reserved for them in the home – sitting, reading, daydreaming, and, above all, minding children.

These, then, by virtue of the fact that few others were given to them, are for Morisot and Cassatt the characteristic spaces and activities of their paintings. This does not mean, however, that they simply reproduced the terms on which they were given. What strikes us now about many of these pictures is their awkward and obliquely unsettling occupation, even disruption, of the spaces represented. The garden and the park are cases in point. Consider Cassatt's *Lydia crocheting in the garden* or, more pertinently (since it deals with an outing in the Bois de Boulogne), Morisot's *Le Lac du Bois de Boulogne* (plate 28). Although the latter is an image of leisure, it can also be construed as an image of entrapment: Pollock has spoken of the use by both artists of a convention of 'shallow depth' and of an effect of 'compression' brought about by the strong foregrounding of the figure, to which we may add the corresponding effect of cutting off the horizon in the background of the picture.[64] The two women are, so to speak, locked into the space they occupy. They are also cut off from land, in a boat whose strongly painted edge (to which the other woman is turned) takes the image's play of connotations beyond that of 'leisure' towards a language of boundaries and separations. Boundary lines – 'balustrade, balcony, veranda or embankment'[65] – breaking up units of space are virtually a Morisot signature; here the division may be said to give particular pictorial force to an implication of being set adrift, in – the relevantly active force of the cliché is recovered here – a kind of no-man's-land.

Finally, there is that other sense of being adrift, of not belonging, staged in the diffident, defensive and withdrawn look of the woman turned to the viewer. The self-absorbed and abstracted look of Morisot's female subjects (notably herself) is perhaps the most remarkable feature of her paintings. It is, of course, not without its ambiguities, and is easily misread as confirming a familiar stereotype of femininity: in the dreaminess that marks a non-belonging to the male world of 'action' there is always the possible implication of a 'natural' condition of passivity and inertia; and we are then not far from the revealing analogy between a purely narrative account of the subject afloat in *Le Lac du Bois de Boulogne* and those contemporary critical descriptions of its painterly qualities as 'floating' (reinforced by more recent references to Morisot's 'fluttering brushstrokes'[66]). But the inwardness of the gaze in Morisot is less the painterly equivalent of a daydreaming Emma Bovary than the refusal of another kind of belonging to another kind of gaze, the appropriating gaze of men and its required rituals of submissive, doll-like display; in the clash between the finery of costume and the air of apparent vacancy on the face, we might read a tacit withdrawal from the circuits of exchange converting women in public space into objects of visual consumption. Women, in the familiar story, are patient sewers and weavers, and so indeed is Lydia in Cassatt's picture. But it is not at all obvious whether this is proposed as a condition naturally assumed or socially imposed, or whether the garden she sits in permits or constrains. By the same token, Morisot's park, through its understated ironies and dislocations, does not so much reproduce as unravel a certain sexual economy of the city and its given spaces of 'retreat'.

The reach of the irony is nevertheless limited. If it stimulates to complex reading on the axis of a gendered ordering of urban space, it is not at all clear that it invites us to anything like the same along the axis of class; and this, as we have seen, would be vital to any deconstruction of the official mythologies of the city's parks. In the work of both Morisot and Cassatt, relations of class get represented, largely via the domestic world of servants and wetnurses. It is a world they handled directly and without the slightest trace of condescension or sentimentality.[67] Yet that very ease can cut both ways and arguably entails a disappearance or absence of important complication; there is little sense in their pictures of what must have been the inflection of a shared domestic space by uneasy hesitations and slidings between solidarity as women and the social barriers of class. If class is there, it does not appear to be there as an *issue* for the painting, in the sense of troubling its terms of representation. This seems particularly so in respect of the park pictures, especially the paintings of the Bois de Boulogne. It might just be possible to read into the positioning and posture of the servant in Cassatt's *Woman and Child Driving* (plate 29) an ironic comment on protocols of deference; though the fact that the servant goes unmentioned in the title suggests otherwise, the picture is certainly somewhat peculiar in its abstracted and even slightly absurd formality; there is nothing quite like it in any of the other Impressionist riding-in-the-park pictures.

It is doubtful, however, that any claims of a similar sort could be made in respect of Morisot's paintings of the Bois de Boulogne, particularly the later ones. In the 1880s Morisot and her husband moved to the western suburb of Passy, and the Bois in the view from Passy, as Adler and Garb observe, became for Morisot 'an extension to her private garden'.[68] Once more public and private fold into one another, but this time in the terms of privilege unproblematically assumed and enjoyed. It reminds us that, if the park meant confinement and constriction, it also meant protection and shelter. There are, as far as I can see, no ironies or dislocations in *Lady with a Parasol Sitting in a Park* (plate 30); it is quite straightforwardly an image of an elegant woman, a *lady*, in a space that seems to be naturally hers, precisely 'Eden' from the point of view of the bourgeoisie and, moreover, without the slightest trace of the artifice that went into its fabrication. It is the myth of Nature in the city bought wholesale. The woman in Morisot's park thus remains ambiguously positioned between a forced exclusion (from the world of men) and a luxurious exemption (from the harsher conditions of the city). But it is doubtful whether her pictures offer themselves to be read as examining that ambiguity. If they imply a questioning of sexual orderings of position and identity within the bourgeoisie, in particular male constructions of femininity, they do not, it would seem, question the bourgeois order as such. In *Lady with a Parasol Sitting in a Park* the Bois de Boulogne is seen more or less as the Emperor wished it to be seen, and as the property of those for whom the Emperor intended it.

III

In *Le Peintre de la vie moderne*, Baudelaire gives an account of the work of Constantin Guys partly in the form of an itinerary through the city. The park figures as one of its staging-posts. As a journey modelled on the sketches of Guys and reflecting, in several of its aspects, one of Baudelaire's more complacent accounts of Parisian *flânerie*, it is perhaps not surprising that, with the barest hint of a possible irony, it gives us a picture of the bourgeoisie in the park more or less on the bourgeoisie's own terms: the 'élégantes familles'; the women 'se traînant avec un air tranquille sur le bras de leurs maris'; the latter strolling with the 'air solide et satisfait' that reveals 'une fortune faite et le contentement de soi-même'; the children playing at 'visiting' and thus 'répétant ainsi la comédie donnée à domicile par leurs parents'.[69] But, if that last detail recalls something of Taine's exasperated observation, Baudelaire's tone here is itself scarcely exasperated, and, if his text is not exactly an acceptance of the image of self-satisfied contentment, neither does it particularly wish to take issue with that image; it simply registers it as a 'fact' of modern life (or, if we wished to cover Baudelaire's traces here, as a fact of Guys's version of modern life).

Yet, if the itinerary described in *Le Peintre de la vie moderne* remains something of an embarrassment, its assumptions, trajectories and boundaries are seriously disrupted by other, far more important moments in the Baudelairian *œuvre*. We have already seen how such disruptions are at the very heart of the project of the prose poem in its intimate and complex relation to the city, and it is to the Baudelairian prose poem that, inevitably, we return yet again, this time to a story of parks and concerts; it is, of course, the story of 'Les Veuves'.[70] Benjamin, in discussion of that other poem of parks and concerts, the verse poem, 'Les Petites Vieilles', reminds us that Baudelaire's reflection on parks is rooted in questions of class and experiences of exclusion: he cites the essay on the worker poet, Pierre Dupont, in which Baudelaire describes an urban working population which, ill from breathing 'la poussière des ateliers', stands outside looking into the private parks of the rich ('qui jette un long regard chargé de tristesse sur le soleil et l'ombre des grands parcs').[71] The public parks – remember Alphand's remarks about the relation between parks and public health – are, in Benjamin's words, 'those open to city-dwellers whose longing is directed in vain at the large, closed parks'.[72] They also, for Benjamin, signify something else, related to the category in Baudelaire's conception of *modernité* to which Benjamin attached very considerable importance – what Baudelaire called 'l'héroïsme de la vie moderne' and which he represented in 'Les Petites Vieilles' through the image of the old woman seeking sustenance for the struggle to survive, simply to go on, from the evening concert in the park; Benjamin adds Proust's majestic claim about these lines ('il semble impossible d'aller au-delà'):

> Ah! que j'en ai suivi, de ces petites vieilles!
> Une, entre autres, à l'heure où le soleil tombant
> Ensanglante le ciel de blessures vermeilles,
> Pensive, s'asseyait à l'écart sur un banc,
>
> Pour entendre un de ces concerts, riches de cuivre,
> Dont les soldats parfois inondent nos jardins,
> Et qui, dans ces soirs d'or où l'on se sent revivre,
> Versent quelque héroïsme au cœur des citadins.[73]

These, then, are the terms of an alternative poetic itinerary through the public spaces of the city, devoted to following the (mis)fortunes of what in 'Les Veuves' are called the 'cripples of life' ('les éclopés de la vie'). 'Les Veuves' is in many ways the natural companion piece of 'Les Petites Vieilles' (though Benjamin himself does not refer to it). The key difference is that the celebration of the 'heroism of modern life' in the verse poem has almost disappeared in the prose poem. In the former the 'citadins' implicitly constitute a community of listeners across whatever differences might otherwise separate them; it is not just the music but its context as social occasion which sustains the old woman.[74] The park of *Le Spleen de Paris*, however, has become almost exclusively a landscape of rejected and damaged life. There is, for instance, the lunatic imploring the marble statue of Venus in the depopulated park of 'Le Fou et la Vénus'.[75] And there are the two widows of 'Les Veuves'. The text begins with a reference to another text (by Vauvenargues on the failed and abandoned lives to be found in the city's 'jardins publics'). This opening move thus already challenges a stereotype: the park as 'retreat' and 'rendezvous' becomes, in Baudelaire's description, 'ces retraites ombreuses' which serve as 'rendezvous pour les éclopés de la vie'; the poem will concern itself not with 'la joie des riches' but with 'tout ce qui est faible, ruiné, contristé, orphelin'. That may appear at first sight as simply a list of stock neo-romantic epithets, replacing one stereotype with another. The final term, however, both resonates and anticipates; 'orphelin' alludes, by implicit contrast, to the theme of happy families strolling in the park while also evoking, by association, the poem's main subject of the correspondingly dispossessed figure of the widow.

Against the background of the imagery we have previously considered (including the text of *Le Peintre de la vie moderne*), the choice of the *widow* is clearly a significant one; it installs at the heart of a whole literary and visual thematics of the park a figure of irreparable loss.[76] This too, of course, can easily generate its own sentimentality and easy fatalism, as it does, for instance, in Paul de Kock's observation: 'Pour cette femme il n'est ni fête, ni dimanche; il n'y a jamais ni promenade, ni plaisir, ni repos, et cependant elle ne se plaint pas.'[77] There is also something of this in Baudelaire's poem, in the suggestion of sufferings 'humblement, silencieusement supportés'. But Baudelaire's way with the theme is also profoundly different; he takes his widows into the park where there is indeed 'promenade', 'fête' and 'repos'. In this respect, the story of the first widow directly echoes the text of 'Les Petites Vieilles': 'Enfin dans l'après-midi, sous un ciel d'automne charmant, un de ces ciels d'où descendent en foule les regrets et les souvenirs, elle s'assit à l'écart dans un jardin, pour entendre, loin de la foule, un de ces concerts dont la musique des régiments gratifie le peuple parisien.' But, if this repeats the terms of 'Les Petites Vieilles', it does not do so completely; what is missing is the critically important emphasis in the verse poem on the sustaining power of the concert ('où l'on se sent revivre') and its link with the idea of the 'heroism of modern life'. Here, although (like the 'stoïques' old women of the verse poem) the old widow displays 'une fierté de stoïcienne', the narrative of 'heroism' has disappeared; the concert is not an occasion of renewal but mere 'consolation' for a condition of radical dispossession, a condition on the edge, outside the given circuits of social, familial and sexual exchange ('la consolation bien gagnée d'une de ces lourdes journées sans ami, sans causerie, sans joie, sans confident, que Dieu laissait tomber sur elle'). That sentence not only designates where the city leaves her but also marks where Baudelaire's text leaves her, as the point where her narrative ends, in abrupt transition to the story of the second widow ('Une autre encore:').

The abruptness of that switch of narrative focus is of course typical of Baudelaire's literary method in the prose poem and, as I have argued in the previous chapter, is to be seen in relation to the crisis and partial collapse of a poetics of 'harmony' generated from literature's prolonged contact with the contemporary city. In the case of 'Les Veuves', we should note the contrast between, on the one hand, the elaborately formal, unifying syntax which unfolds across the two stanzas of the verse poem and, on the other hand, the structuring of the prose poem around two disparate mini-narratives, contextually and thematically related but also roughly juxtaposed as items ('Une autre encore'). There is here a link between manner and matter which constitutes the area of Baudelaire's deep solidarity with his subject. It is not a matter of the easy 'sympathy' shown by Paul de Kock or even Vauvenargues. On the contrary, the tone of the narration, like that of 'La Corde', is expressly designed to insert maximum distance between narrator and subject: 'un œil expérimenté', 'je l'épiai', 'un piquant mystérieux', 'un regard, sinon universellement sympathique, au moins curieux, sur la foule des parias', 'chose intéressante', 'Singulière vision!', 'en passant curieusement auprès d'elle'.

This is the language of Baudelairian 'curiosity' in concentrated dosage. Its purpose is not just to guard against emotionally specious identifications; it is also to create a wilful 'dissonance', not unlike its thematic counterpart in the figure of the second widow with her child, in the crowd yet not of it, at the concert yet excluded (she cannot afford the ticket and so listens through the outer fence). This picks up on the standard discourse of 'mingling' ('la plèbe à laquelle elle s'était mêlée'), but does so with a difference; in yet another variation on the motif of the barrier or the boundary, it emphasizes clash and separation where the official myths emphasized, precisely, 'harmony'. Interestingly, the term 'harmony' appears in the text itself, in the description of the 'veuves pauvres', but, of course, as a presence marking an absence: 'il y a toujours dans le deuil du pauvre quelque chose qui manque, une absence d'harmonie qui le rend plus navrant.' Since 'harmony', as a term for poetry, derives analogically from music, we might then also wish to say, recalling an earlier emphasis, that the very form of Baudelaire's prose poem is in dispute with the ideological representations of its central narrative term – the supposedly binding force of the concert itself.

'Les Veuves' is contemporary with Manet's picture of the concert in the park, *La Musique aux Tuileries* (plate 31), and there have been suggestions that Baudelaire – who, according to Antonin Proust, habitually accompanied Manet on his visits to the Tuileries – may have proposed the subject to the painter. Moreover, Baudelaire is *in* the picture (just as we find Manet, explicitly in the dedication and very possibly in the figure of the painter-narrator, in the prose poem, 'La Corde'). Yet, on the face of it, there is little affinity between text and image.[78] Manet's version seems the natural choice for the committed *boulevardier* he was, and, while it could be read as being close to the spirit of *Le Peintre de la vie moderne* and the worldly sketches of Guys, there is certainly nothing in it of Baudelaire's emphasis in the prose poem on figures of estrangement and dispossession; for example, the matronly figure in the foreground of the picture, with the younger woman and the fussily dressed children, has little in common with Baudelaire's widows; on the contrary she is, precisely and solidly, at the centre of things, in the sense of both pictorial space and social relations (the children, moreover, seem to be playing in ways that confirm Taine's observation).

Delvau, it will be recalled, described the Tuileries as 'le jardin aristocratique par excellence' and referred to the late-afternoon concert as a key part of its tasteful social style.[79] It was, of course, always understood, for example in the coded language of the male-centred journal, *Le Boulevardier*, that the Tuileries was where a gentleman went in pursuit of the *demi-mondaine*.[80] The conventional view, however, was of the park and its concert as accommodating a mixture of persons that was at once worldly and seemly; as an earlier guidebook put it, the Tuileries was in theory open to all ('Aux Tuileries, il n'y a ni type particulier, ni population spéciale') but subject to the strictest rules of decorum: 'on s'y présente comme dans un cercle de bon ton, où les hommes et les femmes sont admis à la condition de s'y conformer aux règles du plus strict décorum.'[81] Manet's picture mimes, in scrupulous detail, just this version of the Tuileries but less as its endorsement than in the mode of ironic comedy, as pure burlesque of modern forms of sociability. *La Musique aux Tuileries* is in my view one of Manet's funniest paintings, not merely 'amusing' in the distanced, slightly condescending manner we might expect from the denizen of the fashionable boulevard culture, but quite radically funny, and it is so by virtue of the intrinsic absurdity built into the picture's surface miming of the protocols of fashionable gathering.

It has been claimed that *La Musique aux Tuileries* is 'hardly a picture of modernity at all' and is rather to be read as relaying an older definition of the 'public realm' as stable, readable, familiar ('a realm in which one recognises friends and relations, and knows precisely how they would wish to be known').[82] The picture is certainly saturated by the social, and specifically by the signs of class ('invading every square inch between the trees'[83]); it is thoroughly urban and, for all its trees and greenery, profoundly anti-pastoral, less nature in the city than nature *as* the city. But surely the important point about its composition concerns the form of this saturation, the manner in which the society of the park is literally, and comically, packed into the picture. The comedy consists in the way the painting 'starts' by reproducing in the foreground something of the idiom of the spacious and the gracious, but then cancels that connotation as it recedes into a sea of impossibly crowded and progressively undifferentiated bodies, beards, dresses and top hats (above all the hats). If it is right to speak of an effect of compression in Morisot and Cassatt, here there is compression to the point of claustrophobia; the trees themselves form a sort of canopy with only a patch of blue sky at the top of the picture as a possible escape route for the eye.

This is a rather different kind of enclosure from the one we saw informing Monet's park imagery. It puts pressure on the pantomimes of etiquette, on the space required for the performance and legibility of social ritual. The absurd crush of bodies says less that the public realm is still intact than that it has fallen apart, into a messy crush of private conversations and dealings. We really have very little idea of what is going on in Manet's park, especially between the men and the women. The painting of the women in the left foreground replicates the signs of 'decorum', but elsewhere the signs are far less clear. Indeed, in the centre, they are virtually unreadable: a man (Manet's brother) is talking to a seated woman, but we can hardly make out the woman at all.[84] That is but the first of a series of perceptual uncertainties trailing across much of the rest of the canvas and which engage other important aspects of the painting. What, for example, do we make of the artists in the picture, crucially Baudelaire, standing under the tree in conversation with Offenbach and Aurélien Scholl? What are they talking about? Does their conversation consist of an 'exchange of literary judgments',[85] the cultured discourse that is one of 'the great protocols of class that everyone here obeys scrupulously', including the poets and composers who have long since rallied to the regime? Or are they perhaps engaged in more dangerous discourse, of the sort that saw Baudelaire in the law courts but five years previously at the trial of *Les Fleurs du Mal*?

There are, of course, no answers and, anyway, the question as to what they are talking about is roughly in the same area of pointless interpretative speculation as the question: how many children had Lady Macbeth? Yet not knowing is what in many respects the painting is about. We cannot say whether it is 'saying' that the artists and poets properly belong here and consequently that their challenge to the values of the bourgeoisie is really a tame and harmless affair, that the artists are gentlemen after all; or whether there is here a tension, an implied absurdity in the masquerade of Artist and Public as peacefully coexisting constituents of 'polite society'. If we incline to the former reading, it is nevertheless true that, although in real life Baudelaire often accompanied Manet to the Tuileries, there is still something prima facie odd about the presence in the picture of the first great *poète maudit*, and something correspondingly odd about his appearance: he is to be seen 'portant un chapeau',[86] presumably as a token of a certain *mondanité*, but, then, the force of the hat as sign is dissipated in its blurred proliferation across the canvas; and the face itself is almost entirely blurred, more a scarcely recognizable smudge than a properly readable physiognomy.[87] It is almost a case of painterly incognito, perhaps analogous to the terms of Baudelaire's own description of the *flâneur* in *Le Peintre de la vie moderne*, but it looks just as much a case of the poet prosecuted for blasphemy and obscenity having been awkwardly and incompletely smuggled into the picture, as if he really does not belong there after all. If this is Manet 'mixing', he also appears to be mixing it in the sense of an intended provocation.

And, finally, what of Manet himself, there on the far left of the picture with his painter friend, de Balleroy, dressed to the nines with his impeccably pressed trousers and cane? The art historians remind us that this echoes Manet's revered Velasquez, specifically a painting attributed to Velasquez (and which Manet copied) in which Velasquez and Murillo appear in a virtually identical position at the left side of the frame.[88] Velasquez was, of course, a painter obsessed with gentility, with the idea of the painter as courtier and of painting not as *métier* but as a noble calling exercised in appropriately noble company. The visual analogy thus implies Manet setting out to create an equivalent image in which, all formality, exquisite manners and monocles, he appears as painter at the court of the modern bourgeoisie. But, as with all Manet 'quotation', the status of the allusions to Velasquez is by no means obvious, and perhaps the more appropriate comparison here is in fact a contrast: with the Velasquez of *La Meniñas*, exercising his calling centre stage surrounded by royalty, whereas Manet's position suggests detachment, at once inside and outside, poised between affiliation and disaffiliation, in reprise of Velasquez perhaps, but as self-ironizing quotation where it is the quoting rather than the quoted image that is the object of the irony. Velasquez looks out from his easel to the king and queen whose portraits he is painting. Manet looks out from his picture at his viewers, in what seems an implied declaration of solidarity between the classy people in the park and the clientele at the Galerie Martinet (on the corner of the fashionable Boulevard des Italiens) where *La Musique aux Tuileries* was exhibited in Manet's first one-man show. Yet, as so often with Manet, appearances may well be deceptive. If there is an implicit social transaction here between painter and viewer through which the viewer is invited into what is assumed and proposed as a socially shared space, there are also obstructions to acceptance of the invitation: as we have seen, there is hardly anywhere for the viewer imaginatively to go; it's too crowded already, ridiculously cramped and squashed, less a court than a *foule* or even a parody of a *foule* and its related nineteenth-century vocabulary of the 'teeming throng' and suchlike. If the park and the concert represent Manet at the court of the modern bourgeoisie, it is a court squeezed and dissolved into farce.

One of the features of the Tuileries conspicuously absent from Manet's picture – apart from a cursory hint in the distance on the extreme right – is the park's statues. This is perhaps significant in that, in several nineteenth-century sources, reference to the statues was one of the means of securing a connection with an aristocratic past (when the Tuileries was the private garden of the King and the court). Manet's 'suppression' of that aspect of the park might well be read as implying a severance of this connection, and thus reinforce what I have claimed regarding the painting's burlesque of the park's so-called 'courtlike setting'.[89] The statues are, however, an important element in the final account of the park that I want to consider, from Jules Vallès's *Le Tableau de Paris*. This may seem a bizarre or uninspiring choice, simply by virtue of the generic limitations of the form, the possibilities of which, on the whole, made for little beyond a kind of journalistic notation. On the other hand, the *tableau* was also one of the founding genres of a certain discourse of 'Paris', starting with Mercier's *Tableau de Paris*, and became increasingly popular throughout the nineteenth century, notably in the period of the July Monarchy. I have referred on many occasions, though only briefly and opportunistically, to the *tableau* and its cognate modes (in particular the *physiologie*) as sources for grasping various aspects of that discourse. Whatever its formal limitations, given the historical centrality of the genre to representations of the city from the late eighteenth century onwards, it seems appropriate to take a slightly closer look at one of its more interesting examples.

Vallès is indeed conscious of the 'tradition' to which his text belongs. In the preface he refers, respectfully, to Mercier as if hailing an ancestor across the divide of a century.[90] In fact, in Mercier's hands, the genre offered something intellectually stronger than mere notation; it effectively invented a form of urban anthropology. One of the names Mercier gives to this enterprise is 'physionomie' (the aim of the *Tableau* is to present 'la physionomie morale de cette gigantesque capitale'[91]). The expression 'physionomie morale' is clearly from the language of eighteenth-century taxonomy, but, as the many generalizing observations of Mercier's text indicate, it should also be understood as designating a project of social representation at once analytical and historical in scope, reflecting Mercier's evident awareness that, in describing and classifying the city, he is also recording the historical emergence of new general forms of urban life, social, commercial and political.

The term *physionomie*, however, also provides a clue to the subsequent literary and ideological guises the genre will assume in the nineteenth century. The notion of *physionomie*, travelling via adaptations of Lavater's theories to social description, produced the *physiologie* (the more common title of the genre in the nineteenth century), devoted to 'reading' the city in the same way that Lavater interpreted faces.[92] The forms of life and their representative 'characteristics' ('types') were now assumed as simply given, read within a more or less unexamined and naturalizing category of social 'variety'. The genre thus quickly lost whatever modest elements it once had of felt connection with historical processes and came to be dominated almost entirely by the 'freezing' functions implicit in the original theatrical and pictorial senses of the word 'tableau'. It was a device for 'framing' and holding aspects of city life within fixed taxonomies and naturalizing descriptions that ranged from amiable picturesque and the tedious clichés of nostalgia for an allegedly 'lost' Paris to direct complicities in officially sponsored propaganda; as Benjamin put it, the essential purpose of the genre was to offer 'soothing little remedies' for the 'disquieting and threatening aspects of urban life'.[93]

On the other hand, although the broad variations in the genre amounted to little more than marginal differences around the category of 'variety' itself,[94] we should nevertheless bear in mind that, as Karlheinz Stierle has pointed out, the nineteenth-century incarnations of the genre are not quite as homogeneous as might at first sight appear.[95] There is a real, if minor, history here (for example, the genre changes from the early to the late July Monarchy, roughly in the direction of a greater interest in 'modernity'), as well as a politics of moderately contested representation (the *Nouveau Tableau de Paris au XIXe siècle*, as the 'republican' counterpart to the quintessentially middle-class *Paris ou le Livre des Cent-et-un*, begins by questioning the latter in terms of a claim to 'le Paris vrai'[96]). And, of course, later in the period the illustrations of Grandville, Gavarni and, above all, Daumier will bring to the genre a sharpness often quite at odds with the relatively innocuous text they accompany.[97]

These alternative possibilities, though heavily constrained (famously in the case of the censorship brought to bear on *La Caricature* and the work of Daumier), are important for understanding what Vallès brought to the genre. Vallès wrote his *Tableau de Paris* (as a series of newspaper articles from 1882 to 1883) on his return to France, after ten years' exile in London, under the amnesty granted to ex-Communards. Much of it reflects a 'Paris' idealized while in exile, and takes the form of an affectionate ramble through a city which in many respects no longer existed other than in memory or which indeed had never existed at all other than in fiction. *Le Tableau de Paris* is steeped in literary allusion (particularly to the novel from Balzac to Zola),[98] and hence is a prime example of a 'Paris' in part inflected by books about Paris. On the other hand, the intertextuality of Vallès's work is no mere exercise in literary reminiscence. What Vallès idealizes makes sense only from the other perspective he brings to the writing of the *Tableau*, the perspective of a lived history dominated by the catastrophe of the Commune. The lost literary Paris is not only explicitly identified as lost but also linked to another loss – that of an assumed historical innocence. From Vallès's point of view, the Paris of Balzac, Gavarni and Daumier – the example of caricature is important here – enjoyed a degree of self-assurance 'dont la sérénité bête faisait rire'. That, of course, simplifies in a number of directions (though Vallès's adjective 'bête' contains the potentially sentimental drift of the simplification). The point, however, is to emphasize a view of contemporary Paris, post-Commune, where the ruling class and its rule are no longer laughing matters ('Aujourd'hui, la bourgeoisie ne fait plus rire').[99]

By the same token, the genre of the *tableau* has lost whatever innocence it could be said to have originally possessed. '*Le Tableau de Paris*', writes Vallès in the preface, 'est à refaire.'[100] His shorthand for the tradition with which he proposes to break is Edmond Texier's *Tableau de Paris* (published in 1852 and later supplemented by the co-authored *Paris, capitale du monde* brought out in 1867 to coincide with the Exposition Universelle). I have previously noted some of the terms on which Texier's books represent Paris in a manner fully coincident with the official representations embodied in the Exposition itself,[101] and it is, of course, therefore no accident that his work has also figured prominently in the discussion of the theme of the park. Texier more or less takes for granted the world he describes; and in the emphasis on the city as sheer 'variety' reproduces exactly the idiom of the genre as it was practised in its heyday during the July Monarchy: 'Ce qu'il possède enfin, ce Paris sans pair, ce sont des personnages fortement caractérisés, des types aussi originaux qu'innombrables, des industries de toutes sortes, où éclate le génie inventif du peuple le plus inventif de la terre; en un mot, les incalculables variétés de toutes ces espèces que nous avons.'[102]

Vallès's undertaking is directed against this easy assumption of a social 'landscape'. He reorientates and extends the range of the genre by thoroughly politicizing it; against the tidily ordered productive city of Texier (the city as 'beehive'), Vallès gives us a city marked by a history of violent political conflict, a map and an itinerary stained with bloodshed. Blood indeed brings us back to the particular theme of the park and to a more precise point of contrast with Texier. There is an astonishing moment in Vallès's novel, *L'Insurgé*, when, on the eve of the Franco-Prussian war, the hero, crossing the Jardin des Tuileries, suffers from a sudden and profuse nose-bleed; it is a harbinger of things to come but also a disturbance to the tranquil image of the park as refuge for mothers and children: 'Je me suis barbouillé dans le bassin. Mais les mères s'en sont mêlées. "Est-ce qu'il a le droit de faire peur aux cygnes et aux enfants?" ont-elles dit, en rappelant leurs bébés dont trois ou quatre étaient harnachés en zouaves.'[103]

This piece of grotesquerie is of course quite against the grain of Texier's fashion-plate image of the Tuileries as the place where well-dressed mothers show off their overdressed children. In his *Tableau de Paris* Vallès in fact devotes a whole section to the parks. His way with them is, for the most part, direct, even brisk in its plain speaking. The Jardin du Luxembourg is sad and dreary beyond measure[104] (and moreover irreparably violated by Haussmann's renovations). The Jardin des Tuileries is a mockery of both the sociable and the bucolic with its 'allées désertes et son immensité sans verdure'.[105] The 'public' concerts are heard, from a distance, by 'les promeneurs à mines lasses, aux habits fatigués, ouvriers et déclassés';[106] the parks are indeed all the poor have, but it is not much, and certainly not had on the same terms as the rich. Against the decorous circumlocutions of Texier and Delvau, Vallès talks bluntly of the Tuileries as a place of prostitution, pausing only to distinguish between the 'courtisanes à vingt sous la caresse' who come in the evening after the afternoon occupancy of the park by the 'courtisanes à vingt mille écus'.[107] And then – to return to our point of departure – there are the statues, which, apart from the briefest of notations, are entirely absent from Manet's painting.

The statues are present in the accounts of both Texier and Vallès. In Texier, they are also the sign of a space marked by 'history', but a history of a particular sort, monumental, testimony to the glory of France ('est-il sous le ciel un morceau de terre plus historique', etc.[108]). Vallès's account is very different; he draws our attention to a statue that is no longer there, long since removed to the safety of the Louvre. Alongside the other statues wearing 'le masque d'une sérénité bête' is Foyatier's statue of the rebel slave, Spartacus, which once faced the Tuileries 'd'un air menaçant', before being prudently removed after the carnage of 1848.[109] Vallès's enthusiasm for the figure of Spartacus is in fact muted (the form of Foyatier's neoclassical sculpture would doubtless have encouraged him in this view), and, in an elaborate reference to an obscure text on the subject by the ultra-conservative Louis Veuillot,[110] Vallès declares a preference for the more radical Vindex. The point, however, is that even Foyatier's statue is a reminder of the troubled history which the contemporary ecumenical

187

mythologies of the urban park wished to efface (which is doubtless why it was removed). If the other statues are meant to signify a certain 'sérénité', Vallès will have none of it: 'Elle a été bousculée, cette sérénité-là, par la marche sanglante de l'histoire.'[111] Blood thus finds its way once more into Vallès's description of the park, but this time not as contingent personal mishap comically upsetting the received imagery, but as the term of a tragic text of history.

It also finds its way into Nature, specifically the flower-beds. A minor history of the nineteenth-century city from the point of view of the theme of 'flowers' remains to be written (it would doubtless start from *Les Fleurs du Mal*).[112] In Vallès's text, the pretty red flowers emphasized by the commentaries and Impressionist painting are trampled by the crush of history and run the colour of blood: 'Car ici, comme au Luxembourg, les fleurs empestèrent la poudre et le sang aux heures tragiques, et le grand jardin fut, sur ses flancs, bordés de blessés et pavés de morts!'[113] This is a new variation on the topos of 'mixture', and it involves not only the content of Vallès's *Tableau* but its very style. Vallès, constrained perhaps by the requirements of journalistic publication, does not exactly inject into his *Tableau* the language of the street in the way he does in his novels. He nevertheless has a striking, and strikingly political, way of 'mixing' the ingredients which make up his metaphors. In his account of the Jardin du Luxembourg, Vallès tells the sad story of the felling by Haussmann's people of the huge and famous tree known as the Pépinière, whose generous shade gave protection to dreamers and paupers: 'Tout comme la place publique, les jardins ont leurs révolutions, et l'on entend, à certaines heures, tomber sur la cime des arbres des coups de haches qui font l'effet de la guillotine sur le cou d'un roi.'[114] Vallès thus describes the felling of the Pépinière as an 'assassination' and also as a regicide. The latter analogy is, of course, odd, and indeed inappropriate, in so far as, on Vallès own highly 'republican' account, the Pépinière was not only the monarch of the Luxembourg trees but also the protector rather than the oppressor of the poor. Yet the logical inappropriateness is itself perhaps testimony to the way historical and political memory has unreflectingly seeped into the texture of Vallès's prose. It certainly comes as something of a stylistic shock to encounter, after long immersion in the blander idiom of the traditional *tableau*, *physiologie*, guidebook and so forth, a description of a tree in a park whose figurative energies are entirely generated from a sense of the city's revolutionary past. It is a perfect example of the way Vallès, with Morisot and Cassatt, Manet and Baudelaire, not only refigures aspects of the official story of the park (and by extension of the city in general), but also transforms the genre which so consistently reproduced and endorsed that story.

188

8

Conclusion: Baudelaire's Watch, or the Fast, the Slow and the Intelligible

I

Choderlos de Laclos, author of the great eighteenth-century novel of 'circulation' – of both desires and letters – was, in his capacity as a military man, also interested in other kinds of circulation. In a memorandum of 1787, *Projet de numérotage des rues de Paris*, he recommended a system of numbering for the streets of Paris in order to facilitate travel about the city and so to save 'le temps que perdent et les personnes à pied et celles en voiture, faute de pouvoir bien ordonner leurs courses, par l'ignorance où elles sont de la position respective des différentes rues'.[1] Though it got nowhere, Laclos's proposal was a sign of the times, of modern times, and was on a par with other notions, recommendations and measures in the period concerned with the need for faster circulation and more efficient use of time in the city. It was, for example, contemporary with the introduction by Lenoir, Lieutenant-General of Police, of the numbering of houses in the capital, for reasons partly to do with 'policing' (in the relevant eighteenth-century senses) but also partly to do with ensuring a more efficient delivery of goods; while Mercier gave over a whole chapter of his *Tableau de Paris* to the importance of the live axle ('Essieux roulans') for the city's system of transport.

These ideas and measures were, moreover, not simply matters of practical policy; they also reflected and anticipated a whole new sense of the nature of life in the city as based on an increasingly accelerating set of rhythms. In the course of the following century the association of the city and speed becomes commonplace. Maxime du Camp will devote the whole of the first volume of his six-volume history of contemporary Paris to the topic of

189

movement and circulation (with chapters on the postal service, the telegraph, carriages, trains and the river). The emphasis will also feature in the discourse of the guidebook and, appropriately enough, will be found in several of the texts commemorating that grand celebration of the modern commercial and technological city, the 1867 Exposition Universelle. Thus, in his contribution to the volume *Paris-Guide*, Edmond About defined life in the modern city in terms of speed: 'les grandes villes, dans l'état actuel de la civilisation, ne sont que des agglomérations d'hommes pressés.'[2] In the same volume, the popular novelist, Paul Féval, made a similar point, figuratively holding the pulse of Paris, watch in hand, though, in his characteristically facile way, declaring the patient to be in excellent health: 'Le pouls de Paris bat cent vingt à la minute, montre en main; ailleurs ce serait une fièvre de cheval. Paris, néanmoins, se porte à merveille.'[3] But perhaps the neatest – and the speediest – illustration of the point is one that involves another timepiece. Anecdotal history has it that Baudelaire removed the hands from his watch, inscribing instead on its face the words: 'il est plus tard que tu ne crois.' This may seem roughly on a par with Nerval's famous lobsters paraded on a leash in the Jardin des Tuileries, yet another gesture in the repertoire of *épater le bourgeois*. But if anecdotally the story of Baudelaire's watch reproduces the terms of a certain *bohème*, symptomatically it is the sort of detail that perfectly illustrates Walter Benjamin's diagnostic 'pre-history of modernity', and it comes as no surprise to find the story cited in the *Passagen-Werk* (culled from prolonged scholarly *flânerie* in the footnotes of Crépet's edition of *Les Fleurs du Mal*).[4] For, beyond merely restating the familiar Baudelairian cliché to the effect that life is short and art is long, it is also a comment on the modern way with clock time, on an urban culture increasingly dominated by a 'Taylorism' of the watch and, more generally, by the values of speed, mobility and circulation.[5]

This, of course, is to end where we began, circling back on the very principle of 'circulation' which, in the introductory chapter, I suggested was at the heart of perceptions and representations of nineteenth-century urban experience. Ideally, I would have wished to end otherwise, to end by opting out of the culture of speed (especially as reflected in the over-heated prose of Féval), by finding some alternative spaces in the city – or, more accurately, in writing about the city – where it might be possible to slow down, spaces not yet thoroughly mythologized and ideologized, and in which therefore one might recover, with Benjamin, some relatively unappropriated and uncontested form of what Susan Buck-Morss has called 'the utopian moment of *flânerie*'.[6] It is, of course, a most dubious notion (as we have seen with the example of the park), carrying the risk of all kinds of bad faith and sentimental delusion (and in any case does not really correspond with the sense of 'utopia' active in the texts of both Benjamin and his remarkable commentator). What these spaces might, temptingly, look like in terms of the major concerns of this book and why, finally, they are nevertheless unavailable, are matters which I shall consider later, although it is worth recalling forthwith that one very good reason why it is inadvisable to attempt ending in this way is that the nineteenth century itself sought to do so in the form of a palpably absurd fantasy: the 1900 Exposition Universelle looked back as well as forwards by building a huge simulacrum of *vieux Paris* complete with winding streets, cobblestones and so on, in which the modern consumer could nostalgically wander in search of lost time.[7]

But if in conclusion I return here to one of my points of departure (the preoccupation with speed), it is not merely to resume an earlier argument, but also to sketch out some new perspectives that bear upon the question of the city today (the so-called 'postmodern' city) and the forms of understanding at our disposal, in a context where it is precisely the principle of 'understanding' itself that is now dramatically in question, and where one reason commonly given for the resistance of the city to intelligible representation is, precisely, that everything in it – from fashions to information – now moves too fast. The point, then, is to suggest, via Benjamin, a continuity, an extension from the idea of Paris as the 'capital of the nineteenth century' into the business of writing about the city in the late twentieth century. In particular, the fact of having found myself writing much of this book in late twentieth-century New York leaves me entirely persuaded of the relevance of those relations and connections (from the city as spectacle to the city as garbage). This chimes well with Benjamin's argument about nineteenth-century Paris as producing, in the phantasmagoria of the arcades and the circulation of the commodity, not only a reflection of the present but also a dream of the future. 'Chaque époque', wrote Michelet (in a remark quoted epigraphically by Benjamin), 'rêve la suivante.'[8] The nature of this dream varies, from the predictive to the fantastic (in Benjamin's gloss, the emphasis is in fact more on the latter, on an imagining less of actual future outcomes than of desired ones, the utopian-paradisiac dream of the commodity culture become the cornucopia of capitalist abundance[9]). But, whether as prophecy or fantasy, in very many of its versions the dream typically involves scenarios of speed.

These scenarios, for the most part, had their source in the material life of the city, the paradigm-case being the effects on sensibility and imagination of the new modes of transport and experience of traffic, in that long history marked by the appearance of the omnibus, the train and finally the automobile (not to mention the exotic and short-lived forms such as the 'vélocipède', popular in the 1870s as a successor to the late eighteenth-century 'vélocifère'). Thus developed what Raymond Williams, describing the emergence of the 'new metropolis', called the city as 'transport network',[10] in which the network and its traffic were to be understood not just as technologies of physical movement but also as 'a form of consciousness and a form of social relations'.[11] Here, taken randomly from the Benjaminian archive of the Arcades Project, are some examples of the diverse ways in which transport in nineteenth-century Paris became an object of attention: Léon Gozlan wrote a 'poème héroïcomique' on the subject of 'le triomphe des omnibus'; Théophile Gautier, describing the omnibus as 'ce Léviathan de la carosserie', caught the emphasis on the speeded-up city (vehicles criss-crossing one another 'avec la rapidité de l'éclair'); in 1838 the Académie des Sciences Morales formally posed as a topic of discussion the question of the influence on 'l'état social' of the 'moyens de transport qui se propagent actuellement'. Finally, there is that odd fact of the novel I mentioned in the introductory chapter as providing the very model of a system of communication whose circuits speed up to the point of running out of control, Balzac's *Splendeurs et misères des courtisanes*: namely, the fact that Vautrin acquires the funds necessary to put Lucien de Rubempré into 'circulation' in Parisian high society by way of a spectacularly successful investment (of convict money) in nothing other than the new systems of public transport.[12]

Had the action of the novel been situated a little later in time, the investment would doubtless have included shares in the railways (Balzac himself played, and – typically – lost, heavily in railway speculation). The locomotive was the very emblem of modernity (Michel Chevalier, the Saint-Simonian apostle of the industrial society, claimed that the construction of railways was to the latter what the building of churches had been to earlier civilizations[13]). It found its way not only into transport systems but also into rhetoric (most famously in Marx's metaphor for revolutions as the 'locomotives of world history'). Above all, the railway train supplies an image and a focus for the ways in which nineteenth-century notions of speed could be said to anticipate (to 'dream') those of the twentieth century, and perhaps we see that join across time nowhere more seamlessly than in the juxtaposition of two instances of that other dream-palace, the World Exhibition. At the 1855 Exposition Universelle in Paris, the locomotive appeared in the following guise: 'Quatre locomotives gardaient l'entrée de l'annexe des machines, semblables à ces grands taureaux de Ninive, à ces grands sphinx égyptiens qu'on voyait à l'entrée des temples . . . tout était en mouvement.'[14] It is then but a step from the sphinx-like locomotives guarding a scene of constant movement at the 1855 Exposition to yet another dream-representation of the future ('the World of Tomorrow'), the advertisement of the Pennsylvania Railroad for transport to the New York World Fair of 1939 (at the opening of which Mayor La Guardia named New York itself as one of the exhibits): 'From the World of Today to the World of Tomorrow in ten minutes for ten cents'.[15]

A more Benjaminian piece of historical montage one could scarcely imagine than the yoking, across the gap of nearly a century, of these two powerful synecdoches for whole cultural formations. The juxtaposition, however, picks up on only one aspect of the developing technology of speed and its corresponding ideological-affective environment, the aspect of celebration. The train as symbol of power was indeed a motif of nineteenth-century literature and painting, either eroticized, as in Huysmans's *Les Sœurs Vatard* and, notoriously but also darkly, in Zola's *La Bête humaine*, or lyricized, as in Monet's Gare Saint-Lazare pictures. On the other hand, it was also an object of anxiety and denunciation, for instance, in the melodramatic anti-industrial imagery of Vigny's poem, 'La Maison du Berger', or the rural nostalgias of Nerval's autobiographical *Promenades et souvenirs*. But the crucial effect of the railway train, or more precisely of railway travel, on literature was in the sphere of subjectivity and perception, in its determining relation to, precisely, a new 'form of consciousness'.

Before the invention of the railways, wrote Benjamin Gastineau in 1861, 'la nature ne palpitait plus . . . les cieux mêmes paraissaient immuables. Le chemin de fer a tout animé. . . . Le ciel est devenu un infini agissant, la nature une beauté en action.'[16] In the view from the carriage window, railway travel generated a new perceptual register, perception speeded up, fluid, blurred, disorientated, which, in its translation to literature, came to inflect the very forms of literary language, from the syntax and rhythms of, say, Verlaine's railway poem, 'Le Paysage dans le cadre des portières'[17], to that canonical moment of early high modernism, the swirl of perception and discourse as the narrator rushes from one window to the other in the Proustian railway carriage.[18] The logical terminus of these developments, in both material life and literary representation, was the automobile and its appearance in the writings of, again, Proust (the 'Journées en automobile') and Virginia Woolf, where, as Williams remarks of the car ride out of London in Woolf's *Orlando*, 'the atomism of the city' is staged not only as 'a problem of perception' but also as one 'which raised problems of identity': 'After twenty minutes the body and mind were like scraps of torn paper tumbling from a sack and, indeed, the process of motoring fast out of London so much resembles the chopping up small of identity which precedes unconsciousness and perhaps death itself that it is an open question in what sense Orlando can be said to have existed at the present moment.'[19]

II

Here, then, along the chain linking carriages, omnibuses, trains and motor cars as the sources and signs of a developing urban phenomenology of speed, we have a convergence of pre-modern and modern (to which later will be added the peculiarly dislocating accelerations of the postmodern) around questions of *identity* ('the chopping up small of identity'). This too is where we began, with *inter alia* two fictional scenes of 'arrival' in the capital (the disorientation felt by Rousseau's Saint-Preux before the 'tourbillon social' of Paris and the identity-threatening, as well as exciting, 'tournoiement parisien' experienced by Balzac's Lucien de Rubempré in his first week in Paris). It is also where, for the most part and in one form or another, we have stayed throughout, that is, with questions of 'identity', in the city, of the city and of its representations. The imagery of modern transport is one further way of giving determinate shape to these questions. Indeed arrivals, along with departures, again evoke the image of the railway, specifically, the railway station – that place *par excellence* of both transit and transitoriness – as a special place of urban movement and encounter; Zola, for instance, introduces a minor modification to the convention of novelistic arrival-in-the-capital by beginning *Au Bonheur des Dames* with his heroine disembarking at the Gare Saint-Lazare (it is, of course, relative to the given convention, a more than minor matter that the character is a *woman*). Trains and stations are also elements – active, moreover, in interesting conjunction with the motif of the department store– in the text which I wish to take not only as a 'terminus' for the nineteenth-century enterprise of 'writing the city', but also as a point of transition and new departure into the twentieth century and the terms of our own preoccupation with the city: Laforgue's extraordinary experiment in what he called 'prose blanche', the 'Grande Complainte de la Ville de Paris':

Bonne gens qui m'écoutes, c'est Paris, Charenton compris. Maison fondée en . . . à louer. Médailles à toutes les expositions et des mentions. Bail immortel. Chantiers en gros et en détail de bonheurs sur mesure. Fournisseurs brevetés d'un tas de majestés. Maison recommandée. Prévient la chute des cheveux. En loteries! Envoie en province. Pas de morte-saison. Abonnements. Dépôt, sans garantie de l'humanité, des ennuis les plus comme il faut et d'occasion. Facilités de paiement, mais de l'argent. De l'argent, bonne gens!

Et ça se ravitaille, import et export, par vingt gares et douanes. Que tristes, sous la pluie, les trains de marchandise! A vous dieux, chasublerie, ameublements d'église, dragées pour baptêmes, le culte est au troisième, clientèle ineffable! Amour, à toi, des maisons d'or aux hospices dont les langes et loques feront le papier des billets doux à monogrammes, trousseaux et layettes, seules eaux alcalines reconstituantes, o chlorose! bijoux de sérail, falbalas, tramways, miroirs de poche, romances! Et à l'antipode, qu'y fait-on? Ça travaille, pour que Paris se ravitaille . . .

D'ailleurs, des moindres pavés monte le Lotus Tact. En bataille rangée, les deux sexes, toilettés à la mode des passants, mangeant dans le ruolz! Aux commis, des Niobides; des faunesses aux Christs. Et sous les futaies seigneuriales des jardins très-publics, martyrs niaisant et vestales minaudières faisant d'un clin d'œil l'article pour l'Idéal et Cie (Maison vague, là-haut), mais d'elles-mêmes absentes, pour sûr. Ah!

l'Homme est un singulier monsieur; et elle, sa voix de fausset, quel front désert! D'ailleurs avec du tact . . .
    Mais l'inextirpable élite, d'où? pour où? Maisons de blanc: pompes voluptiales; maisons de deuil: spleenuosités, rancœurs à la carte. Et les banlieues adoptives, humus teigneux, haridelles paissant bris de vaiselles, tessons, semelles, de profil sur l'horizon des remparts. Et la pluie! trois torchons à une claire-voie de mansarde. Un chien aboie à un ballon là-haut. Et des coins claustrals, cloches exilescentes des *dies iraemissibles*. Couchants d'aquarelliste distinguée, ou de lapidaire en liquidation. Génie au prix de fabrique, et ces jeunes gens s'entraînent en auto-litanies et formules vaines, par vaines cigarettes. Que les vingt-quatre heures vont vite à la discrète élite! . . .
    Mais les cris publics reprennent. Avis important! l'Amortissable a fléchi, ferme le Panama. Enchères, experts. Avances sur titres côtés ou non côtés, achat de nu-propriétés, de viagers, d'usufruit; avances sur succession ouvertes et autres; indicateurs, annuaires, étrennes. Voyages circulaires à prix réduits. Madame Ludovic prédit l'avenir de 2 à 4. Jouets *Au Paradis des enfants* et accessoires pour cotillons aux grandes personnes. Grand choix de principes à l'épreuve. Encore des cris! Seul dépôt! soupers de centime! Machines cylindriques Marinoni! Tout garanti, tout pour rien! Ah! la rapidité de la vie aussi seul dépôt . . .
    Des mois, les ans, calendriers d'occasion. Et l'automne s'engrandeuille au bois de Boulogne, l'hiver gèle les fricots des pauvres aux assiettes sans fleurs peintes. Mai purge, la canicule aux brises frivoles des plages fane les toilettes coûteuses. Puis, comme nous existons dans l'existence où l'on paie comptant, s'amènent ces messieurs courtois des Pompes Funèbres, autopsies et convois salués sous la vieille Monotopaze du soleil. Et l'histoire va toujours dressant, raturant ses Tables criblées de piteux *idem*, – o Bilan, va quelconque! o Bilan, va quelconque . . .[20]

Railway stations and trains are present in Laforgue's text (along with tramways) as figures in the representation of Paris as a vast 'import/export' operation: 'Et ça se ravitaille, import et export, par vingt gares et douanes. Que tristes, sous la pluie, les trains de marchandise!' Traffic and transportation thus appear here as both means and metaphor for other kinds of 'circulation', notably the circulation of the commodity form and the systematic implication of the city at all levels, from public to private, in the logic and language of pure exchange. The goods train, the depot and the customs house constitute but one strand in a multiplicity of superimposed, interacting yet open-ended series of tropes, the most important of which derive from two related creations of the modern capitalist city: the department store ('Ville de Paris' was also the name of the largest department store in the city) and the advertising poster. From this base the text generates a network of commercial terms and images – wholesale, retail, real estate, lease, cash register, rent, credit, mortgages, interest, stocks, balance-sheet – variously, randomly, yet relatedly clustered around the idea of Paris for sale or rent (or close-down).

Of the many forms of this idea evoked by the text's saturation with commercial idiom, one is strictly literary: the commodification of Paris includes 'Paris' as literary commodity. Lewis Mumford, we recall, argued that writing is the city's 'stigmata', that, because of writing and the circulation of fictions, 'life as recorded' tends to take over from 'life as lived', in the mode of 'overdramatisation, illusory inflation and deliberate falsification'.[21] In respect of nineteenth-century Paris, Benjamin remarked – and demonstrated in his own unbelievably copious notes and quotations – that the *flâneur*'s exploration of the city often went by way of a massive textual relay ('an almost infinite number of works'), and that what he saw and felt during his late-afternoon stroll, how he 'constructed' the city, was substantially affected by what he read in the morning.[22] Laforgue gives us a Parisian marketplace that includes the market in literary stereotypes of Paris, here devalued by dint of over-production and over-circulation, as styles for rent ('à louer'), genius at factory prices ('génie au prix de fabrique'), intertext as bargain basement, articles on offer in the 'sales' of the cultural department store, shortly to be going out of business ('en liquidation').[23]

In this densely packed ironic rehearsal of nineteenth-century urban sensibility, the most important intertextual allusions are to the novels of Balzac and the poetry of Baudelaire, or rather to a whole set of attitudes based on the diffusion of 'Balzac' and 'Baudelaire': Rastignac's 'A nous deux maintenant' is picked up here, after its long intertextual journey throughout the nineteenth century, in the absurdly deformed echo of 'A vous dieux', while, more generally, the proliferating list-like quality of Laforgue's style not only repeats the language of the sales catalogue and advertising poster but also parodies the endless notations of realist description in the novel, the idea of writing the city as a kind of inventory or stock-taking of reality, precisely, a 'bilan' ('o Bilan').[24] 'Baudelaire', on the other hand, appears as an advertisement for the second-hand market in genteel 'boredom' ('des ennuis les plus comme il faut et d'occasion'). The plural here is ambiguous: normally it would signify 'troubles', but the sense of 'boredom', along with its specifically Baudelairian connotations, is suggested by virtue of the later 'spleenuosités', a preposterously mannered, neologistic reference to the 'Spleen' poems of *Les Fleurs du Mal* as well as to the prose poems, *Le Spleen de Paris*.

Boredom is, of course, a typical Baudelairian experience, and belongs to the city as – again following Benjamin – the psychological consequence of immersion in the commodity culture, once the latter has been emptied of its hypnotic phantasmagoria and its 'truth' revealed in the paradox of the new as the ever-same. Laforgue, however, takes the experience a stage further or rather turns it reflexively back on itself, implying that 'boredom' is in turn caught up in the very phenomenon to which it is a negative reaction. The plural form of 'ennuis' can thus be read as designating the literary-cultural plurality of available 'boredoms', a range of late nineteenth-century Baudelairian posturings represented as so many brands in the store or, alternatively, as stale items on the 'menu' of literary discourse ('rancœurs à la carte'), a *reductio* of yet another theme introduced in the opening chapter – the gustatory imagining of Paris as a city to be 'tasted'. Laforgue's ironic point is that 'ennui' post-Baudelaire has itself become commodity, empty jingle ('auto-litanies et formules vaines'); it has become Boredom, a mere attitude, cheaply purchased and endlessly recycled, and, of course, nowhere more insistently than in much of the poetry of Laforgue himself; the irony is doubtless self-referential, including as one of its objects Laforgue the consummate performer in the roles of Hamlet and Pierrot, languishing in the tedium vitae of *dies iraemissibles* (a wonderfully parodic echo of both the genre of the requiem and the Baudelairian theme of the *irrémédiable*).

The implication of Laforgue himself in the great game of commodification, and in particular the crossing of commerce and literature in nineteenth-century Paris, also raises questions about what is clearly the most interesting feature of the 'Complainte' – namely, its status as 'prose blanche'. The peculiar notion of blank prose is presumably intended to 'advertise' its freedom from all generic constraint, as being beyond generic classification, beyond even the fluidities of the prose poem and *vers libre*, and so not to be found on the shelves of the literary store. Yet in one key formal respect it resembles the commercial and cultural world of which it speaks: in its aspect of pure *speed*. This is a text not only about speed of circulation but also itself stunningly fast-moving, constituted as a linguistic environment governed by a quite wildly accelerated flow of images and signifiers. Syntactically, there is scarcely a fully formed sentence; instead there is constant ellipsis and fracture, a breathless rush from one phrasally under-formed idea to the next. Lexically and semantically, it works as a version of 'collage',[25] a fragmentary and mobile patchwork of eclectic juxtapositions, migrating morphemes, verbal metamorphoses, puns, neologisms, and so forth.

The 'Complainte' thus 'moves', with a rapidity of textual displacement that echoes the 'rapidité de la vie' the text itself mentions. Indeed its ellipses and displacements occur at such an intensified pace as to become a form of 'circulation' veering towards delirium, where the textual circuits become short circuits, at risk, in the exploded syntax, of textual blowout or – to return to our railway metaphor – of semantic derailment. Alternatively, if the text can be said to stay on track, to travel a 'network', it is as a multi-track journey, at once lateral and linear, a 'railway' network in the sense of Freud's use of the metaphor to describe the work of the unconscious, in particular his notion of 'switch-words' in the language of dreams, which govern and effect a complex, ever-shifting web of associations and mean-ings.[26] Or, in its most verbally exuberant moments, the text slips below the threshold of sense, careers towards babble, pure play with sound, where circulation is reduced to verbal circularity, the 'voyages circulaires' in which the initial 'Bonne gens' finds an echo in the gratuitous near-rhyme of the closing 'Bilan'.

In this sort of writing, questions of 'identity' arise at many levels: the identity of the text (its generic status, its readability), the identity of its object or referent (Paris), the identity of its subject (the 'speaker', the subject of discourse), and the identity of its addressee (in particular of the strangely anomalous, a-grammatical apostrophe in the opening 'Bonne gens qui m'écoutes'[27]). There is here a generalized scattering of identities which may well recall that other sense of 'derailment' we associate with Rimbaldian 'dérèglement' ('transport' as ecstatic undoing of all fixed relation between subject and object).[28] It may also recall certain aspects of Rimbaud's extra-ordinary cityscapes. Rimbaud – that other great poet of speed – also gives us cities that cannot be 'possessed' by a coherent subject. In a truly radical use of the convention of the *tableau* (quite different in formal terms from, say, the journalistic mode of Vallès's *Tableau*), Rimbaud exploits its po-tential for interruption of linear continuity to give us a city as 'a tableau made up of totally heterogeneous sequences';[29] thus the criss-crossing of bridges and metallic structures in 'Ponts' provides no 'bridges' at all for the reader, no recognition points with which the city might be mapped and travelled; or, in the case of 'Métropolitain', the 'éclats' referred to in the text ('éclats de neiges'[30]) could be read as the shattering of the order of representation itself, an instance of what Georges Poulet has called 'la poésie éclatée',[31] or – given the 'sea' images of 'Métropolitain' – as a marker of the self-dissolving activity of the text, its 'identity' dispersed, like Lautréamont's *Maldoror*, in a ceaselessly fluctuating wake of traces.

Laforgue's 'Complainte' in many ways looks like an aggravated form of Rimbaud's already radical dismantlings. But it is important to remember that Rimbaud's fast and fabulous imaginings in 'Métropolitain' not only have the city enveloped in black smoke ('la plus sinistre fumée noire') but also have the poor in the poem's first paragraph ('de jeunes familles pauvres') as arguably an ironic check on an excessively hasty search for proto-modernist poetic 'riches' ('Rien de riche . . . la ville!'). We may also wish to raise similar issues in connection with the flamboyant experimentalism of Laforgue's 'prose blanche'. For it is clearly not enough – although it is certainly true – to say that Laforgue's method anticipates Eliot, Pound, Joyce and suchlike. The explosions of genre and form, and the correspond-ing loss of stable subject-positions for both writer and reader, still leave problematically open the question as to what exactly the implications of this way of representing the city might be. For instance, what do we make of

Laforgue's pastiche of the advertising slogan? It would seem to be fairly obviously pastiche as criticism, in the manner of Rimbaud's mock-sonnet, 'Paris' (from the 'Conneries' section of the *Album Zutique*), which apes the invasion of the urban environment by publicity in the form of a wilfully incoherent collage of poster-text.[32] Similarly, Laforgue's collage-like inventory can be read as a broken mimesis devoted to breaking what Benjamin called the 'ruse' of the advertisement, its aesthetic conversion of 'industry' into the terms of the dream-image; in the inchoate heterogeneity of Laforgue's prose, the flow of 'information' gets close to being pure noise, a simulacrum of capitalist circulation reduced to meaningless proliferation, reification writ large in the ultimately arbitrary list, the unreadable enumeration:[33] 'Et les banlieues adoptives, humus teigneux, haridelles paissant bris de vaiselles, tessons, semelles, de profil sur l'horizon des remparts.'

Accordingly, we could then generalize the linguistic and rhetorical characteristics of the 'Complainte' as the setting in motion of a provocative *counter*-circulation: the syntactic derailments, the lexical inventions and deformations are expressly designed to bring about a denaturalization of 'plain' language, to undermine the 'contract' (of commerce, of language) whereby a stable circulation of signs, money, goods, identities, is guaranteed ('tout garanti'). Laforgue's text tears up the contract enabling a ready 'consumption' of meaning, engenders panic in the markets of sense. On the other hand, engendering panic in the financial markets is exactly one of the moves of the bolder forms of speculative capital. Thus, to pose modern urban reality as a collection of heteroclite signs caught in a permanent semiotic spin may well be a mimesis not as comment on – in the mode of an ironic dramatization – but as symptom of that very reality (or indeed even as an 'effect' of that reality[34]); the neologism, for example, would then be seen not so much as counter-discursive coinage but as another kind of 'coinage', as itself commodity (the 'mot-marchandise'[35]), 'authorial jingles' as catchy new literary tunes. More generally, a method for the denaturalization of the 'natural' is in turn liable to its own naturalization, whereby the loss of intelligible identities becomes a condition taken for granted, even celebrated.[36] The deterritorialized flow of signifiers and the corresponding increases in semantic disorder may lie both parallel to and complicit with certain kinds of urban disorder, with the collapse of information into noise, and a profound loss of control (where 'control' is not just the Foucauldian incarcerator but all more or less settled forms of life). Like the city to which it belongs, Laforgue's department store, though 'in liquidation', never closes ('pas de morte-saison'), but this is not necessarily good pre-modernist news; it may mean that the commercialized space of the city-store finally absorbs everything, including the work which represents it, while appearing to 'advertise' itself as occupying another space altogether, secure in the possession of its distancing irony.

Such a judgement of Laforgue's poem and its cultural significance would, however, be both excessively severe and excessively reductive. If it appears to abandon the prospect of making sense of the city to the radically disconnected, it also hints at buried narratives of connection. Take the following bizarre concatenation: 'Amour, à toi, des maisons d'or aux hospices dont les langes et loques feront le papier des billets doux à monogrammes, trousseaux et layettes, seules eaux alcalines reconstituantes, o chlorose! bijoux de sérail, falbalas, tramways, miroirs de poche, romances!' We appear to be, in bewildering succession, in a hospital (at a birth?), a boudoir (writing monogrammed love letters), a brothel (the harem jewels and fripperies), on a tram, and in a popular cabaret (singing sentimental love songs, the 'romances', in witheringly ironic juxtaposition to the view of the couple-relation staged in the third paragraph). This, of course, is referential guesswork, and leaves a very great deal entirely unexplained. The web of associations, however, evokes yet another 'circuit', and of a sort that once more engages the conditions of 'literature' in the modern city.

The magazine world of the 'billet doux' and the mass-cultural world of the 'romances' coexist with the allusions to 'Balzac' and 'Baudelaire', thus compromising the customary distinctions of 'high' and 'low' culture. More startling is another implied narrative connecting 'high' and 'low' around the material base of literature itself, this time on the axis underground to overground: the 'langes' (nappies) and 'loques' (rags), as that which will furnish the paper on which the 'billets doux' are written, perhaps allow us to read Laforguian ellipsis here as a compressed restoration of a history that otherwise remains for the most part repressed, namely, the history of the economic and social chain linking, for much of the nineteenth century, waste, excrement, the sewer, the ragpicker, his rags, and the production of the paper on which love letters, and literature generally, are normally written. And then there is the odd connecting force of the rhyme in 'Ça travaille, pour que Paris se ravitaille', where 'ça' refers to the 'antipodes', the other side of the world, and the whole story of the 'suppressed connections'[37] which tie the metropolis to its exploited imperialist hinterland (railways also belong to this picture: in the previous decade there had been much talk of a railway running across the Sahara joining Algeria to Senegal, the two most important French colonies).

III

Through suggestive ellipsis and unexpected rhyme, Laforgue's text thus gets to speak of other kinds of 'circulation', to imply the 'system' beneath the patchwork, the connecting histories as well as the disintegrative, antitotalizing fragmentations. The text is thus truly multivalent, at once record, comment, symptom and resistance, laying out, ironizing, playing with, contesting the terms of the city and its representations. This is why the 'Complainte' is an exemplary work with which to conclude, the ideal threshold-text from which to exit from nineteenth-century Paris into the twentieth century and the latter's immensely complicated response to the city. On the other hand, it is not a text that can be inhabited for very long without the onset of a severe bout of vertigo. The temptation is, then, to leave its roller-coaster excitements, and instead to go looking for those alternative spaces to which I alluded earlier, which furnish the attractions of a slower and quieter ending, one that recovers, from the 'war on *flânerie*' declared by the society of speed, something of the so-called 'utopian moment' in the nineteenth-century idea of the urban stroll.

The virtues of moving slowly against those of moving fast through the city were part of the given code of *flânerie*. In the 1872 Larousse *Grand Dictionnaire Universel*, the definition of the verb *flâner* was made to turn on a contrast between the fast and the slow: 'cette ville où règne une vie, une circulation, une activité sans égale, est aussi, par un singulier contraste, celle où l'on trouve le plus d'oisifs, de paresseux et de badauds.'[38] Although the definition conflates distinctions which we have already seen to be important elsewhere (between *flâneur* and *badaud*, for instance), the contrast nevertheless captures an important stress in the discourse of *flânerie*. It was also, perhaps curiously, important to Benjamin himself, as a point of ambivalence and hestitation. For while Benjamin always locates the *flâneur* in a critical account of very specific economic, social and ideological conditions (as 'the spectator of the market' and 'the spy that capitalism sends into the world of the consumer',[39] the *flâneur*, in the standard incarnations, was necessarily male, indolent, exempted not merely from the capitalist world of work but from seeing the imposition of work as the very condition of capitalism), he also construed the idleness of the *flâneur* as 'a protest against the division of labour'.[40] And although the 'protest' is inseparable from the protected conditions under which it is made, it nevertheless had an implication of resistance to the rationalized city of economic modernity, which Benjamin – himself a passionate, compulsive city-walker – valued highly.

Thematically and topically, there were several spaces proposed by nineteenth-century literature and painting as sites of escape within the city from the city and its exhausting rhythms, but, not surprisingly perhaps, two of the most favoured were to be found close to water: the stroll along the Seine or the walk by the canal. The former was difficult to separate from the overlay of cultural and artistic stereotypes on the great river itself (before which even Maupassant went soft at the knees, describing it, in *Les Dimanches d'un bourgeois de Paris*, as 'ce fleuve adorable et doux qui passe au cœur de la France'[41]). Certain river views quickly became part of the canonical imagery of the city – more or less any which included Notre-Dame (thus associating the river with the 'flow' of time and the implied continuity of past and

present), or the view either from or of the Pont-Neuf (an important reference for the novel of Balzac, the urban history of Maxime du Camp, the
painting of Monet and Renoir). The quayside with its shop fronts and
bouquinistes fitted into this scheme quite naturally, especially when it was
essentially a matter of the elegant browsing of Renoir's strollers in the *Quai
Malaquais*. Even Jean Lorrain, perhaps the most desperately neurotic of
the *décadents*, found solace in the standard package of *quai*, *bouquiniste* and
flânerie ('la bonne'): 'Paris, pour moi, ne commence qu'au pont du Louvre;
je ne pourrais pas vivre loin des quais. O les bonnes flâneries dans l'air
frais du matin, devant les étalages des bouquinistes des quais d'Orsay et
Malaquais.'[42]

There were, however, other images, less readily assimilable to the pre-
scribed terms. The improbable riverside *flânes* of Huysmans's M. Folantin
in *A Vau-l'eau* is a case in point, as a sudden, unexpected but also down-
beat release from an otherwise irredeemably desolate world.[43] Or consider
the painting by Armand Guillaumin, *La Seine à Paris* (Cézanne so admired
it that he quoted it in one of his own pictures[44]). Guillaumin painted the
quais from a variety of angles, though he specialized in the working river,
the world of dockers, barges and cranes in the eastern districts from the
Quai de la Rapée to the increasingly industrialized Quai de Bercy. The view
in *La Seine à Paris* (plate 32) is more a picture of leisure, a large and spacious
one, a 'vista' from the Bassin de l'Arsenal; it takes in the compulsory Notre-
Dame, some barges, a rowing boat, factory chimneys and smoke and, as
viewers or strollers, two pairs of working men in conversation, a woman
with a baby and a girl walking beneath the trees. It is an image at once
relaxed and prosaic, stating its elements calmly but matter-of-factly (Huysmans
commented on the way 'les plans s'assurent, les tons hurlants s'apaisent, les
couleurs hostiles se réconcilient' in Guillaumin's paintings[45]); it offers a quiet
assembling of motifs that does not, however, imply the fictions of 'harmony'
and which leaves entirely open questions of 'belonging'. It does not say that
the city 'belongs' to the viewers; the signs of the 'heritage' (Notre-Dame)
are physically too distant for that. But it also does not deny the city to them
or at least not that particular space of leisure, at once ordinary and easily
occupied; indeed the very matter-of-factness of the painting *assumes* the space,
without fuss, while the distance of the 'historic' centre may also be read as
an escape from its hold (there is an oddness of perspective here – Notre-
Dame seems much further away than it actually is). This is worker's *flânerie*,
not exempt from work, but after work, shown, without the slightest sign of
sentimentality, unselfconsciously using the resources of the city to hand.

Nevertheless, despite these efforts to defuse the theme of the riverside
stroll by detaching it from a hugely overdetermined doxa of the River, the
efforts could, in the nature of things, be only partially successful. Verlaine's
early poem, 'Nocturne parisien', tries to play down the legends by contrasting

the Seine with the great rivers of the world and world history; the Seine is 'morne', evil-smelling, repository of dead and rotting bodies; it has nothing ('Toi, Seine, tu n'as rien') beyond two 'quais, et voilà tout', and even the latter are but:

> Deux quais crasseux, semés de l'un à l'autre bout
> D'affreux bouquins moisis et d'une foule insigne
> Qui fait dans l'eau des ronds et qui pêche à la ligne.

This is expressly designed to keep both the literal and literary *flâneur* away. But the perspective of demystification is not sustained, and, with the arrival of sunset, the poem retrieves, along with this familiar stereotype itself, most of the others (including, towards the end of the poem, the cliché of Paris as the 'reine du monde'):

> Oui, mais quand vient le soir, raréfiant enfin
> Les passants alourdis de sommeil ou de faim,
> Que le couchant met au ciel des taches rouges,
> Qu'il fait bon aux rêveurs descendre de leurs bouges
> Et s'accoudant au pont de la Cité, devant
> Notre-Dame, songer, cœur et cheveux au vent![46]

The Seine was finally inseparable from its legends. Indeed, in its most powerful embodiments, the river was not so much a way of exiting from the pressures of the city as the symbol of the city itself, its history, its 'soul'. In the most famous nineteenth-century fictional walk along the quayside (that of Zola's artist, Claude Lantier and his mistress Christine, in *L'Œuvre*), the river and its views come, for Lantier, both to resume the city, its secret essence, its 'soul' ('cette âme de Paris'),[47] and to engender the feverish, impossible and ultimately fatal attempt to capture that essence in art; Claude and Christine start out on a simple lovers' stroll and end up in a nightmare of obsession and suicide, that other form of 'exiting'. The Seine, finally, has to be either the source or the scene of high drama, in particular by way of a long literary association with suicide (it is where Balzac's Raphael de Valentin tries to kill himself and where, perhaps most famously of all, Hugo's Javert succeeds).

If, then, we go in search of the understated, it is better to quit the banks of the Seine altogether. There was, of course, always an alternative river, that anti-Seine, the Bièvre, whose seedy charms were praised, in characteristically mordant prose, by Huysmans (in both the *Croquis parisiens* and *Le Drageoir aux épices*[48]) and, in more sentimentally affectionate register, by Delvau (who managed, by filtering his own childhood experience through reminiscence and reverie, to convert the river's polluted 'eau fangeuse' into the image of 'un ruisselet à l'onde cristalline').[49] But perhaps the true anti-Seine of the nineteenth century, the site of a consciously constructed coun-ter-*flânerie*, was not so much the banks of the other river as those of the canal, in particular the Canal Saint-Martin and the Canal de l'Ourcq. There is not much to report on here: a handful of paintings and drawings, an occasional literary setting, a sketch for a story or just a mere allusion, as, for example, in Baudelaire's declared preference for the Canal de l'Ourcq over the seaside at Honfleur ('Ma promenade préférée est la berge du canal de l'Ourcq'[50]).

On the other hand, the under-representation of the urban canal (outside the city it received a great deal more attention, especially from the painters) is, for the purposes of the present argument, precisely part of its signifi-cance; the fact of its relative marginality in both life and art ensured its relative freedom from colonization by myth, or at least from the kind of myths informing the representation of the Seine. The canal appears as literally and figuratively a backwater, where the water itself often seems quite still, in contrast to the ever-flowing Seine and its association with the large and often turbulent 'movements' of human life and history (Paul de Kock said of the Canal Saint-Martin that 'vous ne croiriez pas être alors dans Paris, cela n'en a ni l'esprit, ni le mouvement, ni le bruit'[51]). There was some attempt to give the canal a certain artistic pedigree (for instance, Stanislas Lépine's *Canal Saint-Martin* was modelled on the Venetian canal and its painterly tradition, by way of Corot and Turner).[52] The echo is nevertheless faint, and virtually disappears in Sisley's two paintings, *Le Canal Saint-Martin* Plate 33 and *Péniches sur le Canal Saint-Martin* Plate 34. The barges pic-ture is primarily a scene of work, plainly stated, the city going about its ordinary business (though the understated quality of the 'déchargeur' suggests that work here may be merely pretext for a more detached interest in 'landscape'). In the other picture, the signs of work have almost completely disappeared: the barges are still there but are not so strongly foregrounded. It is more a scene of leisure (there appear to be two nondescript strollers on the towpath with some onlookers set back on the street). And the nondescript is precisely the important stress of the painting, an image utterly de-dramatized, emptied of myth, but also suffused with that low-key melancholy, so characteristic of Sisley, that generates reverie from a haunt-ing suggestion of lack, a scene without a 'centre' or at its centre a muted sense of pure Absence.

In literature, there is a corresponding paucity of matter. It appears briefly as metaphor for the streets of Paris ('les canaux étroits') in Baudelaire's 'Les Sept Vieillards',[53] but has no sustained life, either figuratively or referentially, in his writings generally. Yet what is lost in quantity is surely compensated for in quality by the fact that surely the greatest beginning in nineteenth-century French fiction is set by the Canal Saint-Martin. This is where, on the opening page of Flaubert's novel, Bouvard and Pécuchet meet, at first in sedentary conversation, then in repeated strolling 'depuis l'écluse d'amont jusqu'à l'écluse d'aval', reluctant to leave if not the spot then certainly each other.[54] This is perhaps in part a personal 'reply' to the opening of the earlier *L'Education sentimentale* (in a boat on the Seine), and hence by extension an ironic farewell from a whole tradition of narrative beginnings (though even *L'Education* equivocates the tradition by beginning with the hero leaving rather than entering the city). Flaubert's canal, as anti-Seine, thus serves as a modest metonymy for what we will later call the anti-Novel (the canal turns up again in the unnamed and unmappable city of Robbe-Grillet's *Les Gommes*).

Certainly, the paradoxical pleasures of ending with Flaubert's beginning, in demythologized *flânerie* with Bouvard and Pécuchet, are almost irresistible. They are, moreover, heightened when additionally spiced with the perverse pleasures of Huysmans's urban walks in the *quartiers populaires* of late nineteenth-century Paris (I use the culinary metaphor advisedly; the smells of food, in particular of *friture*, are an essential constituent of the Huysmanian repertoire and add a further aspect to the theme of 'tasting' Paris). Like Baudelaire, Huysmans was much taken with the Canal de l'Ourcq and included it on the list of 'ces promenades [qui] sont fécondes en apaisements et en rêveries'.[55] Huysmans is, of course, the absolute master of the literary excursion to the out-of-the-way, unpretentious, neglected district, for example, the 'cité Berryer' in the industrial *banlieue* frequented by André, the hero of *En ménage*, or the Quartier Maine-Montparnasse in *Les Sœurs Vatard*.[56] Here, it would seem, are the ultimate places of retreat from the spectacularized and glamorized city; the Huysmanian *quartier* is strictly not for 'sight-seeing', non-touristic, anti-monumental, forlorn and 'flat', but in its very flatness refusing a discourse of *flânerie* at once inflated and exhausted.

Yet, whatever the apparent attractions, we cannot in fact end here, at least not if the governing idea is that 'here' we are somehow beyond the tentacular reach of the great myth-making machine of 'Paris'. Huysmans takes us to a limit point, but only in turn to install his own myths. The *quartier populaire* in Huysmans is also typically *crapuleux*, chlorotic, consumptively sick. This is not merely a comment on levels of illness in working-class Paris; it is a stylistic signature, a mannerism that takes the form of a kind of literary *encanaillement*, an exquisite slumming. A style which zeugmatically joins, as if they were connected not incongruously but 'naturally', the two adjectives in the reference to 'les quartiers poitrinaires et charmants' in *En ménage*[57] belongs entirely to the terms of a certain aesthetic of decadence; and the much-discussed intensity of Huysmans's descriptive prose (modulating from the naturalistic to the surrealistic) is fully consistent with the commitments of that aesthetic. It is, finally, not a retreat at all, but a quest for 'sensation', and it is, of course, decisive to the argument about Huysmans that, if, with him, we visit these districts, we do not stay in them for long; we move on, like André in *En ménage* wandering from one to the other in search of a figment of his own nervous imagination, a paradigm of the deeply neurotic character of fin-de-siècle *flânerie*.[58]

Above all, there is the paradox that overtakes all the others, whereby the Huysmanian adventure itself becomes a standard move or 'turn'. If it is correct to describe Huysmans's Paris as a 'detour' from mainstream *flânerie*, it is so not only topographically but also rhetorically. Michel de Certeau has ingeniously described walking in the city as a 'rhetoric', a series of *tours* (where the latter signifies not only physical 'turns' and 'turnings' but also 'turns of phrase'), and in relation to which therefore the notion of 'de-tour' also has a particular rhetorical value.[59] If, in connection with the literal activity of walking in the city, this is perhaps stretching the validity of tropological analysis to breaking point, its relevance to literary representation will be clear; and, in the case of Huysmans, it will be equally clear what the dominant rhetorical figure is: Huysmans's work redescribes *flânerie* according to the arts of understatement, in the mode of litotes. To go out with Huysmans is therefore to go out obliquely, with a whimper rather than a bang. But it is a whimper that itself soon becomes a markedly literary one, a routine figure for the Modern City. In the emphasis on flatness, the *plat* will eventually acquire the status of platitude,[60] as yet another *idée reçue*, and the idea of 'retreat' will find its place in the cultural *sottisier* of late nineteenth-century retreatism, reduced, jaded, all inertia and paralysis, grey on grey, like the 'tristesse grise' which hangs over Paris in winter in the Goncourt brothers' novel, *Manette Salomon*[61] (though here Flaubert, ever the provocateur, once more turns the tables on the stereotype by setting his canal scene in summer-time, bathed in that characteristically Flaubertian atmosphere, 'la tristesse des jours d'été'[62]).

Moreover, in returning to the particular example of the canal, we should not forget what, in the actual practical and political history of the city, the canal was all about. It was of course primarily about bringing water to the city. In this regard, Napoleon was a prime mover, allegedly stating to his Minister, Chaptal, 'je voudrais faire quelque chose pour les Parisiens', to which came back the eminently practical suggestion: 'Donnez-leur de l'eau.'[63] Thus began the construction of the Canal de l'Ourcq, soon to be caught up in disputes between the engineers and administrators about the organization of flows (broadly, the demand for increased water supply against the claims of river traffic). In short, the canal was from the very beginning integral to the planning of 'circulation' in the city, and it comes as no surprise to read in his *Mémoires* that Louis-Philippe's Préfet, Rambuteau, not only considered the 'service des eaux' as the jewel in the crown of urban administration but also believed his own contributions in this area to be his highest achievement as a public servant.[64] The canal was moreover implicated in other kinds of circulation, this time of bodies rather than of goods. If from the 1840s the banks of the canal became a place of popular sociability, for *promenades*, *fêtes nautiques* and the like, they were also useful as a place of 'retreat' for insurrectionaries; in 1848 the eastern bank of the Canal Saint-Martin served as a refuge for revolutionaries pursued by Cavaignac's troops. This may be called the true form of both counter-circulation and counter-*flânerie*. It was, furthermore, very far removed from the leisurely; in the nature of things, speed was of the essence. The administration learnt its lesson; what we know today as the covered sections of the canal on the Boulevard Richard Lenoir were specifically built to secure access across the canal in the event of future disturbances.[65]

IV

The wish to end by slowing down and to exit via detour thus turns out to be a detour of our own, by which moreover, and paradoxically, we come full circle, back to speed, to Laforgue's collage-city, and from there once more to the connections with our own myths, fears and desires of the contemporary metropolis. These too commonly involve some model of collage (quintessentially New York, which the composer Stockhausen once described as 'social collage'[66]). But the model also has a built-in principle of self-destruct, whereby the city is perceived not simply as collage more or less randomly assembled but also as collage undone, with the glue coming apart, Pound's modern metropolis, for example, as 'a flood of nouns without verbal relations'.[67] This sense of the fixative no longer holding, as life speeds up more and more, has generated the terms of two of our most powerful narratives of the contemporary metropolitan condition: stories of end-time and stories of playtime. In the first, the city careers unstoppably towards a doom-laden finale; in the second, the emphasis on accelerated falling apart remains but is redirected from the catastrophic to the aleatory (Manhattan as the 'aleatory island'[68]), from nightmare to fun, apocalypse to *bricolage*, ruins to waste, to the view of the city as playground and its debris as the material for a kind of urban *fort/da* game of an endlessly 'decentring' sort.

Yet if apocalyptic imaginings and ludic fantasies have acquired pride of place among our postmodern urban shibboleths, they are less novel than we might think. In Baudelaire, for example, there are many scenarios in which the emblematic watch announces not merely that it is later than you think but that the End is near ('Le monde va finir'[69]). 'Ruins' are a favoured motif here, in, for instance, the sketch of a possible prose poem, 'Symptômes de ruine', the dream of a building (as the house of a body and a self) about to collapse, but where the building can also be read as the dream-residue of Haussmann's demolitions converted into a generalized vision of a city falling into ruins.[70] It is a vision that occasionally translates into poetic greatness, famously in 'le Cygne', Baudelaire's magnificent poem of Paris as another Troy-to-be, with its prefiguring of modernity as antiquity not in order to dignify the former with the aura of the latter, but rather to project a history as issuing in the city's death.[71] The general point, however, is that, although in 'Le Cygne' the vision became great poetry, ending scenarios for the city were commonplace in the nineteenth century as a whole, so much so that the literature of apocalyptic *frisson* was also already an object of parody and satire (for instance, in Louis Reybaud's *La Cité de l'Apocalypse*).[72] So too was the idea of the city as a kind of playground. Baudelaire's *flâneur* in 'Le Joujou du pauvre', setting out on his stroll armed with toys for the children of the poor, literalizes the idea into sheer absurdity. Laforgue's 'Complainte', in a brilliant ironic stroke, also alludes to the image of the city as toytown, around the twin ideas of playtime for children and party-time for adults; the department store stocks toys as well as supplying party accessories for the grown-ups ('Jouets *Au Paradis des enfants* et accessoires pour cotillons aux grandes personnes').

My purpose here, however, is not simply to indicate some of the terms on which the nineteenth century can be said to anticipate the late twentieth. It is less to trace a lineage of images and postures (and, in some cases, impostures) than to raise an issue: as the images in question harden over time into received images (while still masquerading as the New), what is the cost, both intellectual and political, of their continuing 'circulation' (the latter itself an increasingly speeded-up phenomenon, largely by virtue of the mass circulation of the photographic image, especially, in a remarkable conjunction of vision and technology, the image of the city-in-motion produced by the use of fast film)? One such potential casualty is the prospect of construing the city as knowable.[73] This too sends us back to Baudelaire and Laforgue, partly in the terms we have already considered but to which certain others may now, in conclusion, be added; in particular, from the Baudelairian repertoire, the metaphor of the sea-without-edges (the city as the unframable and unnavigable 'mer monstrueuse et sans bords' of 'Les Sept Vieillards'[74]) and the even more influential figure of the 'labyrinth'.

The city as labyrinth, in which one gropes like a blind person, without the help of an Ariadne's thread, is an image that has travelled well from the nineteenth century to the theoretical and fictional writing of our own time (in post-war fiction it has made regular appearances from the cities of the *nouveau roman* to the New York of Paul Auster's remarkable novels). Michel de Certeau – in perhaps the most powerful theoretical statement of this point of view – writes of being in the city as akin to moving in 'des labyrinthes mobiles et sans fin'.[75] Yet de Certeau's use of the image is in no sense a warning or a lament for the loss of a knowledge-based orientation, and indeed his more general argument shows just how difficult and complicated the question of the city as object of knowledge, especially systematic knowledge, has become. For de Certeau, knowledge of the city, the idea of the city as intelligible, is inseparable from the institution of panoptic regimes of domination and control. His model – one we have considered in a previous chapter – is the panorama (the 'ville-panorama'), and his example – the view from the World Trade Centre – offers yet another link joining postmodern New York to pre-modern Paris.

In de Certeau's version of the view from on high, the 'scopic' and the 'gnostic' work together to produce a 'fiction du savoir', a series of 'totalisations imaginaires' fuelled by the viewing subject's desire to be but a pure 'point voyant'.[76] Not surprisingly, knowledge here is linked to death; what is seen from on high are mere 'cadavres', a spectral parody of the real thing. Indeed, if the production of the spectacularized city involves the scopic as well as the panoptic regime, it might then make sense to relate the assumed position of masterful and mastering vision common to both regimes to aggression, the impulse to destroy, and hence suggest a link between seeing the city whole and imagining it dead, a hidden and dangerous relation between the totalizing fantasies of the panoramic view and fantasies of destruction at work in the equally insistent nineteenth-century emphasis on prophetic visions of Paris falling into ruins. From de Certeau's image of the 'cadaver', it would seem plausible to construe the view from on high as animated as much by an impulse to annihilate as by a will to administer. The city's life, on the other hand, that which is down below and experienced at ground level, consists of the 'obscur entrelacs des conduites journalières'; against the scopic drive to detached and masterful clarity, there is the lived reality of the city as 'opaque mobilité', as 'migrational' flows that 'échappent à la lisibilité', as heterogeneous movement always in excess of the text of the planned and readable city.[77] For the panorama – as we have ourselves already seen from its nineteenth-century Parisian examples – is, of course, the very image of a certain urban rationality. De Certeau calls it 'la Ville-concept', the creature of a 'totalitarisme fonctionnaliste' bent on installing the order of the fully regulated and regulative city, and rejected by de Certeau in the name not only of an epistemology of the lived, but also of a politics of critique and resistance based on the proliferation in everyday life of 'pratiques microbiennes, singulières et plurielles' and 'les ruses et les combinaisons de pouvoirs sans identité lisible, sans prises saisissables, sans transparence rationnelle'.[78]

The illustrative example de Certeau gives of these practices is once again from the experience of 'circulation', though this time of the pedestrian rather than the vehicular sort, namely the topos of walking, redescribed, as we have seen, as a 'rhetoric', a rhetoric of walking ('une rhétorique piétonnière') which we ourselves might well wish to situate as an energetic and contestatory alternative to the older lexicon of *flânerie*. The rhetoric of walking is a rhetoric of mobility, detour and displacement based on essentially two figures: one is, precisely, *the* figure of displacement, namely, metonymy or synecdoche, the endless encounter of parts for wholes (this, importantly for the general problem of the possibility of knowledge of the city, necessarily retains a relation to some principle of totality); the other is the figure of asyndeton, the figure of disconnection and ellipsis ('supprimant le conjonctif et le consécutif').[79] From these two primary figures of pedestrian rhetoric ('figures cheminatoires') is elaborated a whole strategy of escape from the 'clean' and ordered spaces of panoptic rationality, ensuring an alternative 'circulation', denarrativized and dispossessed, or rather non-possessing; 'marcher', says de Certeau, 'c'est manquer de lieu', and is thus the paradigm of the 'immense experience sociale de la privation de lieu' in the city; it is to move through an 'univers de location', a universe of rented spaces, not settled or owned, where the relation between property and the 'propre', between ownership, cleanliness and identity, is decisively confounded.[80]

In this emphasis on the elliptical, the asyndetic, the rented, we hear, of course, echoes of Laforgue, but here the tone is radically upbeat (there is nothing in it of the genre of the 'Complainte'). It is rather a passionate plea for counter-panoptic urban circulation as a kind of ebullient *errance* directed against the fixities and sedentarities (not to mention the deportations) of the administered city; it is a brand of the *fort/da* game (the latter is de Certeau's own analogy), understood as 'la marche que Freud compare au piétinement de la terre maternelle'.[81] This is the strongest, the most eloquent and the most attractive postmodernist *profession de foi* I know of around the theme of the contemporary city. Not the least of its fetching characteristics is its politically cheerful way with Foucauldian premises; it shares the preoccupation with carceral regimes, but without the dispiriting view that we are hopelessly locked into them, reproducing them even in the (illusory) act of offering resistance to them. It is, moreover, a view with friends from otherwise very different intellectual traditions; it is, for example, close to Kracauer's distinction between urban forms of life as 'fortuitous creations' and those that are 'consciously formed', the former seen as fragmentary and improvised, but with special resources in lived knowledge, experience and memory to pit against the project of the managed city (the classic example for Kracauer was indeed Paris, in opposition to Berlin, the prime example, in which, against the city as 'readable pattern', the 'people are incalculable like its network of streets').[82]

Yet, while it is heartening to encounter the eirenic dismissal of what de Certeau eloquently calls those 'ministres du savoir', guardians of the (decaying) Concept-city, who convert 'le malheur de leurs théories en théories du malheur',[83] there are nevertheless both omissions and simplifications in this account of both how the city is and how it might be. One elision in all the talk of *errance*, asyndeton, lack, 'rented' spaces, and so on, concerns the fact that, as with our introductory metaphor of the Jamesian 'house', there are in fact owners, some of them very large indeed, with correspondingly powerful interests to protect (in this respect, Laforgue's vision of the city as a vast real-estate market is absolutely on target). By the same token, just as we must qualify the fashionable reappropriation of the nineteenth-century ragpicker, as a figure for postmodern *bricolage* with the city's junk, by reminding ourselves of the literal resurgence of widespread scavenging in the late twentieth-century city, so we would have to add to de Certeau's image of 'rented' spaces the image – and the fact – of the homeless, for whom 'walking' the streets reflects less a challenge to the power of those who own the city than one of the miserable effects of that power. And since de Certeau's starting point in his commentary on the city is the politics of the panoramic view, we might also recall here the anti-panorama of Van Gogh's remarkable Montmartre picture (discussed in chapter 3): one reason for also having it on the front cover of a book about the endlessly self-celebrating capital of the nineteenth century is that, although there is of course no way of verifying this, the woman in the right of the painting could well be a homeless person, excluded from the city in the most elementary sense, a huddled, sad prefiguration of the bag lady.

Another difficulty with de Certeau's approach is a potential simplification reducing fast to a kind of intellectual melodrama: the partial assimilation of the question of 'knowledge' to the configurations of *savoir/pouvoir* rests on a now very familiar schematic opposition between 'administration' and 'every-day life', which then comes out as a relatively unexamined opposition between the 'collective' ('le mode collectif de la gestion') as the zone of interrelated power, knowledge and oppression, and the 'individual' ('le mode individuel d'une réappropriation') posed as the sphere of freedom, autonomy and rebellion.[84] In its wholly unexamined forms, this opposition can end by reinstating an old (essentially nineteenth-century) duality of the 'social' and the 'individual', the social *against* the individual, and the consequent loss not only of those notions of community which require us to get beyond the simple opposition of the administered and the free, but also of just about all kinds of solidarity, shared meanings, or even any meaning at all, any possibilities of knowledge other than those associated with the panoptic project. One – by now quite common – consequence of this way of thinking is a view of the city as the space for a very fast-moving postmodern trip. Here, for example, is Michel Deutsch, recycling the notion of the city's indecipherability: 'L'idée de la ville, toujours énigmatique, à la densité sémantique toujours multipliée à l'infini . . . l'idée d'une ville à déchiffrer, en un mot, n'a plus cours.'[85] Indecipherability is not, however, a problem to be tackled, in an effort, perhaps endlessly defeated but always renewed, to understand the city; on Deutsch's view (a view not unrepresentative of a certain brand of postmodernist taste in these matters), it is rather a condition to be welcomed, both condition and effect of high-speed existence become pure high, the vapid euphoria that transforms *flânerie* into floating: 'cette impression euphorique de flotter dans la ville – flotter sans sensation comme dans un téléfilm'.[86] This, of course, simply repeats another long-established *idée reçue* (recalling, for instance – since Deutsch's example is once again New York – the view of Norman Mailer's memorably awful *An American Dream* as a work inviting us to 'thrill to the existential precariousness of the collage'[87]).

It is a mark of the intelligence and seriousness of de Certeau's account that, whatever the difficulties of his argument, they do not lead to this sort of self-indulgence. On the contrary, not only is 'meaning' retained as an important category (the 'significations cachées et familières'[88] with which the encroaching reach of 'alien reason' is stubbornly obstructed); so too is the category of knowledge, the useful kind versus the 'fiction of knowledge', indeed a knowledge which even requires the sense of a 'totality'. If, in the rhetoric of urban movement described by de Certeau, the figure of asyndeton disconnects ('ouvre des absences dans le continuum spatial'[89]), the figure of synecdoche, on the other hand, points to the whole of which it is the representative part, although the former, the totality, can never be apprehended as such (without instituting the tyranny of the imaginary totalization); it is only through its scattered parts that the whole can ever be, though always incompletely, known.

This must, however, mean that to represent the city as a 'labyrinth' is not necessarily to abandon the belief in being able to find one's way around it or to understand the principles on which it has been constructed. The analogy of the labyrinth was, of course, also Benjamin's, who in turn took it not only from Baudelaire but also from Simmel. In Simmel's writings on the city the image is active but problematic: Simmel's method was to describe 'spaces' and 'surfaces', forms of social life presented as a patchwork or web of phenomena, but not differentiated and ordered according to some conceptual or causal hierarchy.[90] The consequence is that we get much complexity but little structure (especially structures of power), or, as Lukács put it, in Simmel we are given a 'labyrinth' rather than a 'system'.[91] Benjamin's approach and method often appear very similar, and he is certainly often, and rightly, billed as a cultural theorist and historian who prefers fragments to wholes, for whom indeed the 'fragment' is the ground of a methodological and philosophical rejection of those 'totalizing' models of social life where totality is assumed as unified, seamless, and fully invulnerable to rupture by what is heterogeneous to it. Yet, in many ways, this dissolves into the terms of a simple opposition what in the reality of Benjamin's writing is at once a complex tension and necessary relation between part

18. Eugène Delacroix, *La Liberté guidant le peuple*, 1831. (Musée Louvre. © photo: Réunion des Musées Nationaux)

20. Jules Chéret, *Exposition universelle de 1889: Le pays des fées*. (Musée Carnavalet: Phototheque © Musées de la Ville de Paris by SPADEM 1992)

19. Honoré Daumier, *Le Gamin aux Tuileries*. (Reproduced by Courtesy of the Trustees of the British Museum, London)

21. Claude Monet, *La rue Montorgueil, fête du 30 juin 1878*, 1878. (Musée d'Orsay. © photo: Réunion des Musées Nationaux)

22. Claude Monet, *Camille au jardin*, 1867. (Musée d'Orsay. © photo: Réunion des Musées Nationaux)

23. Claude Monet, *Le Déjeuner*, c.1873. (Musée d'Orsay.
© photo: Réunion des Musées Nationaux)

24   Claude Monet, *Les Tuileries*, 1876. (Musée Marmottan, Paris; photo: Jean-Michel Routhier)

25. Claude Monet, *Le Parc Monceau, Paris*, 1876, oil on canvas, 59.7 × 82.6 cm. (The Metropolitan Museum of Art, Bequest of Loula D. Lasker, New York City, 1961 [59.206].

26. Claude Monet, *Le Parc Monceau*, 1878, oil on canvas, 72.7 × 54.3 cm. (The Metropolitan Museum of Art, Mr. and Mrs. Henry Ittleson, Jr. Fund, 1959 [59.142].

27. Pierre-Auguste Renoir, *La Promenade: femme et enfants*, c.1874. (Copyright The Frick Collection, New York)

28. Berthe Morisot, *Le Lac au Bois de Boulogne*, 1879, oil on canvas, 45.7 × 75.2 cm. (Reproduced by Courtesy of the Trustees, The National Gallery, London)

29. Mary Stevenson Cassatt, *Woman and Child Driving*, 1881, oil on canvas, 76 × 128 cm. (Philadelphia Museum of Art: The W. P. Wilstach Collection)

30. Berthe Morisot, *Lady in a Park with a Parasol*, 1872. (The Metropolitan Museum of Art, Harris Brisbane Dick Fund, 1948. [48.10.81].)

31. Edouard Manet, *La Musique aux Tuileries*, oil on canvas, 76.2 × 118.1 cm. (Reproduced by Courtesy of the Trustees, The National Gallery, London)

32. Jean-Baptiste Armand Guillaumin, *La Seine à Paris* (Rainy Weather), 1871. Oil on canvas, 126.4 × 181.3 cm. (The Museum of Fine Arts, Houston; The John A. and Audrey Jones Beck Collection)

33. Alfred Sisley, *Le Canal Saint-Martin*. (Musée d'Orsay. © photo: Réunion des Musées Nationaux)

34. Alfred Sisley, *Péniches sur le Canal Saint-Martin*, 1870. (Oskar Reinhart Collection, Winterthur)

and whole. Horkheimer understood this (where Adorno did not) when he described the Arcades Project as an attempt at 'grasping the epoch from the small symptoms of the surface',[92] or, in Benjamin's own terms, the positing of the 'small, individual moment' as a 'crystal' from which can be read or inferred the shape of the 'total event'.[93]

'Moment' here can be read as cognate with de Certeau's 'synecdoche', and hence the emphasis on the fragment as involving less the refusal of totality than its recasting in the terms of what Benjamin called the 'dialectical image'. The dialectical image, while formed from the mobilities of collage (or, rather, montage[94]), nevertheless has as its ultimate objective a moment when the mobilities are suspended, when 'thinking stands still' in order to accede to an act of comprehension. It is a point of 'arrest', the antithesis, precisely, of speed, the point where the procession of images is halted; it is 'the caesura in the moment of thought' from which, in a flash of recognition ('the shock of recognition'), comes understanding of reality.[95] The form of that understanding is, moreover, political, an awakening into rational critique of a hypnotically naturalized social order. The 'labyrinth' thus functions in Benjamin's account as a negative, critical image of the city; it is indeed where you get lost, but lost not so much in the euphoric spin ('thrill') of the indecipherable collage as in the deep narcosis of the commodity phantasmagoria. Benjamin's enterprise can thus be seen as directed towards leading us out of the labyrinth, from obscurity ('blindness') into the light of awakened consciousness.

Such an enterprise is, of course, an immensely difficult one; there is no easy route from part to whole, from the loss of connection to its recovery. As we have seen, the idea of writing the city as suites of metonymies and synecdoches[96] deprived of a route to an intelligible whole has been the major preoccupation and practice of very many of the nineteenth-century texts we have considered, a preoccupation based not on a refusal to understand but on a sense of the city as overtaken by a genuinely thickening opacity and splintering fragmentation. We have also seen the dangers, as well as the aspirations, of a projected totality based on the concept of the 'Peuple', the ideal of the coherent and unified republican city caught up in and devalued by fictions of the Nation, the mother-land (or father-land) that de Certeau's rhetoric of 'walking' asks us to trample on. Finally, we should also remember how, in the narrative cityscapes of the contemporary novel (notably those of Pynchon, Butor and Auster), attempts to map the labyrinth of the city by investment in the principle of 'connectedness' engender paranoia. On the other hand, these difficulties and dangers are not adequately met by simply booking one's trip on the exhilarating flight of the signifier. For, in the case of the city, what has become opaque and obscure is so not only as lived experience (de Certeau's walkers who write their city while being unable to read it) but often as the effect of a will to

213

obscure, whether by the active manipulation of power or, more passively, through unacknowledged complicities in its rule.

Coping with this tension between the lived and the imposed, or just being able to distinguish the two, requires a vastly more complex and differentiated set of categories than the simple opposition of an easily acquired and dogmatic totalization, on the one hand, and, on the other hand, an equally easy surrender to epistemic and political bafflement. Experience, analysis and representation are here confronted with an endlessly negotiable relation, within a constantly shifting terrain, between the knowable and the unknowable, the unknown and the as-yet-unknown, in which we try to get from the opacities of the lived to, in Raymond Williams's words, 'seeing the human and social order as a whole'.[97] Benjamin, like Williams (though in a very different style), insists on 'connection', the bringing to consciousness and knowledge of a system whose deep structures and modes of operation are often hidden, in the form of both a suppression and an oppression; which suppresses the conditions of its own intelligibility (the 'suppressed connections' of Williams's account), including, crucially, the intelligibility of its oppressive character. This is one reason why returning, with Benjamin, to Paris, capital of the nineteenth century, remains important, even indispensable, not just for how we understand the city of today but for how we think, intellectually and politically, in one of the complex 'tenses of the imagination' commended by Williams,[98] about the city of tomorrow.

Notes

CHAPTER 1   INTRODUCTION: PARISIAN IDENTITIES

1   Gustave Flaubert, *Madame Bovary*, *Œuvres*, Pléiade, Paris, 1951, vol. 1, p. 344.
2   ibid., p. 343.
3   Honoré de Balzac, *Le Père Goriot*, *La Comédie humaine*, Pléiade, Paris, 1951–65, vol. 2, p. 1005 (all references to *La Comédie humaine* are to this edition, by volume and page number). Théodore de Banville used the tautologous mode in even more extravagant celebration of the self-evident 'identity' of the city: 'Paris sera Paris, tant qu'entier le monde durera'; *Esquisses parisiennes*, Paris, 1859, p. 47.
4   On the relation between the city and the question of 'identity' (in the various relevant senses), the indispensable starting point remains Raymond Williams's *The Country and the City*, London, 1985 (especially pp. 59, 212).
5   Balzac, 'Avant-propos', vol. 1, p. 7.
6   Maxime du Camp, *Paris, ses organes, ses fonctions et sa vie dans la deuxième moitié du XIXe siècle*, 6 vols, Paris, 1883–98, vol. 1, p. 6.
7   Balzac, *Histoire et physiologie des boulevards de Paris*, *Œuvres diverses*, 3 vols, Paris, 1940, vol. 3, p. 611.
8   Newman, *The Idea of a University*, New York, 1959, p. 160. As critique of this increasingly fashionable view of the city as that which cannot be 'mapped', there is the emphasis on the importance of what the Marxist urban geographer David Harvey has called 'cognitive mapping', *The Urban Experience*, Baltimore, 1989, p. 2.
9   I borrow the term 'parisianisme' from *Les Français peints par eux-mêmes*, ed. E. Curmer, 8 vols, Paris, 1840–2, vol. 1, p. 6; cf. also Richard Sieburth, 'Une Idéologie du lisible: le phénomène des *Physiologies*', *Romantisme*, 47, 1985, p. 47 (for a longer version, cf. *Notebooks in Cultural Analysis*, 1, 1984, pp. 163–99).
10   Alfred Delvau, *Les Dessous de Paris*, Paris, 1860, p. 9; on the theme of 'Paris-sphinx', cf. Richard E. Burton, *Baudelaire in 1859*, Cambridge, 1988, pp. 115–16.
11   Henry James, 'Preface' to *Portrait of a Lady*, London, 1968, p. 18.

215

12   Quoted in David Frisby, *Fragments of Modernity*, Cambridge, 1988, p. 71.
     For further discussion of the city as 'space' (notably via the writings of Henri
     Lefèbvre), cf. Kristin Ross, *The Emergence of Social Space: Rimbaud and the
     Commune*, Minnesota, 1988. The writings of Lefèbvre are also a theoretical
     source for David Harvey's remarkably interesting work on the category of
     urban 'space' (see Harvey, op. cit., pp. 5 and 174–80).

13   Eric Hobsbawm, *The Age of Capital, 1848–75*, London, 1984, pp. 281ff.

14   cf. T. J. Clark, *The Painting of Modern Life: Paris in the Art of Manet and his
     Followers*, London, 1985, p. 49: 'This, I should say, is the essential myth of
     modern life: that the city has become a free field of signs and exhibits.'

15   Henry James, *Roderick Hudson* (Library of America edition), New York, 1983,
     p. 176.

16   cf. Janet Wolff, 'The Invisible *Flâneuse*: Women and the Literature of Mod-
     ernity', *Theory, Culture and Society*, 2, 3, 1985, pp. 37–46. On vagabondage,
     cf. Kristin Ross (who cites Théodore Homberg's classic, *Etudes sur le
     vagabondage*, Paris, 1880), op. cit., pp. 55–9.

17   Alfred Kazin 'The New York Writer and his Landscapes', in Mary Ann Caws
     (ed.), *City Images: Perspectives from Literature, Philosophy and Film*, New York,
     1991, p. 139.

18   Walter Benjamin, *Charles Baudelaire: A Lyric Poet in the Era of High Capi-
     talism*, London, 1973; *Das Passagen-Werk*, *Gesammelte Schriften*, vol. 5,
     Frankfurt, 1982, trans. *Paris, capitale du XIXe siècle: Le Livre des Passages*, Paris,
     1989. In addition, special note should be taken of Susan Buck-Morss's brilliant
     reconstruction-cum-commentary in English, *The Dialectics of Seeing: Walter
     Benjamin and the Arcades Project*, Cambridge, Mass., and London, 1989. Both
     the French translation and Buck-Morss's work became available to me only in
     the final stages of writing this book. I have tried in particular to take them
     into account in the concluding chapter. It is no exaggeration to say that these
     two publications have effected a major transformation of the field of Benjamin
     studies. In addition, one can consult the translation by Richard Sieburth of
     the 'epistemological' section of the *Passagen-Werk* (the 'Konvolut N'), 'Re
     The Theory of Knowledge, Theory of Progress', in Gary Smith, (ed.) *Benjamin:
     Philosophy, Aesthetics, History*, Chicago, 1989. Throughout the main body of
     the book I generally refer to the *Passagen-Werk* as the Arcades Project, while
     page references in the notes are for the most part to the French translation.

19   Balzac, *Illusions perdues*, vol. 4, p. 62. On the relations between the city,
     speed and narrative in Balzac, cf. the interesting remarks of Franco Moretti,
     The Way of the World: The Bildungsroman in European Culture, London, 1989,
     pp. 142ff.

20   Karl Marx and Friedrich Engels, *The Communist Manifesto*, in Marx and Engels,
     Selected Works, London, 1968, p. 38.

21   Friedrich Nietzsche, *Untimely Meditations*, Cambridge, 1983, p. 148.

22   Georg Simmel, 'Fashion', in D. Levine (ed.), *Georg Simmel on Individuality
     and Social Forms*, Chicago and London, 1971, p. 318.

23   Simmel, 'The Berlin Trade Exhibition', quoted in Frisby, op. cit., p. 75.

24   Simmel, 'Rodin', in *Philosophische Kultur*, Leipzig, 1911; quoted in Frisby,
     op. cit., p. 46.

25 cf. Benjamin, *Charles Baudelaire*, p. 117.

26 Simmel, 'Rodin' quoted in Frisby, op. cit., p. 47.

27 Charles Baudelaire, *Le Peintre de la vie moderne*, *Œuvres complètes*, Pléiade, Paris, 1961, p. 1163. All references to Baudelaire's writings are to this edition except where otherwise indicated.

28 ibid., p. 1162.

29 Alfred de Vigny, 'Paris', *Œuvres complètes*, Pléiade, Paris, 1950, p. 162.

30 Balzac, 'Paris en 1831', *Œuvres diverses*, vol. 3, pp. 610–17.

31 Victor Considérant, *Description du phalanstère, ou considérations sociales sur l'architectonique*, Paris, 1834 (Slatkine Reprints, Geneva, 1980), p. 17.

32 Edmond Texier, *Tableau de Paris*, Paris, 1852, 2 vols, vol. I, p. 1; E. Texier and A. Kaempfen, *Paris, capitale du monde*, Paris, 1867.

33 *Paris-Guide*, ed. Louis Ulbach, Paris, 1867, republished 1983 (ed. Corinne Verdet). Victor Hugo's preface is to be found under the title *Paris, Œuvres complètes*, ed. Jean Massin, 18 vols, Paris, 1967–70, vol. 13, pp. 573–609. All references to Hugo's works are to this edition except where otherwise indicated.

34 Hugo, *Paris*, pp. 586–7. This view recurs frequently in Hugo's writings: 'Paris est le centre même de l'humanité', 'Paris est l'éblouissant et mystérieux moteur du progrès universel' (*Actes et paroles*, *Œuvres complètes*, vol. 15, p. 1269, vol. 16, p. 1328).

35 On the idea of the city as the embodiment of 'civilized virtue', cf. Carl Schorske, 'The Idea of the City in European Thought: Voltaire to Spengler', in *The Historian and the City*, ed. O. Handlin and J. Burchard, Cambridge, Mass., and London, 1963, pp. 96ff.

36 cf. below, chapter 5, p. 108.

37 The connection between the idea of Paris as the expanding 'centre of the world' and the ideology of a developing commercial society is directly reflected in the self-descriptions of the contemporary department store as 'the largest stores in the world', cf. Susan Buck-Morss, 'Bigger and Better', *The Dialectics of Seeing*, p. 91. It is no accident that the biggest of them all was called 'Ville de Paris'; cf. below, chapter 8, p. 195.

38 Donald J. Olsen, *The City as a Work of Art*, New Haven and London, 1986, p. x. For similar views, notably in connection with Haussmannization, see François Loyer, *Paris au XIXe siècle: l'immeuble et l'espace urbain*, Paris, 1981.

39 'Préface', *Nouveau Tableau de Paris au XIXe siècle*, Paris, 1834–5, vol. 1, p. v.

40 Olsen, op. cit., pp. 5, 44.

41 ibid., p. 5.

42 David Pinkney, *Napoleon III and the Re-Building of Paris*, Princeton, 1958, p. 72. The figure is potentially deceptive: 'new' here did not just mean physically new parkland created by the municipal authorities; it also included the legal transfer of national property to municipal ownership.

43 *The Builder: An illustrated weekly magazine*, ed. G. Godwin, London, 1869, vol. 27, p. 437; quoted in Olsen, op. cit., p. 233.

44 Didier Gille, 'Maceration and Purification', *Zone*, 1/2, 1986, pp. 226–81, esp. 231. For a representative nineteenth-century view of the relation between the modern city and the principle of 'circulation', cf. Alphonse Alphand, *Les Promenades de Paris*, Paris, 1867–73 (repr. Princeton Architectural Press, 1984),

p. lix: 'A l'origine, les villes se sont développées sans plan, sans prévoyance, au hasard. Aucune des précautions les plus élémentaires ne présidait à la construction des voies publiques; aucune méthode pour l'évacuation des eaux fluviales ou ménagères, pour l'enlèvement des immondices, pour la ventilation, pour l'aérage des maisons. Quant à la circulation, elle s'établissait tant bien que mal, d'une manière à peu près suffisante pour une société peu active, dans des rues étroites, sinueuses, obscures, mal pavées ou sans nulle trace de parage. Mais depuis longtemps, même dans leurs localités où les populations sont moins adonnées au travail industriel, les rues et les ruelles sont devenues insuffisantes, et les larges voies ont été imposées par le développement énorme de la civilisation moderne.' On the theme of 'circulation' in Haussmann's Paris from the point of view of the power of modern capital, see the important work of David Harvey, 'Paris, 1850–1870', in *Consciousness and the Urban Experience: Studies in the History and Theory of Capitalist Urbanization*, Baltimore, 1985, pp. 63–220.

45 cf. Pinkney, op. cit., p. 133.

46 Vigny, 'La Maison du Berger', *Œuvres complètes*, p. 178.

47 A representative example is Proudhon's characterization of Paris as 'la ville neuve, monotone et fatigante de M. Haussmann, avec ses boulevards rectilignes' quoted in Georges Duveau, *La Vie ouvrière en France sous le Second Empire*, Paris, 1946, p. 206; cf. also Clark, op. cit., pp. 30ff.

48 Paul Verlaine, 'Parisien, mon frère à jamais étonné', *Sagesse, Œuvres poétiques complètes*, Pléiade, Paris, 1962, p. 290.

49 Baudelaire, *Les Fleurs du Mal*, p. 82.

50 cf. Philippe Hamon, *Expositions: Littérature et architecture au XIXe siècle*, Paris, 1989, p. 126.

51 For a discussion of the problem of the 'legibility' of the city in the earlier part of the century, cf. Peter Brooks, 'Romantic Antipastoral and Urban Allegories', *The Yale Review*, Autumn 1974, pp. 11–26; and *The Melodramatic Imagination*, New Haven, 1977.

52 Balzac, *Le Père Goriot*, vol. 2, p. 856.

53 Maurice Barrès, *Les Déracinés*, Paris, 1897, p. 233.

54 ibid., p. 207.

55 Marshall Berman, *All That is Solid Melts into Air: The Experience of Modernity*, London, 1985, p. 17.

56 Jean-Jacques Rousseau, *Emile, Œuvres complètes*, vol. 4, Pléiade, Paris, 1959, p. 551.

57 Rousseau, *La Nouvelle Héloise*, ibid., vol. 2, Paris, 1961, p. 255.

58 A. R. J. Turgot, *Œuvres de Turgot et documents le concernant*, ed. G. Schelle, 5 vols, Paris, 1913–23, vol. 4, p. 619.

59 ibid., p. 583.

60 ibid., p. 583.

61 On the relation between property, identity, signs and indices, cf. Roland Barthes, *S/Z*, Paris, 1972, pp. 46–7.

62 Turgot's view will nevertheless find a much later echo in Weber's writings about the city: Weber speaks of 'urban real estate which consists in house ownership to which land ownership is accessory', 'The Nature of the City' in

Richard Sennett (ed.), *Classic Essays in the Culture of Cities*, New York, 1966, p. 32.

63 Henri Lecouturier, *Paris incompatible avec la République*, Paris, 1848, p. 65.

64 Georges-Eugène Haussmann, *Mémoires*, 3 vols, 1890–3; quoted in Louis Chevalier, *Classes laborieuses et classes dangereuses pendant la première moitié du XIXe siècle*, Paris, 1958, p. 460.

65 Anne Querrien, 'The Metropolis and the Capital', *Zone*, 1/2, pp. 219–21.

66 Auguste Cochin, *Paris, sa population, son industrie*, Paris, 1864; quoted in Louis Chevalier, *La Formation de la population parisienne au XIXe siècle, 1809–80*, Paris, 1950, p. 241. The older notion of the city as 'capital' is represented in Texier's view of Paris as centred on a 'people' at once municipal and national in its social and political identity: 'C'est à sa puissance d'universalité que cette vaste capitale a dû de former à elle seule tout un peuple, doué au degré le plus éminent du sens municipal et du sens national, ces deux grands éléments de la civilisation française', *Tableau de Paris*, vol. 1, p. 111.

67 Barrès, op. cit., p. 234.

68 ibid., p. 122. Benjamin also picks up on this theme, quoting from the *Histoire de Paris* by Lucien Debech and Pierre d'Espezel on the alleged effects of Haussmannization (Paris, 1926, p. 438): 'Le Parisien, dans sa ville devenue carrefour, cosmopolite, fait figure de déraciné'. Quoted in *Paris, capitale du XIXe siècle*, p. 153.

69 Clark, op. cit., p. 49.

70 ibid., p. 35.

71 cf. Ross Chambers, 'Are Baudelaire's *Tableaux parisiens* about Paris?', in *On Referring in Literature*, ed. Anna Whiteside and Michael Issacharoff, Bloomington, Indiana, 1987, pp. 99–100.

72 cf. Hobsbawm, op. cit., p. 263.

73 cf. Alain Faure and Jacques Rancière (eds), *La Parole ouvrière 1830–1851*, Paris, 1976.

74 cf. Jacques Rancière, *La Nuit des prolétaires: Archives d'un rêve ouvrier*, Paris, 1981. On disciplinary techniques in the workplace (especially the factory), cf. Michelle Perrot, 'The Three Ages of Industrial Discipline in Nineteenth-Century France', in J. M. Merriman (ed.), *Consciousness and Class Experience in Nineteenth-Century Europe*, New York, 1979, pp. 149–68.

75 Edouard Foucaud, *Paris inventeur: Physiologie de l'industrie française*, Paris, 1844; quoted in Benjamin, *Charles Baudelaire*, p. 38.

76 Jules Michelet, *Le Peuple*, Paris, 1946, p. 60.

77 Simmel, 'The Metropolis and Mental Life', in Sennett (ed.), op. cit., p. 48. Cf. also Simmel's important essay, 'The Sociology of the Senses', quoted in Frisby, op. cit., pp. 55ff.

78 Alain Corbin, *Le Miasme et la jonquille*, Paris, 1982.

79 Lewis Mumford, *The City in History, its Origins, its Transformations, and its Prospects*, London, 1961, p. 470.

80 Raymond Williams, 'Metropolitan Perceptions and the Emergence of Modernism', *The Politics of Modernism*, London, 1989, p. 40.

81 Corbin, op. cit., ch. 2.

82 Simmel, *Soziologie*, Berlin, 1958, p. 486; quoted in Benjamin, *Charles Baudelaire*, pp. 37–8.

83 Frédéric Soulié, 'Restaurants et gargotes', *La Grande Ville, Nouveau Tableau de Paris*, 2 vols, Paris, 1842, vol. 2, pp. 5–24; cf. also Taxile Delord, *Paris-viveur*, Paris, 1854.

84 Alfred Delvau, *Les Plaisirs de Paris*, Paris, 1867, p. 3.

85 Roland Barthes, 'Lecture de Brillat-Savarin', *Le Bruissement de la langue*, Paris, 1984, pp. 293–4.

86 Balzac, *Ferragus, Histoire des treize*, vol. 5, pp. 18–19.

87 The phrase comes from Jean-Pierre Richard, *Poésie et profondeur*, Paris, 1955, p. 10.

88 Emile Zola, *La Curée, Les Rougon-Macquart*, Pléiade, Paris, 1960–7, vol. 1, p. 332. All references to Zola's works are to this edition except where otherwise indicated.

89 Jean-Pierre Richard, *Pages/paysages, Microlectures* II, Paris, 1984.

90 Quoted in Mumford, op. cit., p. 97.

91 ibid., p. 117.

92 ibid., p. 116.

93 Jules Vallès – doubtless from his memory of the Commune – sought to keep alive the notion of Paris as a space of democratic exchange analogous to the Athenian agora: 'Ce boulevard, qui pour ceux qui ne font que passer ou ne regardent pas d'assez près n'est qu'une voie de plaisir ou un rendez-vous de viveurs, ce boulevard, c'est l'*Agora* de notre Athènes. Mais sur l'Agora grec, il ne venait que les privilégiés pour causer de la République devant l'état-major en marbre de statues. Ici devant les tables de zinc ou sur des tabourets de paille, les Parisiens dressent la mercuriale des idées qui ont cours sur le marché des capitales', *Le Tableau de Paris, Œuvres complètes*, vol. 13, Paris, 1971, p. 132.

94 Balzac, *La Vieille Fille*, vol. 4, p. 276.

95 cf. Hugo, 'Réponse à un acte d'accusation', *Les Contemplations*, 2 vols, Paris, 1964, vol. 1, pp. 20–7.

96 On the idea of words as commodities, cf. *Nouveau Tableau de Paris au XIXe siècle*, vol. 6, p. 292: 'Tout le monde échange dans la conversation ces mots trouvés comme une marchandise commode et de bon aloi.'

97 cf. François Furet, *Penser la Révolution française*, Paris, 1978, p. 223.

98 Siegfried Kracauer, *Jacques Offenbach and the Paris of his Time*, London, 1937, p. 63.

99 cf. Michel de Certeau et al., *Une Politique de la langue: la Révolution française et le patois: l'enquête de Grégoire*, Paris, 1975; Renée Balibar and Dominique Laporte, *Le Français national: politique et pratique de la langue nationale sous la Révolution française*, Paris, 1974.

100 Victor Hugo, *Les Misérables*, Pléiade, Paris, 1951, p. 870.

101 cf. Malcolm Bowie, 'Genius at Nightfall: Mallarmé's "Quand l'ombre menaça de la fatale loi"', in Christopher Prendergast (ed.), *Nineteenth-Century French Poetry: Introductions to Close Reading*, Cambridge, 1990, pp. 238–40.

102 Michael Riffaterre, *The Semiotics of Poetry*, Bloomington, Indiana, 1978.

103 Benjamin, *Charles Baudelaire*, p. 100.

104 Charles-Augustin de Sainte-Beuve, 'De la littérature industrielle', *Portraits contemporains*, Paris, 1863, vol. 1, p. 491.

105 This represents what (roughly) we may call the 'Bakhtinian' view of the place of the novel in nineteenth-century urban culture. There is, however, a counter-view. If, on the one hand, the novel, by virtue of its generous inclusiveness, is appropriately described as being 'democratically' open to the heterogeneity of the city, its formal organization can also be said to embody a powerful, and ultimately 'paranoiac', will to domination, a desire to subjugate the heterogeneous to the design of a unified and coherent fictional plot commanded by an all-seeing narrator. The novel, on this view, is close in spirit to the controlling and containing strategies of the panoptic model of representation described by Foucault in *Surveiller et punir*. In his very interesting article ('The Unseen Seer or Proteus in the City: Aspects of a Nineteenth-Century Parisian Myth', *French Studies*, 42, January 1988, pp. 50–68), Richard Burton has posed the omniscient narrator of nineteenth-century fiction as one of several key figures in the construction of the literary-mythological equivalent of the emerging 'régime panoptique'. In terms of the specific link between the city and narrative, Burton takes this a stage further: the ordering plots of fiction are linked to nineteenth-century perceptions of other, more strictly paranoiac kinds of 'plots', the notion – reflected in the recurring nineteenth-century obsession with secret societies and conspirators – that 'a once legible and coherent society confronts its members as a bewildering conundrum which only the theory of a concerted plot can render intelligible' (p. 63). For a more general account of both the possibilities and the problems of construing narrative on the analogy with policing, surveillance and paranoia, cf. my *The Order of Mimesis*, Cambridge, 1986; D. A. Miller, *The Novel and the Police*, Berkeley and Los Angeles, 1988. On the relation of these general questions of narrative to the specific question of the city, cf. also John Bender, *Imagining the Penitentiary*, Chicago, 1987.

106 Renée Balibar, *Les Français fictifs: le rapport du style littéraire au français national*, Paris, 1974; *L'Invention du français*, Paris, 1985.

107 Mumford, op. cit., p. 97.

108 Louis-Sebastien Mercier, *Tableau de Paris*, Amsterdam, 1782 (Slatkine Reprints, Geneva, 1979), 'Préface', vol. 1, p. xvi: 'On a dans la capitale des passions que l'on n'a point ailleurs. La vue des jouissances invite à jouir aussi. Tous les acteurs qui jouent leur rôle sur ce grand et noble théâtre vous forcent à devenir acteur vous-même. Plus de tranquillité, les désirs deviennent plus vifs; les superfluités sont des besoins; et ceux que donnent la nature sont infiniment moins tyranniques que ceux que l'opinion inspire.' For Rousseau's view, cf. Jean Starobinski who says of 'les villes' in Rousseau's writings that they are places 'où les hommes ne vivent que par anticipation', *L'Œil vivant*, Paris, 1961, p. 133.

109 Delvau says of 'la société parisienne' that it 'n'est autre chose après tout que *la Comédie humaine* de Balzac', *Les Plaisirs de Paris*, p. 21.

110 Balzac, *Ferragus*, p. 19.

111 Moretti, op. cit., p. 148.

112 Gustave Flaubert, *L'Education sentimentale*, ed. Edouard Maynial, Classiques Garnier, Paris, 1964, p. 17.
113 Balzac *Le Père Goriot*, p. 1085.
114 Barrès, *Les Déracinés*, p. 86. Elsewhere in Barrès's novel, however, there is serious dispute as to the relevance in late nineteenth-century conditions of the Balzacian model (p. 204); cf. also Vallès, 'En débarquant à Paris, combien de Rubemprés et de Rastignacs . . .', op. cit., p. 743.
115 Georg Lukács, *Theory of the Novel*, Cambridge, Mass., 1971, pp. 74ff.
116 Balzac, *Le Père Goriot*, p. 914.
117 Flaubert, *L'Education sentimentale*, p. 47.
118 cf. Frisby, op. cit. p. 210.
119 Benjamin, *Charles Baudelaire*, p. 69.

CHAPTER 2   FRAMING THE CITY: TWO PARISIAN WINDOWS

1 Lautréamont, *Les Chants de Maldoror*, Paris, 1969, p. 233.
2 Julien Lemer, *Paris au gaz*, Paris, 1861, p. 15.
3 For a discussion of the category of 'spectacle' in the interpretation of nineteenth-century Paris, cf. T. J. Clark, *The Painting of Modern Life: Paris in the Art of Manet and his Followers*, London, 1985, pp. 9–10, 63–64. Clark's point of departure is Guy Debord's seminal *La Société du spectacle*, Paris, 1967.
4 cf. Wolfgang Schivelbusch, *Disenchanted Night: The Industrialization of Light in the Nineteenth Century*, Berkeley, Los Angeles and London, 1988.
5 ibid., p. 132.
6 L. A. Garnier-Pagès, *Histoire de la Révolution de 1848*, Paris, 1861, vol. 4, pp. 305–6.
7 Schivelbusch, op. cit., p. 105.
8 David Pinkney, *Napoleon III and the Re-Building of Paris*, Princeton, 1958, p. 72.
9 On the crossing of the themes of light and enlightenment in connection with the city, cf. Raymond Williams, *The Country and the City*, London, 1985; cf. also Walter Benjamin, 'Types d'éclairage', *Paris, capitale du XIXe siècle*, Paris, 1989, pp. 579ff., and the discussion by Susan Buck-Morss, *The Dialectics of Seeing*, Cambridge, Mass., and London, 1989, pp. 308ff.
10 Gustave Kahn, *Esthétique de la rue*, Paris, 1901, p. 205.
11 For a full discussion of the *Bar* picture, cf. Clark, op. cit., pp. 205–58.
12 Charles Baudelaire, *Les Fleurs du Mal, Œuvres complètes*, Pléiade, Paris, 1961, p. 99. One of Benjamin's more curious observations is that the windows in some of Meryon's engravings resemble eyes staring at the viewer, and, more specifically, the eyes of the poor (that last analogy suggesting, of course, a link with Baudelaire's poem, 'Les Yeux des pauvres), *Paris, capitale du XIXe siècle*, p. 402.
13 cf. below, chapter 4.
14 Charles Duveyrier, *La Ville Nouvelle ou le Paris des Saint-Simoniens*, Paris, 1837;

cf. Maurice Agulhon, *Marianne au combat: Imagerie et symbolique républicaines de 1789 à 1880*, Paris, 1979, p. 57.

15 cf. Rosalind Williams, *Notes on the Underground*, Cambridge, Mass., 1990, pp. 165ff.

16 Siegfried Kracauer, *Jacques Offenbach and the Paris of his Time*, London, 1937, p. 58.

17 Lemer, op. cit., p. 16.

18 Rachel Bowlby, *Just Looking: Consumer Culture in Dreiser, Gissing and Zola*, New York, 1985. On the technology and methods of commodity display in the department store, whereby 'display' is transformed into 'spectacle', cf. H. Pasdermadjian, *The Department Store: Its Origins, Evolution and Economics*, London, 1954; Richard Sennett, *The Fall of Public Man*, New York, 1977, pp. 141ff.; Michael Miller, *The Bon Marché: Bourgeois Culture and The Department Store 1869–1920*, Princeton, 1981; Rosalind Williams, *Dream Worlds: Mass Consumption in Late Nineteenth-century France*, Berkeley, Los Angeles and London, 1982.

19 Quoted in David Frisby, *Fragments of Modernity*, Cambridge, 1988, p. 95. Victor Fournel fantasized a future Paris which would be entirely governed by the logic of 'exposition' as 'un objet de luxe et de curiosité plutôt que d'usage, une *ville d'exposition*, placée sous verre', *Paris nouveau et Paris futur*, 1868, p. 237; quoted in Benjamin, *Paris, capitale du XIXe siècle*, p. 418. On the relation between the shop window and the architectural style of the Exposition Universelle as 'la mise en spectacle généralisée de la ville par une architecture industrielle et *pour des objets industriels*', cf. Philippe Hamon, *Expositions*, Paris, 1989, p. 125.

20 cf. Charles Rearick, *Pleasures of the Belle-Epoque: Entertainment and Festivity in Turn-of-the-Century France*, New Haven and London, 1985, pp. 132–3.

21 Jules Vallès, *Le Tableau de Paris, Œuvres complètes* , vol. 13, Paris, 1971, p. 54.

22 ibid., p. 55.

23 Arthur Rimbaud, 'Ornières', *Illuminations, Poésies complètes*, Paris, 1963, p. 146.

24 Emile Zola, *Au Bonheur des dames*, Pléiade, Paris, 1960–7, vol. 3, p. 492.

25 Baudelaire, *Les Fleurs du Mal*, p. 26.

26 Baudelaire, *Sur la Belgique*, p. 1325.

27 Baudelaire, *Le Spleen de Paris*, p. 288.

28 ibid., p. 278.

29 ibid., pp. 268–9.

30 For a discussion of Baudelaire in terms of the concept of 'pastoral', cf. Marshall Berman, *All That is Solid Melts into Air*, London, 1985, pp. 134ff.

31 On the non-reciprocity of the gaze in this poem, cf. the interesting analysis by Marie Maclean, *Narrative as Performance: The Baudelairean Experiment*, London and New York, 1988, p. 120.

32 This is the only point on which I would disagree with Berman's fine reading of this poem, op. cit., p. 154.

33 cf. Richard Terdiman, *Discourse/Counter-Discourse*, Ithaca and London, 1985, p. 317. For a view of the poem as offering a critique of just this attitude, cf. Jonathan Monroe, *A Poverty of Objects: The Prose Poem and the Politics of Genre*, Ithaca and London, 1987, p. 111.

34 Zola, *La Curée*, Pléiade, vol. 1, pp. 449–51. On the general significance of the view from the window in Zola's novels, cf. Philippe Hamon, *Le Personnel du roman: Le système des personnages dans les Rougon-Macquart d'Emile Zola*, Geneva, 1983, p. 88; on the structural value of the Café Riche episode for *La Curée*, cf. Henri Mitterand et al., *Genèse, structures et style de la Curée*, Paris, 1987, pp. 145–6.

35 Zola's great *tour de force* in the description of the illuminated city from the point of view of commodity display is, of course, the description of the Passage des Panoramas in *Nana*, Pléiade, vol. 2, p. 1259.

36 cf. Michael Riffaterre's distinction between the 'code-regard' and the 'code-coup d'œil', *Essais de stylistique structurale*, Paris, 1971, p. 362.

37 Edmond Duranty, *La Nouvelle Peinture: à propos du groupe d'artistes qui expose dans les Galeries Durand-Ruel* (1876), Paris, 1946, p. 46.

38 Alain Corbin, 'Commercial Sexuality in Nineteenth-Century France: A System of Images and Regulations', *Representations*, 14, 1986, p. 217.

39 Griselda Pollock, 'Modernity and the Spaces of Femininity', *Vision and Difference: Femininity, Feminism and Histories of Art*, London and New York, 1988, ch. 3.

40 'Women did not enjoy the freedom of incognito in the crowd. They were never positioned as the normal occupants of the public realm. They did not have the right to look, to stare, to scrutinize or watch', ibid., p. 71.

41 This, of course, is Wordsworth's point in respect of the London crowd as 'an undistinguishable world . . . differences that have no law, no meaning and no end' (*Prelude*, Book 7); cf. Raymond Williams, op. cit., p. 151.

42 Zola, *L'Œuvre*, Pléiade, vol. 4, pp. 206, 74–5.

43 Mary Ann Caws (ed.), 'Introduction', *City Images. Perspectives from Literature, Philosophy and Film*, New York, 1991, p. 1.

CHAPTER 3   THE HIGH VIEW: THREE CITYSCAPES

1 For details, cf. F. Robichon, 'Le panorama, spectacle de l'histoire', *Le Mouvement social*, 131, April–June 1985, pp. 65–86; *The Panorama Phenomenon* (exhibition catalogue), The Hague, 1981.

2 Francisque Sarcey, *L'Indépendance belge*, 1 August 1880, quoted in Robichon, op. cit., p. 80.

3 Quoted in Robichon, op. cit., p. 69.

4 Edouard Detaille, *Carnets*, 1899, quoted in Robichon, op. cit., p. 78.

5 Michel de Certeau, *L'Invention du quotidien, vol. 1: Arts de faire*, Paris, 1980, p. 173. It was from the principle of instant 'readability' that Walter Benjamin linked the panorama and the *physiologie* (describing the latter as a 'panorama literature'), *Charles Baudelaire*, London, 1973, p. 35.

6 *Panorama voyageur, vue de Paris*, 'Notice historique et explicative', Paris, 1928, p. ix.

7 De Certeau, op. cit., p. 173.

8 cf. Robichon, op. cit., p. 67.

9 cf. Charles Rearick (on the panorama *Tout-Paris* at the 1899 Exposition

Universelle): 'The panorama *Tout-Paris*... made sight-seeing easy', *Pleasures of the Belle-Epoque*, New Haven and London, 1985, p. 173.

10 Quoted in Henry René d'Allemagne, *Les Saint-Simoniens 1827–1837*, Paris, 1930, p. 308.

11 cf. Pierre Citron, *La Poésie de Paris de Rousseau à Baudelaire*, 2 vols, Paris, 1964, vol. 2, pp. 122–3.

12 Ernest Renan, *Prière à l'Acropole* (1876), Paris, 1956, p. 11.

13 Alexis Martin, *Paris: Promenades dans les vingt arrondissements*, 1890, p. vi.

14 Maxime du Camp, *Paris, ses organes, ses fonctions et sa vie dans la deuxième moitié du XIXe siècle*, 6 vols, Paris, 1883–98, vol. 1, pp. 14–15. The obstruction to the high view over the city effected by the city's smoke was in fact a theme going back to Louis-Sebastien Mercier (*Tableau de Paris*, Amsterdam, 1782, Slatkine Reprints, Geneva, 1979, vol. 1, p. 17); in the nineteenth century it was frequently associated, by all shades of political opinion, with the idea of the moral 'filth' of the city (cf., for example, Henri Lecouturier, *Paris incompatible avec la République*, Paris, 1848, p. 19; Victor Considérant, *Description du phalanstère*, Paris, 1834, Slatkine Reprints, Geneva, 1980, p. 42).

15 ibid., p. 11.

16 Robert Hughes, *The Shock of the New*, New York, 1987, p. 14.

17 Edmond and Jules de Goncourt, *Manette Salomon*, Paris, 1979, p. 18.

18 J. K. Huysmans, 'Vue des remparts du Nord-Paris', *Croquis parisiens*, Paris, 1981, p. 113; on the view over the industrial Plaine Saint-Denis, cf. also the poem by Jean Ajalbert, 'Gennevilliers', *Sur le vif*, Paris, 1886, quoted in T. J. Clark, *The Painting of Modern Life*, London, 1985, pp. 161–2.

19 cf. Victor Hugo, *Paris*, where Paris is seen as the sum of Athens, Rome and Jerusalem ('Paris est la somme de ces trois cités'), *Œuvres complètes*, ed. Jean Massin, 18 vols, Paris, 1967–70, vol. 13, p. 591.

20 Maurice Barrès *Les Déracinés*, Paris, 1897, p. 431.

21 ibid., p. 446.

22 Auguste Barbier, 'L'Indifférence', *Le Diable à Paris*, Paris, 1845–6, p. 307.

23 Renan, op. cit., p. 11.

24 Emile Zola, *Deux définitions du roman*, *Œuvres complètes*, Paris, 1966–9, vol. 10, pp. 273–83.

25 Renan saw in the Exposition Universelle a degraded analogue of the ancient Greek festival, the former, as Benjamin put it, a version of the latter minus the 'poetry' (Ernest Renan, *Essais de morale et de critique*, Paris, 1859, pp. 356–7; quoted in Walter Benjamin, *Paris, capitale du XIXe siècle*, Paris, 1989, p. 215.

26 Arthur Rimbaud, 'Villes', *Illuminations, Poésies complètes*, Paris, 1963, p. 148.

27 cf. Citron, op. cit., esp. vol. 1, pp. 174–6.

28 Théophile Gautier, *Caprices et zigzags*, Paris, 1845, quoted in Benjamin, *Paris, capitale du XIXe siècle*, p. 116; cf. also the apocalyptic prophecy of Blanqui in *La Patrie en danger* at the time of the Siege of Paris ('Paris, c'est Babylone usurpatrice et corrompue, la grande prostituée que l'envoyé de Dieu, l'ange exterminateur, la Bible à la main, va balayer de la face de la terre'), quoted in ibid., p. 793.

29 Charles Baudelaire, *Œuvres complètes*, Pléiade, Paris, 1961, p. 310.

30 Balzac described the panorama as a 'charlatanisme mécanique', *Lettres sur Paris* (1831), *Œuvres diverses*, 3 vols, Paris, 1940, vol. 2, p. 125.

31 Honoré de Balzac, *La Fille aux yeux d'or*, Pléiade, Paris, 1951–65, vol. 5, pp. 255–69. For the most part I shall concentrate the analysis on the first two pages. Where no references are indicated, it should be assumed that quoted text is from these two pages.

32 Georges Poulet, *Etudes sur le temps humain: la distance intérieure*, Paris, 1952, pp. 166–7.

33 *La Grande Ville, Nouveau Tableau de Paris*, 2 vols, Paris, 1842, vol. 2, p. 2. On the *flâneur* (specifically Delvau) as one who reads the city like a geologist, cf. Benjamin, *Paris, capitale du XIXe siècle*, pp. 452–3.

34 Léon Gambetta, *Discours et plaidoyers politiques*, 1880–5, quoted in Clark, op. cit., p. 154.

35 On the fragility and arbitrariness of the Balzacian model of 'causal' narrative grounded in an appeal to natural science, cf. Gérard Genette's discussion of the 'motivation' of Balzac's plots in terms of the notion of a 'vraisemblable artificiel', cf. 'Vraisemblance et motivation', *Figures II*, Paris, 1969, p. 79. On the relation of Genette's formal account of Balzacian narrative to the dynamic properties of a developing capitalist society, seen as a constantly mobile, desire-laden heterogeneity that is always in excess of stable narrative framing, cf. Franco Moretti, *The Way of the World*, London, 1989, pp. 159ff.

36 On the motif of the mask in this description of Paris, cf. Diana Festa-McCormick, *The City as Catalyst*, London, 1979, pp. 21–3.

37 For an example in the *Comédie humaine* of the panoramic view of Paris as the happy combination of urban and pastoral, cf. *La Femme de trente ans*, Pléiade, vol. 2, pp. 775–6.

38 Marcel Proust, 'Sainte-Beuve et Balzac', *Contre Sainte-Beuve*, Paris, 1954, p. 228.

39 Roland Barthes, *S/Z*, Paris, 1972, p. 221.

40 cf. Pierre Michel, 'Paris pyroscaphe: Mythe de Paris et thermodynamique dans *La Fille aux yeux d'or*', in Roger Bellet (ed.), *Paris au XIXe siècle: Aspects d'un mythe littéraire*, Lyon, 1984; Christopher Prendergast, 'Balzac's Steam-Engine: Energy and Entropy in the *Comédie humaine*', *Degré second*, 1977.

41 Georges Charbonnier, *Entretiens avec Claude Lévi-Strauss*, Paris, 1960.

42 Baudelaire, *Œuvres complètes*, p. 317.

43 cf. Citron, op. cit., pp. 159ff.

44 Paul de Kock, *La Grande Ville*, vol. 1, pp. 137ff.

45 Hugo, *Notre-Dame de Paris*, Pléiade, Paris, 1973, p. 137.

46 First published in 1857 (in *Le Présent*) under the title 'Paysage parisien', it was included, in reworked form and under the title 'Paysage', in the 1861 edition of *Les Fleurs du Mal*. Richard Burton argues that it may well go back to the 1830s and that its original setting was in fact Lyon rather than Paris, 'Baudelaire and Lyon: a Reading of "Paysage" ', *Nottingham French Studies*, 28, 1, Spring 1989.

47 On the values of the articulated 'e', cf. Clive Scott, *A Question of Syllables*, Cambridge, 1986, pp. 86–116.

48 In the essay *Peintres et aqua-fortistes* of 1862 Baudelaire, in a discussion of the

work of Meryon, talks of the fusion of industrial smoke with the stone and spires of the city (*Œuvres complètes*, p. 1149); the idea of the city as harmonious 'landscape' thus seems to have stayed with him until quite late.

49   cf. Benjamin, *Charles Baudelaire*, p. 143: 'In the *spleen*, time becomes palpable; the minutes cover a man like snow-flakes.'

50   On the motif of the 'pivot' in this poem (dead centre at the moment of 'shutting' the window) and elsewhere in the period, cf. Philippe Hamon, *Expositions*, Paris, 1989, p. 192.

51   Baudelaire, 'Moesta et errabunda', *Les Fleurs du Mal*, pp. 60–1.

52   Burton, op. cit., pp. 32–3.

53   Baudelaire, *Le Peintre de la vie moderne*, p. 1159.

54   Friedrich Schiller, *On Naïve and Sentimental Poetry*, New York, 1980.

55   ibid., pp. 145ff.

56   Burton, op. cit., p. 36.

57   Théophile Gautier, *Emaux et camées*, Paris, 1947, p. 114. Ross Chambers notes that 'Paysage' echoes Gautier's poem but that 'it does so in a clearly ironic and distanced fashion', 'Baudelaire's Street Poetry', *Nineteenth-Century French Studies*, 13, 4, Summer 1985, p. 255.

58   cf. Ross Chambers, 'Trois paysages urbains: Les poèmes liminaires des Tableaux parisiens', *Modern Philology*, 80, 4, May 1983.

59   Baudelaire, 'Crépuscule du matin', *Les Fleurs du Mal*, p. 99. As a transformation of a poetic topos, Baudelaire's way with dawn over the city might be compared with Wordsworth's 'Composed upon Westminster Bridge' ('This City now doth, like a garment, wear / the beauty of the morning'); the ultimate poetic negation of the 'pastoral' theme of dawn over the city is arguably Rimbaud's 'Chant de guerre', where the dawn red sky is, as Kristin Ross puts it, the 'false sun of incendiary bombing over Paris and its suburbs' *The Emergence of Social Space: Rimbaud and the Commune*, Minnesota, 1988, p. 141.

60   Baudelaire, 'A une mendiante rousse', *Les Fleurs du Mal*, p. 81.

61   cf. Susan Buck-Morss, *The Dialectics of Seeing*, Cambridge, Mass., and London, 1989, p. 183.

62   Zola, *Le Ventre de Paris*, Pléiade, Paris, 1960–7, vol. 1, p. 713.

63   ibid., p. 733.

64   ibid., p. 633.

65   F. W. J. Hemmings, *Emile Zola*, Oxford, 1953, p. 81.

66   Zola, *Le Ventre de Paris*, pp. 633–4.

67   cf. Kenneth Cornell, 'Zola's City', *Yale French Studies*, 32, 1964.

68   Philippe Hamon, *Le Personnel du roman*, Geneva, 1983, p. 70.

69   Zola, *Le Ventre de Paris*, pp. 626–33.

70   The reader of the *Rougon-Macquart* will encounter Lantier in Les Halles again, moreover, in the context of yet another narrative beginning (the opening pages of *L'Œuvre*), where Zola significantly describes Lantier as an 'artiste flâneur': 'Il s'était oublié à rôder dans les Halles, par cette nuit brûlante de juillet, en artiste flâneur, amoureux du Paris nocturne', Pléiade, vol. 4, p. 12.

71   Huysmans takes Zola's painter (and quotes Zola's text) as an exemplary

spokesman for the idea of 'modern art', *L'Art moderne, Œuvres complètes*, Paris, 1928–34, vol. 6, p. 246.

72   cf. J. Noiray, *Le Romancier et la machine*, Vol. 1, Paris, 1981, pp. 241ff.

73   cf. François Emile-Zola et Massin (ed.), *Zola photographe*, Paris, 1979.

74   Clark, op. cit., p. 75.

75   cf. Ralph T. Coe, 'Camille Pissarro in Paris: A Study of his Late Development', *Gazette des Beaux-Arts*, February 1954, p. 116.

76   Quoted in Marie-Thérèse Barrett, '*Le Ventre de Paris*, Claude Lantier and Realist Themes of Food and Markets in Seventeenth and Nineteenth-Century Painting', in J.-M. Guien and A. Hilton (eds), *Emile Zola and the Arts*, Washington, 1988, p. 48.

77   The juxtaposition (and perhaps implied blending) of 'old' and 'new' Paris was a common nineteenth-century theme in architectural writing. A favoured topos here was the bridge as a means of 'passage' joining one to the other; for example, the Pont des Arts, a metallic structure serving as a symbol of 'modernity' but also leading across the river into the Ile de la Cité (the very heart of 'old' Paris), was for many years the frontispiece of the newspaper, *L'Illustration*, cf. Hamon, *Expositions*, p. 124.

78   Hamon, *Le Personnel du roman*, p. 88. David Baguley, on the other hand, notes that the important relation here is not one of doubling but of contrast, *Naturalist Fiction: The Entropic Vision*, Cambridge, 1990, p. 193. Cf. also Baguley, 'Le supplice de Florent: à propos du *Ventre de Paris*', *Europe*, April–May 1968, pp. 91–6.

79   Noiray, op. cit., pp. 290ff.

80   Michel Serres, *Feux et signaux de brume*, Paris, 1975.

81   cf. Leon Deffoux and Emile Zavie, *Le Groupe de Médan*, Paris, 1924, p. 16; on the general implications of this for 'naturalist description', cf. Baguley, op. cit., pp. 184–203.

82   'In Morisot's painting the city is alien and apart from the women', Kathleen Adler and Tamara Garb, *Berthe Morisot*, Ithaca, 1987, p. 109.

83   For an extended account of Manet's *Exposition Universelle de 1867*, cf. Clark, op. cit., pp. 60–6.

84   Meyer Schapiro, *Van Gogh*, New York, 1983, p. 55.

CHAPTER 4   PARIS UNDERGROUND

1   Antonin Proust, *Edouard Manet, Souvenirs*, Paris, 1913, p. 94.

2   ibid., p. 94.

3   ibid., p. 95.

4   For an interesting discussion of this obsession, cf. Rosalind Williams, *Notes on the Underground*, Cambridge, Mass., 1990. Walter Benjamin was of course fascinated by the topic of Paris underground, notably the catacombs and the Métro (cf. in particular section C of *Paris, capitale du XIXe siècle*, Paris, 1989, 'Le Paris antiquisant, catacombes, démolitions, déclin de Paris'). Benjamin's interest in the literal forms of Paris underground was essentially as metaphor for the 'underground' of the mind and for the 'archaeological' project of

excavating the layered strata of collective mental life, dream and phantasmagoria.

5   Catherine Gallagher, 'The Bio-Economics of *Our Mutual Friend*', *Fragments for a History of the Human Body, Zone*, 5, 1989, p. 361.

6   This anecdote figures in Alain Corbin, 'Introduction' to the English translation of *Le Miasme et la jonquille* (trans. *The Foul and the Fragrant*), Cambridge, Mass., 1986, pp. 2–3.

7   Philippe Muray, *Le Dix-neuvième siècle à travers les âges*, Paris, 1984, pp. 22ff.

8   This is from the 'Adresse au Conseil Municipal du 27 mai 1881' signed by Lafitte, Magnin, Bernard et al.; quoted in Philippe Ariès *Essai sur l'histoire de la mort en occident du moyen age à nos jours*, Paris, 1975, p. 152.

9   A.-J.-B. Parent-Duchâtelet, *Rapport sur le curage des égouts Amelot, de la Roquette, Saint-Martin et autres . . .* , Paris, 1820; *Essai sur les cloaques ou égouts de la ville de Paris, envisagés sous le rapport de l'hygiène publique et de la topographie médicale de cette ville*, Paris, 1824; *Les Chantiers d'équarrissage de la ville de Paris envisagés sous le rapport de l'hygiène publique*, Paris, 1832; *Rapports sur les améliorations à introduire dans les fosses d'aisance et les voiries de Paris*, Paris, 1833. All these reports are collected in *Hygiène publique, ou mémoires sur les questions les plus importantes de l'hygiène appliquée aux professions et aux travaux d'utilité publique*, 2 vols, Paris, 1836.

10 Eugène Belgrand, *Les Travaux souterrains de Paris*, 5 vols, Paris, 1873–87.

11 David Pinkney, *Napoleon III and the Re-Building of Paris*, Princeton, 1958, p. 134.

12 Victor Considérant, *Description du phalanstère*, Paris, 1834, repr. Geneva, 1980, p. 42.

13 Alain Corbin, *Le Miasme et la jonquille*, Paris, 1982, part 1, ch. 2.

14 Pierre Chauvet, *Essai sur la propreté de Paris*, Paris, 1797, p. 18.

15 Parent-Duchâtelet, *Hygiène publique*, vol. 2, p. 259, quoted in Louis Chevalier, *Classes laborieuses et classes dangereuses pendant la première moitié du XIXe siècle*, Paris, 1958, p. 252. This passage is also briefly discussed by Charles Bernheimer, *Figures of Ill Repute: Representing Prostitution in Nineteenth-Century France*, Cambridge, Mass., and London, 1989, p. 9.

16 Louis Veuillot, *Les Odeurs de Paris*, Paris, 1867.

17 Corbin, *Le Miasme et la jonquille*, part 2, chs 1 and 2.

18 Michel de Certeau speaks of the rationalized modern city as the 'production d'un espace propre: l'organisation rationnelle doit donc refouler toutes les pollutions physiques, mentales ou politiques qui la compromettraient', *L'Invention du quotidien*, vol. 1, Paris, 1980, p. 17.

19 Quoted in Chevalier, op. cit., p. 112.

20 Didier Gille, 'Maceration and Purification', *Zone*, 1/2, 1986, p. 233.

21 Félix Nadar, *Quand j'étais photographe*, Paris, 1900, p. 120.

22 Pierre Citron, *La Poésie de Paris de Rousseau à Baudelaire*, 2 vols, Paris, 1964, vol. 1, p. 179.

23 Quoted in J.-J. Poulet-Allemagny, 'Notice historique', in *Le Paris souterrain de Félix Nadar*, ed. Philippe Néagu, Paris, 1982, p. 61.

24 Roland Barthes, *La Chambre claire*, Paris, 1980.

25 Nadar, op. cit., pp. 106–7.

26 Shelley Rice, in a very interesting article on Nadar's underground photography, stresses the 'orderly aspect' of Nadar's catacombs, as an image celebrating the triumph of 'culture' over 'the ravages of nature', 'Souvenirs', *Art in America*, September 1988, p. 164.

27 Nadar, op. cit., p. 120.

28 Rice, op. cit., p. 166.

29 ibid., p. 166.

30 cf. Emile Gérards, *Paris souterrain*, 1909.

31 cf. Citron, op. cit., vol. 1, p. 408.

32 Claude Lachaise, *Topographie médicale*, Paris, 1822, quoted in Chevalier, op. cit., p. 82.

33 Honoré-Antoine Frégier, *Des classes dangereuses de la population dans les grandes villes*, Paris, 1840, quoted in Chevalier, op. cit., p. 159.

34 ibid., quoted in Chevalier, op. cit., p. 371. The attempt, both discursive and practical, to close off the 'dangerous classes' from the rest of society, is also one of the main themes of Foucault's *Surveiller et punir*. In political terms, a key figure for the association of revolution with the 'underground' metaphor was Blanqui: Gustave Geoffroy, Blanqui's biographer, spoke of his subject's 'politique de catacombes' (*L'Enfermé*, Paris, 1926, vol. 1, p. 72, quoted in Benjamin, op. cit., p. 123). Alexis de Tocqueville, in a famous piece of pure vitriol, said of Blanqui that 'il semblait avoir vécu dans un égout et en sortir; on me dit que c'était Blanqui', *Souvenirs*, Paris, 1893, p. 181. Blanqui himself commented on the strategy of separating off different groups in the city's population by way of the example of the military garrison and the metaphor of 'contagion': 'On y tient ses soldats en garnison, à l'abri de la contagion populaire', quoted in Benjamin, op. cit., p. 167.

35 Quoted in Chevalier, op cit., p. 459.

36 Walter Benjamin, *Charles Baudelaire*, London, 1973, p. 19.

37 Baudelaire, *Paradis artificiels, Œuvres complètes*, Pléiade, Paris, 1961, pp. 327–8.

38 cf. Benjamin, *Paris, capitale du XIXe siècle*, p. 352.

39 It should, however, be recalled that, though associated with inaugurating the tradition of urban picturesque, Mercier's actual account of the ragpicker is characteristically more complex and more interesting; in particular, Mercier reverses the code that insists, in its very modes of social description, on the hierarchical separation of groups and 'levels' of society by linking the ragpicker's 'underground' activity to the production of 'high' culture (the rags the former collects provide the material for the paper-making on which literature depends for its very material existence): 'Ce vil chiffonnier est la matière première qui deviendra l'ornement de nos bibliothèques et le trésor précieux de l'esprit humain', Louis-Sebastien Mercier, *Tableau de Paris*, Amsterdam, 1782, repr. Geneva, 1979, vol. 2, p. 271.

40 Victor Fournel, *Ce qu'on voit dans les rues de Paris*, Paris, 1858, pp. 327–8. Le Play also described the ragpickers' world as 'savage' ('obéissant aux instincts de la vie sauvage'), *Les Ouvriers européens*, Paris, 1855, p. 462. For a more general discussion of the place of the term 'sauvage' in the language and ideology of

nineteenth-century social description, cf. Chevalier, op. cit., especially part 3, chs 1–4.

41 Jean-Pierre Richard talks – largely in connection with *Les Nuits d'Octobre* – of Nerval's 'longue errance parisienne' as a 'véritable descente aux enfers', *Poésie et profondeur*, Paris, 1955, p. 27.

42 Alexandre Privat d'Anglemont, *Paris-anecdote*, Paris, 1854, p. 217. For an interesting discussion of Privat d'Anglemont, see Jerrold Seigel, *Bohemian Paris: Culture, Politics and the Boundaries of Bourgeois Life*, New York, 1986, pp. 136–49.

43 Corbin, *Le Miasme et la jonquille*, p. 171.

44 Frégier, op. cit., p. 110.

45 Jules Janin, *Un Hiver à Paris*, Paris, 1843, p. 201.

46 Karl Marx, *The Eighteenth Brumaire of Louis Bonaparte*, in Karl Marx and Friedrich Engels, *Selected Works*, London, 1968, pp. 136–7. Marx also includes 'vagabonds' (and 'their *lazzaroni* character') in his list.

47 Jeffrey Mehlman, *Revolution and Repetition: Marx/Hugo/Balzac*, Berkeley and Los Angeles, 1977, p. 77.

48 For some interesting remarks on this aspect of the writings of Marx and Engels, cf. Peter Stallybrass and Allan White, *The Politics and Poetics of Transgression*, London, 1986, pp. 125–48, and Stallybrass, 'Marx and Heterogeneity: Thinking the *Lumpenproletariat*', *Representations*, 31, Summer 1990, pp. 79ff.

49 Benjamin, *Charles Baudelaire*, p. 22.

50 All but one of the above are quoted by Chevalier, op. cit., pp. 55, 175, 181, 142, 162, 142. The exception is the remark by Louis Blanc, *L'Organisation du travail*, 4th edn, Paris, 1845, p. 25. Chevalier also claims that this is a language specifically characteristic of the first half of the nineteenth century and that it effectively disappears after 1848 (op. cit., pp. 92 and 468). This, however, curiously overlooks the widespread invasion, in the second half of the century, of the language of social description (notably in accounts of the urban 'crowd' and the revolutionary 'mob') by terms and analogies drawn from biology, along with the corresponding fears and fantasies of regression to 'savage' or animal 'origins'; cf. Susanna Barrow, *Distorting Mirrors: Visions of the Crowd in Late Nineteenth-Century France*, New Haven and London, 1981; Daniel Pick, *Faces of Degeneration*, Cambridge, 1989. In the sphere of imaginative literature, Zola's novels in particular were, at least to some extent (systematically, others would argue), implicated in this way of thinking and describing social reality; cf. especially Naomi Schor, *Zola's Crowds*, Baltimore, 1978.

51 Eugène Sue, *Les Mystères de Paris*, Paris, 1963, p. 1. The nineteenth-century popular novel worked from and explored a whole imaginary of the underground city; cf. Roger Caillois, who speaks of the 'importance prépondérante des caves et des souterrains', 'Paris, mythe moderne', *Nouvelle Revue française*, 25, 284, 1 May 1937, p. 686, quoted in Benjamin, *Paris, capitale du XIXe siècle*, p. 123.

52 Sue, op. cit., p. 2. For a brief but illuminating comment on this moment of Sue's novel from the point of view of ideological strategies of enclosure and

surveillance, cf. D. A. Miller, *The Novel and the Police*, Berkeley and Los Angeles, 1988, p. 77.

53 Honoré de Balzac, *Le Père Goriot, La Comédie humaine*, Pléiade, Paris, 1951–65, vol. 2, p. 911.

54 Stéphane Mallarmé, 'Le Tombeau de Charles Baudelaire', *Poésies*, Paris, 1945, p. 70.

55 Benjamin, *Charles Baudelaire*, p. 100.

56 Lautréamont, *Les Chants de Maldoror*, Paris, 1969, pp. 87–8.

57 R. Ricatte, *La Création romanesque chez les Goncourt*, Paris, 1953, p. 280.

58 Victor Hugo, *Les Misérables*, Pléiade, Paris, 1951, p. 1318. All subsequent references to *Les Misérables* are to this edition.

59 Chevalier also claims that these were the terms and tropes of working-class belief and self-representation, as essentially an internalization of the dominant bourgeois discourse (cf. *Classes laborieuses et classes dangereuses*, part 2, ch. 3). In fact, the positions adopted in much working-class self-description (for example, in the worker press of the 1840s and 1850s) were far more varied and complex than Chevalier's reductive internalization thesis allows for. Working-class accounts of the contemporary social world have certainly to be seen in relation, and reaction, to bourgeois discourse, but in the form of a very complicated series of tactical moves, sometimes imposed, sometimes chosen (more often an uneasy and unstable mix of the two). Cf. Alain Faure and Jacques Rancière (eds), *La Parole ouvrière 1830–1851*, Paris, 1976.

60 Chevalier, op. cit., pp. 89ff.

61 ibid., pp. 94ff.

62 Victor Hugo, *Politique*, Paris, 1985, pp. 199–206.

63 Hugo's recommendation was 'avoir les populaces en dédain et les peuples en amour', *Discours de réception à l'Académie française, Œuvres complètes*, ed. Jean Massin, 18 vols, Paris, 1967–70, vol. 6, p. 161. His reply to Vinçard is cited by Chevalier, op. cit., p. 92.

64 Frédéric Soulié made similar remarks about the language of the porters and vendors at Les Halles, *La Grande Ville, Nouveau Tableau de Paris*, 2 vols, Paris, 1842, vol. 2, p. 29.

65 The ideological perspective in which Hugo brings all these issues together (the masses, language and the 'light' of redemption) is clearly stated in the question asked and the answer given in his meditation on his own novel, *Philosophie, commencement d'un livre*: Hugo asks by what right he can entertain the project 'pour clarifier la populace et en extraire le peuple, pour constater l'innocent dans le voyou, pour chercher le rayon jusque dans le cloaque, pour retrouver le Verbe jusque dans l'argot'. The answer, of course, is because 'Je crois en Dieu', *Œuvres complètes*, vol. 12, p. 72.

66 'Notes et variantes', *Les Misérables*, pp. 1743–4.

67 Jean Cocteau, *Œuvres complètes*, Lausanne, 1946, vol. 10, p. 21. Jean-Paul Sartre, *L'Idiot de la famille*, Paris, 1971–2, vol. 1, p. 841, quoted in Victor Brombert, *Victor Hugo and the Visionary Novel*, Cambridge, Mass., 1984, p. 3.

68 Georges Piroué, *Victor Hugo romancier ou les dessus de l'inconnu*, Paris, 1964, p. 137.

69 cf. Louis Villermé, *Tableau de l'état physique et moral des ouvriers*, 2 vols, Paris,

1940, and the discussion of Villermé's report in W. H. Sewell, *Work and Revolution in France: The Language of Labor from the Old Régime to 1848*, Cambridge, 1980, pp. 224ff.

70 Brombert, op. cit., pp. 101–2.

71 Baudelaire, *Œuvres complètes*, p. 1681.

72 cf. Brombert, op. cit., p. 4.

73 Quoted in Pierre Albouy, *Mythographies*, Paris, 1976, p. 132.

74 Quoted in Claudette Combes, *Paris dans les Misérables*, Nantes, 1981, p. 265.

75 Hugo, *Discours de réception à l'Académie française*, p. 160.

76 cf. Claude Habib, '"Autant en emporte le ventre!"', in Anne Ubersfeld and Guy Rosa (eds), *Lire les Misérables*, Paris, 1985, pp. 133–49.

77 Quoted in Michel Dansel, *Paris incroyable*, Paris, 1936, pp. 105–6.

78 Marcel Proust, *A la recherche du temps perdu*, Pléiade, Paris, 1954, vol. 3, p. 834.

CHAPTER 5 INSURRECTION

1 Gustave Flaubert, *L'Education sentimentale*, ed. Edouard Maynial, Classiques Garnier, Paris, 1964, p. 295. All references are to this edition.

2 Maurice Agulhon refers to this moment of *L'Education sentimentale* as an illustration of the 'honeymoon' period of 1848, *1848 ou l'Apprentissage de la République 1848–1852*, Paris, 1973, p. 47.

3 Marx called it the period of the 'universal brotherhood swindle', *The Eighteenth Brumaire of Louis Bonaparte*, in Karl Marx and Friedrich Engels, *Selected Works*, London, 1968, p. 165.

4 It was already a question in the early July Monarchy. The anonymous author of 'Le Flâneur à Paris, par un flâneur' distinguished between the street as a site of political struggle and a place of *flânerie*, or alternatively resolved the opposition into the terms of the latter (insurrection as 'spectacle' for the *flâneur*, which will of course be one of the forms of Frédéric Moreau's relation to the events of 1848), *Paris, ou le Livre des Cent-et-un*, 15 vols, Paris, 1831–4, vol. 6, p. 107.

5 cf. Jeanne Gaillard, *Paris, la ville 1852–1870*, Paris, 1977; cf. also T. J. Clark, *The Painting of Modern Life*, London, 1985, pp. 39–41.

6 cf. The 'faubourgs', wrote Daniel Stern, are 'le foyer de toutes les révolutions populaires . . . ce labyrinthe de rues et de carrefours qu'habite et que connaît à peu près exclusivement la population ouvrière', *Histoire de la révolution de 1848*, Paris, 1862, p. 112.

7 Victor Hugo, *Paris, Œuvres complètes*, ed. Jean Massin, 18 vols, Paris, 1967–70, vol. 13, p. 586. Cf. also Henri Lecouturier, *Paris incompatible avec la République*, Paris, 1862, p. 6: 'Paris est bien la ville du monde la plus révolutionnaire par nature. Pour lui, les révolutions sont un besoin.' For a counter-view, cf. Maxime du Camp, 'S'il n'y avait à Paris que des Parisiens, il n'y aurait pas de révolutionnaires', quoted in Walter Benjamin, *Paris, capitale du XIXe siècle*, Paris, 1989, p. 164.

8 Jules Vallès, *La Rue, Œuvres complètes*, Paris, 1971, vol. 10; cf. Roger Bellet,

'Rue de Paris et Tableau de Paris, vieux Paris et Paris révolutionnaire chez Jules Vallès', in Bellet (ed.), *Paris au XIXe siècle: Aspects d'un mythe littéraire*, Lyon, 1984, pp. 138–9.

9   Hugo, *Actes et paroles III*, *Œuvres complètes*, vol. 15, p. 1286.

10 cf. Bellet, 'Rue de Paris et Tableau de Paris', p. 139.

11 Vallès, *Le Cri du peuple*, *Œuvres complètes*, vol. 7, p. 108.

12 Hugo, *Paris*, p. 586.

13 Agulhon, op. cit., p. 8.

14 ibid., pp. 62–4.

15 Stern, op. cit., p. 111.

16 Alphonse de Lamartine, *Histoire de la révolution de 1848*, 2 vols, Brussels, 1849, vol. 1, pp. 2–3.

17 ibid., p. 335.

18 ibid., p. 305.

19 ibid., vol. 2, p. 478.

20 Richard Sennett gives an interesting account of how Lamartine 'succeeded in imposing what were middle-class standards . . . on a working-class audience', *The Fall of Public Man*, New York, 1977, p. 230.

21 In *Les Misérables*, Hugo described the June insurrection in terms very similar to those of Lamartine: 'la populace livre bataille au peuple. . . . Il fallut la combattre [cette émeute], et c'était le devoir, car elle attaquait la République', Pléiade, Paris, 1951, pp. 1217–18.

22 Lamartine, 'Considérations sur un chef-d'œuvre ou le danger du génie', quoted in Hugo, *Œuvres complètes*, vol. 12, pp. 1608, 1616.

23 Quoted in Victor Brombert, *Victor Hugo and the Visionary Novel*, Cambridge, Mass., 1984, p. 110.

24 'On se redit, pendant un mois, la phrase de Lamartine sur le drapeau rouge, "qui n'avait fait que le tour du Champ de Mars, tandis que le drapeau tricolore", etc.', *L'Education sentimentale*, p. 295.

25 Quoted in Maria Amalia Cajueiro-Roggero, 'Dîner chez les Dambreuse: "La réaction commençante"', in Maurice Agulhon et al., *Histoire et langage dans L'Education sentimentale*, Paris, 1981, p. 75.

26 Jules Michelet, *Nos Fils*, Paris, 1870, p. 364.

27 cf. Jean Pommier, *Les Ecrivains devant la révolution de 1848*, Paris, 1948, p. 72: 'Le premier devoir de Michelet dès lors, n'était-il pas de continuer son *Histoire*, de procurer au plus tôt à la Révolution nouvelle l'image complète d'une époque qui devait être la monitrice du présent?' Michelet himself described 1848 as the 'jeune sœur' of 1789, 'Préface de 1868', *Histoire de la Révolution française*, 2 vols, Paris, 1979, p. 37.

28 Michelet, *Journal*, quoted in Roland Barthes, *Michelet par lui-même*, Paris, 1965, p. 161.

29 Michelet, *Journal*, vol. 4, Paris, 1976, p. 182.

30 Michelet, *Histoire de la Révolution française*, vol. 1, pp. 144–56, and especially the sequence from the beginning to 'Va, paisible, que t'importe? Quoiqu'il t'arrive, mort, vainqueur, je suis avec toi!'; Flaubert, *L'Education sentimentale*, pp. 286–7 (especially the passage from 'Le bruit d'une fusillade le tira très brusquement de son sommeil' to 'le perron de trois marches restait vide').

31 For a discussion of the distinction in these terms, cf. Hayden White, *Metahistory*, Baltimore and London, 1973. I do not, of course, mean by this that, on other considerations, the distinction does not matter; cf. Hayden White, *The Content of the Form: Narrative Discourse and Historical Representation*, Baltimore and London, 1990, pp. 44–5.

32 François Furet, *Penser la Révolution française*, Paris, 1978, p. 115.

33 Michelet, 'Introduction', *Histoire de la Révolution française*, vol. 1, p. 51.

34 For a detailed discussion of Michelet's ambivalent relation to the Bible and Christianity – rejected as doctrine yet replicated as narrative – cf. Lionel Gossman, 'Michelet's Gospel of Revolution', *Between History and Literature*, Cambridge, Mass., and London, 1990, pp. 201ff.; Frank Paul Bowman, 'Michelet et les métamorphoses du Christ', *Revue d'histoire littéraire de la France*, 74, 1974, pp. 43–4. Cf. also Hayden White, *Metahistory*, p. 152.

35 Furet, op. cit., p. 76. Cf. also Paul Viallaneix, *La Voie royale: essai sur l'idée de peuple dans l'œuvre de Michelet*, Paris, 1959; and Barthes refers to Michelet's version of the 'peuple' by way of Luther's *Herr Omnes* (op. cit., pp. 159–61). Interestingly, the same expression turns up in Alfred Delvau's account of the *murailles révolutionnaires* of 1848: 'Œuvre collective qui a pour auteur monseigneur tout le monde, *mein herr omnes* [sic], comme disait Luther', *Les Murailles révolutionnaires*, Paris, 1852, vol. 1, p. 1.

36 Michelet, 'Préface de 1847', *Histoire de la Révolution française*, p. 32.

37 Given Michelet's famous notion of history-writing as a 'resurrection', a giving voice to the dead, it is worth recalling that this is also one of the functions associated with the figure of prosopopoeia. Cf. J. Hillis Miller, 'Topography and tropography in Thomas Hardy's "In Front of the Landscape"', in R. Machin and C. Norris (eds), *Poststructuralist Readings of English Poetry*, Cambridge, 1987, pp. 346–7. Miller points out, however, that prosopopoeia, as well as 'raising the ghosts from the dead', also 'kills them again'.

38 Furet, however, reminds us that, in so far as Michelet's idea of history as 'resurrection' reflected a desire to get 'inside' the past, to see the past from the point of view of the past, his conception was non-teleological, op. cit., p. 117.

39 The critical literature on this aspect of Flaubert's narrative way with history is, of course, very extensive. One can usefully consult the following: Jean Bruneau, 'Le rôle du hasard dans *L'Education sentimentale*', *Europe*, 485, 1969, pp. 101–7; J.-P. Duquette, *Flaubert ou l'architecture du vide*, Montreal, 1972, pp. 91ff.; Duquette, 'Flaubert, l'histoire et le roman historique', *Revue de l'histoire littéraire de la France*, 2–3, 1975, pp. 344–52; Eugenio Donato, 'Flaubert and the Question of History', *Modern Language Notes*, 91, 5, October 1976, pp. 850–70 (Donato picks up the Flaubert–Michelet relation by way of their respective interest in ancient history, as reflected in Michelet's *Histoire romaine* and Flaubert's *Salammbô*); Michel Crouzet, '*L'Education sentimentale* et le genre romanesque', in Maurice Agulhon et al. (eds), *Histoire et langage dans l'Education sentimentale*, Paris, 1981, pp. 77–110. From a study of the corrections and variants of the manuscript version of the novel, one can trace the elaboration of Flaubert's methods in the very process of composition itself (many of the textual revisions take the form of a suppression of causal

conjunctions and other markers of narrative coherence), cf. *L'Education sentimentale*, ed. Michael Wetherhill, Classiques Garnier, Paris, 1984, p. 587.

40 cf. ibid., p. 586.

41 Hugo, *Les Misérables*, p. 1113.

42 Daniel Stern's text on 1848 (which Flaubert read) once more provides the counter-example to Flaubert. Consider, for example, the syntax and rhetoric surrounding the use of the pronoun 'on' in the account of the funeral procession to the Place de la Bastille after the massacre of 23 February: 'Arrivés sur la place de la Bastille, on dépose les cadavres au pied de la colonne de Juillet; les torches consumées s'éteignent; on se disperse. Les uns courent dans les églises et sonnent le tocsin; d'autres frappent aux portes des maisons et demandent des armes. On aiguise le fer; on coule du plomb; on fabrique des cartouches. Le fantôme de la république se dresse dans ces ombres sinistres; la royauté chancelle', op. cit., p. 142. For some interesting remarks on Flaubert's use of the pronoun 'on', cf. Jean-Luc Seylaz, 'Un aspect de la narration flaubertienne: quelques réflexions sur l'emploi du "on" dans *Bouvard et Pécuchet*', *Flaubert et le comble de l'art: Nouvelles recherches sur 'Bouvard et Pécuchet' de Flaubert*, Paris, 1981, pp. 23–30.

43 Hugo, *Les Misérables*, p. 1114.

44 cf. *L'Education sentimentale*, ed. Wetherhill, pp. 585–6.

45 Roland Barthes, *Le Degré zéro de l'écriture*, Paris, 1972, p. 32.

46 By one of those wonderful 'accidents' of the signifier, Flaubert's use of this image to suggest a blur, an illegibility in historical experience, finds itself literally reproduced in the very manuscript of his own notes for the 1848 sequence in *L'Education sentimentale*: after the entry 'maison criblée' (where 'criblée', of course, means riddled with bullets), the editor of the notes draws our attention to '[(un mot illisible)]'!, 'Scénarios et brouillons', in *L'Education sentimentale*, ed. Wetherhill, p. 637.

47 Compare this moment with Vallès's description of the tracery of bullets on a wall in the Boulevard Poissonnière fired during the 1848 insurrection; in Vallès's account, it appears as a sign invested with maximum historical and political legibility: 'comme une grande affiche sur laquelle les balles avaient écrit ineffaçablement l'histoire de l'assassinat', *Le Tableau de Paris*, *Œuvres complètes*, vol. 13, p. 40.

48 Raymond Williams, *Modern Tragedy*, London, 1966, p. 64.

49 The 'ironic' is, of course, one of the major figures in Hayden White's tropological classification of modes of historical discourse, *Metahistory*, pp. 37–8.

50 Flaubert, *Correspondance* (Conard edition), Paris, 1926–33, vol. 1, pp. 261–2.

51 Flaubert, *L'Education sentimentale*, p. 288.

52 cf. *L'Education sentimentale*, ed. Wetherhill, p. lxii and p. 482.

53 Flaubert, *L'Education sentimentale*, p. 16.

54 ibid., p. 140.

55 ibid., p. 308.

56 ibid., p. 303.

57 Marx, *Eighteenth Brumaire*, p. 98: 'the Revolution of 1848 knew nothing better to do than to parody now 1789, now the revolutionary tradition of 1793–1795.' For a detailed account of Marx and Flaubert in terms of the

representation of 1848 by way of the principle of ironic 'emplotment', cf. Hayden White, 'The Problem of Style in Realistic Representation: Marx and Freud', in Berel Lang (ed.), *The Concept of Style*, Ithaca, 1987; cf. also Richard Terdiman, *Discourse/Counter-Discourse*, Ithaca and London, 1985, pp. 198–226.

58 Alexis de Tocqueville, *Souvenirs*, Paris, 1893, p. 75: 'Nos Français, surtout à Paris, mêlent volontiers les souvenirs de la littérature et du théâtre à leurs manifestations les plus sérieuses. . . . Ici l'imitation fut si visible que la terrible originalité des faits en demeurait cachée. . . . Les hommes de la première révolution étaient vivants dans tous les esprits, leurs actes et leurs mots présents à toutes les mémoires. Tout ce que je vis ce jour-là porte la visible empreinte de ces souvenirs; il me semblait toujours qu'on fût occupé à jouer la Révolution française plus encore qu'à la continuer.'

59 cf. T. J. Clark *The Absolute Bourgeois: Politics and Artists in France 1848–1851*, London, 1982, especially chs 1 and 2.

60 ibid., p. 27 (on Leleux and Meissonnier): 'They record a revolution emptied of meaning.'

61 cf. ibid., pp. 25ff.

62 At a public meeting, Pellerin gives us politics and painting in the following terms: 'Je voudrais savoir un peu où est le candidat de l'Art dans tout cela? Moi, j'ai fait un tableau' (Flaubert, *L'Education sentimentale*, p. 307); the 'tableau' is of course the picture displayed in M. Dambreuse's salon during the latter's 'republican' moment: 'Cela représentait la République, ou le Progrès, ou la Civilisation, sous la figure de Jésus-Christ conduisant une locomotive, laquelle traversait une forêt vierge' (ibid., p. 300).

63 Tocqueville, op. cit., p. 52.

64 Flaubert, *L'Education sentimentale*, p. 336.

65 ibid., p. 59.

66 ibid., p. 292.

67 ibid., p. 291. The prostitute appears also on the barricades, as both literal event and, in certain accounts, as figure of the 'monstrous' in revolutionary convulsions. Cf. the fascinating account by Neil Hertz, *The End of the Line: Essays on Psychoanalysis and the Sublime*, New York, 1985, pp. 163–4.

68 The identification of the *blague* as a standard feature of 'Parisian' discourse and indeed the *blagueur* as a distinctive Parisian type went back to the *physiologies* and the *tableaux* of the 1830s and 1840s. Cf. M. le Comte J. A. de Maussion, 'De la blague parisienne', *Paris, ou le Livre des Cent-et-un*, vol. 12, pp. 243–5; Paul de Kock, 'Les Blagueurs', *La Grande Ville, Nouveau Tableau de Paris*, Paris, 1842, vol. 1, pp. 293–4: 'La manie de blaguer s'est répandue à Paris de façon déplorable.'

69 Walter Benjamin, *Charles Baudelaire*, London, 1973, p. 14: 'The seeds of the *culte de la blague* which reappears in Georges Sorel and has become an integral part of fascist propaganda, are first found in Baudelaire.'

70 Jean-Paul Sartre, *L'Idiot de la famille*, Paris, 1971–2, vol. 3, p. 448.

71 From the very beginning, Flaubert conceived of Hussonnet as 'blagueur et sceptique', 'Scénarios et brouillons', *L'Education sentimentale*, ed. Wetherill, p. 589.

72 Flaubert, *L'Education sentimentale*, p. 27.
73 ibid. pp. 288–92. Flaubert states, on more than one occasion, that the 'people' is the very antithesis of the 'human': 'Le peuple est une expression de l'humanité plus étroite que l'individu . . . et la foule est ce qu'il y a de plus contraire à l'homme', *Carnets*, 2, quoted in *L'Education sentimentale*, ed. Wetherhill, p. 483; cf. also Flaubert *Correspondance*, vol. 3, p. 356: 'je ne peux admirer le peuple, et j'ai pour lui, en masse, fort peu d'entrailles parce qu'il en est, lui, totalement dépourvu. Il y a un cœur *dans l'humanité*, mais il n'y en a point *dans le peuple*, car le peuple, comme la patrie, est une chose morte.'
74 Flaubert, *L'Education sentimentale*, p. 296. On the negative association of the *blagueur* with ineffectuality and impotence in the later nineteenth century (notably in the work of the Goncourt brothers and Zola), cf. Philippe Hamon, *Expositions*, Paris, 1989, pp. 174ff.
75 cf. Stirling Haig, *Flaubert and the Gift of Speech*, Cambridge, 1986, p. 127.
76 Flaubert, *L'Education sentimentale*, p. 159.
77 ibid. p. 346.
78 ibid. p. 347.
79 ibid. p. 383. It is accordingly ironic that Frédéric, precisely in the course of a conversation in the Dambreuse salon, should characterize the journalists of the left as 'des imbéciles ou des blagueurs', p. 34.
80 Flaubert, *Correspondance*, vol. 3, p. 37.
81 Flaubert, *L'Education sentimentale*, p. 28.
82 ibid. p. 177.
83 cf. Lea Caminiti (ed.), *Dictionnaire des idées reçues* (Edition diplomatique des trois manuscrits de Rome, Naples et Rouen), Paris, 1966, p. 147.
84 Flaubert, *L'Education sentimentale*, p. 416.
85 cf. Brombert, op cit., pp. 112–13. The emphasis is also to be found in Vallès: 'Je n'oublierai pas que ce Paris qui souffre a la belle santé du rire. . . . Le petit Joe de Dickens se contente de pleurer et de mourir: Gavroche blague et épaule', quoted in Bellet, 'Rue de Paris et Tableau de Paris', p. 146. We should not, however, forget here the sheer weight of cliché which this association carries in the nineteenth century (cf., for example, Maussion, op. cit., p. 244: 'C'est l'amour de la blague qui a fait les révolutions de toutes les couleurs').
86 Flaubert, *L'Education sentimentale*, p. 320.
87 Ann Herrschberg-Pierrot has shown how in the composition of *L'Education sentimentale* Flaubert circled hesitantly and uneasily around these naturalizing analogies for the revolutionary crowd (notably the comparison with animals and the sea); the latter appear abundantly in the *brouillons*, but are often suppressed or heavily attenuated in the final version, 'Le Travail des stéréotypes dans les brouillons de la "Prise des Tuileries"', in Agulhon et al. (eds), op. cit., pp. 43–61. For further discussion of Flaubert's involvement with political stereotypes, cf. Henri Mitterand, 'Discours de la politique, politique du discours dans un fragment de *L'Education sentimentale*', in Claudine Gothot-Mersch (ed.), *Flaubert et la production du sens*, Paris, 1975, pp. 125–41.
88 Flaubert, *Correspondance*, vol. 6, p. 287.
89 cf. Antoine Compagnon, 'Comme si le cœur de l'humanité tout entière avait

battu dans sa poitrine', in Dominique Laporte (ed.), *Bouvard et Pécuchet centenaires*, Paris, 1981, pp. 28–9.

90 Flaubert, *L'Education sentimentale*, p. 427.

91 ibid., p. 18.

92 On the question of beginnings and endings in *L'Education sentimentale*, cf. Edward W. Said, *Beginnings: Intention and Method*, New York, 1975, p. 148. Victor Brombert describes the ending of Flaubert's novel as a 'retrospective prolepsis' but, if this reverses our formula for 'farce', it does not reverse anything else: for Brombert the point of Flaubert's ending is to confirm its beginning, in the form of a negative telos which looks back to a past as object of nostalgia and to a future from which all potential for change has been cancelled in advance (*The Novels of Flaubert: A Study of Themes and Techniques*, Princeton, NJ, 1966, p. 140); for a similar view, cf. Charles Bernheimer, *Figures of Ill Repute*, Cambridge, Mass., and London, 1989, p. 143.

93 Flaubert, *Correspondance*, vol. 2, p. 379.

94 Jay Bernstein argues that the ordering of the historical narrative is effectively governed by just such a negative telos. According to Bernstein, Flaubert wrote the temporality of 1848 'backwards', from the perspective of the 'dead' time of 1849–51: 'Flaubert transposes the "time" of the defeat of the revolution and the republic into the revolutionary period itself', 'The "time" of 1848: Lukács on Flaubert's *Sentimental Education*', in F. Barker et al. (eds), *1848: The Sociology of Literature*, Colchester, 1978, p. 139.

95 Gustave Flaubert, *Souvenirs, notes et pensées intimes*, Paris, 1965, p. 90. It is also in this early text that Flaubert offers the following defence of the joke: 'Une plaisanterie est ce qu'il y a de plus puissant, de plus terrible, elle est irrésistible – il n'y a point de tribunal pour en rappeler ni la raison ni le sentiment – une chose en dérision est une chose morte, un homme qui rit est plus fort qu'un autre qui a une peine' (p. 72).

96 Gille Henry, *L'Histoire du monde, c'est une farce, ou la vie de Gustave Flaubert*, Condé-sur-Noireau, 1980. In both the early correspondence and the juvenilia, statements in the form of that adopted by Henry for his title are of course legion: 'Je m'ennuie, je voudrais être crevé, être ivre, ou être Dieu, pour faire des farces' (*Agonies, Œuvres complètes*, Paris, 1964, p. 158); 'cette plaisanterie bouffonne qu'on appelle la vie' (*Correspondance*, vol. 1, p. 14); 'J'en suis venu à regarder le monde comme un spectacle et à en rire' (ibid., vol. 1, p. 30); 'ce ridicule intrinsèque à la vie humaine' (ibid., vol. 1, p. 262). For a discussion of the significance of this attitude in the juvenilia, cf. Jonathan Culler, *Flaubert: The Uses of Uncertainty*, Ithaca, 1974, ch. 1. In the light of the more general value Henry (along with many others) wishes to give to the recurrence of this sort of thing in Flaubert, it is worth recalling the identification the later Flaubert offers in the correspondence between the *blagueur* and the *poseur*: 'Nous sommes tous des farceurs, et des charlatans. Pose, pose et blague partout', *Correspondance*, vol. 4, p. 20.

97 Quoted in Cajueiro-Roggero, op. cit., p. 76.

98 cf. Stephen Heath, 'Literary Theory, etc.' *Comparative Criticism*, 9, 1987, pp. 301–2.

99 Paul Virilio, *Vitesse et politique*, Paris, 1977, pp. 13ff. These were also the

terms of Lamartine, who spoke of the 'partie nomade, flottante et débordée des villes, qui corrompt par son oisiveté sur la place publique, et qui roule, à tout vent des factions, à la voix de celui qui crie le plus haut', *Le Passé, le Présent, l'Avenir de la République*, Paris, 1850, p. 31.

100 Flaubert, *L'Education sentimentale*, p. 57; Hussonnet's remark continues: 'une lorette est plus amusante que la Vénus de Milo.'

CHAPTER 6 NOISY AND HYSTERICAL SCENES: POETRY IN THE CITY

1 Guillaume Apollinaire, *Alcools*, Paris, 1920, p. 7.

2 James Joyce, *Portrait of the Artist as a Young Man*, London, 1988, p. 180.

3 Marcel Proust, *A la recherche du temps perdu*, Pléiade, Paris, 1954, vol. 3, pp. 116ff.

4 Leo Spitzer, 'Intuition and Philology', in René Girard (ed.), *Proust: A Collection of Critical Essays*, Englewood Cliffs, NJ, 1962, pp. 97–103.

5 Paul de Kock, *La Grande Ville, Nouveau Tableau de Paris*, 2 vols, Paris, 1842, vol. 1, p. 116.

6 Victor Fournel, *Les Cris de Paris*, Paris, 1887, pp. 44ff.

7 ibid. p. 67.

8 George Sand, 'La rêverie à Paris', *Paris-Guide*, ed. Louis Ulbach, Paris, 1867, repr. Paris, 1983 (ed. Corinne Verdet), p. 50.

9 Amédée de Tissot, *Paris et Londres comparés*, Paris, 1830, pp. 172–3, quoted in Walter Benjamin, *Paris, capitale du XIXe siècle*, Paris, 1989, pp. 467–8. Michelet rang an important change on the cliché of Paris as the 'capital' of everything in calling it also 'la capitale du bruit', quoted in Pierre Citron, *La Poésie de Paris de Rousseau à Baudelaire*, 2 vols, Paris, 1964, vol. 1, p. 412.

10 Charles Baudelaire, *Les Fleurs du Mal, Œuvres complètes*, Pléiade, Paris, 1961, p. 85.

11 ibid. p. 91.

12 Baudelaire, *Œuvres complètes*, pp. 1543–4.

13 Baudelaire, *Le Spleen de Paris, Œuvres complètes*, p. 262. Page references for individual poems from *Le Spleen de Paris* are to this edition and hereafter are given parenthetically in the main text.

14 Baudelaire, *Sur la Belgique, Œuvres complètes*, p. 1323.

15 Baudelaire, *Les Fleurs du Mal*, p. 88.

16 On the metrics of this line, cf. Ross Chambers, 'The Storm in the Eye of the Poem', in Mary Ann Caws (ed.), *Textual Analysis: Some Readers Reading*, New York, 1986, pp. 158–9; Clive Scott, *French Verse-Art: A Study*, Cambridge, 1980, pp. 91–2.

17 I. A. Richards, *Practical Criticism*, New York, 1929, p. 299.

18 On the relation between poetry, the city and 'noise' in Baudelaire, cf. especially Ross Chambers, 'Baudelaire's Street Poetry', *Nineteenth-Century French Studies*, 13, 4, Summer 1985, pp. 244–59.

19 Edgar Allan Poe, 'The Poetic Principle', *Literary Criticism of Edgar Allan Poe*, ed. Robert L. Hough, Lincoln, Nebraska, 1968, p. 40.

20 Samuel Taylor Coleridge, *Biographia Literaria*, Oxford, 1973, p. 56.
21 Baudelaire, 'Notes nouvelles sur Edgar Poe', *Curiosités esthétiques*, Classiques Garnier, Paris 1962, p. 636.
22 Baudelaire, 'Théophile Gautier', *Œuvres complètes*, p. 698.
23 cf. Richard Terdiman, *Discourse/Counter-Discourse*, Ithaca and London, 1985, p. 304: 'Baudelaire's identification of his prose poem with the city seizes a fundamental truth of the new genre's determination.' One would have to add, however, that 'genre' is exactly what that 'truth' places in question.
24 Barbara Johnson, *Défigurations du langage poétique: la seconde révolution baudelairienne*, Paris, 1979, pp. 41–50.
25 cf. Chambers, 'Baudelaire's Street Poetry', p. 244: 'Baudelaire uses synecdoche, not to reconstitute a missing unity, but to express its disintegration.'
26 cf. Graham Chesters, 'Baudelaire and the Limits of Poetry', *French Studies*, 32, 4, October 1978, pp. 420–34.
27 Walter Benjamin, *Charles Baudelaire*, London, 1973, p. 140.
28 cf. Paul de Man, *The Rhetoric of Romanticism*, New York, 1984, p. 249; Jonathan Culler 'Intertextuality and Interpretation: Baudelaire's "Correspondances"', in Christopher Prendergast (ed.), *Nineteenth-Century French Poetry: Introductions to Close Reading*, Cambridge, 1990, pp. 118–37.
29 Baudelaire, 'A Arsène Houssaye', *Œuvres complètes*, p. 229. Since noise is crucially an issue (for instance, in Baudelaire's example of converting 'stridency' – the 'cri strident' of Houssaye's 'Vitrier' text – into 'song'), it is interesting to compare the letter to Houssaye with the latter's own memories of Paris as a quasi-pastoral space of 'silence', *Confessions*, Slatkine Reprints, Geneva, 1971, vol. 1, p. 304. It is, of course, also interesting to contrast Baudelaire's reference to Houssaye's 'Vitrier' with the edgy, violent and distinctly un-'song'-like tones of his own poem, 'Le Mauvais Vitrier', in *Le Spleen de Paris*.
30 Suzanne Bernard remarks, specifically in connection with the terms 'heurtée' and 'soubresauts de la conscience' in the letter, on the idea of a literary style geared to certain 'ruptures de ton ou dissonances', but then adds – quite mistakenly in my view – that this idea is not translated into the actual practice of the Baudelairian prose poem, it being thus poetic business as usual (*Le Poème en prose de Baudelaire jusqu'à nos jours*, Paris, 1959, p. 130). In 'Asmodée', his contribution to *Paris, ou Le Livre des Cent-et-un*, Jules Janin spoke of 'notre civilisation moderne si *heurtée*' (my italics), 15 vols, Paris, 1831–4, vol. 1, p. 15. Walter Benjamin suggests that this passage from the letter to Houssaye reflects the link between the experience of the city (the 'metropolitan masses') and the 'figure of shock', *Charles Baudelaire*, London, 1973, p. 119.
31 For a discussion of this poem, cf. Marshall Berman, *All That is Solid Melts into Air*, London, 1985, pp. 155ff.
32 Baudelaire, 'A Arsène Houssaye', p. 229; cf. Johnson, op. cit., p. 27.
33 Baudelaire, *Les Fleurs du Mal*, pp. 27–8.
34 ibid., pp. 84–5.
35 On the *flâneur*, cf. Benjamin, *Charles Baudelaire*, pp. 35–66; Richard E. Burton, 'The Unseen Seer or Proteus in the City', *French Studies*, 42, January 1988, pp. 59–61; Robert L. Herbert, *Impressionism: Art, Leisure and Parisian*

Society, New Haven and London, 1988, pp. 33ff.; Richard Sieburth, 'Une Idéologie du lisible', *Romantisme*, 47, 1985, pp. 53–8; Susan Buck-Morss, *The Dialectics of Seeing*, Cambridge, Mass., and London, 1989, pp. 185–7 and 304–7.

36 Baudelaire, *Œuvres complètes*, p. 1321.

37 'Le Flâneur à Paris, par un Flâneur', *Paris, ou le Livre des Cent-et-un*, vol. 6, pp. 96–7. Jules Janin described the word 'flâneur' as 'un mot tout parisien pour représentér une passion toute parisienne', *Un Hiver à Paris*, Paris, 1843, pp. 191–2.

38 Baudelaire, *Correspondance*, Paris, 1973, vol. 2, p. 583.

39 The other title Baudelaire considered was *Le Rôdeur parisien*, *Œuvres complètes*, p. 1597.

40 'Il (le flâneur) est maître de son temps et de lui-même, il savoure le plaisir de respirer, de regarder, d'être calme au milieu de cette agitation empressée', *Paris, ou le Livre des Cent-et-un*, vol. 6, p. 101.

41 Benjamin, *Charles Baudelaire*, p. 36.

42 ibid., p. 37.

43 ibid., p. 41. The author of 'Le Flâneur à Paris' speaks of the 'regard investigateur' of the *flâneur*. On the relation between the *flâneur* and the detective, cf. especially, Herbert, op. cit., pp. 43ff.

44 Benjamin described the *flâneur* as a 'connoisseur of human nature', *Charles Baudelaire*, p. 40.

45 Edmond Texier, 'Introduction', *Tableau de Paris*, Paris, 1852, p. iv.

46 Benjamin, *Charles Baudelaire*, p. 54; cf. Baudelaire, *Mon cœur mis à nu*, *Œuvres complètes*, p. 1287: 'Qu'est-ce que l'homme supérieur? Ce n'est pas le spécialiste. C'est l'homme de loisir et d'éducation générale.' 'Specialization', its problems and its paradoxes, is a recurring theme of the literature of *flânerie*. The author of 'Le Flâneur à Paris', addressing the question of the division of labour in contemporary Paris, remarks on the paradox whereby idleness itself becomes a specialized function in the city's economy of 'occupations' ('le flâneur au dix-neuvième siècle est flâneur, et rien de plus', *Paris, ou le Livre des Cent-et-un*, vol. 6, p. 98); Marc Fournier, in his entry for *La Grande Ville* ('Les Spécialités parisiennes'), said of the word 'spécialité': 'voici un des mots les plus révolutionnaires et les plus pétulants de notre patois parisien', vol. 2, p. 57.

47 Victor Fournel, *Ce qu'on voit dans les rues de Paris*, 1858, p. 261: 'Quelle bonne et douce chose que la flânerie, et comme le métier de badaud est plein de charmes et de séductions.' This synonymy of *flâneur* and *badaud* somewhat contradicts the passage cited by Benjamin (*Charles Baudelaire*, p. 69), in which Fournel distinguishes the two categories. The terms are clearly unstable in the general discourse, though the insistence on the *flâneur* as a subject of active and skilful monitoring of the urban environment remains constant.

48 Louis Huart, *Physiologie du flâneur*, Paris, 1842, pp. 16ff. Huart here echoes and refines the distinctions between *flâneur* and *badaud* proposed by Auguste Lacroix, 'Le Flâneur', in *Les Français peints par eux-mêmes*, ed. E. Curmer, 8 vols, Paris, 1840–2, vol. 3, p. 66. On these distinctions and their sources, cf. Burton, op. cit., p. 59, and Sieburth, op. cit., p. 53.

49 Huart, op. cit., p. 125.

50 'Le Flâneur à Paris', p. 101.

51 Honoré de Balzac, *La Fille aux yeux d'or*, Pléiade, Paris, 1951–65, vol. 5, p. 268. We might recall here again the description of the *flâneur* in 'Le Flâneur à Paris' as someone who '*savoure* le plaisir de *regarder*' (my italics). Sieburth also points out the analogical relation between the *physiologie* and the theme of food, in particular the core idea of the former as a 'dish' served to the consumer, op. cit., pp. 43–5.

52 Fournel, op. cit., p. 261.

53 T. J. Clark, *The Painting of Modern Life*, London, 1985, p. 108.

54 The key study is Alain Corbin, *Les Filles de noce: misère sexuelle et prostitution aux 19e et 20e siècles*, Paris, 1978.

55 cf. Citron, op. cit., vol. 2, pp. 108ff. Cf. also, on the motif of 'Paris-putain', Richard E. Burton, *Baudelaire in 1859*, Cambridge, 1988, pp. 107ff.

56 Balzac, *Ferragus*, Pléiade, vol. 5, p. 19.

57 On the theme of prostitution in nineteenth-century French literature (especially the novel), cf. Charles Bernheimer, *Figures of Ill Repute*, Cambridge, Mass., and London, 1989.

58 cf. Stephen Heath, 'Family Plots', *Comparative Criticism*, 5, 1983, pp. 318–22.

59 Quoted in Clark, op. cit., p. 109.

60 Alexandre Dumas, 'Filles, lorettes et courtisanes', *La Grande Ville*, vol. 2, pp. 317, 373, 346.

61 For an extended discussion of *Olympia* in these terms, cf. Clark, op. cit., ch. 2.

62 Benjamin, *Charles Baudelaire*, p. 34.

63 Baudelaire, *Le Peintre de la vie moderne*, *Œuvres complètes*, p. 1160.

64 Baudelaire, 'Projets de préface pour *Les Fleurs du Mal*', *Œuvres complètes*, p. 186.

65 Leo Bersani suggests a scenario in which 'psychic penetrability is fantasized as sexual penetrability', *Baudelaire and Freud*, Berkeley, Los Angeles and London, 1977, p. 12.

66 Jean Starobinski, 'Le Dédommagement et l'irréparable', in *Le Lieu et la formule: Hommage à Marc Eigeldinger*, Neufchatel, 1978, pp. 128–41.

67 Nathaniel Wing, *The Limits of Narrative*, Cambridge, 1986, p. 39.

68 ibid., p. 40.

69 Benjamin, *Charles Baudelaire*, pp. 117–8.

70 Jean–Paul Sartre, *Baudelaire*, Paris, 1963, p. 188.

71 Benjamin, *Charles Baudelaire*, p. 62.

72 Huart, op. cit., pp. 118, 123.

73 Paul de Kock, *La Grande Ville*, vol. 1, p. 6.

74 Edmond et Jules de Goncourt, *Journal*, 9 vols, Paris, 1912, vol. 1, p. 346.

75 Xavier Feyruet, 'Courrier de Paris', *L'Illustration: Journal Universel*, 38, 24 August 1861, p. 114.

76 Alexis Martin, *Paris: Promenades dans les vingt arrondissements*, 1890, p. vi.

77 Edmond de Goncourt, *La Fille Elisa*, Paris, 1877, p. 64.

78 On the different meanings of the category of 'chance' from the bourgeois to the worker, cf. Benjamin, *Paris, capitale du XIXe siècle*, p. 531.

79 Baudelaire, 'Notes nouvelles sur Edgar Poe', p. 638.
80 Baudelaire, *Fusées, Œuvres complètes*, p. 1254.
81 Baudelaire, *Les Fleurs du Mal*, p. 79; cf. Chambers, 'Baudelaire's Street Poetry', p. 246.
82 Baudelaire, *Le Peintre de la vie moderne*, p. 1158.
83 ibid., p. 1160.
84 Baudelaire, *Les Fleurs du Mal*, p. 89.
85 Baudelaire, *Salon de 1846, Œuvres complètes*, p. 952.
86 Benjamin, *Charles Baudelaire*, pp. 113ff. Richard Sennett poses this as a general condition of life in the nineteenth-century city (*The Fall of Public Man*, New York, 1977, p. 140).
87 Harold Rosenberg, 'Discovering the Present', *New Yorker*, 10 February 1961, p. 92.
88 Baudelaire, *Fusées*, p. 1260.
89 Benjamin, *Charles Baudelaire*, pp. 46, 125.
90 Wing, op. cit., p. 21.
91 Baudelaire, 'Le Mauvais Vitrier', *Le Spleen de Paris*, p. 239.
92 Baudelaire, 'Madame Bovary', *Œuvres complètes*, p. 654; cf. also the description of the world of Edgar Allan Poe as 'l'hystérie usurpant la place de la volonté, la contradiction établie entre les nerfs et l'esprit, et l'homme désaccordé au point d'exprimer la douleur par le rire', 'Edgar Poe, sa vie et ses œuvres', in *Curiosités esthétiques*, p. 616.
93 Baudelaire, *Mon cœur mis à nu*, p. 1265.
94 Baudelaire, *Le Peintre de la vie moderne*, p. 1159.
95 Baudelaire, 'Notes nouvelles sur Edgar Poe', p. 595.
96 cf. Baudelaire, 'La Destruction', *Les Fleurs du Mal*, p. 105.
97 Bersani, op. cit., p. 129.
98 Baudelaire, *Le Peintre de la vie moderne*, p. 1160.
99 I borrow this expression from Teresa Brennan, *History after Lacan* (forthcoming).
100 Baudelaire, *Mon cœur mis à nu*, p. 1296. On the 'courant froid' in Baudelaire, cf. Charles Mauron, *Le Dernier Baudelaire*, Paris, 1966, p. 43.
101 Sartre, op. cit. p. 208.
102 Siegfried Kracauer, *Jacques Offenbach and the Paris of his Time*, London, 1937, p. 215.
103 Baudelaire, *Le Peintre de la vie moderne*, p. 1160.
104 cf. Jonathan Monroe, *A Poverty of Objects*, Ithaca and London, 1987, p. 108.
105 Baudelaire, 'Notes nouvelles sur Edgar Poe', p. 1068.
106 Baudelaire, *Le Peintre de la vie moderne*, p. 1160.
107 Benjamin, *Charles Baudelaire*, p. 98 ('He always avoided revealing himself to the reader').
108 Baudelaire, *Le Peintre de la vie moderne*, p. 1161.
109 cf. Berman, op. cit., p. 136.
110 Baudelaire, *Les Fleurs du Mal*, p. 74.
111 Baudelaire based his story on a macabre episode in Manet's life. The boy whom Manet used as a model for *Le Gamin* hanged himself in Manet's studio. Cf. Michel Butor, *Histoire Extraordinaire*, Paris, 1961, ch. 15.

112 Bersani, op. cit., p. 134.

113 Bersani proposes, specifically in connection with the prose poems, an interesting relation between sadism and 'realism', the 'detachment' of the latter being cognate with cruelty of the former, op. cit., pp. 106ff.

114 The relation between the high, pseudo-classical formality of Baudelaire's style and the containment of incipient hysteria is beautifully captured in Alcide Dusolier's description of Baudelaire as 'un Boileau hystérique', *Nos gens de lettres*, 1864, p. 119, quoted in Benjamin, *Paris, capitale du XIXe siècle*, p. 318.

115 Roland Barthes, *S/Z*, Paris, 1972, pp. 104–5.

116 For a review of hostile critical response, cf. Johnson, op. cit., pp. 13ff. The hostility was almost certainly related to the prose poem's equivocation of settled generic expectations, as the paradox of a 'genre' which, in Johnson's words, 'ne peut être nommé que par une expression qui fait éclater la notion même de genre' (p. 9).

117 cf. Mary Ann Caws and Hermine Riffaterre (eds.), *The Prose Poem in France*, New York, 1983.

118 Quoted in Georges Blin, *Le Sadisme de Baudelaire*, Paris, 1948, p. 163.

119 On Baudelaire's prose poems as narrative, cf. Michel Butor, 'Le roman et la poésie', *Répertoire*, 2, Paris, 1964. Butor argues, somewhat implausibly, that it is possible to read the prose poems as a novel. The implausibility of this view has been remarked by Michel Beaujour, 'Short Epiphanies: Two Contextual Approaches to the French Prose Poem', in Caws and Riffaterre (eds.), op. cit., pp. 43–4; cf. also the interesting article by Margaret Evans, 'Laurence Sterne and *Le Spleen de Paris*', *French Studies*, 42, 2, April 1988, pp. 165–76.

120 Jonathan Monroe emphasizes the 'teleological narrative aspect' of the individual prose poems (while equally stressing the absence of a larger coherence in the collection as a whole), op. cit., p. 123. But even at the level of the articulation of the individual text, the claim is doubtful; certainly 'Mademoiselle Bistouri' is a dramatic counter-example.

121 Baudelaire, 'L'Exposition Universelle de 1855', *Œuvres complètes*, p. 698.

122 cf. D. Aynesworth, 'Humanity and Monstrosity in *Le Spleen de Paris*: A Reading of "Mademoiselle Bistouri"', *Romanic Review*, March 1982, p. 215.

123 The phrasing here is in fact that of the sketch of the letter to Houssaye, normally referred to as the 'Canevas de la dédicace' for *Le Spleen de Paris*, *Œuvres complètes* p. 311.

124 Wing, op. cit., p. 22.

125 On this point, I am in agreement with R. G. Cohn's view that 'to hypostatize the fragment is just as sterile as its opposite, a pretentious claim to completeness', 'Baudelaire's Beleaguered Prose Poems', in Caws (ed.), *Textual Analysis*, p. 119.

126 Baudelaire, 'A Arsène Houssaye', p. 229.

127 Walter Benjamin, 'The Storyteller', *Illuminations*, New York, 1969, pp. 88–9, and *Charles Baudelaire*, pp. 112–13.

128 Edmond and Jules de Goncourt, *Journal*, vol. 2, p. 492.

129 cf. Fredric Jameson, 'Baudelaire as Modernist and Postmodernist: The Dissolution of the Referent and the Artificial "Sublime"', in Chaviva Hosĕk

and Patricia Parker (eds), *Lyric Poetry: Beyond New Criticism*, Ithaca, 1985, p. 255.

130 Morse Peckham, *Man's Rage for Chaos: Biology, Behavior and the Arts*, New York, 1967, pp. 13ff.

131 Benjamin, *Charles Baudelaire*, p. 114; cf. Jonathan Arac, 'Walter Benjamin and Materialist Historiography: Romanticism, Experience and the City', *Critical Genealogies*, New York, 1987, pp. 174–214; Edward J. Ahearn, 'The Search for Community: The City in Hölderlin, Wordsworth and Baudelaire', *Texas Studies in Literature and Language*, 13, Spring 1971, pp. 71–89.

132 Church bells were, of course, a natural choice for representing city noise as 'harmony' and, moreover, through the religious association, for suggesting a nostalgic sense of shared, communal identity. They were particularly favoured in the poetry of Esquiros and Banville (cf. Citron, op. cit., vol. 1, p. 412). In his poem, 'La Cloche fêlé', Baudelaire is doubtless in part writing in conscious rejection of this use of the motif.

133 Baudelaire, *Salon de 1846*, p. 951.

134 Michael Hamburger, *The Truth of Poetry*, London, 1969, p. 268.

135 cf. also the line describing the ragpicker in 'Le Vin des chiffonniers' ('Vomissement confus de l'énorme Paris'), *Les Fleurs du Mal*, p. 101.

136 In the opening pages of *Ferragus*, Balzac rings the changes on the theme of Paris as 'monster', but as a term in the idiom of the 'poetry' of Paris ('le plus délicieux des monstres', 'cette monstrueuse merveille'), pp. 18–19. In his contribution to *Paris, ou Le Livre des Cent-et-un*, Jouy asks the decidedly rhetorical question; 'quel écrivain voudrait se charger de ce monstre?', 'Politique', vol. 1, p. 246.

137 Baudelaire, *Correspondance*, vol. 2, p. 615.

138 Baudelaire, *Salon de 1859*, p. 1061.

139 Baudelaire, *Salon de 1846*, pp. 948–9.

140 Baudelaire, *Le Peintre de la vie moderne*, p. 1160.

141 Baudelaire, *Mon cœur mis à nu*, p. 1284.

CHAPTER 7 A WALK IN THE PARK

1 Gustave Flaubert, *Bouvard et Pécuchet*, *Œuvres*, Pléiade, Paris, 1951, vol. 2, p. 986.

2 Quoted in J. M. and B. Chapman, *The Life and Times of Baron Haussmann*, London, 1957, p. 197.

3 Alphonse Alphand, *Les Promenades de Paris*, Paris, 1867–73 (reprinted Princeton Architectural Press, 1984), p. lix.

4 On the modes of 'enchantment' employed by nineteenth-century capitalism to counter and mask its own 'disenchanted' character (in the Weberian sense), cf. Susan Buck-Morss, *The Dialectics of Seeing*, Cambridge, Mass., and London, 1989, p. 254; interestingly, Walter Benjamin includes the 'winter garden' on his list of the topoi of the collective phantasmagoria, *Paris, capitale du XIXe siècle*, Paris, 1989, p. 423.

5 Charles Rearick, *Pleasures of the Belle-Epoque*, New Haven and London, 1985, pp. 3–18.

6 *Le Temps*, 15 July 1880, quoted in ibid., p. 14.
7 Auguste Montagu, *Manuel politique du citoyen français*, Paris, 1881, p. 323. Cf. Rearick, op. cit., pp. 27ff.; Kristin Ross, *The Emergence of Social Space*, Minnesota, 1988, pp. 47ff; Jacques Rancière, *La Nuit des prolétaires*, Paris, 1981.
8 cf. T. J. Clark, *The Painting of Modern Life*, London, 1985, pp. 229ff.
9 Jules Vallès, *Le Tableau de Paris, Œuvres complètes*, vol. 13, Paris, 1971, p. 136.
10 cf. Theodore Reff, *Manet and Modern Paris*, Chicago and London, 1982, p. 250.
11 Denis Brogan, *The Development of Modern France*, vol. 1: *From the Fall of the Empire to the Dreyfus Affair*, New York, 1966, p. 187.
12 Camille Pelletan, *La Justice*, 16 July 1880, p. 1.
13 Siegfried Kracauer, *Jacques Offenbach and the Paris of his Time*, London, 1937, p. 331.
14 Rearick, op. cit., p. 5.
15 Camille Pelletan, *La Justice*, 24 May 1880, p. 1.
16 cf. Nicholas Green, 'Rustic Retreats: Visions of the Countryside in Mid-Nineteenth-Century France', in Simon Pugh (ed.), *Reading Landscape*, London, 1990, pp. 166–8.
17 cf. chapter 1, p. 9.
18 Edouard André, 'Les Jardins de Paris', *Paris-Guide*, ed. Louis Ulbach, Paris, 1867, repr. Paris, 1983 (ed. Corinne Verdet), p. 60.
19 Robert L. Herbert, *Impressionism: Art, Leisure and Parisian Society*, New Haven and London, 1988, p. 145.
20 cf. Patrice Boussel et al., *Dictionnaire de Paris*, Paris, 1964, p. 337.
21 Herbert, op. cit., p. 144.
22 Baron Ernouf, *L'Art des Jardins: Parcs-Jardins-Promenades*, Troisième édition avec le concours de Alphonse Alphand, Paris, 1886, p. 348.
23 Edmond Texier, *Tableau de Paris*, Paris, 1852, vol. 1, p. 302.
24 Jules Simon, *Souvenirs de jeunesse*, quoted in P. Audebrand, *Faisons la chaîne*, Paris, 1890, pp. 3–4.
25 Théodore de Banville, *Mes Souvenirs*, Paris, 1882, quoted in Daniel Oster and Jean Goulemot (eds), *La Vie parisienne: Anthologie des mœurs du XIXe siècle*, Paris, 1989, p. 174.
26 A. Trébuchet, 'Rapports généraux des travaux du Conseil de Salubrité depuis 1829 jusqu'en 1839', *Annales d'hygiène publique et de la médecine légale*, 1841, vol. 25, p. 75.
27 Texier, op. cit., vol. 1, p. 304.
28 Alfred Delvau, *Les Plaisirs de Paris*, Paris, 1867, p. 39.
29 David Pinkney, *Napoleon III and the Re-Building of Paris*, Princeton, 1958, pp. 94ff.
30 Ernouf and Alphand, op. cit., p. 347.
31 George Sand, 'La rêverie à Paris', *Paris-Guide*, p. 51.
32 Clark, op. cit., p. 214.
33 Jules Michelet, *Le Peuple*, Paris, 1946, pp. 152, 153.
34 Louis-Sebastien Mercier, *Tableau de Paris*, Amsterdam, 1782, Slatkine Reprints, Geneva, 1979, vol. 2, pp. 155–6.

35 Quoted in Victor Fournel, *Le Vieux Paris*, Paris, 1887, repr. 1979, pp. 176–7. Mercier, on the other hand, in the 'Longchamp' chapter of his *Tableau de Paris* stressed that social 'mingling' did not entail social misrecognition (vol. 2, pp. 53–5).

36 Richard Sennett, *The Fall of Public Man*, New York, 1977, p. 40.

37 Delvau, op. cit., p. 32.

38 Paul de Kock writes of the *commis* who dresses up as a gentleman to go out, but who always remains recognizable, if only from the awkward newness of his clothes (allowance must, of course, be made here for Paul de Kock's own assumption of detached and effortless superiority), *La Grande Ville, Nouveau Tableau de Paris*, 2 vols, Paris, 1842, vol. 1, pp. 230–1.

39 Clark, op. cit., p. 213 (quoting Louis Veuillot).

40 cf. ibid., p. 67. The Goncourt brothers had their own version of the park (their example was the Jardin des Plantes) as a site of social mixing: 'Du monde allait dans le Jardin des Plantes, montait au labyrinthe, un monde particulier, mêlé, cosmopolite, composé de toutes les sortes de gens de Paris, de la province et de l'étranger, que rassemble ce rendez-vous populaire', Edmond et Jules de Goncourt, *Manette Salomon*, Paris, 1979, p. 17.

41 Clark, op. cit., p. 258.

42 Trébuchet, op. cit., pp. 75–6.

43 Alphand, *Les Promenades de Paris*, p. lix.

44 Pinkney, op. cit., p. 94.

45 cf. Jeanne Gaillard, *Paris, la ville 1852–1870*, Paris, 1977, p. 18.

46 Adeline Daumard, *Maisons de Paris et ses propriétaires parisiens au XIXe siècle 1809–80*, Paris, 1965, pp. 85–91.

47 Honoré de Balzac, *Œuvres diverses*, 3 vols, Paris, 1940, vol. 2, p. 317.

48 Delvau, op. cit., p. 37.

49 ibid., pp. 31, 35, 45, 41, 44, 32, 27.

50 Claudette Combes, *Paris dans les Misérables*, Nantes, 1981, p. 97.

51 On the topic of springtime in the Jardin du Luxembourg, Hugo repeats the 'edenesque' image of the park: 'Le printemps est un paradis provisoire; le soleil aide à faire patienter l'homme', *Les Misérables*, Pléiade, Paris, 1951, p. 1267.

52 Meyer Schapiro, 'The Nature of Abstract Art', *Marxist Quarterly*, January–March 1937, p. 83; repr. *Modern Art: Nineteenth and Twentieth Centuries*, New York, 1978.

53 Clark speaks of the 'uterine stillness' of some of these pictures, op. cit., p. 195.

54 Herbert, op. cit., p. 180. Much of my argument here about Monet's park pictures is indebted to Herbert's book (along with Paul Tucker's *Monet at Argenteuil*, New Haven and London, 1982, and Joel Isaacson, *Monet: Le Déjeuner sur l'herbe*, London, 1972). However, given this emphasis in Herbert's own argument, it is correspondingly difficult to understand how he can also present Monet as a hero of modernity, at once representing and celebrating the emancipation of a hitherto culturally disenfranchised middle class (the latter notion becomes even more peculiar when the model of 'emancipation'

on offer is access to the forms of leisure exemplified by the aristocratic 'picnic', op. cit., pp. 176–7).

55 Théodore Duret, 'Les Intransigeants et les Impressionistes', *L'Artiste*, November 1877, pp. 298–9; quoted in Herbert, op. cit., p. 261.

56 cf. Clark, op. cit., p. 179.

57 cf. Tucker, op. cit., p. 163.

58 Fredric Jameson, *The Political Unconscious*, Ithaca, 1981, pp. 236–7.

59 Herbert, op. cit., p. 188.

60 Texier, op. cit., pp. 305–6.

61 Hippolyte Taine, *Notes sur Paris*, Paris, 1867, p. 78.

62 Guy de Maupassant, *Bel-Ami*, Paris, 1973, p. 307.

63 Griselda Pollock, *Vision and Difference*, London and New York, 1988, pp. 55ff.

64 ibid., p. 63.

65 ibid., p. 62.

66 Herbert, op. cit., p. 151.

67 cf. Linda Nochlin, 'Morisot's Wet Nurse: The Construction of Work and Leisure in Impressionist Painting', *Women, Art and Power and Other Essays*, New York, 1988, pp. 37–56.

68 Kathleen Adler and Tamara Garb, *Berthe Morisot*, Ithaca, 1987, p. 124.

69 Charles Baudelaire, *Le Peintre de la vie moderne, Œuvres complètes*, Pléiade, Paris, 1961, p. 1186.

70 Baudelaire, *Le Spleen de Paris, Œuvres complètes*, pp. 244–7.

71 Baudelaire, 'Pierre Dupont', *Œuvres complètes*, p. 610.

72 Benjamin, *Charles Baudelaire*, pp. 73–4.

73 Baudelaire, *Les Fleurs du Mal, Œuvres complètes*, pp. 86–7.

74 We might contrast Baudelaire's hard-won and ever fragile notion of the 'heroism of modern life' with Alphonse Daudet's saccharine view of the concert in the park: 'Rien de joli au Luxembourg, aux Tuileries, par ces premiers joyeux soleils, par ces premiers frissons de verdure, comme la sortie des bébés et des nourrissons de une à deux heures de l'après-midi', *Souvenirs d'un homme de lettres*, Paris, 1888, p. 191.

75 Baudelaire, *Le Spleen de Paris*, pp. 236–7.

76 On the motif of 'Paris-veuve', cf. Richard E. Burton, *Baudelaire in 1859*, Cambridge, 1988, pp. 126–8.

77 Paul de Kock, *La Grande Ville*, vol. 1, p. 385.

78 Kathleen Adler, for instance, quotes from 'Les Veuves' only that passage which mentions the pleasures of the park and the concert, which, of course, gives a misleading view of a poem whose main focus is on what or who is excluded from the scene of pleasure, *Manet*, London, 1986, p. 41.

79 Delvau, op. cit., pp. 32, 40.

80 Reff, op. cit., p. 20.

81 *Guide des promenades*, Paris, 1855, quoted in *L'Impressionisme et le paysage français* (exhibition catalogue), Paris, 1985, p. 219.

82 Clark, op. cit., p. 64.

83 ibid., p. 64.

84 Adler describes the 'central area' as 'almost impenetrable at first glance', op. cit., p. 44.
85 Clark, op. cit., p. 64.
86 For information on Manet's portraits of Baudelaire (including two 'en chapeau'), cf. *Manet* (exhibition catalogue), Paris, 1983, pp. 156–7.
87 cf. Benjamin on Courbet's problems with painting Baudelaire: 'Courbet se plaignait de ne pouvoir achever le portrait de Baudelaire. Celui-ci avait chaque jour une physionomie différente', *Paris, capitale du XIXe siècle*, p. 273.
88 Adler, op. cit., p. 41.
89 Reff, op. cit., p. 15.
90 Vallès op. cit., p. 725.
91 Mercier, op. cit., Préface, p. 111.
92 cf. Richard Sieburth, 'Une Idéologie du lisible: le phénomène des *Physiologies*', *Romantisme*, 47, 1985, p. 47 (cf. also *Notebooks in Cultural Analysis*, 1, 1984).
93 Benjamin, *Charles Baudelaire*, p. 37
94 Ibid., p. 40.
95 Karlheinz Stierle, 'Baudelaire and the Tradition of the *Tableau de Paris*', *New Literary History*, 11, 2, Winter 1980, pp. 350–1.
96 *Nouveau Tableau de Paris au XIXe siècle*, Paris, 1834–5, vol. 1, p. v. The editors of *La Grande Ville* wrote in their introduction that 'un *tableau* de Paris est un livre qui devient nécessaire une fois au moins tous les cinquante ans', vol. 1, p. 1. For an exceptionally interesting discussion of the history of the genre of the *Tableau* and related forms, from this and other points of view, see Patricia Parkhurst Ferguson 'Reading Revolutionary Paris' in *Literature and Social Practice*, ed. Philippe Desan, Priscilla Parkhurst Ferguson and Wendy Griswold, Chicago, 1981, pp. 32ff.
97 cf. Judith Wechsler, *The Human Comedy*, London, 1982, ch. 1.
98 cf. Roger Bellet, 'Rue de Paris et Tableau de Paris, vieux Paris et Paris révolutionnaire chez Jules Vallès', in Bellet (ed.), *Paris au XIXe siècle: Aspects d'un mythe littéraire*, Lyon, 1984, p. 146.
99 Vallès, op. cit., p. 197.
100 ibid., p. 726.
101 cf. chapter 1, pp. 6–7.
102 Texier, op. cit., p. iv.
103 Jules Vallès, *L'Insurgé*, *Œuvres complètes*, Paris, 1971, vol. 4, pp. 145–6.
104 Vallès *Tableau de Paris*, p. 327.
105 ibid., p. 330.
106 ibid., p. 318. The great exception for Vallès is the café-concert on the Champs-Elysées: in its forms of popular irreverence and vitality 'on retrouve pourtant l'esprit et l'âme de la ville, son âme de patriote et son esprit d'ironie', p. 339.
107 ibid., p. 330.
108 Texier, op. cit., p. 305.
109 Vallès, *Tableau de Paris*, pp. 331–2.
110 Louis Veuillot, *L'Esclave Vindex*, *Œuvres*, vol. 5, Paris, 1925.
111 Vallès, *Tableau de Paris*, p. 332.
112 cf. Philip Knight, *Flower Poetics in Nineteenth-Century France*, Oxford, 1986; on the literature of 'flowers' in the nineteenth century, cf. also Benjamin,

Paris, capitale du XIXe siècle, p. 403. The great parody of nineteenth-century flower poetry was, of course, Rimbaud's 'Ce qu'on dit au poète à propos de fleurs', cf. Ross, op. cit., pp. 83–5.
113 Vallès, *Tableau de Paris*, p. 332.
114 ibid., p. 325.

CHAPTER 8   CONCLUSION: BAUDELAIRE'S WATCH, OR THE
FAST, THE SLOW AND THE INTELLIGIBLE

1 Choderlos de Laclos, *Œuvres complètes*, Pléiade, Paris, 1979, p. 598.
2 Edouard About, 'Dans les ruines', *Paris-Guide*, ed. Louis Ulbach, Paris, 1867, repr. Paris, 1983 (ed. Corinne Verdet), p. 33.
3 Paul Féval, 'La Vie à Paris', ibid., p. 20.
4 Walter Benjamin, *Paris, capitale du XIXe siècle*, Paris, 1989, p. 401.
5 Walter Benjamin, *Charles Baudelaire*, London, 1973, p. 54.
6 Susan Buck-Morss, *The Dialectics of Seeing*, Cambridge, Mass., and London, 1989, p. 344.
7 cf. Charles Rearick, *The Pleasures of the Belle-Epoque*, New Haven and London, 1985, p. 139.
8 Benjamin, *Paris, capitale du XIXe siècle*, p. 36.
9 cf. Buck-Morss, op. cit., p. 116.
10 Raymond Williams, *The Country and the City*, London, 1985, p. 287.
11 ibid., p. 296.
12 Benjamin, *Paris, capitale du XIXe siècle*, pp. 160, 452, 618, 451.
13 Quoted by Benjamin in ibid., p. 614.
14 A. S. Doncourt, *Les Expositions Universelles*, Lille-Paris, 1989, p. 53, quoted in *Paris, capitale du XIXe siècle*, Benjamin, p. 207.
15 Quoted in Peter Conrad, *The Art of the City: Views and Versions of New York*, New York and Oxford, 1984, pp. 248, 265.
16 Benjamin Gastineau, *La Vie en chemin de fer*, Paris, 1861, p. 50, quoted in Benjamin, *Paris, capitale du XIXe siècle*, p. 604.
17 Paul Verlaine, *La Bonne Chanson, Œuvres poétiques complètes*, Pléiade, Paris, 1962, p. 146; cf. Ross Chambers, 'Training for Modernity: Verlaine's "Le Paysage dans le cadre des portières"', in Christopher Prendergast (ed.), *Nineteenth-Century French Poetry*, Cambridge, 1990, pp. 157–77; cf. also Claude Pichois, *Vitesse et vision du monde*, Neuchatel, 1973.
18 cf. Gérard Genette, 'Proust palimpseste', *Figures I*, Paris, 1966, pp. 51–2.
19 Williams, op. cit., pp. 241–2.
20 Jules Laforgue, 'Grande Complainte de la Ville de Paris', *Complaintes*, Paris, 1979, pp. 129–31; trans. Peter Collier, 'Nineteenth-Century Paris: Visions and Nightmares', in Edward Timms and David Kelley (eds), *Unreal City*, Manchester, 1985, pp. 41–2.
21 Lewis Mumford, *The City in History, its Origins, its Transformations, and its Prospects*, London, 1961, p. 97.
22 Benjamin, *Paris, capitale du XIXe siècle*, p. 435.
23 The metaphorical association of literature and the shop, or the idea of literature

as shop (what Philippe Hamon calls the 'texte-magasin') was fairly widespread in the later nineteenth century, cf. Hamon, *Expositions*, Paris, 1989, pp. 97ff.

24 Given Laforgue's massive awareness of Villon, there may well also be here an allusion to the inventory-like quality of Villon's *Testament*; Villon, the great poet of medieval Paris, writes his testament as, precisely, an inventory ('item. is its refrain). Laforgue's 'Bilan' would then be both an echo of Villon and its parodic deformation, the language of poetic testament ending in the meaningless lists of department store stock-taking. I am grateful to Richard Sieburth for having drawn my attention to this possible allusion.

25 cf. Collier. op. cit., p. 40; Hamon, op. cit., p. 130.

26 Sigmund Freud, *The Interpretation of Dreams*, London, 1976, pp. 456, 495–6, 536, 557, 677.

27 If we discount the possibility that Laforgue here intends the specialized sense of 'gens' as a singular feminine noun (deriving from Latin *gens* as 'clan' or 'family'), the form of the apostrophe is wilfully a-grammatical or at least anomalous: it deploys a noun that is always plural and normally masculine (though taking the feminine 'bonnes'), thus playing simultaneously with the peculiar gender-history of the noun as well as with rules of number and hence subject/verb agreements. The consequence is, of course, a radical indeterminacy of 'identity' from the very beginning of Laforgue's text.

28 Arthur Rimbaud, *Poésies complètes*, Paris, 1963, p. 220.

29 Marc Blanchard, *In Search of the City: Engels, Baudelaire, Rimbaud*, Sarratoga, 1985, p. 143.

30 Rimbaud, 'Métropolitain', *Illuminations, Poésies complètes*, p. 154.

31 Georges Poulet, *La Poésie éclatée: Baudelaire, Rimbaud*, Paris, 1980.

32 Rimbaud, 'Paris', *Album Zutique, Poésies complètes*, pp. 78–9; cf. Kristin Ross, *The Emergence of Social Space*, Minnesota, 1988, p. 151; Hamon, op. cit., p. 130.

33 cf. Edward Said's summary of Lukács's account of reification as 'articulation under capitalism which he sometimes characterizes as if it were a gigantic itemized list', *The World, the Text and the Critic*, Cambridge, Mass., 1983, p. 232.

34 Peter Collier suggests that the 'heteroclite listing' of Laforgue's text 'seems clearly shown as the *effect* of a generalised capitalist commodification of experience', 'Poetry and Cliché', in Prendergast (ed.), op. cit., p. 211 (my italics); to pose the writing as an 'effect' of this sort risks reinstalling simple base/superstructure models and explanations of literary discourse.

35 Cf. chapter 1, note 96.

36 On this point, cf. Raymond Williams, *The Politics of Modernism*, London and New York, 1989, pp. 34–5.

37 Williams, *The Country and the City*, p. 149.

38 Quoted Benjamin, *Paris, capitale du XIXe siècle*, p. 468.

39 ibid., p. 445.

40 ibid., p. 445.

41 Guy de Maupassant, *Les Dimanches d'un bourgeois de Paris, Œuvres complètes*, Paris, 1968, vol. 1, p. 339.

42 Jean Lorrain, *Fards et poisons*, Paris, 1903, quoted in Marie-Claire Bancquart, *Images littéraires du Paris 'fin-de-siècle'*, Paris, 1979, p. 207.

43 cf. Jean-Pierre Richard, 'Quais de Seine', *Pages/paysages, Microlectures II*, Paris, 1984, pp. 101–8.

44 cf. John Rewald, *Studies in Impressionism*, London, 1985, p. 105.

45 J. K. Huysmans, *L'Art moderne, Œuvres complètes*, Paris, 1928–34, vol. 6, pp. 259–60.

46 Paul Verlaine, 'Nocturne parisien', *Poèmes saturniens, Œuvres poétiques complètes*, pp. 83–6.

47 Emile Zola, *L'Œuvre*, Pléiade, Paris, 1960–7, vol. 4, p. 214.

48 In *Le Drageoir aux épices*, Huysmans describes the Bièvre as 'un monde à part, triste, aride, mais par cela même solitaire et charmant', Paris, 1975, p. 385.

49 Alfred Delvau, *Au bord de la Bièvre*, in A. Suarès, *Delvau, Huysmans, Monthouard: La Bièvre*, Paris, 1922, p. 26.

50 Quoted in Pierre Citron, *La Poésie de Paris de Rousseau à Baudelaire*, 2 vols, Paris, 1964, vol. 2, pp. 359–60.

51 Paul de Kock, *La Grande Ville, Nouveau Tableau de Paris*, 2 vols, Paris, 1842, vol. 1, p. 297.

52 cf. Christian Lassalle, 'Iconographie du paysage des canaux en France dans les domaines de la peinture, de la carte postale et de la photographie', in *Un Canal . . . des Canaux* (exhibition catalogue), Paris, 1986, p. 371.

53 Charles Baudelaire, *Les Fleurs du Mal, Œuvres complètes*, Pléiade, Paris, 1961, p. 83.

54 Gustave Flaubert, *Bouvard et Pécuchet, Œuvres*, Pléiade, Paris, 1951, vol. 2, p. 713.

55 J. K. Huysmans, *Pages retrouvées*, Paris, 1975, p. 421.

56 Marie-Claire Bancquart defines Huysmans's representation of the Quartier Maine-Montparnasse in *Les Sœurs Vatard* as 'un Paris aussi "autre" qu'une ville étrangère', op. cit., p. 162.

57 J.-K. Huysmans, *En ménage*, Paris, 1975, p. 135.

58 cf. Bancquart, op. cit., p. 164.

59 Michel de Certeau, *L'Invention du quotidien*, vol. 1, Paris, 1980, p. 183.

60 cf. Hamon, 'Le plaqué et le plat', op. cit., pp. 55–94.

61 Edmond et Jules de Goncourt, *Manette Salomon*, Paris, 1979, p. 174.

62 Flaubert, *Bouvard et Pécuchet*, p. 713.

63 Quoted in Jean-Marc Léri, *Les Canaux de Paris*, Paris, 1982, p. 311.

64 Quoted in Lassalle, op. cit., p. 371.

65 cf. Léri, op. cit., p. 312; Georges Duveau, *La Vie ouvrière en France sous le Second Empire*, Paris, 1946, p. 204.

66 Quoted in Conrad, op. cit., p. 307. On the 'postmodern' city as 'collage' from the point of view of architectural theory and practice, cf. David Harvey, *The Condition of Postmodernity: An Enquiry into the Origins of Cultural Change*, Oxford, 1989, pp. 82–3.

67 Ezra Pound, review of Jean Cocteau's *Poésie 1917–20, The Dial*, January 1921.

68 Conrad, op. cit., pp. 300ff.

69 Baudelaire, *Fusées, Œuvres complètes*, p. 1262.

70 Baudelaire, 'Plans et projets de petits poèmes', ibid., p. 317.

71 cf. Richard E. Burton, *Baudelaire in 1859*, Cambridge, 1988.

72 cf. Citron, op. cit., vol. 2, pp. 19–40.

73 cf. Jonathan Crary, 'J. G. Ballard and the Promiscuity of Forms', *Zone*, 1/2, 1986, p. 159: 'In the late 1960s the legibility of the city appeared near a threshold of oblivion. Discourses on urbanism multiplied seemingly in inverse proportion to the dissolution of the city's coherence . . . (u)rbanism collided with that moment in capitalism when the rationalization of built space became secondary to the problems of speed and the maximization of circulation.'

74 Baudelaire, *Les Fleurs du Mal*, p. 84.

75 De Certeau, op. cit., p. 172. For a discussion of the theme of the 'labyrinth' in connection with the city and its architectures, cf. Manfredo Tafuri, *The Sphere and the Labyrinth: Avant-Gardes and Architecture from Piranesi to the 1970s*, Cambridge, Mass., and London, 1990. Interestingly, David Harvey takes de Certeau's view from the World Trade Centre as one of his own starting points, but – in an important reinflection – less to repeat de Certeau's reduction of totalizing knowledge to a form of voyeurism or panoptic megalomania than to emphasize the importance of seeking a point from which to try to see the city in its interrelations; it thus stands for one side of the 'hardest of intellectual labors . . . the building of a theoretical apparatus through which we might understand the city as a whole while appreciating the multiple confusions to which daily urban experience is always prone', *The Urban Experience*, Baltimore, 1989, pp. 1–2.

76 De Certeau, ibid., pp. 172, 174, 173.

77 ibid., pp. 173, 174.

78 ibid., pp. 178, 177.

79 ibid., p. 186.

80 ibid., pp. 198, 189.

81 ibid., p. 198.

82 Quoted in David Frisby, *Fragments of Modernity*, Cambridge, 1988, pp. 138–9.

83 De Certeau, op. cit., p. 177.

84 ibid., p. 179.

85 Michel Deutsch, *Parhélie*, Paris, 1988, pp. 17–18.

86 ibid., p. 18.

87 Conrad, op. cit., p. 308.

88 De Certeau, op. cit., p. 189.

89 ibid., p. 186.

90 cf. Frisby, op. cit., p. 86.

91 Quoted in ibid., p. 86.

92 Quoted in ibid., p. 200.

93 Walter Benjamin, 'Re The Theory of Knowledge, Theory of Progress' ('Konvolut N' of the *Passagen-Werk*), trans. Richard Sieburth, in Gary Smith (ed.), *Benjamin: Philosophy, Aesthetics, History*, Chicago, 1989, p. 48.

94 In the adaptation of 'montage' from its origins in film to practices of writing, the former has often been treated as if it were more or less synonymous with 'collage'. It is, however, probably important to insist on a distinction here:

whereas collage tends to imply merely 'pattern' assembled, often randomly, from bits and pieces, montage is more closely associated with projects of representation; montage produces and works with a representational image, which it questions, dismantles, ironizes, reconstitutes, explores and so on. But, as (mobile) representation, the purpose of the vigilantly experimental moves of montage is not simply to play at endgames or other games; it is also to seek and create knowledge of the object.

95   Benjamin, *Paris, capitale du XIXe siècle*, p. 67; *Illuminations*, New York, 1969, pp. 262–3.

96   I have proceeded here as if metonymy and synecdoche were the same thing. It may, however, be important to our understanding of city-writing to consider them as, in significant ways, quite different: metonymy would be more the figure of contiguity, adjacency and succession; its dimensions would be 'horizontal' and temporal, denoting a chain of movements and substitutions without totalization (unless gathered up in a teleologically ordered narrative); synecdoche, on the other hand, would be placed in the 'vertical' dimension and be more the figure in which part is seen to relate to whole. De Certeau's text in fact consistently uses the term 'synecdoche'.

97   Williams, *The Country and the City*, p. 149.

98   Williams, 'Tenses of the Imagination', *Writing in Society*, London, 1984, pp. 259–68.

Appendix: Translations

Translations are given here for most of the French text quoted in the main body of the book (French text quoted in the notes is not translated). I have used as far as possible published translations, although I have also amended these where it has seemed to me necessary in the interests of accuracy. In particular I have drawn on the following translations: Balzac, *La Fille aux yeux d'or*, Herbert J. Hunt; Baudelaire, *Les Fleurs du Mal*, Richard Howard; Baudelaire, *Le Spleen de Paris*, Frances Scarfe; Baudelaire, *L'Art romantique, Curiosités esthétiques*, P. E. Charvet; de Certeau, *L'Invention du quotidien*, Steven Rendall; Flaubert, *Madame Bovary*, Gerard Hopkins; Flaubert, *Bouvard et Pécuchet*, A. J. Krailsheimer; Flaubert, *L'Education sentimentale*, Robert Baldick; Hugo, *Les Misérables*, Norman Denny; Laforgue, 'Grande Complainte de la Ville de Paris', Peter Collier; Mallarmé, 'Le Tombeau de Charles Baudelaire', Anthony Hartley; Michelet, *Histoire de la Révolution française*, Charles Cocks; Rimbaud, *Illuminations*, Oliver Bernard; Sartre, *Baudelaire*, Martin Turnell; Verlaine, 'Nocturne parisien', C. F. MacIntyre; Zola, *La Curée*, A. Texeira de Mattos; Zola, *Le Ventre de Paris*, David Hughes and Marie-Jacqueline Mason. Otherwise translations are either my own or by Carina Yervasi.

Chapter 1   Introduction: Parisian Identities

p. 1. Flaubert, 'She read Balzac and George Sand, seeking in their pages satisfaction by proxy for all her longings. Even at meals she sat with a book before her, turning the pages while Charles ate his meal and chatted.'

p. 1. Flaubert, 'What kind of a place was this Paris? What a boundless name!'

p. 2. Balzac, 'Paris is Paris, you see. This saying explains my life.'

p. 2. Maxime du Camp, 'Paris is registered, catalogued, numbered, surveyed, brightened, cleaned, directed, groomed, administered, arrested, judged, imprisoned, buried.'

p. 2. Balzac, 'There are as many dress styles as there are men, and as many personalities as there are dress styles.'

p. 6–7. Texier, 'the eye of intelligence, the brain of the world, a summary of the universe, a commentary on man, the citification of humankind'.

256

p. 7. Hugo, 'Paris is the place on the whole face of the earth where one best hears the shivering of the sails of progress.'

p. 8. *Nouveau Tableau de Paris*, 'Who has investigated the entrails of the city, examines the wounds of its body like a doctor.'

p. 11. Balzac, 'Paris is an ocean. You may cast the sounding-line, but you will never fathom its depth.'

p. 11. Barrès, 'a scattered multitude of individuals, without social relation, without life-rules, without purpose'.

p. 11. Barrès, 'Paris is not for us an apprehendable universe; it is pure disorder.'

p. 12. Rousseau, 'I'm beginning to feel the drunkenness that this agitated, tumultuous life plunges you into. With such a multitude of objects passing before my eyes, I'm getting dizzy. Of all the things that strike me, there is none that holds my heart, yet all of them together disturb my feelings, so that I forget what I am and who I belong to.'

p. 13. Turgot, 'the indelible place they occupy on the soil'; 'they belong to no place'; 'mobile wealth is as fugitive as talent.'

p. 13. Lecouturier, 'There is no such thing as a Parisian society, there are no Parisians. Paris is but a camp of nomads.'

p. 14. Cochin, 'There are still inhabitants of Paris, there are no more citizens.'

p. 14–15. Barrès, 'The true heritage of the French is a common nature, a social and historical product in which all of us participate.'

p. 29. Flaubert, 'You will succeed, I'm sure of it. Remember Rastignac in the *Comédie humaine.*'

p. 30. Flaubert, 'What does that mean, reality?'

CHAPTER 2 FRAMING THE CITY: TWO PARISIAN WINDOWS

p. 31. Lautréamont, 'The shops of the rue Vivienne display their riches to awe-struck eyes. Lit by numerous gas-lamps, the mahogany caskets and gold watches flood the windows with wreaths of dazzling lights.'

p. 31. Lemer, 'Glittering shops everywhere, splendid displays, cafés covered in gilt and permanent lighting. . . . The shops put out so much light that one can read the paper as one strolls.'

p. 32. Kahn, 'the street of today, the Polychromatism of the street, produced from the colours of the façades, the posters and the lights.'

p. 33. Baudelaire, 'Now the lamp / that glowed at midnight seems, like a bloodshot eye, to throb and throw a red stain on the room.'

p. 34. Lemer, 'One takes a walk, one strolls in all those streets where commerce maintains every evening a splendid display of lights.'

p. 35. Vallès, 'No other city in the world offers the spectacle of the Parisian boulevards, especially at certain times. In the evening, when the gas lights are lit, when the theatres, café-concerts, open bazaars, the bars for both rich and poor, light their signs and lamps, when the windows of the great clubs blaze, and the electric trails of light look like a river of silver on the pavement, who then would speak of the bright lights of Venice and of the radiant splendours of the Orient?'

p. 35. Vallès, 'The whole of contemporary life shimmers all along the great glass fronts of the arcades, iridescent with cheerfully coloured advertisements.'

p. 36. Baudelaire, 'There is no sight with greater depth and mystery and variety, more obscurely suggestive, more brightly revealing, than a window lit up by a candle.'

p. 36. Baudelaire, 'With her face and dress and movements, with almost no clues at all, I have reconstituted that woman's history, or rather her legend, and sometimes I tell it over to myself in tears.'

p. 36. Baudelaire, 'Perhaps you will ask me, "Are you sure that legend is the true one?" But does it matter what the reality outside myself is, so long as it can help me to live, to feel that I am, and what I am?'

p. 37. Baudelaire, 'The café glittered all over with lights. The new gas-jets cast their incandescent novelty all round, brightening the whiteness of the walls, the dazzling planes of a multitude of mirrors, the gilt of all the mouldings and cornices, the rosy-cheeked pageboys drawn along by harnessed dogs, the ladies laughing at the falcons perched on their wrists, the nymphs and goddesses balancing baskets of fruit and pâtés and game on their heads, the Hebes and the Ganymedes offering little cups of Bavarian cream or multicoloured pyramids of ices – all history and mythology were exploited in the service of gluttony.'

p. 38. Baudelaire, 'We had each sworn that our every thought would be common to us both, and that from now on our twin souls would be one.'

p. 38. Baudelaire, 'Directly opposite to where we sat, a harmless fellow who must have been in his forties stood in the roadway. He had a tired face with a grizzled beard, and was holding a small boy by the hand, and carrying a child, too small for walking yet, on the other arm. He was playing the nursemaid, taking his children out for an evening airing. They were all in rags. Their three faces were strikingly serious, with their three pairs of eyes fixed on the new café, all with equal wonderment though varying in expression according to their age.'

p. 38. Baudelaire, 'Not only was I moved by that family of eyes, but I felt a little ashamed of our array of glasses and decanters, all so much bigger than our thirst.'

p. 38. Baudelaire, 'I just can't stand these people with their eyes as wide open as gates. Could you not ask the head waiter to see them off?'

p. 39. Baudelaire, 'So you see how hard it is to understand one another, my dear angel, how incommunicable our thoughts are, even between those who love each other.'

p. 42. Zola, 'and it was especially in the centre of this burning focus that they saw the pallid faces and pale smiles of the passers-by.'

p. 43. Zola, 'and look at them, Maxime and her, with the curious glance of famished people peering through a keyhole.'

CHAPTER 3 THE HIGH VIEW: THREE CITYSCAPES

p. 46. Sarcey, 'Education by visual means cannot be encouraged enough . . . in this regard, the panorama was a useful tool of popular instruction.'

p. 47. Detaille, 'The panorama is a bit like the theatre, you must paint with broad brushstrokes and be readable to everyone.'

p. 47. De Certeau, 'the fiction which converts the city's complexities into the readable and freezes its opaque mobility into a transparent text.'

p. 47. *Panorama voyageur*, 'From this vantage point, the view encompasses the entire horizon at a distance of several leagues, and at the same time plunges down into the capital, at the centre of which the viewer is situated. The choice of this position is not arbitrary; it was intended to place the spectator at the centre of the city he wishes to know.'

p. 48. Chevalier, 'the panoramas and dioramas that would unite in a single point all space and all time'.

p. 48. Renan, 'a place where perfection exists . . . it appeared before me as the ideal crystallized in Pentelicus white marble.'

p. 48. Martin, 'conceived acording to a plan clear enough to encompass the totality and to make out the details at a single glance.'

p. 49. Du Camp, 'The endless fog of bluish smoke from the five hundred thousand chimneys floats above the rooftops, envelops the city in a haze, blurs the details, distorts the buildings and produces an inextricable confusion.'

p. 49. Du Camp, 'The panorama is clear and precise, its perspective maintains quite distinct planes which conserve exact proportions in the distance; all is clear, explained and understood.'

p. 49. Goncourt brothers, 'Paris was below them, to the right, to the left, everywhere.'

p. 50. Huysmans, 'From high up on the ramparts, the marvellous and terrible view of the flattened plains can be seen spreading out to the edge of the city. On the horizon, in the sky, round, brick-built chimneys belch puffs of soot into the clouds, while down below, just above the flat roofs of the workshops covered with bitumen sheets and corrugated iron, trails of hissing white vapour escape from thin tubes of steel.'

p. 51. Renan, 'a thing which existed but once . . . that will never be seen again'.

p. 51–2. Rimbaud, 'I thought I could judge the depth of the city. This was the marvel I was unable to understand: what are the levels of the other districts above or below the acropolis?'

p. 52. Baudelaire, 'With a contented heart, I climbed the hill from which one can survey the city in its breadth – hospitals and brothels, purgatory, inferno, prison-houses, where every monstrosity blossoms like a flower.'

p. 53. Balzac, 'Here then we find ourselves led into the third circle of that hell which will one day have its Dante.'

p. 53. Balzac, 'for it is not simply in jest that Paris has been called an inferno. You must take the term at face value.'

p. 54. Balzac, 'A few reflections on Paris as a moral entity may help to explain the reasons for its cadaverous physiognomy'; 'Few words are necessary to assign a physiological cause . . .'; 'Perhaps before we analyse the causes which create a special physiognomy for each category of this intelligent and mobile nation, we ought to put a finger on the generally operative cause.'

p. 55. Balzac, 'There, social nature, forever in the crucible, once one task is accomplished, seems to urge itself to a new effort, like Nature herself.'

p. 55. Balzac, 'What is Paris other than a vast cornfield whose waving stalks are incessantly swayed this way and that by the winds of self-interest – a swirling harvest of men and women which the scythe of death cuts down more ruthlesssly than anywhere else, even though it springs up again as dense as ever: a sea of faces, twisted, contorted, exuding through every pore of the skin the toxic lusts conceived in the brain?'

p. 55. Balzac, 'not so much faces as masks: masks of weakness or strength, masks of misery or joy or hypocrisy, all of them drained of vitality, all of them bearing the ineffaceable mask of panting greed.'

p. 56. Balzac, 'There all is smoke, fire, glare, ebullience; everything flares up, falters, dies down, burns up again, sparkles, crackles and is consumed.'

p. 58. Balzac, 'the boilers of the magnificent seaships which cleave the waves'.

p. 58. Balzac, 'Paris is indeed a very fine ship, carrying a cargo of intelligence. . . . No doubt this stout craft may pitch and roll, but she ploughs her way across the billows of humanity . . . calls out from the height of her topsails through the voices of her learned men and artists: "Forward! March onward! Follow me!"'

p. 59–60. Baudelaire

Landscape

To make my eclogues proper, I must sleep
hard by heaven – like the astrologers –
and being the belfries' neighbour, hear in my dreams
their solemn anthems fading on the wind.
My garret view, perused attentively,
reveals the workshops and their singing slaves,
the city's masts – steeples and chimneypots –
and above that fleet, a blue eternity . . .

How sweet to see the first star in the sky,
the first lamp at the window through the mist,
the coalsmoke streaming upward, and the moon
shedding a pale enchantment on it all!
From there I'll watch the easy seasons pass
and when the tedious winter snows me in,
I'll close my shutters, draw the curtains snug,
and build my Spanish castles in the dark,
dreaming of alluring distances,
of sobbing fountains and of birds that sing
endless obbligatos to my trysts –
of everything in Idylls that's inane!
A revolution down in the street will not
distract me from my desk, for I shall be
committed to that almost carnal joy
of fastening the springtime to my will,
drawing the sun from my heart, and by my zeal
persuading Paris to become a south.

p. 66. Baudelaire 'Shivering dawn, in a wisp of pink and green'.

p. 67. Zola, 'He delighted in the immense stretch of sky he had before his eyes, the vast areas of Les Halles which brought to his mind, amid the strangled streets of the city, a faint vision of the seashore, the still and slate-grey waters of a bay barely stirring with the far-off rolling of the swell.'

p. 67. Zola, 'a satiated and digesting beast, a well-stuffed Paris brooding on its fatness, heavily supporting the empire.'

p. 67–8. Zola, 'All around him the sun seemed to set the vegetables afire. He no longer recognized that tender watercolour which had come in the paleness of the dawn. The plump hearts of the lettuces were ablaze, the row of greens burst into wonderful life, the carrots bled, the turnips became incandescent, in this triumph of fire.'

p. 68. Zola, 'his stomach, racked and twisted by the red-hot pangs.'

p. 68. Zola, 'The sea was still rising. . . . Blind, drowned, his ears ringing, his stomach crushed by all that he had seen, guessing at the presence of new, unfathomable wells of food, he prayed for mercy and he was seized by the pain and madness of thus dying of hunger in the midst of a Paris gorged with food, at this fulgurant awakening of Les Halles. Large, hot tears started from his eyes.'

p. 69. Zola, 'the whole epoch was to be found here. . . . Then Claude declaimed against romanticism; he preferred his piles of cabbages to the rags and tatters of the Middle Ages. . . . Old slums must be razed to the ground and room made for the modern.'

p. 70. Pissarro, 'the impresssion of the whole . . . to bring everything together by placing tones everywhere'.

p. 70. Zola, 'The artistic aspect is Les Halles, the modern market, the gigantic still lifes of the pavilions, the avalanche of food that occurs every morning in the centre of Paris.'

p. 70. Zola, 'But Claude in his enthusiasm had climbed on to the bench.'

p. 70. Zola, 'And here, this is where I breakfast, or at least where my eyes do.'

p. 71. Zola, 'He was a mere thing, battered, swept along at the mercy of the incoming tide.'

p. 71. Zola, 'Once again the blazing fires deep in his chest took hold of him.'

p. 71. Zola, 'They appeared like some modern machine of immeasurable dimensions, a steam-engine, or a cauldron intended to perform the digestive processes of an entire nation.'

p. 72. Zola, 'the river of green which seemed to flow down the bed of the street like the torrents of autumn rains'.

Chapter 4   Paris Underground

p. 74. Manet, 'I would have Paris-Markets, Paris-Railroads, Paris-Bridges, Paris-Underground, Paris-Racetracks and Gardens.'

p. 77. Considérant, 'a great manufactory of putrefaction'.

p. 77. Chauvet, 'centre of science, the arts, fashion and taste', 'centre of stench'.

p. 78. Parent-Duchâtelet, 'If you then imagine the kind of gases likely to be given off by piles of carcasses with much of the offal still clinging to them, as well as the emanations generated from a soil soaked for years with blood and animal sweat and urine, and from the blood itself left to clot in some yard or other with no drain, and from the waste matter from the gut-dressing and skin dryers' shops nearby; if you multiply the degrees of stench indefinitely by comparing them with the stink that all of us have smelled sometimes when passing the decaying carcass of a dead animal we may have happened upon, you will get only a faint idea of the truly repugnant reek from this sewer, the foulest imaginable.'

p. 79. Bruneseau, 'Health of body reflects cleanliness of soul. . . . The cleanliness of a city reflects the purity of the inhabitants' morals'.

p. 80. Nadar, 'thanks to its perfect ventilation', 'that outlet for the endless putridities of a great capital'.

p. 80. Rambuteau, 'It would be in some way provocative to expose thus to view piles of bones, . . . to offer to public curiosity such a spectacle, unworthy of a civilized people.'

p. 81. Nadar, 'What human vanity, what pride could survive before this ineluctable final promiscuity of our remains?'

p. 84. Frégier, 'under the heading of the dangerous classes those individuals who foment popular sedition.'

p. 84. Thiers, 'It's the mob, not the people, that I wish to exclude; it is this heterogeneous mob, this mob of vagabonds with no avowed family and no known domicile.'

p. 85. Fournel, 'an instinctive fear in the respectable city-dweller, who looks on them as a race of the outcast and the damned.'

p. 85. Privat d'Anglemont, 'Down there, far away, in the depths of an unimaginable district . . . in a district where no one has ventured, there exists something incredible, curious, strange, desolating and admirable. . . . It is a city within a city, a population lost in the midst of another population.'

p. 85. Janin, 'in the tribe of the underworld', 'to seek his fortune amid those foul rags that have no name in any language'.

p. 86. Janin, 'a swarming and oozing population that beggars description'; de Girardin, 'an underground city', 'like reptiles in a marsh'; Proudhon, 'this vast cesspool, this place of masters and lackeys, thieves and prostitutes'; Barbier, 'the sewer of the world', 'savage races amidst its bustling, witty, elegant, polite inhabitants'; Blanc, 'the faces one meets are full of ferocity and bestiality'; Buret, 'extreme poverty is a relapse into barabarism'; Considérant, ' the bourgeoisie recognized it perfectly when they screamed, in an agony of fear: "the barbarian is at the gate."'

p. 87. Sue, 'We are going to try to place before the reader certain episodes of barbarians as much beyond the pale of civilization as the savage tribes.so well painted by Cooper. Only the barbarians of which we speak are amongst us. . . . These men have their own manners, their own women, their own language, a mysterious language, full of deadly images, of metaphors dripping with blood.'

p. 88. Mallarmé, 'the sewer's sepulchral mouth, slobbering mud and rubies'.

p. 88. Hugo, 'Today the sewer is clean, cold, straight and correct . . . the filth is well behaved.'

p. 89. Hugo, 'The history of mankind is reflected in the history of cloaca. . . . The sewer of Paris was a formidable ancient thing, both sepulchre and refuge. Crime, intelligence, social protest, liberty of conscience, thought and theft, everything that human laws pursue or have pursued has been hidden in it.'

p. 89. Hugo, 'Through the cloaca it reconstructs the city. . . . From what remains it rediscovers what has been, good, bad, false, true.'

p. 90. Hugo, 'the sewer has been the disease of Paris, the evil in the city's blood.'

p. 90. Hugo, 'This four-man syndicate was known to the underworld by the name "Patron-Minette".'

p. 90. Hugo, 'the sewer cleaner sweeping the mud and the ragpicker collecting rags'.

p. 90. Hugo, 'in the deepest recesses of that ancient Paris of the poor and destitute, which lay hidden beneath the brilliance of the rich and fortunate Paris, there was to be heard the sombre growling of the masses.'

p. 91. 'Utopias are born in these subterranean channels.'

p. 91. Hugo, 'I did not say "rabble", but "rabbles"; to my way of thinking the plural is important. There is a gilded rabble just as there is a rabble in rags.'

p. 92. Hugo, 'rabble, down-and-outs, riff-raff, mobocracy'.

p. 92. Hugo, 'the language of poverty'; 'that debased idiom streaming with filth'; 'that diseased vocabulary'; 'a sort of repellent animal intended to dwell in darkness, which has been dragged out of its cloaca.'

p. 92. Hugo, 'some kind of fantastic bestiality'; 'in the light of thought'; 'the unintelligible immersed in shadow'

p. 93. Hugo, 'You are the social disease . . . we want to cure you. . . . Bravo! shouted the solemn group. Thank you! said the one who seemed to be the leader.'

p. 93. Hugo, 'What is the turmoil in a city compared with that of the human heart?'

p. 93. Hugo, 'The direction of the sewers in general follows that of the streets above them.'

p. 93. Hugo, 'a maze to which the only key is itself'; 'a grotesque jumble of eastern letters'; 'a sort of Chinese puzzle'.

p. 93. Hugo, 'fog, miasma, haze, blackness'.

p. 93. Hugo, 'But for this he would have needed a detailed knowledge of the enormous living organism of the sewer, in all of its networks and openings; but, and here we must insist, he knew nothing of the terrifying system in which he walked.'

p. 93–4. Hugo, 'If Jean Valjean had any notion of what we here describe.'

p. 94. Hugo, 'He was walking through a riddle'

p. 94. Hugo, 'Would he find a way out, and in time?'

p. 94. Hugo, 'He went anxiously but calmly ahead, seeing and knowing nothing, trusting to chance, or to Providence.'

p. 94. Hugo, 'That is how God evens things out. He watches us all from above and knows what he is doing amid his splendid stars.'

p. 95. Hugo, 'the eye of the dramatist must be everywhere at once.'

p. 95. Hugo, 'It is honest money. You can be rich with an easy mind.'

p. 95. Hugo, 'It was evident that Marius had his doubts about the origin of those six hundred thousand francs and perhaps feared that they had come from some discreditable source.'

p. 95. Hugo, 'To be a false signature in flesh and blood'.

p. 98. Hugo, 'a vaccine which inoculates progress and preserves from revolutions.'

p. 98. Hugo, 'He was like those creatures of the night feeling their way in the void, and lost in the veins of an underground cave of shadows.'

p. 99. De Montjau, 'The Metropolitan railway is anti-national, anti-municipal and threatens the glory of Paris.'

CHAPTER 5 INSURRECTION

p. 102. Flaubert, 'Frédéric gave the Marshal his arm, and they strolled through the streets together.'

p. 102. Flaubert, 'There was a carnival gaiety in the air . . . nothing could have been more enchanting than Paris in those first days.'

p. 103. Hugo, 'What therefore does Paris have? Revolution.'

p. 104. Hugo, 'I am for the Commune in principle and against the Commune in practice.'

p. 104. Hugo, 'Without . . . 89, the supremacy of Paris is an enigma.'

p. 105. Stern, 'the extreme manifestation, the most complete expression until now of that organic movement which . . . has tried since 1789 . . . to substitute human law for divine law.'

p. 105. Lamartine, 'a continuation of the first with fewer elements of disorder and a greater element of progress. In one as in the other, it is a moral idea erupting into the world. This idea is the people.'

p. 106. Lamartine, 'I will not relate the different battles of those days.'

p. 107. Michelet, 'After the terrible and murky affair of 24 June, 1848, bent, overwhelmed with sorrow, I said to Béranger: "O, who will be able to speak to the people? . . . Without that we shall die."'

p. 107. Michelet, 'I was born of the people, I have the people in my heart. . . . But the people's language, its language was inaccessible to me. I have not been able to make the people speak.'

p. 107. Michelet, 'I glanced through Flaubert's *Sentimental Education* or story of a young man. . . . Cold and indecisive. . . . Riots of 1848, very cold.'

p. 108. Michelet, 'Versailles, with an organized government, a king, ministers, a general and an army, was all hesitation, doubt, uncertainty, and in a state of the most complete moral anarchy. Paris, all commotion, destitute of every legal authority, and in the utmost confusion, attained, on the 14th of July, what is morally the highest degree of order, unanimity of feeling.'

p. 109. Michelet, 'A light broke upon every mind, and the same voice thrilled through every heart: "Go! and thou shalt take the Bastille!"'

p. 109. Michelet, 'No one proposed. . . . No one, I repeat. . . . But all believed and all acted.'

p. 110. Michelet, 'Old men who have had the happiness and the misery to see all that has happened in this unprecedented half-century . . . declare . . . that the 14th of July alone was the day of the whole people.'

p. 110. Michelet, 'Then let that great day remain one of the eternal celebrations of the human race, not only as having been the first of deliverance, but as having been superlatively the day of concord!'

p. 111. Michelet, 'What took place at the Palais-Royal, at the Hôtel de Ville, is well known; but what would be far more important to know is what took place in the heart of the people. There, however, we can guess.'

p. 111. Michelet, 'The future and the past both gave the same reply; both cried Advance!'

p. 112. Flaubert, 'Further on he noticed three paving-stones in the middle of the road-way, presumably the beginnings of a barricade.'

p. 112. Flaubert, 'Suddenly, out of an alley, there rushed a tall, pale young man, with black hair hanging down over his shoulders, and wearing a sort of singlet with coloured dots. He was carrying a long infantry musket and running along on tiptoe, looking as tense as a sleepwalker and as lithe as a tiger.'

p. 112. Hugo, 'At the barricade of the rue des Ménétriers . . . a fair-haired young man without a cravat went from one barricade to another passing on orders.'

p. 113. Flaubert, 'Every now and then an explosion could be heard.'

p. 113. Flaubert, 'and while aides-de-camp came and went at the Tuileries, while Monsieur Molé, who was constructing a new cabinet, failed to reappear, while Monsieur Thiers tried to form another, and while the King dillied and dallied, finally giving Bugeaud complete authority only to prevent him from using it, the insurrection grew in strength, as if directed by a single hand.'

p. 114. Flaubert, 'Men harangued the mob at street corners with frenzied eloquence.'

p. 114. Flaubert, 'by the morning, Paris was covered with barricades.'

p. 114. Flaubert, 'the people . . . had taken possession of the strongest strategic positions. Quietly and rapidly, the monarchy was disintegrating all by itself.'

p. 114. Flaubert, 'Now the mob was attacking the guard-house at the Château-d'Eau, to liberate fifty prisoners who were not there.'

p. 114. Flaubert, 'A huge barricade blocked the rue de Valois.'

p. 114. Flaubert, 'The smoke hanging over it broke up; men rushed at it with wild gestures and disappeared.'

p. 115. Flaubert, 'The guard-house replied, although nobody could be seen inside.'

p. 115. Flaubert, 'and the monument, with its two storeys and two wings, its fountain on the first floor and its little door in the middle, was beginning to show white pockmarks where the bullets had struck.'

p. 115. Flaubert, 'Its flight of three steps remained empty.'

p. 116. Flaubert, 'Fresh groups of workers kept coming up, driving fighters towards the guard-house. The firing became more rapid. The wine merchants' shops were open, people went into them from time to time to smoke a pipe and drink a glass of beer, and then came back again to fight. A stray dog began to howl. This raised a laugh.'

p. 116. Flaubert, 'and as it was customary for every person in the public eye to model himself on some famous figure, one copying Saint-Just, another Danton, and yet another Marat, he himself tried to resemble Blanqui, who in his turn imitated Robespierre.'

p. 117. Tocqueville, 'these old paintings that they want to force into new frames always come out badly.'

p. 118. Flaubert, 'he was fitted out by the tailor of the Ecole Polytechnique.'

p. 118. Flaubert, 'Frédéric urged a military cadet to intervene. The cadet did not understand, and indeed seemed to be half-witted.'

p. 120. Flaubert, ' "What nonsense," grumbled a voice in the crowd. "A mere joke. Nothing significant." '

p. 120. Flaubert, ' "All the same," a gentleman observed in a loud voice, "people are paying far too much attention to the Revolution. They're publishing dozens of histories and books about it." '

p. 120. Flaubert, 'there must be more serious subjects of study.'

p. 120. Flaubert, 'the spokesman for a reactionary club ... by poking fun at the principles of '89'.

p. 120. Flaubert, 'Besides, this was no time for joking, as Nonancourt pointed out, recalling the death of Monsignor Affre and that of General Bréa.'

p. 120. Flaubert, 'Hussonnet, who was to write a report of the funeral for the newspapers, even made a joke out of all the graveside speeches.'

p. 121. Flaubert, 'from the point of view of a supreme joke; that is, as God sees them, from above'.

p. 121. Flaubert, 'That's just an old dodge of the government's, to scare the middle classes.'

p. 121. Flaubert, 'That idiot gets on my nerves. As for the paper's point of view, my opinion is that the clearest and fairest thing to do is have no point of view at all.'

p. 121. Flaubert, 'Artists – laugh at everything they say. All jokers.'

p. 121. Flaubert, 'They talked freely, shouting jokes and insults at the soldiers, but going no further.'

p. 122. Flaubert, 'in its depths one could sense an incalculable strength, an elemental force.'

p. 122. Flaubert, 'Nevertheless, it is necessary to respect the masses, however inept they may be, because they contain the seeds of an incalculable fertility. Give them liberty, but not power.'

p. 123. Flaubert, 'All burst out laughing, amused by his embarrassment; thinking they were making fun of him, he fled.'

p. 123. Flaubert, 'This reference to an adventure they had shared amused them. They roared with laughter as they walked along the street.'

CHAPTER 6   NOISY AND HYSTERICAL SCENES:
POETRY IN THE CITY

p. 126. Apollinaire, 'Shepherdess O Eiffel Tower your flock of bridges is bleating this morning.'

p. 126. De Kock, 'the noise one hears incessantly could serve as an alarm-clock.'

p. 126. Fournel, 'the raw and discordant chant made from the thousand cries of Paris.'

p. 127. De Genlis, 'scarcely intelligible, excessively sad and melancholy, and almost in a minor key.'

266

p. 127. Sand, 'In the air, in the look, in the sound of Paris, there is an indescribable something, a particular influence which is not found elsewhere'; 'the confusion of sounds which blend into harmony.'

p. 127. Tissot, 'the intolerable noise that twenty thousand vehicles make day and night in the streets of Paris'.

p. 127 Baudelaire, 'shuddering to the noise'; 'at the sight of those discordant limbs'.

p. 127. Baudelaire, 'And close your ear to the roar.'

p. 128. Baudelaire, 'the extraordinary music of our astonishing cities. . . . In the depth of the forest, enclosed beneath a canopy of trees like the vaults of sacristies and cathedrals.'

p. 128. Baudelaire, 'Brussels, a noisier city than Paris. . . . Paris, infinitely larger and busier, gives out but a humming sound, vast and vague and velvety, so to speak.'

p. 128. Baudelaire, 'The traffic roared around me, deafening!'

p. 129. Baudelaire, 'It is, moreover, the character of true poetry to have a regular flow, like the great rivers as they approach the sea, at once their death and their extension into the infinite, and to avoid hurry and jolting. Lyric poetry takes wing, but always, with a supple and rhythmical movement. Everything that is brusque and broken displeases it.'

p. 130. Baudelaire, 'Everything here has its appropriate measure of light and delicious dark, of harmony itself.'

p. 130. Baudelaire, 'The draperies speak an unvoiced language, like flowers, like skies, like setting suns.'

p. 131. Baudelaire, 'It is above all from the experience of great cities, from the intersection of their innumerable relations, that this obsessive ideal is born.'

p. 131. Baudelaire, 'Which of us has not, in his moments of ambition, dreamed of the miracle of a poetic prose, musical though without rhythm and without rhyme, sufficiently supple and articulated to adapt to the lyric movements of the soul, to the undulations of reverie, to the sudden starts of consciousness.'

p. 132. Baudelaire, 'As I was crossing the road just now as fast as my legs would carry me, hopping through the mud and the chaos of traffic with death hurtling at me from every direction at once, some sharp movement of mine made my halo fall off my head and roll in the dirt on the road.'

p. 132. Baudelaire, 'We may cut where we like – I, my reverie, you, the manuscript, the reader his perusal.'

p. 133. Baudelaire, 'they dance – against their will, the creatures dance – / sad bells on which a merciless Devil tugs.'

p. 133. Baudelaire, 'and my soul / went dancing on, an old and mastless scow / dancing across a black and shoreless sea.'

p. 133. Baudelaire, 'strolling, so dear to peoples endowed with imagination'.

p. 133. Baudelaire, 'a new Joseph Delorme, latching his rhapsodic thought on to the haphazard moments of his stroll'.

p. 134. Texier, 'this fertile, instructive, stimulating, animated strolling, full of emotions, recollections and lessons'.

p. 135. 'Le Flâneur à Paris', 'to occupy his eyes, provoke his thoughts, infuse his existence with movement, away from which the mind languishes'.

p. 135. Balzac, 'the happy and indolent sort of strollers, the only people truly content in Paris, and who taste in it mobile poetry at every moment'.

p. 135. Fournel, 'Strolling is good and sweet. . . . Whoever has tasted it once can never be filled, and keeps returning to it, just as one returns to a first love.'

p. 137. Dumas *père*, 'the queen of all civilizations'; 'this fallen being'; 'which cannot be classified in any known genre'.

p. 139. Baudelaire, 'He who is easily married with the crowd knows febrile raptures.'

p. 139. Baudelaire, 'the coupling of a given noun with a given adjective, analogous or contrary'.

p. 139. Baudelaire, 'Like those lost souls which wander in search of a body to inhabit, he can enter the personality of anyone he likes. For him alone, everything is vacant.'

p. 140. Baudelaire, 'Multitude and solitude: equal and interchangeable terms for the active and fertile poet'.

p. 140. Baudelaire, 'The solitary walker lost in thought derives a strange intoxication from this universal communion.'

p. 141. Baudelaire, 'There are times when it is salutary to teach the self-satisfied mortals of this world, if only to deflate their self-conceit for a moment, that there are forms of happinesss of a higher quality than their own, more vast and more refined than theirs. Founders of colonies, pastors of nations, missionary priests exiled to the far ends of the earth, no doubt know something of such mysterious intoxications; and in the heart of the vast family created by their genius, must sometimes laugh at those who pity their unquiet fortunes and their chaste lives.'

p. 142. Sartre, 'Baudelaire, the man of crowds, was also the man who had the greatest fear of crowds.'

p. 143. Huart, 'the greatest charm of strolling is the encounter with the unexpected.'

p. 143. De Kock, 'let us stroll haphazardly.'

p. 143. Goncourt, 'I am stranger to what is coming, to what is, as I am to these new boulevards without turnings, without chance perspectives, implacabale in their straight lines.'

p. 144. Goncourt, 'Ordinarily in Paris, it is the chance climb . . . of a staircase yawning in the night . . . the angry contact . . . of two bodies that will never meet again.'

p. 144. Baudelaire: 'that unexpected element, strangeness, which is like the indispensable condiment of all beauty.'

p. 144. Baudelaire, 'the irregular, that is, the unforeseen, surprise, astonishment, are an essential and typical feature of beauty.'

p. 144. Baudelaire, 'Scenting a chance rhyme in every corner'.

p. 144. Baudelaire, 'the soul which gives itself entire, all poetry and charity, to the unexpected, to the unknown passer-by'.

p. 144. Baudelaire, 'he rushes out into the crowd in search of a man unknown to him whose face, which he had caught sight of, had in a flash fascinated him.'

p. 145. Baudelaire, 'Thus the lover of universal life moves into the crowd as though into an enormous reservoir of electricity.'

p. 145. Baudelaire, 'O fugitive beauty / from your swift glance I am suddenly reborn.'

p. 145. Baudelaire, 'Parisian life is fertile in poetic and marvellous subjects.'

p. 146. Baudelaire, 'And I drank, in spasm as a madman trembles.'

p. 146. Baudelaire, 'that humour – hysterical according to the medical men, but satanic according to those who think on a higher plane'.

p. 146. Baudelaire, 'Hysteria! . . . this mystery, unsolved as yet by the Faculty, which takes the form, in women, of a feeling of rising and choking oppression (to mention only the main symptom), and which produces, in men of nervous temperament, every form of impotence and also a capacity for all kinds of excess,'

p. 146. Baudelaire, 'I cultivated my hysteria with ecstasy and terror.'

p. 147. Baudelaire, 'I felt my throat tighten with a sort of frightening hysteria.'

p. 147. Baudelaire, 'every sublime thought is accompanied by a nervous shock, of greater or lesser strength, which echoes even in the cerebellum.'

p. 147. Baudelaire, 'In vain they struggle, in vain they conform to the world, its prudence and its guile; they will perfect their armour, seal every exit, hang mattresses over the windows against the projectiles of chance; but the Devil will get in through the keyhole.'

p. 147. Baudelaire, 'a brilliantly lit underground residence, which displayed a luxury which none of the finest mansions in Paris could rival'.

p. 148. Baudelaire, 'At last I am allowed to relax in a bath of darkness! First, a double turn of the key in the lock: I have a feeling that this turn of the key will amplify my solitude, and strengthen the barricades which now protect me from the outside world.'

p. 148. Baudelaire (La Bruyère), 'The calamity of not being able to be alone.'

p. 148. Baudelaire (Pascal), 'Almost all our misfortunes come from not being able to stay in our rooms.'

p. 148. Baudelaire, 'all the panic-stricken individuals who seek happiness in movement and in a prostitution I would call *fraternitary*, if I were to speak the fine language of my century.'

p. 149. Baudelaire, 'Fucking is wanting to enter another, and the artist never steps outside himself.'

p. 149–50. Sartre, 'True, he became a little agitated in 1848, but he did not take any real interest in the Revolution. He simply wanted to see General Aupick's house set on fire.'

p. 150. Baudelaire, 'When you set out in the morning, intent on having a ramble along the main roads, you should fill your pockets with a few little contraptions, such as a cardboard Punch and Judy which is worked by a string, or a couple of blacksmiths hammering on an anvil, or a rider whose horse's tail is a tin whistle; then, outside the cafés or under the trees, you can offer them as a tribute to the poor anonymous children you meet on your way.'

p. 150. Baudelaire, 'one of those urchins in whom, for all that, an impartial observer might discern some trace of beauty – if only, just as the connoisseur's eye may sense an ideal painting beneath a carriage-painter's coats of varnish, he could wipe away the repulsive patina of poverty.'

p. 151. Baudelaire, 'Meanwhile the two children were laughing together like brothers, both of them showing teeth of quite equal whiteness.'

APPENDIX: TRANSLATIONS

p. 151. Baudelaire, 'The observer is a prince enjoying his incognito wherever he goes.'

p. 152. Baudelaire, 'He admires the eternal beauty and astonishing harmony of life in capital cities, a harmony so providentially maintained in the tumult of human liberty.'

p. 152. Baudelaire, 'For I – am I not a dissonance / in the divine accord, / because of the greedy Irony / which infiltrates my soul?'

p. 152. Baudelaire, 'Now, if there is any such thing as a self-evident, ordinary and unchanging phenomenon about which we cannot possiby deceive ourselves, it is surely maternal love. It is just as hard to imagine a mother without maternal affection as light without heat.'

p. 153. Baudelaire, 'the agreeable shock of novelty before the hard fact'.

p. 153. Baudelaire, 'our worst sorrows are those for which we cannot find words.'

p. 153. Baudelaire, 'she was now overcome with a sort of tenderness for the instrument of her son's death, and she wanted to treasure it as a horrible but cherished memento.'

p. 153. Baudelaire, 'I understood at last why the mother had been so eager to snatch the rope from me, and the sort of commercial deal with which she intended to console herself.'

p. 154. Baudelaire, 'Once the boy was cleaned up, he became quite charming. The life he led in my studio seemed like a seventh heaven to him, compared with his miseries in the family hovel.'

p. 154. Baudelaire, 'Later on, when we had to undress the corpse to prepare it for burial, the rigor mortis was so advanced that, unable to straighten the limbs, we had to cut and tear the clothes away, to take them off.'

p. 155. Baudelaire, 'this young fellow . . . hanged on the wardrobe door'; 'the little devil had used a very thin rope'.

p. 155. Baudelaire, 'She now said she wanted to see her son's body. To tell the truth I could not stop her from wallowing in her misfortune, and refuse her that last morbid consolation.'

p. 155. Baudelaire, 'I forgot to mention that in the meantime I had called for help, but all my neighbours had refused to lend me a hand – in that respect being slaves to the habits of civilized humanity, who never, I have no idea why, want to involve themselves in hanged people's affairs.'

p. 156. Baudelaire, 'He came and posed for me on several occasions, and I soon turned him into a little gypsy, or an angel, or a mythological Cupid. I painted him carrying a wandering minstrel's viol, the crown of thorns, the nails of the Passion, the torch of Eros.'

p. 158. Baudelaire, 'I'd like him to come and visit me with his doctor's bag and his overall, perhaps even with a splash of blood on it.'

p. 158. Baudelaire, 'What strange happenings we find in a great city, if one roams about with one's eyes open.'

p. 158. Baudelaire, 'I am passionately fond of mystery because I never despair of unravelling it.'

p. 158–9. Baudelaire, 'Oh Lord, Creator, you, the Almighty, who lets us do whatever we will, you, the Judge who forgives us, you who are so full of motives and full of causes, and who have perhaps filled my mind with a taste for horror in

270

order to convert my heart, like a healing lancet; O Lord, have pity of the insane, the madmen and madwomen! O Creator, can there be such a thing as monsters in the eyes of Him who alone knows why they exist, who knows both how they are made as they are, and how they could *not* have been made?'

p. 159. Baudelaire, 'Slice into any number of fragments, and you will find that each can exist independently.'

p. 160. Goncourt brothers, 'We could baptize our present genre of novels and those of which we dream for the future as a prose poem of sensations.'

p. 161. Baudelaire, 'I love you, foul city, who with your harlots and hoodlums offer delights which godless, commonplace minds can never understand.'

p. 162. Baudelaire, '*Les Fleurs du Mal* with much more freedom, details and mockery'.

p. 162. Baudelaire, 'Fancy is all the more dangerous the easier and more open it is; dangerous like prose poetry, like the novel, it resembles the love inspired by a prostitute and which degenerates quickly into puerility and baseness; dangerous like all absolute liberty.'

p. 162. Baudelaire, 'the chaos of an exhausting and sterile freedom . . . the anarchic liberty which glorifies the individual'.

p. 163. Baudelaire, 'a bent for disguises and masks, hatred of domesticity and a passion for travel'.

p. 163. Baudelaire, 'to domicile oneself in numbers'; 'To be away from home, and yet to feel at home anywhere'; 'makes the whole world into his family'.

p. 163. Baudelaire, 'abhorrence of home [is] a great sickness.'

CHAPTER 7 A WALK IN THE PARK

p. 165. Pelletan, 'The whole population of all classes and all nuances of opinion took an active and joyous part without the slightest manifestation of excess or disorder.'

p. 165. Montagu, 'Work ennobles, idleness debases.'

p. 166. Pelletan, 'a dazzle of garlands and a decorative foliage of flags fluttering and flickering in the wind . . . as if some incomprehensibly joyous tricolour spring had broken out over the city'.

p. 167. Alphand/Ernouf, 'One forgets momentarily the concerns of everyday life.'

p. 167. Texier, 'green enclosed spaces where [Paris] brought together all the treasures of the country, the most majestic trees, the greenest grass, the most richly coloured and scented flowers.'

p. 167. Banville, 'one was a thousand leagues from the cares and busy trifles of the city.'

p. 168. Alphand, 'this truly democratic work . . . corresponds to the tendencies of the modern outlook and to the legitimate aspirations of democracy.'

p. 168. Sand, 'walk through the public gardens: all those common and dangerous individuals form a benevolent crowd, submitting to a general influence, a gentle population, trusting, polite, almost fraternal.'

p. 169. Delvau, 'not to take these elegant men and women for what they are not, but rather for what they most likely are, false dandies and painted women'.

pp. 170. Trébuchet, 'where city-dwellers of all ages could go to enjoy the benefits of sunshine and to breathe a purer air than that in their homes'.

p. 170-1. Alphand, 'where the air circulates more freely'; 'absolutely necessary in the interior of large cities from the point of view of public health'.

p. 171. Balzac, 'the cordial familiarity which exists between all the inhabitants of the capital, without distinction of rank or condition'.

p. 171. Delvau, 'In Paris, the parks . . . are equally visited by strollers of all conditions, ages, styles.'

p. 175. Taine, 'The Tuileries are a salon, an open-air salon, where little girls learn the ploys, the social graces and the calculating attitudes of the world; the art of coquetry, of simpering and of never being compromised.'

p. 178. Baudelaire, 'this sickly population which swallows the dust of factories . . . which casts a long, sorrow-laden look at the sunlight and shadows of the great parks'.

p. 178. Baudelaire:

> Little old women! I remember one
> I had trailed for hours, until the sky
> went scarlet as a wound, and she sat down
> lost in thought on a public-garden bench,
>
> listening to the tunes our soldiers play –
> brazen music for daylight's waning gold
> (and yet such martial treasures stir the soul,
> granting a kind of glory to the crowd).

p. 179. Baudelaire, 'These shady sanctuaries are where life's cripples come together.'

p. 179. Baudelaire, 'everything that is enfeebled, ruined, mortified or orphaned'.

p. 179. De Kock, 'For this woman, there is never holiday or Sunday; there is neither leisured stroll, nor pleasure, nor rest, and yet she does not complain.'

p. 179. Baudelaire, 'Finally, in the afternooon, under a balmy autumn sky, one of those skies from which regrets and memories swarm down, she went and sat all by herself in a park, at some distance from the crowd, to listen to one of those concerts with which regimental bands regale the Paris masses.'

p. 180. Baudelaire, 'the well-earned consolation for one of those dreary days spent without friend or chat, without moment of joy or someone to confide in, which God dropped on her.'

p. 180. Baudelaire, 'the poor person's mourning always has something missing, some lack of harmony which makes it the more distressing.'

p. 181. *Guide des promenades*, 'In the Tuileries, there is neither a particular kind of person, nor a special population'; 'one introduces oneself as in a refined social circle, where men and women are admitted on condition that they conform to the rules of the strictest decorum.'

p. 186. Texier, 'What it really possesses, this Paris without equal, are characters with very marked personalities, types as original as they are countless, all kinds of work and activity in which the inventive genius of the world's most inventive people bursts forth, in short, the incalculable varieties of all the types at our disposal.'

p. 187. Vallès, 'I cleaned myself off in the pond. But the mothers interfered. "What right does he have to frighten the swans and the children?" they said, remembering that three or four of their children were decked out in coloured uniforms.'

p. 187. Vallès, 'the strollers with tired looks, in faded clothing, workers and the *déclassés*'.

p. 187. Texier, 'is there a more historic piece of earth under the sun?'

p. 188. Vallès, 'This serenity was upset by the bloody march of history.'

p. 188. Vallès, 'For here, as in the Luxembourg Gardens, the flowers reeked of powder and blood at these tragic moments, and the great garden was bordered with the injured and paved with the dead on all sides.'

p. 188. Vallès, 'As with the public square, the parks have their revolutions, and at certain times, one hears the fall of the axe in the tree tops, which sounds like the guillotine falling on the neck of a king.'

CHAPTER 8 CONCLUSION: BAUDELAIRE'S WATCH, OR THE FAST, THE SLOW AND THE INTELLIGIBLE

p. 189. Laclos, 'the time lost by both pedestrians and coach travellers, as a result of being unable to organize their errands due to ignorance of where they are relative to the different streets'.

p. 190. About, 'capital cities, in their current state of development, are but agglomerations of busy men.'

p. 190. Féval, 'The pulse of Paris beats a hundred and twenty to the minute, watch in hand; elsewhere that would be a mighty fever. Paris, nevertheless, is in fine form.'

p. 190. Baudelaire, 'It is later than you think.'

p. 192. Doncourt, 'Four locomotives guarded the entrance to the annexe for machines, resembling those great bulls of Nineveh, those great Egyptian sphinxes that one saw at the entrance of temples . . . everything was in movement.'

p. 193. Gastineau, 'nature did not quiver . . . the sky seemed immutable. The railway incited everything into movement. . . . The sky became an infinitely active mass, nature a form of beauty in action.'

p. 194–5. Laforgue 'Listen, my friends, I give you Paris, including loony bins. Founded in the year dot, going cheap. Winner or universal runner-up in every exhibition, 9000-year lease. Wholesale or retail building sites of hand-made happiness. By appointment to throne-loads of royals. Highly recommended. Prevents precocious balding. Lotteries! Expeditions to the provinces. We never close. Subscriptions. Agent for genteel second-hand suffering, guaranteed untouched by human heart. Credit given as long as it's cash. Cash, my friends!

And it feeds and importexports through a score of customstations. Sad rain, goods train. All yours, gods and other surplices, church props and confetti, service on the third floor, going up, ineffable customer! All yours, darling, love, its golden sickbeds and ragged nappies will do for monogrammed loveletters, bottom drawers and babyclothes, the only salts that really cleanse, oh anorexia! Harem jewels, tassels, trams and pocket mirrors, fiction! And down under by the way, they're working so that Paris eats . . .

Besides, that ever-tactful Lotus, Love, upslides its tactile tongue between the slightest cobble-cracks. The sexes are locked in hand-to-mouth combat, preened in serried ranks, and camouflaged as regulation window-shoppers, wielding their silver-plated cutlery. There's a Venus, or one of her fly-traps, to ambush your average pen-pusher, and a maenad or two to maudlin the occasional Christ on the run. And down amid the rite-fully abused shrubbery of the somewhat pubic gardens, the martyred billers and vestal cooers deliver their goods quick as a wink to the lowest bidder, chalk it up to Mssrs Ideal and Son (all contributions to Head Office in a self-addressed envelope FAO Them Up There, please), while carefully taking leave of their actual selves, my dear. God, what an oddly behaved sort of gent is Man! And as for the female of the species, that schoolboy in drag, that sawdust-brained doll . . . which reminds me how touching they . . . how touching them . . .

But the unuprootable elite, whence? whose? Linen whorehouses, wedding derangements, mourning unlimited, bitchuperation, à la carte resentments. And foster suburbs, lice-ridden peat, old nags munching broken crocks, and shards and soles and silhouettes across the fortified skyline. And rain! Three tea towels in an attic fanlight. A dog is barking at that ball up there. And cloisterphobic corners, clanging inconciliable *dies wearies.* Sunsets in society pastels of bankruptcy gemstock. Genius at factory prices, juggling with empty authorial jingles by cigarette-light. Twenty-four hours a day aren't enough for the discreet elite! . . .

Again the public cries arise. Please note, mortgages are off, float the Panama Canal. Good buys, wise guys. Credit on or off demand, purchase of real and ephemeral estate and usury; loans on life or otherwise insurance; timetables, directories, gifts. Round trips at reduced prices. Mme Ludovic foretells the future from 2 to 4. Toys in the *Children's Paradise* and party accessories for grown-ups. Large selection of battered principles. More cries! Sole agent! Celebratory suppers for the nth performance. Marinoni circular machines! Everything guaranteed, everything free! And life goes faster! Sole agent . . .

Second-hand calendars, months and years. And autumn sods off into the Bois de Boulogne, winter freezes the pauper's beans on flower-paintless plates. May's a laxative, the heatwave's dirty beachy breezes bleach expensive dresses. Then as we live in cashdown times there come the courteous guys who undertake and autopsy and raise their hats to the old one-cat's-eyed sun. And history goes on making up and crosssing out its moth-holed repetitive accounts – Down, balance-sheet, down boy!'

p. 201. Larousse, 'this city, governed by a rhythm of life, a circulation, an unexampled pace of activity, is also, by a strange contrast, the city in which one finds the greatest number of the idle, the lazy and loungers.'

p. 201. Maupassant, 'this sweet and adorable river that passes through the heart of France'.

p. 202. Lorrain, 'Paris, for me, begins only at the Pont du Louvre; I couldn't live far from the quays. O the good time of strolling in the fresh morning air, in front of the stall displays and the booksellers of the Quai d'Orsay and the Malaquais.'

p. 202. Huysmans, 'the planes become steady and the strident tones calm.'

APPENDIX: TRANSLATIONS

p. 203. Verlaine:

> You, Seine, have nothing. Two quays, and that's all,
> two dirty quays with musty old bookstalls
> littered from beginning to end, and a low crowd
> makes rings in the water, fishing with line and rod.
>
> Yes, but when evening has thinned out the loungers,
> stupefied with drowsiness and hunger,
> and sunset reddens the sky with freckles, then
> how it fetches the dreamers forth from lair and den,
> to lean on the Pont de la Cité and dream,
> heart and hair to the wind, near Notre-Dame!

p. 204. De Kock, 'you would not then believe yourself to be in Paris; the place has neither the spirit, nor the movement, nor the noise of the city.'

p. 205. Flaubert, 'from the lock upstream to the lock downstream'.

p. 205. Huysmans, 'these walks [which] are so rich in soothing reveries'.

p. 206. Napoleon, 'I would like to do something for the Parisians'; Chaptal, 'Give them water.'

p. 209–10. De Certeau, 'fiction of knowledge'; 'murky, intertwining, daily behaviours'; 'opaque and blind mobility'; 'microbe-like, singular and plural practices'; 'ruses and combinations of powers that have no readable identity'; 'to walk is to lack a place'; 'the immense social experience of lacking a place'; 'a universe of rented spaces'.

p. 210. De Certeau, 'the walk that Freud compares to the trampling underfoot of the mother-land'.

p. 210. De Certeau, 'ministers of knowledge'; 'transmute the misfortune of their theories into theories of misfortune'.

p. 211. Deutsch, 'the idea of the city as always enigmatic, packed with a semantic density stretching to infinity . . . in a word, the idea of the city as an object to be deciphered is no longer valid.'

p. 212. Deutsch, 'the euphoric feeling of floating in the city – floating without sensation as in a telefilm'.

p. 212. De Certeau, 'opens gaps in the spatial continuum'.

Index